Heritage of Conquest:
Thirty Years Later

Heritage of Conquest
Thirty Years Later

Edited by
Carl Kendall, Stanford University
John Hawkins, Brigham Young University
Laurel Bossen, University of Pittsburgh

University of New Mexico Press
Albuquerque

Library of Congress Cataloging in Publication Data
Main entry under title:

Heritage of conquest.

   Includes bibliographies and index.
   1. Ethnology—Central America—Addresses, essays,
lectures. 2. Ethnology—Mexico—Addresses, essays,
lectures. 3. Central America—Social life and customs—
Addresses, essays, lectures. 4. Mexico—Social life
and customs—Addresses, essays, lectures. 5. Central
America—Social conditions—Addresses, essays, lectures.
6. Mexico—Social conditions—Addresses, essays,
lectures. 7. Indians of Central America—Social
conditions—Addresses, essays, lectures. 8. Indians
of Mexico—Social conditions—Addresses, essays,
lectures. I. Kendall, Carl, 1947–   . II. Hawkins,
John, 1946–   III. Bossen, Laurel, 1945–   .
GN564.C46H47   1982   306'.0972   82-20171
ISBN 0-8263-0639-X

Manufactured in the United States of America.
First edition

Contents

Foreword

In nineteenth-century Europe, scholars who studied American Indian peoples, cultures, and history called themselves Americanists, and in 1875 held their first international congress in Nancy, France. Thereafter, congresses were held every second or third year in different European cities. The Eleventh International Congress of Americanists, in 1895, was the first to be held in the New World, in Mexico; thereafter the congresses alternated regularly between Europe and the Americas. The thirteenth was held in New York in 1902 and the fifteenth in Quebec in 1904, after which the New World congresses were held mainly in Latin America. Washington, D.C., hosted the nineteenth in 1915 and New York the twenty-third (1928) and the twenty-ninth (1949).

The New York congress in 1949 was the occasion for a first major assessment of the cultural anthropology of Mesoamerica, published as *Heritage of Conquest.* Thirty years passed before the congress again came north, this time to Vancouver, August 10–17, 1979. At this congress a new generation completed a review of what had been learned about Mesoamerica in thirty fruitful years.

I had myself organized the 1949 Viking Fund Seminar that resulted in *Heritage of Conquest,* and I edited the book. Although I was consulted occasionally as the present book proceeded, I did not know the results until I read it in page proof. I had thought to write about what had become of our science in thirty years, but I found that the authors of the new book had themselves done this at every point and had summarized the comparisons so well that I was left without that task. Hindsight from the 1980s is clearer than foresight from the 1950s, especially when blessed with a tenfold increase of available data against which to test the accumulating hypotheses and changing ideas.

The original *Heritage of Conquest* is kept in print by Littlefield, Adams and Co. and tells its own story, all details of which can be found in archives of the University of Chicago. Suffice it to say here that I had been working closely with anthropologists in Guatemala since the mid 1930s and in Mexico since 1942. The data on the Maya peoples of Chiapas and Guatemala were accumulating in notebooks and cried to be pulled together. In 1948 it seemed opportune to use the approaching 1949 Congress, when interested colleagues and students would converge on New York, to bring some order out of our notebooks. All of us knew a great deal about the lives of our respective clusters of Indians and something of their non-Indian neighbors. When we gathered in New York to compare notes, the problem was stated as follows:

> We have all seen different parts of the elephant—different parts of Middle America or different kinds of people; and, though we reinforce our senses with the tools of our discipline, we use different tools and so see different things. In short, we are what good scientists must first be—specialists.
>
> That all of us together may reveal the elephant that none of us has seen, to put our special information into the perspective of the whole—that is the idea of the Seminar. A few of us have forsaken our modesty to commit to paper our ideas about the whole of Middle America, in the certainty that we must be wrong in much of what we think, but with the hope that if others with different

experience will correct us where they can, we shall become much less wrong about much more of what we think.

Our only fear is that somebody will be afraid to correct us—that somebody who could help us with his knowledge keeps his peace for fear of offending—that somebody will forget that the only authority which science and scholarship can respect is the authority of knowledge. To discourage misplaced courtesy and false modesty that could spell failure for this enterprise—that is the purpose of these remarks.

So challenged, the thirty-two "49ers" listed below began a week of unabashedly critical discussions that resulted in a volume that could tolerate, if not always withstand, the searchlights of a later generation. Readers of the excellent book before us now will in turn judge the work of the thirty years that followed.

SOL TAX

Chicago
October 1982

Participants in the Viking Fund Seminar

CONTRIBUTORS

RALPH BEALS. University of California. Fieldwork: Yaqui-Mayo of Sonora; Mixe of Oaxaca; Mountain Tarascan of Michoacán.

FERNANDO CAMARA BARBACHANO. University of Puerto Rico. Fieldwork: Tzeltal and Tzotzil groups of Chiapas; Chacaltianguis and Tuxtilla, Veracruz; Andean communities in Peru.

JULIO DE LA FUENTE. Museo Nacional de Mexico. Fieldwork: Extended research among the mountain and valley Zapotec of Oaxaca; the Otomí of Hidalgo; the Huastec of Veracruz; the Quechua of Peru.

JOHN P. GILLIN. University of North Carolina. Fieldwork: San Luis Jilotepeque (Pokomán) in Eastern Guatemala; Carib òf British Guiana; Indian and non-Indian communities in the Andes.

CALIXTA GUITERAS HOLMES. Museo Nacional de Mexico. Fieldwork: Tzeltal and Tzotzil groups in Chiapas; Huastec and Nahua of Northern Veracruz.

PAUL KIRCHHOFF. University of Washington. Field of interest: Ancient Middle America.

GERTRUDE PROKOSCH KURATH. Michigan Folklore Society. Fieldwork: Mexico.

BENJAMIN D. AND LOIS PAUL. Harvard University. Fieldwork: San Pedro la Laguna, Guatemala.

ROBERT REDFIELD. University of Chicago. Fieldwork: Tepoztlan, Morelos; Maya of Yucatan; Midwest Highlands of Guatemala.

SOL TAX. University of Chicago. Fieldwork: Chichicastenango and Panajachel, Midwest Highlands of Guatemala; Zinacantan, Chiapas.

CHARLES WISDOM. University of Connecticut. Fieldwork: Chorti of Eastern Guatemala.

PARTICIPANTS IN THE DISCUSSIONS

GEORGE M. FOSTER. Smithsonian Institution. Fieldwork: Sierra Popoluca of Veracruz; Tzintzuntzan (Tarascan-Mestizo) of Michoacán; Spain.

ANTONIO GOUBAUD CARRERA. Guatemalan Ambassador to the United States; formerly Director of the National Indian Institute of Guatemala. Deceased, March, 1951. Fieldwork: Kekchi of San Juan Chamelco, Alta Verapaz, and other Guatemalan communities.

WIGBERTO JIMENEZ MORENO. Museo Nacional de Mexico. Fieldwork: Mexico.

BERNICE KAPLAN. Detroit, Michigan. Fieldwork: Paracho, Michoacán, Mexico.

ISABEL KELLY. Smithsonian Institution. Fieldwork: Lowland Totonac of the Papantla area of Veracruz, Mexico.

ARDEN R. KING. Middle American Research Institute. Fieldwork: Alta Verapaz, Guatemala.

DOROTHY LOUISE KYTE. Columbia University. Fieldwork: Los Morros, Guerrero, and general reconnaissance of Guerrero, Mexico.

GABRIEL LASKER. Wayne University. Fieldwork: Physical anthropology in Mexico.

JUNE HELM MACNEISH. University of Chicago. Fieldwork: Los Angeles, a Mestizo community in Tamaulipas.

DONALD MARSHALL. Peabody Museum.

J. ALDEN MASON. University of Pennsylvania. Fieldwork. Tepecano and Tepehuan of the Sierra Madre Occidental.

DANIEL F. RUBIN DE LA BORBOLLA. Director, Museo Nacional de Mexico. Fieldwork: Mexico.

DORIS Z. STONE. Costa Rica. Fieldwork: Northern Guaymi of Panama; Talamancan tribes, Boruca, Guatuso, and Chorotega of Costa Rica; the Lenca, Payo and Suma of Honduras, and the Matagalpa of Nicaragua.

FRANZ TERMER. Museum für Völkerkunde, Hamburg. Fieldwork: Guatemala, Mexico, Honduras and Salvador.

FRANCES TOOR. Mexico. Fieldwork: Mexico and Peru.

MELVIN M. TUMIN. Princeton University. Fieldwork: Pokoman of San Luis Jilotepeque, Eastern Guatemala.

ALFONSO VILLA ROJAS. Papaloapan Commission. Fieldwork: Quintana Roo; Yucatan, Tzeltal of Chiapas.

CHARLES WAGLEY. Columbia University. Fieldwork: Northwestern Guatemala (Santiago Chimaltenango), and Brazil.

MARK HANNA WATKINS. Howard University. Fieldwork: Cakchiquel of Guatemala.

NATHAN L. WHETTEN. University of Connecticut. Fieldwork: Rural Mexico and Guatemala.

Acknowledgments

Any effort that extends over several years—from conception through publication—incurs many debts. Many who helped are named in the overview to this volume, but I must especially mention Professor Sol Tax, who, despite ill health, encouraged the volume and participated in its planning. This work is dedicated to Sol and Gertrude Tax. My debt to the contributors, and especially Professor Norman B. Schwartz, is great.

Support for the organization of the symposium that led to this volume was provided during a postdoctoral year in the Department of Anthropology and the Medical Anthropology Training Program, Michigan State University. Special thanks are due Dr. Arthur Rubel, director of the Medical Anthropology Training Program, and Dr. Bernard Gallin, chairman of the Department of Anthropology, both of Michigan State University. The volume would never have reached the publisher without the efforts of my coeditors, Professor John

Hawkins, Department of Anthropology, Brigham Young University and Professor Laurel Bossen, Department of Anthropology, University of Pittsburgh. Special thanks are due Martin Hickman, dean of the College of Family, Home, and Social Sciences at Brigham Young University, who generously provided the university's word-processing facilities for preparation of the manuscript. I wish to thank Professor John Sorenson, chairman, Department of Anthropology, Brigham Young University, for his support, both financial and collegial, during my stay in Provo. Dr. Stan Taylor, Center for International and Area Studies, Brigham Young University, kindly provided additional office services. The Institute for Communications Research, Stanford University, and Professor Dennis Foote kindly gave me the time to complete the manuscript in Provo. Finally I must thank Professor Hawkins, his wife Carol Lee, and their children for their generous hospitality.

Carl Kendall
August 1981
Provo, Utah

Overview of the Volume

This volume explores changes in Mesoamerican anthropology, and changes in Mesoamerica, that have occurred since the publication of *Heritage of Conquest* in 1952. The volume is not an encyclopedia, but rather a diverse sampler of new topic areas and new approaches in anthropology.

The new topic areas include state and regional analysis, women's studies, demography, urbanization, historical studies, education, and medical anthropology. The new approaches include economic and political class analysis, decision modeling, national-level survey research, structuralist and phenomenological symbolic studies, and semiotic analysis.

The papers cluster easily in three areas of social theory. The first group of papers explores the large-scale forces and institutions that shape and constrain social life. The second group explores the richness and flexibility of local life in terms of available choices and the premises for choosing. The third group delves into the internalized cultural ideas that underlie and define perception and action.

Part I, *The Regional Perspective: The Articulations of State, Region, and Locale,* deals with the macrosocial and exogenous (from the perspective of the community) factors that are now shaping so much of Mesoamerican life. These include the ramifying ties of government and national and multinational economic institutions that affect the rural people of Mesoamerica. These exogenous factors, if they did not in the past, are expanding their control over local political and economic sectors. They are becoming a significant component of the politicojural domain of events in rural Mesoamerica. Their effects are both transient and uneven, and therefore require historical documentation and careful regional comparisons.

Part II, *Mesoamerican Institutions: New Modes of Analysis,* deals with domestic functions such as enculturation, household partition, and health-seeking behavior. The traditional topics of kinship and postmarital residence are treated with new (for Mesoamerica) approaches, and the bureaucratic institutionalization of education and health are discussed.

Part III, *Symbolism and Culture: Some Recent Approaches,* addresses the indigenous religious domain of Mesoamerican life. The papers demonstrate a number of new approaches to the analysis of symbols in this domain and demonstrate the links between these symbols and the national order of events characterized in Sections I and II.

By examining the political, economic, and regional-level world in Part I, the practical world of Part II, and the internal subjective world of Part III, the volume reveals a broad picture of Mesoamerican life and Mesoamerican scholarship. The whole is then ably summarized by Professor Norman B. Schwartz, in his afterword.

History

The present volume is a collaborative effort in the fullest sense. Dr. Sol Tax and Dr. Fernando Cámara first suggested a Mesoamerican resynthesis at the American Anthropological Association meetings in Washington, D.C., November 1976. Drs. Tax and Cámara were original participants in a symposium entitled Heritage of Conquest, sponsored by the Wenner-Gren Foundation for Anthropological Re-

search in August and September of 1949. The symposium was sub-
sequently published (1952) as *The Heritage of Conquest*. Nearly thirty
years had passed since that first symposium, and the original participants felt that perhaps the time had come to review the changes in
Mesoamerican scholarship.

The original participants in the symposium (as Dr. Schwartz mentions in his afterword to this volume) shared, if not a common paradigm for research, at least a familiarity with each other's works. In
organizing the Second Heritage of Conquest symposium, however,
the problem immediately arose of maintaining close agreement of
themes and papers in the face of increasing diversity and specialization within Mesoamerican studies, and indeed within contemporary
anthropology.

There are indications of this diversity at every turn. A number of
reviews, including that of Chambers and Young (1979), demonstrate
the quantity of publications found in Mesoamerican anthropology.
To their community-study review could be added the publications
in comparative and regional studies in Mesoamerican archaeology,
linguistics, the development literature, and the work of historians
and demographers. National and international health agencies have
conducted investigations as well, often incorporating anthropologists.
Increasingly activist perspectives were being taken by scholars in
Mexico and Guatemala to aid indigenous peoples and other deprived
groups in their struggles for social justice. How then to characterize
Mesoamerican anthropology?

An effort was made to define the scope of a Mesoamerican review
at the Society for Applied Anthropology meetings in Mérida, Mexico in 1978. An executive committee met to discuss ways to implement the thirty-year review of *Heritage of Conquest*.[1] The committee
noted that the original volume was novel in a number of ways, including the push for synthesis from the contributors, and the broad
appeal of the topics. Dr. Cámara voiced hope for the production of a
second volume that would incorporate these and other innovations.
They concluded that the second volume would build on the first by
expanding the focus of the volume in three directions: (1) by ques-
tioning the original definitions of the area and divisions into topic
areas, (2) by attempting to synthesize recent work in Mesoamerica,
and (3) by looking at the implications of anthropology for the future
of the region.

The committee agreed with Sol Tax that the new volume should use the same base as the 1949 conference, focusing on social anthropology and ethnology in Mesoamerica. Moreover, they concluded that the core areas could be expanded both topically and geographically, and be subjected to a number of different intellectual approaches, incorporating such recent developments as ecological, cognitive, symbolic, structuralist, activist, and applied and optative studies.

There was substantial agreement in the committee about the format of the volume. There was less consensus about the topics for the content. New topics included linguistics, ethnohistory, population studies and population processes, a session on anthropology in development, a session on the role of women in Mesoamerica.

One member expressed some fear that the session could grow too large and encyclopedic, and the committee considered ways to narrow the focus of the meetings and still include a broad range of opinions.

Thus the common goal of the second symposium and subsequent volume was to be a nonencyclopedic review of traditional and new topics. But the problems inherent in such an undertaking proved difficult. It was clear that Mesoamerican anthropology had grown enormously, and that the peoples with whom anthropologists had worked were undergoing profound changes. It was also apparent that anthropologists' perspectives were diverse, and that they did not share a common paradigm for anthropology. Neither were they necessarily familiar with each other's works, as had been true for the participants in the original Heritage conference. The original *Heritage of Conquest* contained presentations from scholars who were familiar with the archaeology, history, linguistics, and ethnography of their day. Wisdom, for example, was originally trained as an archaeologist but did ethnographic fieldwork in Jocotán. The diversity apparent in the original volume seemed to derive not from the disparate paradigmatic commitments but from different ethnographic contexts.

By contrast, participants in the second symposium represent more divergent approaches that reflect the overall growth of the field, and a flowering of new theoretical interests. Faced with this variety, some scholars felt that fruitful communication would be difficult, and a natural winnowing of the volume occurred. Ultimately, the participants in this volume include those who held that, despite their apparent diversity, the significance of the Mesoamerican ethnographic tradition would remain a unifying force.

Mesoamerica, to claim a parallel with J. Davis's (1977) discussion of the Mediterranean, has been fertile ground for anthropology. From Las Casas to John Lloyd Stephens to Redfield, the area has been explored for clues to the significant "other" of our ethnographic imagination. As comparative sociology, notions such as the folk society, the culture of poverty, and the open and closed corporate community have had a large impact on anthropology. Mesoamerica's proximity to North America has meant that the region is the site of much peripatetic fieldwork, even for scholars with specialties in other areas. For example, both Tylor and Malinowski published work on Mexico. More recently, Victor Turner has worked in Mexico, although these scholars are primarily known for contributions elsewhere. Although well studied and richly documented, the diverse materials of the many Mesoamerican studies have not been successfully synthesized.

Our volume does not achieve this goal, but it is a beginning. By juxtaposing the new topics and perspectives of these papers with the topics and papers of the original *Heritage of Conquest* volume, it is hoped we will have satisfied some small part of J. Davis's prescription that "each ethnographer who pursues knowledge within his area of interest should pay attention to what his predecessors have done and what his successors will require of him" (1977:16).

NOTES

1. The executive committee included Fernando Cámara, chair, Sheila Cosminsky, Barbara Dahlgren, Munro Edmunson, Carl Kendall, Alfredo Méndez-Domínguez, Emma Pérez-Rocha, Michael Salovesh, and Sol Tax.

REFERENCES

Chambers, Erve J., and Philip D. Young
1979   "Mesoamerican Community Studies: The Past Decade," *Annual Review of Anthropology* 8:45-69.
Davis, J.
1977   *People of the Mediterranean: An Essay in Comparative Social Anthropology* (London: Routledge and Kegan Paul).

I

The Regional Perspective: The Articulations of State, Region, and Locale

Introduction

An emphasis on the impact of political-economic institutions and social processes radiating from centers "outside" the local field site underlies much of the changing approach to Mesoamerican anthropology. Since the early sixties, the impact of the state and of regional structures of domination has gained substantial recognition. The early works (Stavenhagen and Aguirre Beltrán, for example) argued that the state is instrumental in regional exploitation, and also contributes to the marginalization of rural peoples. The more recent research, pursuing this theme, explores the impact of the macrolevel social and economic structures and their attendant ideological changes upon domains of community and family life that anthropologists formerly analyzed in relative isolation.

The four papers in this section deal with different topics—state impact, sexual stratification, national censuses, ethnic demography, and urban history. Until recently all of these topics were unconventional in anthropology. All of them share, however, a perspective that permits them to examine "causal and conditioning factors" emanating from beyond the perspective of the local community (Russell 1913). All are comparative. And all are concerned with process and history.

A concern with history and with comparison is not new to anthropology. In fact, anthropology developed "intensive studies of limited areas" (Fortes 1953:16) in response to a highly speculative stage of ethnological investigation that ranged across economic, legal, political, and religious topics as well as tribe, nation, race, and history. Fortes describes the nature of this response in his *History of Social Anthropology at Cambridge,* a report coterminous with the publication of the first *Heritage of Conquest.* "Now good ethnography," he observed, "must be local, particular, and circumstantial. It must, as Malinowski wrote, take in the "imponderabilia of actual life and typical behavior" (1953:27). Indeed, Sol Tax had advocated a move in this direction as early as 1937. Opposing the implicit treatment of indigenous language groups as homogenous or organized cultural units, Tax maintained that local diversity was such that "the study of ethnology of Guatemala must start with the study of the cultures of municipios as individual units" (1937).

Given the legitimacy of this concern, much of the anthropological profession passed through a period of retreat from the investigation of larger issues and institutions that impinge upon such localized units (see Harris 1968) or the historical context of their development. The rejection of speculative generalizations and pseudohistory, however, need not entail a complete loss of historical and integrating perspectives. Indeed, the works of a growing group of scholars, from Gunder Frank (1967) and Wallerstein (1974, 1980) at the world-system level to Aguirre Beltrán (1967) and Stavenhagen (1975) at the regional-national level, have shown that we cannot ignore the impact of external political and economic forces upon our local cultural "units." Nor can we understand such larger system processes and their impact on the microenvironment without reference to a careful history of the changes in these institutions. Indeed, at a time when the indigenous peoples of western Guatemala are under attack from their own government, no scholar can avoid the implications of state penetration seen in a historical context.

As Corbett and Whiteford point out in the first article of this volume (State Penetration and Development in Mesoamerica, 1950-1980), the need to trace state development in Mexico is due to the increasing impact of the state and state-supported capitalist growth in rural areas, a fact that merits consideration even in ethnographies of a limited area. They show that the description of this process requires careful attention to institutional history, because policy is often developed behind closed doors and far away from the anthropologist's field site. Fieldwork in rural areas of Mexico and Guatemala demonstrates that markets and services that originate in state or regional centers are important for local populations, and affect their lives.

Corbett and Whiteford further maintain that links between the state and regional development underlie changes in land tenure, political structure, and agricultural labor relations in the rural community. They explore this process in terms of three kinds of penetration into the rural locales: structural, cultural, and institutional. Tracing these processes upward to the center, the authors discuss important features of Mexican history and government which shape national policy. Tracing them downward, they demonstrate the unanticipated consequences of these interventions. Their report demonstrates the full range of possibilities open to researchers who would pursue such linkages. Within the community, the different interventions have effects that can be studied systematically; outside the community the policies can be seen as satisfying regional, national, or international interests. Anthropologists will always be called on to evaluate how programs are working "out there," and the paper provides an excellent framework for this examination, as Dr. Schwartz points out in the Afterword.

Outside penetration is also evident in the economic and cultural expansion of capitalism, a process which generates new forms of social relations and increased stratification. Bossen's paper (Sexual Stratification in Mesoamerica) argues that this expansion has distinctive and pronounced negative effects upon women. She maintains that many of these effects were heretofore unrecognized or misunderstood because the status of women was attributed to strictly local, if not purely domestic, cultural factors. The increased mobility of rural and urban populations is taken as an opportunity to explore how changing economic environments affect women's roles, and how women are incorporated into a new division of labor and dependency. Bossen reviews the sparse treatment of women in the original *Heritage of Conquest* volume and assesses the more recent literature on women in Mesoamerica. The systematic analysis of changes in women's status in the labor force and corresponding changes in the social relations of production demonstrate that the investigation of larger changes can be fruitful to understanding sexual stratification in its local forms.

Bossen's paper is unusual in that it includes a number of communities representing both rural and urban contexts. Not only does her work integrate community-level data into a regional perspective, but it opens up a major area of research on sexual stratification that for too long has been lost in the shadow of ethnic stratification.

Early's paper (A Demographic Survey of Contemporary Guatemalan Maya) summarizes a much larger study of three Guatemalan national censuses. Early addresses broad questions of cultural geography that were certainly of concern to the original Heritage of Conquest symposium: How many Maya are there in Guatemala? Where are they? How are they changing?

The increasing penetration of the state in Guatemala and Mexico has brought in its wake periodic massive surveys of rural peoples that can provide a wealth of information for anthropologists. Survey research methodology is a natural partner of macrosocial studies. But the use of survey research by anthropologists has been hampered by the incompatibilities between fieldwork data and survey data, due to the obstacles for census projects inherent in the field. For example, the limited linguistic interaction provided in questionnaire administration is new and alien to many rural environments; census items are not properly pretested; tables or proxy lists for the selection of random samples are not available; and interviewers are not dependable.

Nevertheless, Early shows how anthropologists can bring to these investigations and analyses much expertise, often in the form of what survey researchers call pilot studies. This expertise is essential for "conceptualization" and "objectification" of variables. Anthropologists must, as well, participate in the debate concerning the parameters of their subject area. Early's report helps define the Maya, in a contemporary sense, much as Kirchhoff's review of archaeological evidence defines Mesoamerica in the original *Heritage of Conquest* volume.

The difficulty of such analysis is sketched in Early's paper. Indicators of Indian identity were developed by the National Census Bureau for each census, but these indicators changed from census to census. Furthermore, little in the way of analysis was conducted to validate these indicators for Guatemala as a whole. Although changes in these indicators can be shown, the question remains, how sensitive are these indicators and what do their apparent changes signify? Early promises to answer these questions in a forthcoming book.

Kemper and Royce (Urbanization in Mexico: Beyond the Heritage of Conquest) trace the pattern of urbanization through history in several Mexican sites. Urbanization is another topic that received relatively short shrift in the original volume, although Redfield's work in the Yucatán was seminal for the description of rural and urban locales. The result, though, of Redfield's famous work was a turning away from urban studies, as Hawkins's paper later in this volume demonstrates.

Kemper and Royce's paper is a study of the historiography of urbanization as well as a description of the urbanization process itself. Although the term urbanization implies a process that evolves through time, its social scientific characterization remains elusive. As Kemper and Royce point out, the urban centers themselves are related to each other, as well as to rural locales, growing and shrinking with a rhythm of their own. The linkage of these centers and peripheries constitutes an element of the field of social organization that was, until recently, rarely treated in the anthropological literature.

These four papers exemplify ways in which the gap between the study of small communities and the study of national social and economic change can be bridged. The state, the expanding capitalist economy, demographic trends, and urbanization are brought to the analysis of economic, sexual, ethnic, and rural-urban divisions that anthropologists confront at the microlevel. These papers represent an important shift in emphasis that is surely essential to a contemporary understanding of the heritage of conquest in Mesoamerica.

REFERENCES

Aguirre Beltrán, Gonzolo
1967   *Regiones de refúgio: El desarrollo de la comunidad y el proceso domini-cal en Mestizoamerica* (Mexico: Instituto Nacional Indigenista).

Fortes, M.
1953   *Social Anthropology at Cambridge Since 1900* (Cambridge: Cambridge University Press).
Gunder Frank, André
1967   *Capitalism and Underdevelopment in Latin America* (New York: Monthly Review Press).
Harris, Marvin
1968   *The Rise of Anthropological Theory* (New York: Thomas Y. Crowell).
Russell, B.
1913   *On the Notion of Cause,* Proceedings of the Aristotelian Society 13 (new series):1-26.
Stavenhagen, Rodolfo
1975   *Social Classes in Agrarian Societies,* trans. Judy Adler Hellman (New York: Doubleday, Anchor Press).
Tax, Sol
1937   "The Municipios of the Midwestern Highlands of Guatemala," *American Anthropologist* 39:423-44.
Wallerstein, Immanuel
1974   *The Modern World-System I: Capitalist Agriculture and the Origins of European World-Economy in the Sixteenth Century* (New York: Academic Press).
1980   *The Modern World-System II: Mercantilism and the Consolidation of the European World-Economy, 1600-1750* (New York: Academic Press).

1

State Penetration and Development in Mesoamerica, 1950–1980

Jack Corbett
Southwest Texas State University
and
Scott Whiteford
Michigan State University

A notable feature of social change in the twentieth century has been the transformation of the state from an institution with limited responsibilities centered on system maintenance to an activist institution continuously mobilizing and allocating resources in pursuit of a broad array of societal goals. Elites and masses have come to expect high levels of governmental output (although their priorities may differ), and failure by the government to make the expected effort may lead to the withdrawal of support or open opposition to national authorities. The state is expected not only to defend its citizens and protect them from harm, but to secure their welfare through the promotion of broad-gauge socioeconomic development. The need to satisfy a variety of expectations places a premium on rational management and effective use of resources, which in turn leads political systems to emphasize control and implementation capabilities. Thus, political leaders seek to ensure that demands made upon the government will not outstrip its ability to respond, and that decisions made at the center will be carried out. The organizational requirements of an activist government foster a need to develop a communications and compliance network by penetrating all sectors and aspects of society, particularly those where its authority and capabilities traditionally have been weak. Thus penetration, often in the form of organizational or institutional linkages, serves both control and developmental functions.

In Mexico, the rise of the activist state has been superimposed upon a heterogeneous society with a long history of conflict between those who centralize power and influence, and those preferring cultural, economic, or political autonomy. It is a conflict epitomized by tensions between Mexico City and regional interests. Center-periphery conflict is a recurring theme in Mexican history, taking forms ranging from the formation of social or political alliances to manipulation of economic resources. On occasion, the conflict takes the form of overt violence. After the Mexican Revolution, the suppression of the Cristeros and various regional strongmen opened the way for an expansion of central authority, a central authority now buttressing its legitimacy through programmatic responses to the Revolution's rallying cry of "Land and Bread." The modernization focus of the Mexican government did not necessarily require a confrontation with other institutions and interests, but rather their capture or cooptation (Anderson and Cockcroft 1966; Hellman 1978).[1] In addition, the central government began formally to institutionalize linkages with heretofore peripheral social aggregates by creating bureaucratic units. The government used these links to shape the character, pace, scope, and intensity of development and to limit or restrain adverse feedbacks. To many policymakers and elites, the Mexican Revolution is a vivid, harsh object lesson of what can happen when social change and developmental processes escape their control.

The policies and programs of the Mexican government must be placed in the context of international pressures and relationships. Mexico's course of modernization through dependent capitalism has led to the accumulation of a significant international debt and government emphasis on capital-intensive agricultural and industrial growth (Barkin 1978). State elites utilizing a dependent capitalist model of modernization have extended state power; at the same time they have utilized this power to remove obstacles to the expansion of capitalism (Esteva 1980).

The process of penetration and integration calls attention to a critical conceptual problem in anthropology, linking different levels of analysis. Mesoamerican research during the 1950s was dominated by the community paradigm in which the community was the largest unit of analysis. This paradigm conceptually bounded the research both methodologically and theoretically, ignoring the penetration of economic and political institutions, linkage mechanisms, and exploitation. The focus was closely tied to the community-development methods of applied anthropology during that period.

Research skills and concepts necessary for work within a community are not always transferable to the analysis of relationships between segments of the community and external actors. The study of culture tends to be holistic and bounded, with the community serving as a convenient and manageable unit of analysis (Schwartz 1978:235). There is no doubt that a generation or two ago, transactions between most communities and the larger societal environment were fewer in number and less central to community life than they are today. In such circumstances the practice of abstracting the community from its broader setting to facilitate the study of cosmology or social dynamics may have been possible without doing violence to key elements in the system or process. But the notion of the isolated community, probably never justifiable empirically or heuristically, has become increasingly anachronistic in an era characterized by aggressive penetration efforts by the national government and an expanding web of economic relationships.

The community paradigm in Mesoamerican research began to shift as anthropologists like Wolf (1957) and Adams (1964) developed frameworks to analyze the nature of integration and conflict between different levels of society. During the same period, studies by North American political scientists dealt almost exclusively with national-level institutions and processes, ignoring the complexity of the interaction between the state and the subordinate political and economic systems of the communities. The Marxian analysis of underdevelopment stemming from the work of Gunnder Frank (1967, 1969) and Samir Amin (1975), among others, led to a series of studies concerning the penetration of capitalism and the role of the state.

The striking conceptual contribution of the Mexican social scientists emerged during the 1970s. Those writing in the Marxist tradition, such as Stavenhagen (1960), Gonzales (1972), Warmen (1976), and Palerm (1980) shifted from the community paradigm and focused on how economic and political forces impinge upon local systems. The political economy perspective, emphasizing diachronic instead of synchronic analysis, placed the processes in a historical perspective (Barkin 1978) and even included historical analysis, a dimension neglected by many American social scientists. The attention given by Latin American scholars not only to local-national political linkages, but also to the interaction between local political systems and broader patterns of economic organization and control is of particular importance. Batra et al. (1976), Eckard Goege (1979), and Sergio de la Peña (1981) develop this theme well.

The conceptual framework presented in this article focuses on the political dimension of the expansion of state power and its impact on the local-level actors and institutions. Like other aspects of the social and natural environment, the political domain presents sources of stress: a set of constraints and an array of opportunities for different segments of the population. The notion of state penetration may be broken down into at least three categories: ideological penetration, institutional transformation, and structural penetration. These general categories may overlap in practice: the establishment of a school in an Indian community (structural penetration) facilitates the teaching of Spanish (cultural penetration). As the discussion of structural penetration below will show, it is possible to subdivide the general categories of penetration into analytically distinct subunits.

Categories of State Penetration

IDEOLOGICAL PENETRATION

If the government goal of integration has been to create a more homogeneous, unified population, then a critical concern must be the assimilation (or at least the acceptance) of dominant-sector values and behavior by the groups that are the targets of penetration. Efforts to foster such integration date back to obligatory conversions to Catholicism in the sixteenth and seventeenth centuries, and to elimination of the community landholding system in the mid-nineteenth century. Post-Revolution attempts include numerous programs to teach Spanish to Indian monolinguals (Heath 1971), patriotic rituals and symbolic acts to develop a sense of national identity, aggressive promotion of consumerism and consumption of manufactured goods, and a gradual shift from corporatist or collective value patterns to individualism—from maintaining one's position in a stable community to "getting ahead" on an individual basis. This is not to argue that traditional values are superior or that new behaviors are inherently pernicious, but to emphasize that ideological penetration works consistently to break down buffers to interaction and to make target groups more receptive to national values.

INSTITUTIONAL TRANSFORMATION

Institutional transformation involves the capture of traditional institutions for purposes of penetration and integration. One clear case is the gradual undercutting of traditional community autonomy as the central government extends its control over local government bodies. This may involve regulation of budgets and taxes, introduction of new standards of criminal justice or recruitment practices, or the reduction in local policy discretion through guidelines and supervision. The net effect is to maintain the form of the traditional institution while converting its function to service as an administrative arm of the state. Market systems, once a means of exchange among peasants and a source of the cash income needed to buy occasional necessities, increasingly serve as a means to distribute manufactured goods to peasants and to tie them more tightly to the national cash economy (Beals 1975, Cook and Diskin 1975). Through fees and taxes, markets support an administrative superstructure which then mobilizes participants to support government policies (Waterbury 1970). Institutional transformation enables external groups and agents to use the authority of traditional institutions to influence decisions and secure compliance.

STRUCTURAL PENETRATION

Whereas institutional transformation refers to changes in existing institutions, structural penetration means the creation of new structures supporting integration. Integration may not be their formal or principal function, but the new structures work in that direction. Although new structures show considerable variation in their specific form—they may be roads or political parties, for example—they share the common characteristic of linking the penetrators and the penetrated. That is, they increase the volume of interaction. Again, this does not mean that such ties are always negative or disadvantageous to peripheral groups, only that the frame of reference for choices or decisions tends to swing from the local to the national level. Specific kinds of linkages are outlined below.

1. Services. A major thrust of Mexican social and economic policy since the Revolution has been to extend services such as education, health care, and agricultural credit to rural areas. Early administrations neglected southern Mexico, but since the 1950s this neglect has diminished, although the region still lags behind the rest of the country in socioeconomic indicators and service levels. Basic services provide a developmental base, and at the same time the local population becomes sufficiently dependent upon them that their reduction or withdrawal is perceived as a serious threat. The key, however, is that services appear to the local population to be a desirable benefit of integration and serve as a stimulus and opening for other kinds of integrative activities (Grindle 1977).

2. Infrastructure. The comments regarding services also apply to infrastructure development in the form of roads, electrification, and water supplies, for example. Infrastructure investment is instituted to improve communications and economic productivity, and to facilitate interaction between local producers and national markets. Heavy investments in roads, electricity, and the like may also initiate conflict between policymakers and communities or local groups. The latter may see themselves as forced to pay for projects of greater utility to outsiders than to themselves. And local producers may find that roads or similar projects make it possible for outsiders to undercut them in local markets, a fate that has been hard on many of the local crafts once found throughout southern Mexico.

3. Organizations. Among new organizational linkages, perhaps the most widely recognized and influential has been the ejido system. Ejidos combine a variety of social, economic, and political facets to give them a far-ranging influence over their members (Ronfeldt 1973). In addition, structure and policy for ejidos originate in the Mexican cabinet, linking the system to the highest levels of national decision making. It is possible to conceptualize organizational linkages as existing on a continuum, from the multidimensional organizations with coercive power, such as ejidos, through intermediate organizations, such as peasant unions or marketing groups, down to essentially voluntary associations with only a limited sphere of influence.

Social networks provide a critical dimension in linking state institutions and local-level organizations. Networks facilitate the exchange process by which the state allocates resources for political and economic compliance (Carlos and Anderson n.d.:24). Peasants may adroitly capture resources from the state or play one state agency off against another with the aid of effective networks. Nevertheless, this is part of a system of control. Networks are both vertical and horizontal in nature, linking communities and sectors to regional or national levels of power through brokers or caciques (Bartra 1975). Populations without effective networks tend to be left out of the state reallocation process.

4. Political Parties. To legitimize its continuing control of the political system, the Partido Revolucionario Institucional (PRI), the dominant party in Mexico, has attempted to extend its influence into almost every hamlet and civic group in the country. The party exists to mobilize support for the government and to co-opt or choke off potential opposition (Hansen 1971; Johnson 1978). The PRI is in an anomalous position in that it is not an "official" body, yet because of its relationship to political power it constitutes a major intrusion into almost every sector of society. Other parties exist, but their activities in most of Mesoamerica are much weaker, and their influence far more restricted, than those of the PRI. While it is not a totalitarian party, its organization and internal processes are far more sensitive to inputs from the top than from the masses. It is the penetrative instrument par excellence (Corbett 1980a). Not surprisingly, then, even communities and groups willing to accept service or infrastructure penetration often will resist penetration and control by the PRI.

It should be noted that penetration is facilitated by changes and preferences within the target groups or communities, which view it as bringing new opportunities or desirable improvements in the quality of life, such as better health care or a higher standard of living. Acceptance may reflect new aspirations or perceptions, or a response to pressures from population growth or environmental change. Marketing opportunities may stimulate receptivity to or a desire for resources only available outside the local system, e.g., credit or irrigation. Thus even in the absence of systematic efforts at penetration from outside, the peripheral populations of Mesoamerica might gradually find integration desirable. On the other hand, the loss of autonomy may expose groups or communities to a decline in the quality of life and a condition of permanent dependency and internal colonialism. Integration can bring either substantial benefits or dismal exploitation or both.

Oaxaca: Development and the Politics of Penetration

The persistence of traditional society in Oaxaca makes it a mecca for scholars and tourists, but it also reflects the low level of development and long neglect by the central government. Oaxaca ranks at or near the bottom on almost every list of socioeconomic indicators, and in some cases the gap between Oaxaca and national standards is growing rather than diminishing. The state has a long history of resistance to domination by the center and a sense of autonomy that influences local responses to federal initiatives. Despite its prominence in nineteenth-century Mexican politics, in many respects Oaxaca has been a backwater since the Revolution, especially in its inability to compete for public and private investment. Topography and other physical factors make development expensive (road and power-line construction cost twice the national average), so cost-benefit ratios have favored other regions. The state's peripheral role in the Revolution left it without powerful families, such as the Calles and Obregons of Sonora, or other political influence over the allocation of scarce national resources. Finally, most peasant communities in Oaxaca valued stability over development, just as local elites preferred not to unleash change that might disturb the existing social order.

Over the past generation local and national perspectives have shifted to favor more extensive development in Oaxaca. Reasons for this shift range from population growth and ideological penetration to a recognition of the problems and opportunities in disparities of development (Corbett 1980b). However, different groups attach different values to different forms of development while the state's continued inability to command large-scale external funding makes it impossible to attend to all needs simultaneously. Furthermore, many people in Oaxaca believe that the population at large bears the social and financial costs, but that the benefits will accrue to a few. Indeed, a common complaint holds that development projects more closely reflect the priorities of the agencies involved and the interests of powerful groups outside the state than they do local needs. Consequently there have been numerous center-local conflicts over the process, substance, and cost/benefit distributions of development programs: federal agencies seek to assure maximum local participation in cost sharing, while local interests respond that low levels of development leave them with few resources to contribute. To a degree, the national government finds itself in a double bind, as both low levels of development and its responses to low levels of development provoke dissatisfaction and conflict. These tensions are aggravated by the authoritarian paternalism in Mexican political culture, which leads central authorities to regard target populations as manipulable supplicants, and to repress rather than accommodate dissent. It is not surprising, therefore, that the government has turned to penetration via institutional transformation and structural penetration as a means of securing compliance and support.

INSTITUTIONAL TRANSFORMATION

Although rarely given explicit attention by anthropologists, pressures for institutional transformation have had a major influence for a generation on community political systems. The civil-religious hierarchy that long governed most Oaxaca municipios generally has been superseded by secular local government, and traditional community autonomy is on the wane (Iszaevich 1973; Lees 1973; Ugalde 1973; Corbett 1974). A steady stream of correspondence and circulars flows from Mexico City to even the most remote municipio, directing local authorities to collect or disseminate information, carry out specific administrative tasks, or provide programmatic support—mobilize labor, for example, or collect the community's share of development costs. Working through local institutions rather than abolishing them or creating an extensive field network permits external actors to draw upon the legitimacy of tradition. The ayuntamiento and related offices also provide local-level administrative capabilities, however rudimentary, across 570 municipios and all linguistic groups, a burden that would weigh heavily upon government agencies. Linkages with the center are not codified or formalized, but pressures for compliance range from implicit threats of sanctions against the entire community to direct public abuse of ayuntamiento members. Thus the frame of reference for community government is shifting from internal system maintenance to the management of relations with external government actors. As a result, municipio authorities find themselves with additional responsibilities and less freedom of action. As the locus and focus of decision making shifts from the ayuntamiento to external bodies, the moral authority of local leaders and institutions, long the key element in community governance, has declined. The importance of bureaucratic power and patron-client relations has, in turn, increased.

Penetration raises special problems for the *presidente municipal,* as it involves major changes in the substance of the role with few outward alterations in the form. Dennis (1973) suggests that one crucial aspect of change is the increasing importance of a middleman function, assuring smooth interaction between the community and more inclusive political systems. Under the civil-religious hierarchy the *presidente* stood at the apex of the community political system, drawing upon accumulated knowledge and prestige to supervise ritual, resolve disputes, and represent the community in its limited interaction with the outside world. Tradition defined appropriate conduct, and the legitimacy of the *presidente* was enhanced by close formal ties to community religious institutions. Today the *presidente* must cope with a much wider range of problems within a shorter time horizon, usually without the guidance of tradition in decision making and without the additional legitimacy once provided through the civil-religious hierarchy. Rather than represent community interests to external agencies, the *presidente* comes under pressures from these to act as their *de facto* agent within the community. To do so would violate traditional norms of officeholding, undermining the authority of the *presidente* and raising the spectre of cleavage within the community. Yet failure to respond to outside pressures may expose the *presidente* to charges of ineptitude, misconduct, or obstructionism, and to possible punitive measures by the agencies involved. Thus while the formal position of *presidente municipal* has changed little since the Revolution, the need to serve multiple and sometimes conflicting constituencies places a great strain upon individuals who fill it, and it is not surprising that several studies report a declining willingness to hold public office (Kearney 1972; Corbett 1974, 1977; Whitecotton 1977).

STRUCTURAL PENETRATION

To the casual observer the most obvious signs of structural penetration are the new roads, schools, power lines, and water systems that have proliferated around the state since the 1950s. Particularly impressive is the expansion of services and physical infrastructure in such formerly isolated and ignored parts of the state as the tropical lowlands bordering Veracruz or along the Pacific Ocean. The recent completion of the coastal highway from the Guerrero state line to Salina Cruz will open extensive areas to agriculture, tourism, and resource development. One outgrowth of recent developmental policies has been a gradual redistribution of population and economic power away from the old core of the Sierra, Mixteca Alta, and Central Valley in favor of the tropics to the north and east (Corbett 1980b). A second outgrowth has been the conversion of land that was formerly almost worthless because of access problems into a valuable commodity, a transformation giving rise to machinations by speculators and well-connected entrepreneurs who hope to replace subsistence farms and ejidos with agribusiness or luxury resorts.

The steady expansion of services and infrastructure, whether attributable to community request or macro-level planning, invariably fosters organizational penetration through the proliferation of boards or commissions to oversee or participate in operations or maintenance. Schools, potable water, CONASUPO stores, electricity, irrigation, and other products of development all spawn bodies that must work with government agencies, and in doing so they serve as communications links between the national government and the community. Such linkages can far outweigh, numerically, the formal relationship between the ayuntamiento and other levels of government. Ugalde (1973) found 132 permanent civic offices in Diaz Ordaz, enough to require 25 percent of the adult males to participate in community governance at any one time. Of course not all these offices permit penetration by extralocal agencies, but the figure provides some insight into the potential complexity of local systems as they begin to experience development. Nor are the impacts solely quantitative (1973:86). Lees points out that the intrusion of the federal government into local water-resources management has introduced a fundamental change in the locus of authority at the municipio level: "water control officials [members of the community] are set apart from other public officials in the community because they are delegates of the state and federal government agencies." She notes that water is a special case, but a centralizing government could seize upon this model to pursue penetration through other service or development areas.

Expanding political party activity (especially by PRI) is a less obvious form of penetration. The PRI controls recruitment for political office at the state and national levels and in urban areas, and seeks to expand its influence over local positions in rural communities. Effective control over the ayuntamientos provides a means of (1) blocking or co-opting dissent, and (2) mobilizing community residents to show support for the regime through the ballot box or through public displays such as campaign rallies. Mobilization has become especially important as other signs of political discontent, such as electoral abstentions or guerrilla activities, become increasingly evident. The PRI's ability to fulfill welfare functions and its close relationship with the bureaucracy provide the leverage necessary to recruit community-level committees and local influentials (teachers or ayuntamiento members) by exchanging its assistance for their support.

In practice the PRI's influence has been less than its dominant position would suggest, for the very notions of "party" and "linkage," with their implications of divisiveness and interaction, conflict with deeply ingrained community norms. Whatever the short-term, instrumental benefit to a few, most communities have little enthusiasm for increasing their vulnerability to external manipulation or imposing further strain on a system of social relations already buffeted by other forms of change. Community unity and harmony, though often idealized images rather than accurate descriptions of reality, still offer some protection against a penetration which has rarely displayed much sympathy for the needs of the campesino. Yet with the decline in corporate values, and continuing penetration in other ways, it is unclear how long communities will withstand party penetration and the attendant subordination of local political life to external political control.

Penetration and the Future of Development in Oaxaca

There is no reason to expect the coming decades to bring a reduction or reversal in the pressures for penetration. Population growth, a rising sensitivity to relative deprivation, and other factors will contribute to increased local demands for development, demands that inevitably mean higher levels of interaction between social groups or communities in Oaxaca and the central government. The central government's inability to satisfy all demands simultaneously, the need to resolve conflicting demands, and tensions over the proper distribution of development costs and benefits will reinforce the current tendency to emphasize political control. The political turmoil in Oaxaca in 1977, which resulted in the removal of Manuel Zarate Acquino as governor, could be attributed in part to struggles between local and Mexico City interests over which would benefit from development expenditures in various parts of the state. The PRI, which maintains its position less through public enthusiasm than through disarray on the part of its opponents, may feel pressed to pursue more aggressive programs of political mobilization. And technocratic governments (such as that of José López Portillo), which place a premium on stability and rationally organized development, may be expected to sustain policies facilitating penetration.

Structuring the Local Environment:
The Expanding Role of the State and Commercial Agriculture

The following case study examines transformation and structural penetration in the sugar zone of the Tehuacán Valley, Puebla, Mexico. While the process of expanding state power in the countryside and the coopting of peasant institutions has been occurring at an accelerated pace throughout Mexico, its nature and intensity vary between regions and within regions. The character of the uneven expansion is linked to the role of local regions and subregions within the dependent capitalist economy. The number of state-controlled programs and their impact is usually greater in zones of commercial agriculture. More marginal regions that are not integrated into the multiple government programs are often linked to the capitalistic production process as labor reserves (Stavenhagen 1978). These structural factors play an important role in generating the constraints to which individuals and groups adapt. Patterns of economic activity, community organization, and social relationships reflect adaptation to the constraints.

State involvement in sugar production in Mexico can be traced back to the colonial period, but the twentieth century witnessed a major expansion of state power and new ways in which it is utilized. In the late nineteenth century, with the expanding world demand for sugar and the accompanying technological changes in the processing of cane, Mexico emerged as a major exporter of sugar. During this period sugarcane was grown on the vast haciendas and foreign capital played an important role. By 1900 competition between Mexican sugar producers had become intense, and the growers of Morelos, Puebla, and Veracruz allied themselves in order to hold down production levels and maintain prices (Womack 1969:79). By 1908 sugar prices had doubled. It was during this period that the haciendas of the Tehuacán Valley through a series of manipulations gained control of water and land previously held by the Indian communities, and thus expanded sugar production. The disenfranchised population became laborers on the haciendas, cultivating and harvesting the cane. They were often organized by local caciques, who served as recruiters *(contratistas)*. At this time the bourgeoisie extended its power and wealth by manipulating the state system.

The Mexican Revolution brought major changes to the sugar region of Mexico. Most foreign capital was driven out of the industry, and the large haciendas were eventually converted to ejidos. In the sugar zones, rural populations were allocated ejido lands and irrigation water. At the same time, they were restricted in their ability to use their land or irrigation water as a commodity in the capitalist market (Singelmann n.d.:4). Ejidos were formed on the sugar-producing haciendas in the late 1930s. The sugar mills, on the other hand, remained in the hands of the former hacienda owners.

Using a variety of techniques to maintain political control, the mill owners remained powerful caciques, but only with the sanction of the federal government that had left them in possession of the mills. In the early 1940s, national legislation was passed which greatly strengthened the mill owner position and profoundly affected peasant communities and their economies. One such law, passed in 1943, forced peasants living in specified areas near the mills to grow sugar cane and to sell it to the designated mills. In effect, the national government forced peasants to grow sugar cane and created a monopoly buyer. Within a year, legislation followed allowing the price paid by the mill to the peasant to be linked to the wholesale price of sugar paid to the mill owners on the national market. The latter price was kept low by the government. All government credit and technical inputs created for the cane growers were funneled through the mill owners instead of being delivered directly to the peasants. Peasants who failed to comply with the law lost their rights to ejido lands, irrigation water, credit, and a sure market for their product. The payoff for the central government was that the mill owners were able to maintain the facade of tranquillity in the countryside as well as to guarantee sufficient production of sugar. Equally important, the government was able to hold down the price of sugar consumed domestically, and produce enough sugar for the expanding export market (Purcell 1979).

In the Tehuacán Valley the legislation abruptly ended the peasants' conversion of cane lands to the cultivation of corn, beans and vegetables. All of these were basic subsistence crops, but during the dry season they had a high market value in Mexico City and Puebla. The return on the land planted with these crops was considerably higher than when planted in sugar cane. Moreover, when the land was planted with other crops it absorbed much more labor, particularly family labor. By contrast, sugar cane requires intensive amounts of work during specific periods, but during most of the year requires little labor. The cultivation of sugar cane not only lowered the income per hectare of land, but reduced family participation in agriculture. Furthermore, it created a higher level of underemployment, generating permanent migration out of the region to the metropolitan centers.

In 1958 the national government froze sugar prices in an effort to control soaring prices. The price freeze remained in effect until 1970, and severely reduced the real income of *cañeros* (cane growers) since Mexico was experiencing inflation during this period. To increase productivity, the *cañeros* needed capital to invest in fertilizers, herbicides, water, and labor. Fertilizer was purchased from the mills at discount prices made available by the government, but many *cañeros,* short of funds, sold their fertilizer and used the money to pay for household goods or food. Others used the fertilizer for crops they had planted outside the cane zone. As a result, their cane productivity remained low, further reducing their income from sugarcane and leading to greater dependence on the government and the mill owner intermediary.

During this whole period, an increasing percentage of sugar in Mexico was being incorporated into soft drinks and processed food by an expanding processed food industry, much of which was foreign owned. By 1975, 41 percent of the sugar in the country was being used by the soft drink, cereal, bread, and cracker industries, which were experiencing tremendous expansion (Perez n.d.:76). These companies were constituents of the Ministry of Industry and Commerce. More important, assisting the sugar production industry fit the government policy of keeping food prices low, particularly in the rapidly expanding and politically sensitive urban areas. The per capita consumption of sugar rapidly increased during this period, climbing from 41 pounds in 1944 to 88.6 pounds in 1979 (Estadística Nacional de México 1976:24).

Social and political control became increasingly linked to the economic organization implemented by the government. The small size of the *cañero* landholdings and the low price paid for their cane left them with limited annual income. There were two important sources of credit—private moneylenders and the mill owners—but the two systems were interrelated. The mill owner manipulated credit as well as jobs and support for state and regional political positions in order to create a patron-client system with the most influential peasant leaders. In turn, the peasant leaders were able to use the system, yet remained dependent on the mill owner. Several became important moneylenders on their own, using money received from the mill owner.

Political networks were also built at the regional and state level through the clientage system. With the mill administrators' support, select peasant leaders were elected to important regional government or state offices, where they made key contacts in the government bureaucracy. These ties enabled them to demonstrate their importance to the *cañeros* and to enhance their roles as leaders. The administrator benefited by creating a patron-client relationship with the leaders, allowing him to have some input in *cañero* programs as well as being able to divide the peasants. Of course, a network system of this nature is always one of conflict and adjustment over time.

Today the cane growers are members of the Confederación Nacional Campensina (CNC), which in turn is officially linked to the PRI. The *cañeros* feel that the CNC is unresponsive to their needs and unsympathetic to the economic hardships created by the government control of sugar prices. The common feeling is that the CNC leaders work more closely with the administrators of the mills than with the *cañeros*. Yet the CNC receives support from the *cañeros* because it is the only organization linking cane growers from the various ejidos that sell cane to the mill. Two rival unions, the Consejo Agrarista Mexicano and the Unión de Productores de Caña de la República Mexicana, have failed to generate peasant support in the Tehuacán Valley, as mill administrators and government officials have refused to deal with the unions. The *cañeros* feel that the CNC leaders at least have access to the government, and have not shifted their support away from the CNC.

The penetration of government control in the sugar zone is multifaceted. On one level the *cañeros* are controlled by the very nature of the production system, including the pricing mechanism and the distribution of land and water rights. On another level their own union is officially linked to the party system that dominates the political arena of Mexico. Because the crop they raise is important to the government, their region is allocated good roads, electricity, schools, credit, and technical advice. Yet they are bound by the state to raise sugarcane, selling it to a monopoly buyer at low prices.

One other population is important to the production of sugarcane—the seasonal workers who harvest the cane. It is estimated that more than 114,600 men work annually as cane cutters in Mexico. Along with cotton, the sugar harvest absorbs more seasonal labor than any other crop in Mexico. Although cane growers may cut their own cane, it is much more common for the growers or the mill management to hire workers to do the hard labor associated with the harvest. More than 80 percent of the men who cut the cane migrate to work to the sugar zone from non-sugar-growing regions (Estadística Azucarera 1977:23).

In the Tehuacán Valley many workers come from nearby villages that are either too cool or lack sufficient irrigation water to grow cane economically. These villages include both ejidos and private landholding systems. In theory, they should receive the same government services (such as credit, technical assistance, and other supports) as the *cañeros,* but they do not. The ecologically more marginal ejidos and communities have undergone less institutional transformation, and less ideological and structural penetration than the regions with greater comparative ecological advantages. Thus local resources appear to be a critical factor in explaining regional or subregional variations in the strength of center-periphery ties (Carlos nd.:3). But marginal regions play a critical economic role in the system of production as a labor reserve for capitalist agriculture. Government services function to lock a significant segment of the population into seasonal subsistence production, a base from which they must seasonally migrate to work in commercial agriculture. The formation of the ejidos allowed many families to remain on the land instead of moving to the city, but poverty keeps them dependent on wage labor during part of the year.

Variations at the subregional level are also reflected culturally. In the major communities south of the city of Tehuacán most people speak Nahuatl as well as Spanish and identify themselves as Indian. Most families with access to land are involved with subsistence production based on family labor, although commercial agriculture is important too. Traditional forms of organization such as *mayordomias* play an important role in their lives. In contrast, in the principal mill town in the sugar zone, where Nahuatl was once spoken, the only language spoken today is Spanish. There are no *mayordomias,* and the population identifies itself as mestizo. The central organization is the union. Agriculture is capitalist in nature, with little subsistence production practiced. Few *ejidarios* cut their own cane; they hire nonunionized laborers, usually from outside the community, to do the work.

The exclusion of seasonal workers from the unions and from potential political linkages to the national government has been generated at two levels. On the local level, the capitalist nature of production has led to a division within the peasantry between the employers, *cañeros,* and the employees, the cane cutters. Although it can be argued that both work for the mills as laborers, one group growing the cane, the other cutting the cane, most *cañeros* feel that the cane cutters work for them. Cane cutters are often regarded as outsiders, socially and ethnically distinct from the *cañeros.* Only when the *cañeros* call a strike do they expect allegiance from the seasonal workers, although incentives are seldom included. The seasonal workers view the *cañeros* as being fortunate to have productive lands and government inputs, and often resent *cañero* disdain of the harvest work. Ideologically, there is no sense of class unifying the seasonal workers. As semiproletarians, their demands or desires are more directed toward obtaining land in their home area than toward improving the conditions of work away from home (Paré 1976:199). Furthermore, mobilization of seasonal workers is always difficult because the means of production and the living and work space are controlled by the growers, leaving workers with limited resources and scant security or sense of territory.

On the national level, the government is committed to keeping production costs down, and seasonal labor, excluded from the union structure, has little recourse for demanding higher wages or improved working conditions. Elite state representatives are not inclined to develop another political force, knowing a divided or disorganized work force is more easily controlled.

Efforts to organize seasonal workers in the Tehuacán Valley have a long history. The first unions on the sugar haciendas were organized in 1918 and included both permanent and seasonal workers, but they did little to help the seasonal workers. When the seasonal workers attempted to unionize on their own, they were kicked out of the union, but continued to work on the haciendas. When Vicente Lombardo Toledano formed the Confederación de Obreros y Campesinos de México, in an effort to break with the Calles controlled Confederación Regional de Obreros Mexicanos (CROM), efforts were made to mobilize the seasonal workers. At the same time the permanent workers' unions on the haciendas in the valley remained committed to CROM. As the conflict between the two national unions intensified, the hostility served to augment already existing antagonisms between permanent and temporary workers at the local level. In 1933, the CROM union forced the haciendas to ban unionized seasonal workers from working on the haciendas. When the haciendas were confiscated in 1937 and 1938 the mills remained in private ownership. The cane growers joined the Confederación Nacional Campesina, an arm of the government. The seasonal workers who were hired to harvest the cane were never incorporated in the CNC. As a result, agricultural producers can depend upon access to an unorganized, poorly paid, seasonal work force that can maintain itself during the nonharvest season. These seasonal workers are truly the *hijos abandonados* (abandoned sons) of the Mexican Revolution.

The Tehuacán case outlined here suggests the uneven penetration of central government programs in the same region. Yet in this case the *política azucarera* (sugar policy) is a product of specific strategies of the Mexican government. Communities in the sugar zone are controlled by regulations, while neighboring communities are indirectly controlled by intentional neglect. These are not two different strategies of the central government, but the outcome of the same approach to development through the strategies of peripheral capitalism.

Conclusion

The two case studies presented in this paper have focused on only a limited dimension of state penetration in rural Mexico, yet together they point to the importance of a broader framework for examining community organization and social relationships. The paper suggests several directions and guidelines for future research in Mesoamerica. We need more attention to state penetration as a process, and to its actual impact. This is particularly true where penetration may offer benefits to some while imposing costs on others. Thinking in terms of costs and benefits raises a question of equity, and it may not be inappropriate to inquire as to what degree penetration contributes to or impedes the attainment of the social justice goals of the Mexican Revolution. Research on penetration also means a move away from the prevailing paradigm, a paradigm that grows at least in part out of the strict "community studies" orientation. This paradigm has been of considerable utility for certain kinds of research, but needs to be complemented with a broader perspective when dealing with questions of social or economic change. There is also need for a more conscious focus on the future, so that our research asks not simply "where have these communities (groups, processes, etc.) been?" in a descriptive-analytic sense, but identifies salient processes, forms of penetration, and potential consequences. Doing so would not only strengthen future studies, but might also benefit the people and communities who have so often welcomed us and assisted our research.[2]

NOTES

1. We are distinguishing between *modernization* and *development. Modernization* consists in increased technological capacity. In the context of capitalism, modernization is an inherently uneven process which creates greater dependence and subordination of regions and populations to urban-industrial centers and elite classes. *Development* is a process in which structural changes lead to more equitable distribution of power and resources, resulting in increased standards of living of the population as a whole. This change can include increased technological efficiency in productive or service sectors.

2. Research in Oaxaca was funded by the Tinker Foundation. The material on the Tehuacán Valley is based on a research project of the Centro de Investigaciones Superiores of the Instituto Nacional de Antropología y Historia. Scott Whiteford is grateful to Serigio Quesada, Consuelo Ocampo, and Luis Emilio Henao, for their participation on this project. We would like to thank Sergio Quesada, Luis Vargas, Andrew Whiteford, Art Rubel, and Joe Spielberg for their comments on sections of this article.

REFERENCES

Adams, Richard N.
1962   "The Community in Latin America: A Changing Myth," *The Cennial Review* 6:3409-39.
1967   "Nationalization," in *Social Anthropology,* ed. M. Nash, Vol. 6 of *Handbook of Middle American Indians,* ed. R. Wauchope (Austin: University of Texas Press).
Anderson, Bo, and James D. Cockcroft
1966   "Control and Cooperation in Mexican Politics," *International Journal of Comparative Sociology* 7:1.
Arias, Patricia, and Lucia Bazan
1979   *Demandas y conflicto: el poder político en un pueblo de morelos* (Mexico City: Editorial Nueva Imágen).

Barkin, David
1978   *Desarollo regional y reorganización campesina* (Mexico City: Editorial Nueva Imágen).
Bartra, Roger, et al.
1975   *Caciquismo y poder político en el méxico rural* (Mexico City: Siglo XXI Editores).
Beals, Ralph
1975   *The Peasant Market System of Oaxaca, Mexico* (Berkeley and Los Angeles: University of California Press).
Boege, Eckart
1979   *Desarollo del capitalismo y transformación de la estructura de poder en la región de tuxtepec, Oaxaca* (Mexico City: Instituto Nacional de Anthropología y Historia).
Carlos, Manuel
n.d.   "A Cross-regional Approach to Intervillage Political Systems, Regional Development, and Center-periphery Ties in Rural Mexico," paper presented at Thirty-eighth Annual Meeting of the Society for Applied Anthropology, 1978, Mérida, Mexico.
Carlos, Manuel L., and Bo Anderson
n.d.   "Political Brokerage, Network Politics, and the Mexican State: Community-National Linkages and Processes," unpublished paper.
1981   "Political Brokerage and Network Politics in Mexico. The Case of a Dominance System," in *Networks, Exchange, and Coercion: The Elementary Theory and Application,* ed. David Willer and Bo Anderson (New York: Elsevier).
Corbett, John G.
1974   "The Context of Politics in a Mexican Community: A Study in Constraints on System Capacity" (Ph.D. diss., Stanford University).
1977   "Role Conflict as a Constraint on Local-level Decision-Making in Mexico," in *The Politics of Culture,* ed. R. Smethermen (San Diego: Companile Press).
1980a   "Linkage as Manipulation: The Dominant Party in Mexico," in *Political Parties and Political Linkages: A Comparative Perspective,* ed. Kay Lawson (New Haven: Yale University Press).
1980b   *Dimensions of Development in Oaxaca* (Nashville: Vanderbilt University Publications in Anthropology).
De la Peña, Sergio
1981   *Capitalismo en cuatro comunidades agrarias.* (Mexico City: Siglo XXI Editoriales).
Del Castillo, Gustavo V.
1979   *Crisis y transformación de una sociedad tradicional* (Mexico City:

Centro de Investigaciones Superiores del Instituto Nacional de Anthropología e Historia).

Dennis, Philip A.
1976   "The Oaxacan Village President as Political Middleman," *Ethnology* 12:4.

Estadística Azucarera
1979   *El azúcar en numeros* (Mexico City: U.N.P.S.A.).

Estadística Nacional de México
1976   *Consumos aparentas de productos agropecuarios* (Mexico City).

Esteva, Gustavo
1980   *La batalla en el méxico rural* (Mexico City: Siglo XXI Editoriales).

González, Luis
1972   *San José de Gracia* (Austin: University of Texas Press).

Grindle, Merilee S.
1977   *Bureaucrats, Politicians, and Peasants in Mexico* (Berkeley and Los Angeles: University of California Press).

Hansen, Roger D.
1971   *The Politics of Mexican Development* (Baltimore: Johns Hopkins University Press).

Heath, Shirley B.
1971   *Telling Tongues: Language Policy in Mexico* (New York: Teachers College Press).

Iszaevich, Abraham
1973   *Modernización en una comunidad oaxaqueña del valle* (Mexico City: Sep/Setentas).

Johnson, Kenneth F.
1978   *Mexican Democracy: A Critical View*, rev. ed. (New York: Praeger Publishers).

Kearney, Michael
1972   *The Winds of Ixtepeji: World View and Society in a Zapotec Town* (New York: Holt, Rinehart and Winston).

Lees, Susan
1973   *Sociopolitical Aspects of Canal Irrigation in the Valley of Oaxaca.* Memoirs of the Museum of Anthropology (Ann Arbor: University of Michigan).

Nash, Manning, ed.
1967   *Social Anthropology.* Vol. 6. of *Handbook of Middle American Indians,* ed. R. Wauchope (Austin: University of Texas Press).

Palerm, Angel
1980   *Anthropología y marxismo* (Mexico City: Editorial Nueva Imagen).

Perez Zozaya, Felipo
n.d.   "Situación actual de la industria azucarera nacional y sus

perspectivas." Quoted in Susan Kaufmann Purcell, "Business-Government Relations in Mexico: The Case of the Sugar Industry," *Comparative Politics* 13:232.

Purcell, Susan K.
1981   "Business-Government Relations in Mexico: The Case of the Sugar Industry," *Comparative Politics* 13:211-33.

Ronfeldt, David
1973   *Atencingo: The Politics of Agrarian Struggle* (Stanford: Stanford University Press).

Schwartz, Norman B.
1978   "Community Development and Cultural Change in Latin America," in *Annual Review of Anthropology,* ed. B. J. Siegel, A. R. Beals, and S. A. Tyler (Palo Alto, Calif.: Annual Reviews).

Singelmann, Peter
n.d.   "Peripheral Capitalist Development and the Transformation of Rural Class Relations: The Role of Peasant Cane Growers in the Mexican Sugar Industry," paper presented at national meeting of the Latin American Studies Association, 1979, Pittsburgh.

Stavenhagen, Rodolfo
1960   *Las clases sociales en las sociedades agrarias* (Mexico City: Siglo XXI).
1978   "Capitalism and the Peasantry in Mexico," *Latin American Perspectives* 5:27-37.

Ugalde, Antonio
1973   "Contemporary Mexico: From Hacienda to PRI, Political Leadership in a Zapotec Village," in *The Caciques: Oligarchical Politics and the System of Caciquismo in the Luso-Hispanic World,* ed. Robert Kern (Albuquerque: University of New Mexico Press).

Warman, Arturo
1972   *Los campesinos, hijos predilectos del régimen mexicano* (Mexico City: Editorial Nuestro Tiempo).
1976   *Y venimos a contradecir* (Mexico City: CIS-INAH).

Waterbury, Ronald
1970   "Urbanization and a Traditional Market System," in *The Social Anthropology of Latin America,* ed. Walter Goldschmidt and Harry Hojier (Los Angeles: Latin American Center, University of California).

Whitecotton, Joseph W.
1977   *The Zapotecs* (Norman: University of Oklahoma Press).

Whiteford, Scott, and Luis Emilio Henao
1979   "Irrigation, Resource Conflict and Selective Migration," in *Mi-*

gration Across Frontiers: Mexico and the United States, ed. Robert Kemper and Fernando Camera (Albany: State University of New York, Mesoamerican Series).

Whiteford, Scott, and Sergio Quesada

n.d.   "A Peasantry Divided: A View from Below of Political Linkage Systems and the Sugar Industry in Mexico," paper presented at national meeting of the Latin American Studies Association, 1979, Pittsburgh.

1980   "Irrigación descentralizada, desarrollo y cambio social," *América Indígena* 40:58-72.

Wolf, Eric

1953   "La formación de la nación," *Cier Sociales* 4:50.

1956   "Aspects of Group Relations in Complex Society: Mexico," *American Anthropologist* 58:1056-78.

Womack, John, Jr.

1972   *Zapata and the Mexican Revolution* (Harmondsworth, Eng.: Penguin Books).

2
Sexual Stratification in Mesoamerica

Laurel Bossen
University of Pittsburgh

The subject of sexual stratification in Mesoamerican ethnology is relatively new, despite the fact that our popular culture has long been intrigued by sexual stereotypes of the dashing, dominant Latin male, darting from one conquest to another, and the long-suffering submissive female, silently accepting her fate, tending her children, and waiting for her man to come home. North Americans have smugly believed that Mesoamerican sexual inequality was a distinct variety, an extreme form based in the Latin tradition. In this discussion, I do not propose to concentrate on the validity or fallaciousness of these persistent stereotypes, but rather to show how the topic of sexual inequality and stratification in Mesoamerica has emerged in the last three decades since the first Heritage of Conquest seminar. By sexual stratification, I refer to a systematic social inequality between the sexes, manifested in hierarchical relationships which consistently confer greater access to rewards, resources, and power on one sex, particularly in the economic and political spheres. An added dimension of systems of sexual stratification is the development of ideologies which reinforce and rationalize sexual differentiation and inequality.

One of the important findings of recent research on women is that sexual inequality appears to be increasing in many of the world's underdeveloped areas (Boserup 1970). This may be seen as a product of an ongoing "conquest" in Mesoamerica. The expansion and penetration of capitalist relations is transforming sex roles throughout Mesoamerica in peripheral as well as central regions. Men and women who were traditionally economic partners in informal subsistence production are increasingly drawn into a new kind of sexual division of labor, one that more systematically separates them. As the modern market system grows and dominates the economy, men are recruited to its new, formal occupations while women are disproportionately confined to the informal subsistence sphere. The subsistence sector to which women are confined is not destroyed; rather it is maintained in a weakened state as a buffer and cheap labor reserve for the more volatile capitalist sectors. Hence, women are less able than men to obtain direct benefits from the expansion of capitalism in Mesoamerica, and their partnership with men is transformed into an economic dependency which mirrors the disparate relationship between the traditional subsistence and modern market sectors.

This paper outlines the present scope and significance of research pertinent to the study of sexual stratification in Mesoamerica, and examines some recent changes in focus not only in the approach to sexual inequality, but also in the approach to problems of change and capitalist development. While a comprehensive theory of sexual stratification in Mesoamerica is still out of reach, my objective here is to synthesize some of the diverse research findings and to consider their theoretical implications. Beginning with sexual stratification as it was understood and dealt with thirty years ago, I examine recent research, including some of my own data, drawn from peasant, plantation, and urban sectors in Mesoamerica. Taken together, this research illustrates how women are selectively confined to the subsistence sectors within the modern system, and supports the view that women experience increased sexual stratification and dependency with the expansion of the capitalist system.

A Thirty-Year Perspective

Thirty years ago, anthropologists at the first Heritage of Conquest symposium were notably unconcerned with the problem of sexual stratification. Sex roles were not among the special topics selected for comparative treatment. Participants concentrated on untangling the relationships between pre-Columbian, Hispanic, and modern cultural elements in order better to define the Mesoamerican culture area and to analyze ethnic interaction and acculturation. Their occasional remarks on sex roles did not systematically address the problem of economic and social inequality between the sexes (nor that of economic and social inequality between classes). To the extent that women were granted direct attention, it was generally within the constrictive framework of the Western androcentric tradition, 1950s style. Women were viewed as passive, domestic beings, whose primary importance was recognized only in the realms of marriage, sexual services, and child raising. It was accepted as natural that women should be discussed in descriptions of the life cycle and family structure, but not in descriptions of the economy or political structure.

This is not to say that these original participants were completely oblivious to the existence of differing patterns of sex roles or to the fact that these patterns might be undergoing change. Ethnic differences in sex roles received some attention from Gillin, who noted that Indian men's attitudes toward women are more cooperative than authoritarian, in contrast to Ladino men whom he found to be authoritarian and more distant toward women, rejecting any attempts by women to share in public life (1952:202). Sol Tax, in particular, in his discussion of economics and technology raised some interesting questions regarding sex roles and change. Tax observed that Indian women play an important and distinctive role in marketing and that new commercial opportunities could affect the position of women (1952:59). He proposed that the sexual division of labor and the proportion of time spent on economic and noneconomic activities should be compared for different towns, and suggested that in communities that are heavily dependent on agriculture alone, women would have a lower position for lack of a personal source of cash income (1952:59, 63).

Despite these brief observations and attempts to generalize regarding ethnic differences and changes in sex roles, discussion at the seminar consistently veered away from posing sexual stratification as a research problem. The problem of the day was acculturation, and participants usually reframed their observations in these terms. In this context, it was noted that Indian women retain indigenous clothing fashions and other traditions longer than Indian men. Again, it was Tax who posed the problem of cultural change as differentially affecting women and men. He speculated that, in general, women's customs change more slowly than men's, and suggested that "technology connected with women in the household lasts longer" (1952: 271). Noting local variations in the acceptance of technological innovation by one sex or the other, there was mild consensus among the discussants that Mesoamerican men are less "Indian" than women in most regions. To account for the alleged conservatism of Indian women, discussants maintained a stereotype of female passivity (see Kaplan and Wisdom's remarks in Tax 1952:27, 272) and turned their discussion from female attitudes toward change to male attitudes toward females, suggesting that men would generally try to prevent women from changing. Gillin suggested that men's attitudes toward women and toward Ladinos may be "the core of the acculturation problem" (Tax 1952:273). Although these challenging remarks suggest that male-female relations were of critical importance to the processes under discussion, there was no effort to compare systematically women's economic, political, or social roles with respect to men, to discover women's attitudes toward change and how they could be related to the changing status of women.

This glimpse at the state of the subject thirty years ago suggests the extent to which ethnographers had at hand indications of profound differences in the impact of conquest and culture change on women and men. But as Chiñas (1971) has pointed out, women were not then considered as ethnographic subjects. There is no doubt that ethnographers of the 1950s and 1960s perceived sexual stratification in Middle America; it was simply not considered a major topic worthy of special investigation, particularly compared to topics such as ethnic and race relations. The failure to define sexual stratification and changing relations between the sexes as a research problem persisted into the 1960s. The publication of the *Handbook of Middle American Indians* volumes on *Social Anthropology* (M. Nash 1967) and *Ethnology*

(Vogt 1969) again gathered comprehensive comparative data on a wide range of special topics, but the problem of sex roles and stratification was not explicitly formulated (Chiñas 1971). While the more complete ethnographic and ethnological coverage continued to reveal intriguing variations in women's status and activities, sexual stratification was still not considered important enough for systematic examination. The few studies of women's roles and status conducted during the 1960s received little notice (Maynard 1963, Hellbom 1967).

Roughly ten years ago, attendant upon the growth of the North American women's movement, a direct interest in the changing status of women and the issue of sexual equality began to develop in anthropology as well as in most other social sciences. In 1971, Chiñas reviewed the anthropological literature for Mesoamerica and decried the lack of adequate information on the economic roles of women, the lack of comparison and analysis of women's status in the different indigenous cultures, and the failure to treat women as ethnographic subjects. Her own work on the Zapotecs emphasizing the role of women within an indigenous peasant community brought greater attention to the significance and problems of studying women's status in different contexts (1973). Since then, other studies have appeared which are beginning to fill in the many gaps in our knowledge about the manifestations of sexual inequality and the factors that contribute to the development and maintenance of sexual stratification in Mesoamerica.

The recent interest in discovering the variations in the status of women has been accompanied by an important change in emphasis. There is growing awareness that sexual inequality cannot be understood solely from cultural traditions and family roles, but that it is intimately linked to society's overall economic and political structure and must be analysed in these terms. Male dominance is less often taken for granted as an invariant characteristic of Mesoamerican cultures; increasingly it is examined as a variable that can be magnified or diminished by socioeconomic change. Moreover, there is a new appreciation of the considerable variety and change in sex roles at different levels of social organization: the community, the region, or the nation. Equally important, there is now greater interest in the way sexual stratification is related to class and ethnic stratification. Increasingly, sexual stratification is placed alongside class, ethnicity, and race as crucial to our understanding of domination and exploitation in complex, stratified societies. Emphasis on these improvements, however, should not obscure the fact that the mainstream of anthropology does not yet pay sufficient attention to the economic, political, and social condition of the female half of the population.

I will now describe how recent research has improved our knowledge of the status of women in Mesoamerica and our understanding of sexual stratification in three sectors: the peasantry, the plantation system, and urban society. I begin with research carried out in traditional anthropological settings, the Indian peasant communities. This is followed by sections dealing with the plantation and urban contexts.

The Indigenous Peasant Sector

Research on Mesoamerican peasant communities has frequently suggested that sexual stratification is not pronounced in traditional Indian populations dedicated to subsistence agriculture. Apart from the formally stratified political and legal structure linking these communities to the national society, daily life seems to be characterized by a high degree of social and economic cooperation and complementarity. The relationship between Indian men and women is frequently described as a partnership based upon mutual dependency, where the work of both sexes is valued and respected. This type of economic relationship between the sexes appears to be most closely linked to peasant subsistence production, where a man is tied to his land in order to be productive, and where he cannot effectively farm it without female partnership. In many traditional Indian communities, a man is not considered a full adult within the community until he is married (Slade 1975). No amount of "sowing of wild oats" can make him a man; he can only establish this identity when he coordinates the appropriate productive resources—land, male labor (his own), and female labor—in order to constitute a new household, a new unit of economic and social production. These economic and social constraints which act to promote partnership among Indian men and women are generally much weaker among the Ladino population who, even if peasants, are typically less confined to subsistence production, and less dependent on the male-female bond in order to form a unit of production. It is the more commercial, individualistic Ladino male who values machismo and strives to achieve manhood through opportunism both in economic and social relationships.

For the Indian woman, the recognized importance of her labor to the production unit and the future labor of the offspring she produces provide her with economic security as a woman, quite distinct from the overall security of the household itself. This security is based on the strong demand for female labor. A man who fails to share rewards and decision-making powers with his female counterpart risks crippling his own productive potential should she decide to leave him for another man. (His dilemma is nicely summed up by a recent pop song in which a farmer bemoans his fate: "You picked a fine time to leave me, Lucille—with four hungry children and crops in the field.") In traditional peasant societies, unless there is a significant surplus of women, men cannot afford to lose their wives.

This model of complementary roles can be greatly changed as integration with the market economy and national society increases. Many different kinds of factors can alter and transform the relations between the sexes. Increased communication and transportation bring new technology, new commercial patterns, migration, and educational opportunities. These changes do not necessarily affect traditional sex roles in balanced or identical ways. They may displace and devalue the labor of one sex while offering improved opportunities to the other. In some cases, the roles of both sexes may be transformed but may retain roughly the same value.

Maynard's research (1963) comparing the roles of Indian women and Ladinas in Palín, Guatemala, concerns the relationship between sexual inequality, ethnicity, and economic change. Palín is a town experiencing massive contact with modern commercial and capitalist forces. In the town center, composed of approximately two-thirds Pokomam-speaking Indians, a majority of the Indian males work at agricultural occupations, combining subsistence farming and wage labor on neighboring plantations. Palín is located in a region of coffee and sugar plantations, right on the main highway between Guatemala City and its major port. Daily bus and train service, as well as the local demand for plantation labor, have obviously influenced the commercial and employment opportunities of its inhabitants.

Maynard finds important economic differences between the Indian women and Ladinas, even though they both play significant economic roles. The Indian woman provides an important contribution to the household because male income is inadequate. She is an economic partner to her husband, providing domestic services, but she also makes major contributions to the household's cash fund. She markets the household produce, engages in commercial weaving, and performs seasonal wage work on coffee plantations. Although comprehensive data on male and female earnings are lacking, it appears that women's potential earnings from marketing (around 50¢/day) and wage work on coffee plantations (around 40¢/day for sorting) compare favorably with the incomes earned by male agricultural wage laborers (50-80¢/day).[1] Commercial weaving is done by about one-fourth of the Indian women, but sales seem to bring lower returns unless tourist "windfall" prices are obtained. The lower returns to weaving in Palín probably account, in part, for the decline of this traditional craft.

In assessing the economic role of Indian women, it is important to recognize that their economic activities have recently been altered by the market economy and modern technology. In Palín, the traditional time-consuming task of hand-milling corn has been displaced by electric corn mills owned by a few town dwellers, while the traditional weaving of cloth has been displaced by cheaper manufactured textiles for both men's and women's clothes. The once general demand for women's weaving within the town has now been reduced to a small number of traditionalists, some Ladino customers, and the occasional tourist buyer. While Palín Indian women thus lost or are losing two of the major productive functions—both to be replaced by modern consumer goods and services—their location on a major highway and in the coffee zone provides them with new sources of cash income. Palín women simply expanded their traditional produce and food-marketing role, and owing to their highway location, were able to counteract their declining value as subsistence producers with their cash income as marketers. Since they did not become economically dependent, but continued to complement the work of their farming husbands and to acquire cash income to meet increased cash expenses, the Indian women of Palín have not experienced increased sexual stratification within their community.

In contrast, Ladinas—whether wealthy or lower class—are not economic partners to their men on the same order. Maynard argues that among the Ladinos, the machismo complex promotes a higher degree of male infidelity and economic irresponsibility toward their wives and children. Her references to the higher regional mobility of Ladino males who are less tied to the land[2] indicate that they would not have the same type of productive partnership with their wives as that found among Indian farmers. With more individualized occupations for men, Ladinas more commonly experience male abandonment or irresponsibility,which force women to become economically active themselves. According to Maynard, roughly 90 percent of the Ladinas of Palín earn cash income and, owing to male default, they are frequently the main support of their families (1963:250). They run stores and small businesses if they have some capital, or wash clothes and work as cooks and servants if they lack capital.

While Maynard portrays the Indian woman's economic options as restricted, this appears to be true for both sexes. Indeed, the Indian women who engage in interurban marketing may have wider economic horizons than their farmer-husbands (1963:183). In contrast, the Ladina's economic position is limited by "a lack of economic opportunities," by "traditional attitudes about the inferiority of women," and by her role as homemaker (326). Both within and outside Palín, it is clear that Ladino men have privileged access to specialized occupations and paid positions as municipal officials, professionals, police, medical and religious personnel, and industrial employees. Only a few professional positions are open to women, and these are in the modern jobs stereotyped for women: teaching, nursing, and clerical work. Economic stratification by sex and ethnicity is indicated by the fact that Indian women, Indian men, and Ladina women are overwhelmingly limited to informal self-employment, or intermittent noncontract work that is both low paying and insecure. Regarding change, Maynard warily observes:

A factor that may alter the rights of the Indian women is the trend toward Ladinoization. This would mean a decrease in the Indian men's sense of responsibility for their families of procreation and thus threaten the stability of the nuclear family and the security of the women (1963:210).

Indeed, the Ladino family is often cited for its fragility and the weak commitment of the male (with female-headed households approaching 30 percent of all families) when compared to the Indian family where a much smaller proportion (10-15 percent) are characterized by male absence (Maynard 1963, 1974; Adams 1960:34).[3]

Chiñas's study (1973) of women's roles among the Isthmus Zapotecs of Mexico describes a changing Indian community which is *de facto* a dependent barrio of a larger mestizo market center. The Zapotecs of San Juán maintain a clear divison of labor by sex. The men are primarily involved in agriculture, practicing mixed cash and subsistence farming, and using colonial Spanish ox-and-plow technology, irrigation,and increasing mechanization. The women control the preparation and sale of foods in the nearby mestizo market where the local elite purchases their products. Like the women of Palín, the Zapotecs find their marketing opportunities are enhanced by the proximity of the Pan-American highway and the tourist trade, as well as by regular bus connections with larger urban market centers. The women's traditional economic functions of grinding corn and weaving cloth have similarly been displaced by modern corn mills and manufactured cloth, while their favorable market location has enabled them to take advantage of internal food markets to earn significant cash income. Incomes of full-time marketers are comparable to the daily wages of an unskilled Zapotec male in agricultural wage labor. Again, the displacement of women's traditional production has been somewhat compensated by self-employment in marketing.

While certain elements of Zapotec culture are retained (96 percent are still Zapotec speakers), this community cannot be said to depend on a traditional Indian economic system or divison of labor. As in Palín, cash crops, male labor migration, new technology, and commercial integration via the highway have produced many changes. Again, despite the appearance of an ongoing economic equality between the sexes, there are indications that the modern cash economy and occupational structure offer the men wider and better opportunities. First, Chiñas observes that "men probably produce more income per man hour than women when they are employed, but tend to be underemployed compared to women" (1973:40).[4] That is, women have to work longer hours to earn the same income as men. Second, in a list of specialized occupations for 194 men and 174 women, Chiñas found twice as many different occupations for men as women, suggesting a wider range of local opportunities. Third, it was found that:

No women are employed for wages, jobs which are highly prized because any type of regular income, no matter how little, is thought to be economically advantageous compared to self-employment. Women normally do not acquire the skills for wage and salary work. If they do, as in the case of the schoolteacher, they may not find a position because competition from men will be keen (1973:31).

It is most significant that Zapotec women are limited to informal self-employment with all the disadvantages this entails, while men have at least some access to formal jobs both within and outside the community. Moreover, the system of education both reflects and reinforces the different opportunities open to each sex. The literacy rate for men is twice as high as for women (1973:22).

A report from a Guatemalan village of Quiché speakers (Cosminsky and Scrimshaw 1976) shows yet another pattern of economic change as it affects sex roles. In Santa Lucia Utatlán, Indian women have very few opportunities to earn cash income. The men do most of the agricultural work on small subsistence plots while women provision and prepare food. The women's weaving role has been displaced by factory-made cloth. Women's loss of traditional productive importance does not appear to be compensated by any substantial new source of cash income. The women do engage in marketing of processed food, embroidered blouses, and small household surpluses, but the scale of these activities and the returns are very low; women are not considered an important source of cash income. The men migrate to compensate for inadequate subsistence production by working on plantations and by becoming traveling merchants. This situation would appear to be leading to increased economic dependence of women of their husbands. The authors report that the stability of the family is decreasing as the mutually dependent division of labor is replaced by male migratory labor and trade. Within the community, however, a man still depends on his wife to fulfill complementary economic, political, and religious roles.

Turning now to my own research in a more isolated community of Mam Indians, T'oj Nam,[5] in highland Guatemala, we find some similarities in the changing position of women. In this community, the traditional economic partnership of Indian men and women remains quite strong due to the heavy dependence on subsistence farming. As in many other highland communities, their productive base in agriculture is threatened by land pressure and the fragmentation of plots into *minifundias* (subminimal family farms). The continued use of traditional handwoven clothing by both sexes means that women's traditional textile production has not yet been replaced by factory-made clothing, though hand-spun cotton has been almost completely replaced by factory-made threads. Moreover, much of the rural population must still hand-grind their corn. While both men and women have some opportunities to commercialize their surplus production of corn and textiles, the return to the independent corn farmer who can sell to a national market is significantly higher than the return to the independent weaver who can sell only to a sporadic tourist market where textile prices generally yield less than a subsistence income. More precisely, the local wages for male agricultural labor are 50-75¢ a day, while the returns for farming one's own land are normally between $1.30 and $2.00 and the returns on rented coastal land between $2.00 and $4.00 per day. My calculations show that for most Indian women, weaving for sale is scarcely viable, yielding a return of about 36¢ per day for an eight-hour day.[6] While 65 percent of the townswomen occasionally weave for sale, this activity merely disguises or palliates a condition of underemployment. The few women who are successful with textiles are actually more committed to commerce in that they resell or "put out" textiles.

Since poor road transportation has not brought the women or men of this peripheral town significant local commercial opportunities, both Indian men and women supplement their inadequate subsistence base with migratory labor on coffee and cotton plantations. This type of labor does not contribute to sexual stratification given that it is available to both men and women, and workers are paid by piece rates so that incomes by sex are fairly equal. Despite this overall low level of economic stratification by sex among the Indians of this town, the advent of a small number of superior economic opportunities has introduced important disparities between the sexes, particularly among the more acculturated Indians. For instance, formal paid positions with the municipal government or as extension agents of the national government, where they have not been filled by Ladinos, have gone exclusively to Indian males. The most lucrative positions open to Indians, as labor contractors, teachers, translators, medical personnel, and agricultural promoters have not been held by Indian women. The instigation and the means (education and training) to fill these positions with Indians have frequently come from outsiders who have consistently selected men. Not one Indian woman from this village has yet enjoyed access to a formal job with regular pay. Moreover, a number of Indian women indicate that their husbands, who enjoy these higher cash incomes, tend to consume much of their cash earnings in individualistic, rather than household, expenses. This case, as the others already discussed, supports the proposition that the new division of labor between formal and informal employment which is beginning to appear within the Indian communities (in Palín, in the Zapotec community, and T'oj Nam) introduces a new basis for sexual stratification.

The Plantation Sector

Compared to the anthropological interest in peasant communities, the plantation communities have been understudied in Mesoamerica. The growth of both permanent and seasonal rural proletariats has not yet been matched by proportional growth in research into the nature of the relationship between the plantation economy and the social organization of the populations affected. Perhaps the reason for this lack of study is that plantations are business enterprises in which traditional cultural patterns are more obviously limited than in the peasant context. The hierarchical structure of plantations means that the researcher must increasingly take into account such untypically anthropological concerns as "business administration" and consider its impact on plantation community culture. For the subject at hand, the scarcity of plantation studies in Mesoamerica is compounded by the customary inattention to women's position.

Information on women's adaptation to plantation life as well as to the experience and exigencies of migratory wage labor is truly rare. In presenting the available research on this subject, it is necessary to issue a preliminary warning about the dangers of overgeneralizing on the basis of a few initial studies. Plantation communities, despite their shared commercial orientation and profit motives, exhibit a great variety of organizational patterns and policies. Their use of labor, and the social institutions which they promote or tolerate, may be influenced by differences in cash crop, in capital investment and plantation size, in the need for permanent, migrant, skilled, or unskilled labor, as well as by the cultural origins of owners, managers, and workers. Nonetheless, this brief look at the information available will reveal some important aspects of sexual stratification in plantation communities and will suggest some general trends which, if confirmed by further research, have implications for the overall structure of the national economic and social system.

Cosminsky and Scrimshaw (1976) have given us one of the few reports on women's status in plantation society. Their research deals with a Guatemalan sugar cane and coffee plantation with some 690 residents. This population, which includes about 62 percent Indians, primarily of Quiché origin, has an equal number of males and females. The economic base for the resident population includes both wage work and the right to cultivate small plots of plantation land for household use. This dependent form of subsistence farming helps to maintain the residents during slack periods of plantation work when they have very little cash income.

The sexual division of labor for this subsistence farming involves shared activities and the mutual dependency that is often found in the highland communities of Indian peasants. The women have considerable domestic responsibilities, aid in the planting and harvesting of crops, and perform the marketing. It appears that they no longer weave, and it is also likely that the hand-milling of maize with stones has also been replaced by labor-saving power mills or the metal hand-turned mill. Both sexes also perform wage labor, in which there appears to be a more pronounced sexual division.

Men work in the sugar cane fields and in the coffee fields at the peak season, accompanied by other males and often by their sons. Women and children pick coffee and dry bagazo (sugar cane) in season, the latter being part of the processing of panela. In the slack season, the ganadores (temporary male workers), women, and children go to nearby fincas (farms), where the season is longer and coffee crops larger. The women have control over the cash which they and their children earn (Cosminsky and Scrimshaw 1976:7).

Roughly 75 percent of the female population aged twelve and over earn cash income, primarily as wage workers on the plantation. Girls start to earn money at around age twelve, and their average yearly earnings peak between ages fifteen and nineteen when they earn around $70 per year. Women's earnings fall between $38 and $50 per year for most other age groups except women over age sixty, when they again climb to $70 per year.

The low level of women's annual wage income indicates that they are unemployed most of the year, called into service mainly during the coffee harvest. Although details on male income are not provided, the authors mention that the male wage is $7 per week, which with steady employment would yield a yearly income of $364. In fact, males also suffer seasonal unemployment, for some are *colonos*, permanent workers, and others are *ganadores*, temporary workers. Nonetheless, their privileged position in the labor force is revealed by the following breakdown for sources of total household wage income (Cosminsky and Scrimshaw 1976:11).

Males age 16 and over	67.2%
Females age 16 and over	17.7%
Children under 16	15.1%
Total	100.0%

Compared to adult females, adult males earn 3.8 times as much wage income.

Some women (and probably men as well) have alternative sources of cash income through commercial ventures. Seven women with the highest incomes include entrepreneurs with considerable capital investment, and a regularly employed maid who earns $25 per month, or $310 yearly. Together, these seven women earn just slightly more than the total group of 145 women who work for wages ($7,582 as compared to $7,447). Apart from these exceptional cases, women must depend heavily on men for cash income. Notably, the economically active women on this plantation are almost completely limited to informal work as temporary harvest labor or as self-employed vendors. The lack of adequate employment opportunities is further supported by the fact that roughly half of the girls between ages fifteen and nineteen leave the plantation to work in other areas, primarily as domestics in the cities.[7] The continued importance of women in subsistence activity and the fact that most women earn small cash incomes through wage labor do not appear to compensate for women's grossly inferior cash incomes within the plantation economy. The existence of a few successful entrepreneurs should not obscure the strong evidence of economic stratification by sex in the wage-earning sector. Taken together, women's cash incomes from all sources do not approach the level of male wage income.

My own research on two Guatemalan plantations shows a similar stratification of men's and women's economic roles, albeit with certain modifications (Bossen 1979). On a small coffee plantation with some twenty-four permanent workers, all were male with the exception of the domestic servant. The minimal pay for unspecialized regular workers is around $28 monthly. Women and children are able to find wage employment only during the coffee harvest which lasts only a few months. Paid at piece rates, they can earn approximately as much as a man for a full day of work. Also at harvest time, a few resident women are able to turn a little extra cash income by operating stores with a small stock that cater to the temporary influx of migrant workers. During the remainder of the year, women perform domestic services designed to economize on a small cash income. All households are heavily dependent upon cash for food, clothing, and household equipment. The economizing activities of many of the women (such as hand-sewing cotton dresses and shirts to save the cost of paying a seamstress with a machine) merely mask a condition of female underemployment within the household. Yet the fact that male incomes are low, that local housing and services are minimal (homes lack running water), and that the infrastructure for local commerce and consumerism is poorly developed in this relatively remote region, means that improvements in the male standard of living still come primarily from the wife's domestic services. Restaurants, bars, movies, prostitutes, and other entertainments are too distant to have much impact on local life.

Research on a large sugar and coffee plantation reveals some important similarities and differences. At Canaveral, there are some 500 permanent workers, of whom three are females. Moreover, the seasonal workers and migrant workers that are hired are all male with the exception of women who work as cooks.[8] This large plantation community is like a town in itself, but it is also located near an urban center. The population is almost completely dependent on cash incomes. The permanent workers belong to a union which, through collective bargaining, has achieved a relatively high level of wages and benefits for both the agricultural and sugar factory workers. Cash incomes range from $38 to $132 per month, to which are added a certain measure of job security and extra bonuses during the harvest as well as good housing, health and educational benefits. While significant numbers of women endeavor to earn cash income, opportunities are extremely limited.[9] Women do not find employment in the seasonal harvest, agricultural maintenance work, in the sugar factory or office jobs. The only capacities in which women are hired are cooking, nursing, and domestic service in which they find a small number of jobs.[10] Thus the women must turn to informal occupations in order to earn money. They run small stores that cater to the workers, they take in washing, and they prepare meals for widowers and bachelors, or snacks to sell to the workers on their breaks. Women's traditional domestic tasks have been considerably eased by the presence of power corn mills, running water, electricity, and manufactured clothing. But this increased efficiency does not seem to have led to greater productivity, primarily because there are no local enterprises to absorb female labor.

As on the other plantations, the earning potential of resident men and women shows a sharp contrast. Whereas economically active men (including permanent and temporary workers) average $59 per month plus noncash benefits, economically active women average only $25 monthly. Women have considerably lower cash incomes than men primarily because they are confined to the informal sector. Of the economically active men, 76 percent are on the company payrolls, whereas less than 6 percent of the economically active women are paid by the company. Economically, most women are very dependent on men who have access to company jobs. But again, men do not have to share all of their gains with the household. The location of this plantation near an urban center means that there are ample opportunities for men who withhold income from their families to spend it for self-indulgent purposes. The city is noted for its flashy restaurants, bars, and brothels, which beckon the throngs of male plantation workers and migrants on payday. While this is not the place to delve into the manifestations of the machismo complex, suffice it to say that it is fully developed at this plantation (see Bossen 1978). The concepts of shared economic activities, cooperative household production, and mutual dependency do not apply here; within the level of the plantation working class we find a two-tiered economic system characterized by male dominance and female dependency. [11]

The data from these Guatemalan plantations indicate that the degree of female economic participation can vary greatly from nearly zero to a very high level of participation in seasonal wage labor and supplementary subsistence production. What appears to be a constant finding is that the plantations are primarily interested in male labor. Thus men are able to obtain whatever regular positions are available, while women are shuttled in and out of the labor force according to the fluctuating needs of the plantation enterprise. As capitalist institutions, plantations employing wage labor are not compelled to concern themselves with the economic condition of working women who lose their source of income when the harvests are over. Since women respond to plantation employment when it is offered, it follows that the secondary status of women in the plantation labor force is largely a product of managerial or institutional decisions, not the workers' cultural tradition.

For landless rural populations, a steady job is a crucial resource, and lack of access to this "resource" puts women into a lower economic strata as dependent wives. This systematic difference between female and male access to regular plantation employment provides the infrastructure for a myriad of social and cultural expressions of male freedom and dominance with respect to women. For example, at Canaveral, many men allocate part of their earnings to the enjoyment of movies, sports, drinking, or the purchase of bicycles or motorcycles, but they express strong opposition to wives who might seek similar ways to amuse themselves. On the more modern plantations, women's dependence on male wages is further aggravated when traditional domestic products are replaced by industrial consumer goods that require cash.

The Urban Sector

While the plantation sector has received limited attention, massive urban migration and population growth have inspired heightened interest in Mesoamerican cities in the last thirty years. Much of the recent research has been concerned with the causes of migration, the adjustments of migrants to urban life, the eruption of squatter settlements, and the proliferation of marginal populations and unemployment alongside modern urban corporations and industries. There is widespread dissatisfaction with earlier models of economic development which predicted that industrial capitalist growth could provide employment and increase the standard of living for the masses of rural and urban poor. The evidence that the modern sector does not provide sufficient housing or modern jobs for these marginalized populations is accompanied by a parallel recognition that acculturation and acceptance of modern values are not enough to guarantee integration and acceptance within the modern urban socioeconomic structure. Moreover, evidence is accumulating that women are most severely affected by the transition from rural subsistence to urban wage work and unemployment.

It is often observed that two levels can be distinguished among the urban poor. One is composed of what may be called the "industrial workers," a privileged level with formal jobs and a measure of job security, while the other is called the "marginal population," a disadvantaged population that is confined to informal, insecure jobs or self-employment (Lomnitz 1977:12). As Lomnitz defines it, marginality has two characteristic features:

> 1) It lacks a formal articulation or insertion in the urban industrial process of production, and 2) it suffers from chronic insecurity of employment. This core group has also been called by Latin American economists the *informal* sector. . . . In general, marginal entrepreneurs are self-employed and marginal laborers are freelancers. Neither group is normally covered by social security (1977:13).

This division between workers with industrial or formal work and those who have marginal employment takes on particular significance with respect to the different employment opportunities of urban women and men.[12] Lomnitz observes that "the borderlines between the marginal proletariat and the industrial proletariat are blurry. . . . There are sometimes industrial workers as well as marginals within the same family" (1977:13). If one takes not the family, but the individual male and female worker as the unit of classification, the lines of division become somewhat clearer. Several studies of the urban poor in both Mexico City and Guatemala City show that jobs in the formal sector, or jobs that could lead into the formal sector are largely reserved for male workers, while women are more completely and permanently restricted to the informal labor market where poverty and economic insecurity are the most extreme.

In referring to some of this research, I maintain that we must not simply look at sexual stratification as a holdover from traditional peasant societies. We must consider the evidence that the structure of modern capitalist society bears responsibility for contemporary forms of sexual stratification by creating urban job ghettoes (on the model of developed societies) where the greatest burdens of low pro-ductivity employment and unemployment are shouldered by women. Although men as well as women are found in marginal occupations, for women it is a no-exit position. Men have a much better chance to move into higher-paying jobs and to be admitted to the ranks of skilled industrial workers.

The analysis of sexual stratification in Mesoamerican cities has been advanced by several different kinds of research. One is the microsocial approach, or the community study, which is conducted within de-fined neighborhoods or among identifiable subgroups within the city. Another is the macrosociological approach which utilizes national census data. Drawing on these different types of research, I shall concentrate upon some important findings concerning the nature of sexual stratification within the urban working class.

Arizpe (1975) has drawn attention to the situation of the Indian women sidewalk venders in Mexico City, the so-called Marias who have migrated from indigenous communities. Her investigation of the conditions which lead to migration and of the reasons Indian women take to street-vending as a means of livelihood are cast within the larger context of Mexican rural and urban opportunities for both men and women. She notes that the reason the "Marias" have cap-tured public attention is the striking visual impact of women in in-digenous dress, a symbol of Mexico's pre-Hispanic heritage, and their condition of impoverishment and vulnerability at the doorstep of the modern office buildings and shops of Mexico City. Arizpe maintains that their economic situation is shared by vast numbers of marginalized people who are no longer so conspicuous because they have traded or abandoned their colorful village clothing for undistinctive urban outfits.

Arizpe compares four rural Indian communities, both Mazahua and Otomí, in terms of the conditions which give rise to urban migration, particularly the migration of Indian women street venders. Although we are not given much information on the traditional sexual division of labor within the rural communities, it is evident that their subsistence production is no longer sufficient, and both sexes are seeking ways to increase cash income. Wage work opportunities within the villages, however, are rare and low paying. In one of the communities, male agricultural laborers reportedly earn 10 to 12 pesos daily, while women field laborers earn only 8 to 9 pesos "for physically exhausting labor of 12 hours per day" (1975:70, 76). In one village, proximity to a factory that produces electrical parts provides women with additional local employment possibilities. In a factory of 1,500 workers, the majority are single women, earning relatively high wages that range from 28 to 35 pesos per day. Significantly, this village is the only one of the four studied by Arizpe from which Indian women do not migrate to become ambulant venders on the streets of Mexico City. Although a particularly high percentage (25.4 percent) of the female population migrates, Arizpe maintains,

> The young women who have been workers come to the city seeking more elaborate jobs than those of domestic servant or ambulant vender. (1975:113)
> Thanks to their skills, they have succeeded in incorporating themselves fully in the industrial occupation structure and in the urban society of Mexico City (1975:47).[13]

The Indian women from the other villages have had less contact with modern work; their villages lack nearby factories offering female employment, and they also lack good highway connections with Mexico City. When these women migrate, they sell in the city streets because they are not accepted into any other kind of occupational niche. This is partly because they lack education, language skills, or formal job experience, but also because many of them are married or accompanied by small children and therefore cannot even get work as domestic servants. While these women are generally seen vending alone or with children, Arizpe reports that as many as two-thirds live with husbands or lovers. While widowed, separated, or single women tend to sell in groups with other women, married women may work as a team with their husbands who carry their cargo and watch out for the vender from a distance. In this way, maximum sympathy from clients and somewhat less harassment from the police may be achieved. If the woman is detained by the police, then the husband assumes care of the merchandise.

Arizpe found certain general similarities in the occupational options of Indian migrants to the city, but these options also show some significant differences for men and women. Migrant men have some hope of finding work, even if they are unskilled. They can be hired as unskilled construction workers or cargo carriers and earn a daily wage. While their work may be intermittent, the wages for such unskilled male workers are normally around 40 pesos a day, although sometimes migrants may receive as little as 20 or 25 pesos per day. For unskilled women, there is practically no employment other than domestic service, which is normally closed for the majority of Indian women who have dependents. Moreover, the wages of young women in domestic service may be as little as 150 pesos per month. Thus women become street venders or beggars. It is reported that the Indian woman street seller's income averages around 20 pesos per day, ranging from 5 to 50 pesos (Peltier and Galvan 1971, as cited by Arizpe 1975:138).

Migrant women face the most extreme economic insecurity when they must create their own employment as illegal street venders, with little capital and lots of competition. As Arizpe observes:

> Generally, the politics of job creation are directed toward absorbing male labor power. In consequence, there is an enormous female unemployment that it is hoped will be absorbed by domestic service. But married women and women with children are excluded from this work. That is, approximately 85 percent of the indigenous women in the city. (Arizpe 1975:135, referring to report by Peltier and Galvan 1971).

Among these Indian migrants, we find some overlap and cooperation between jobless women and men who turn to street vending.
But access to the wage sector and to better jobs is sex stereotyped
and more rewarding to men. Women's economic position is wholly
informal. The concentration of population in Mexico City gives them
a chance to earn an uncertain, but sometimes "successful" livelihood
using their village marketing skills in an urban environment where
competition from other marginal venders and shop owners, and the
harassment of police make their daily survival precarious. But Arizpe
asserts that female unemployment in the Federal District is "more
flagrant than that of the male." Concerning the demand for female
labor, she states that "in fact, it does not exist" (1975:152). Thus
while migrant men may share a marginal unemployed or underemployed status with the women, this study suggests that the migrant
women are more firmly anchored to the bottom strata.

The evidence that sexual stratification is a condition of urban
integration by migrants is extended by Lomnitz's study (1977)
of Cerrada del Condor, a shantytown settlement on the periphery of
Mexico City. This research deals with a population that is presumably mestizo, and of which about one-third were born in the Federal
District. Lomnitz found that 12.4 percent of the households in this
settlement are headed by women,[14] and that 35 percent of the wives
earn some cash income (1977:64, 69). Regarding the occupations
and economic standing of women, she informs us:

> Most households headed by women derive their income from
> domestic service. Such women either work as maids or as
> laundrywomen. Other typically female economic activities include
> tortilla making and street selling (flavored shaved ice, nopales, or
> lunches for construction workers on building sites). The income
> level of households headed by women tends to be significantly
> lower (1977:65).

Fathers, or male heads of household, are the sole wage earners in
only 46 percent of the households sampled. Occupational histories
of male heads of nuclear families show that 82 percent of male migrants of peasant background start out as unskilled laborers. Over
time, the occupational distribution of these migrants comes to re-

semble closely that of nonmigrants. While as many as one-third of the men remain in the unskilled category all their lives, it is evident that many migrant men acquire special job skills, and even if they may still lack secure jobs, they do "begin to gain access to other forms of employment" (1977:67). Lomnitz found the following distribution of occupations by sex for heads of households.

Table 1.   Occupations by Sex for Heads of Households, Cerrada del Condor

Occupation	155 Men (%)	22 Women (%)
Unskilled worker	32.9	4.5
Skilled free-lance worker	31.0	—
Industrial worker	10.3	—
Service worker/servant	3.2	54.6
Commerce (venders & shopkeepers)	4.5	18.2
Employee	5.1	4.5
Property owner with rental income	3.3	4.5
Unemployed	9.7	—
Housewife (no independent income)	—	13.6
Total	100.0	99.9

Source: Adapted from Table 4.1 in Lomnitz 1977:64.

It is noteworthy that only males are shown as having access to industrial jobs (10.3 percent). Moreover, as few as 4.5 percent of the men are service workers, in contrast to the majority of the economically active women, 54.6 percent, who work as servants. Also, the use of the category of "housewife" to describe 13.6 percent of female household heads with no independent income suggests that these women have a higher rate of unemployment than male household heads with 9.7 percent reported as unemployed.

Although Lomnitz did not provide systematic data on women's earning power, there are indications that it is significantly below the men's. At the time of her study, 1969-71, the legal minimum wage was 32.50 pesos ($2.60 US) a day, or a minimum of 975 pesos a month, but she notes that "the legal minimum wage applies actually to male occupations only. Service jobs normally filled by women or children are subject to conventional wages which rarely reach the legal daily amount" (1977:78). Despite the minimum daily wage, men often lack steady work so that all but two men sampled had monthly incomes that were the equivalent of a minimum wage or less. Lacking explicit data for women, it is nonetheless clear from comparing tables that households headed by women working in service occupations tend to fall into the lowest economic category (see Tables 4.1 and 4.8 in Lomnitz 1977). An important finding, however, is that the households in the highest economic level were also those with the most earners per household. The marginality and economic insecurity of both male and female workers means that long-term success depends on having multiple sources of income per household. The economic data for this shantytown show that a large proportion of migrants of both sexes occupy marginal positions, but they also show that the urban employment structure fosters economic stratification by sex as measured by occupational choice, the legal minimum wage, and income levels.

My own research in the shantytown of San Lorenzo[15] in Guatemala City provides further insights on the position of women among the urban poor. This settlement shares some general similarities with the previous case in terms of its overall standard of living, the percentage of urban migrants (about 75 percent), and the marginal quality of their housing and occupational status. At the same time, there are important differences. First, San Lorenzo is a "true" squatter settlement. Unlike Cerrada del Condor where most people pay rent (implying some recognized rights to remain as long as they pay), San Lorenzo is located on land that was illegally invaded and occupied by poor people precisely because they could not afford to pay rent. Lacking legal titles, they must defend their homes not only against urban officials but also against claims of other squatters. Second, San Lorenzo is located in the central city rather than on the periphery. This has important consequences in terms of job access and informal commercial opportunities. Like the Mexican "Marias" who squat on central city sidewalks to profit from the concentrated purchasing power of the capital, the people of San Lorenzo are also strategically placed to obtain marginal job opportunities and commerce should they fail to obtain or hold formal jobs. Finally, San Lorenzo has twice as many economically active women as Cerrada del Condor, although the percentage of households without male heads is only slightly higher (at 16 percent). In San Lorenzo, approximately 70 percent of the adult women earn cash income, while 6 percent of the women describe themselves as unemployed and another 14 percent as housewives. Men in the settlement are 86 percent economically active, and 11 percent unemployed. The reasons for the substantially higher rate of female economic activity as compared to the Mexican example are unclear. It could reflect greater economic marginality among San Lorenzo families and a more general need by women for supplementary cash income. It could also reflect the central location of San Lorenzo which probably offers more opportunity for women to earn cash in middle-class homes and central business districts than in peripheral settlements. In any case, the high proportion of women earning cash income would suggest a significant basis for sexual equality within this shantytown.

Analysis of the occupational distribution, however, shows important similarities with the urban poor in Mexico City, particularly with respect to the sexual division of labor. In San Lorenzo, 85 percent of the economically active women work in the sales and service sector, primarily as self-employed venders or as domestic employees. In contrast, only 33 percent of the men are in sales or services, while 60 percent are artisans, workers and operatives.

Table 2.   Occupational Distribution of Economically Active Population by Sex for Two Shantytowns

Economic Category	Cerrada del Condor*		San Lorenzo	
	Males %	Females %	Males %	Females %
Artisans, workers, & operators	81	5	60	14
Sales & services	9	84	33	85
Other	10	11	8	1
Total	100	100	101	100
(No. of cases)	(140)	(19)	(117)	(91)

*Data from Cerrada del Condor refer to economically active heads of households and are based on Table 4.1 (Lomnitz 1977:64).

Table 2 above shows that polarization or stratification by sex between two major occupational categories is pronounced in both groups. Although sales and services absorb a good deal more male labor in San Lorenzo than Cerrada del Condor, this may reflect the fact that the San Lorenzo sample includes employed minors and single males whose first jobs are often informal services. In contrast, the higher proportion of males in the artisan-worker category in Cerrada del Condor may reflect the improved occupational status of a more mature sample of heads of households. In San Lorenzo, it was observed that men hold a greater variety of jobs than women in both major categories of employment. Moreover, more than twice as many men (26 percent) as women hold jobs in established institutions (with ten or more employees) where job security and benefits are likely to be greater.

As in Cerrada del Condor, domestic service provides the bulk of female employment in the cash economy. Domestic employees and laundresses account for 35 percent of female employment, while another 27 percent prepare and sell food in marginal enterprises. Of 90 women sampled, more than 80 percent are working in a domestic environment, although nearly half are not working in their own homes. It is extremely rare for men to work in a domestic setting. This strongly implies that for women the small-scale domestic mode of production has been only partially transformed by the urban economy. Women now earn wages, but they rarely obtain work in the large-scale enterprises where larger sums of capital are invested in production. The overwhelming majority of women continue to work in labor-intensive activities where their productivity is enhanced by very little modern technology or capital investment.

The clearest sign of sexual stratification in San Lorenzo is the difference between male and female cash earnings. For males, cash incomes average $53 a month, while women average $20 a month. Thus men's cash incomes are approximately two-and-a-half times as great as those of women. The difference in incomes is somewhat exaggerated, however, in that men's employment tends to be more irregular than women's, so that men may have several weeks or months of steady employment followed by a layoff. Self-supporting women tend to have marginal incomes that do not permit much time between jobs. But they also accept such low incomes that they can generally find work in a shorter time. The low wages of domestic servants have stimulated an increase in the supply of marginal jobs in the private homes of the urban middle class. Women who work in unskilled jobs such as tortilla making or domestic service often earn as little as 50 to 75 cents per day for around 12 hours of work. In contrast, an unskilled male who is hired on a construction site will generally be paid around $2.00 to $2.25 for a 10-to-12-hour day. Even though women sometimes receive additional benefits such as meals as part of their pay, there is no doubt that they must work longer hours to earn a given amount of money.

Out of sheer economic necessity, the women of San Lorenzo play a critical economic role within the shantytown. As they cannot fully count on anyone else to be able to maintain them and their children, they seek to commercialize their labor and skills. It is their low-paying marginal work that tides the family over when male unemployment, alcoholism, or inconstancy reduces the family budget. At the rock-bottom level of the subsistence wage, they can usually support themselves if they have good health. Yet the fact that women are not totally dependent on men, and that men also occupy marginal positions should not blind us to the inequality that exists within this community. It is evident that with only 20 percent of the economically active population employed in established institutions (with ten or more employees), San Lorenzo is not well integrated into the urban-industrial core of the economy. But to the small extent that better-paying jobs have appeared, they have favored male workers. If this pattern of integration is maintained, sexual stratification and female dependency is the likely outcome.

The foregoing research on various migrant and marginal populations that have participated in the rapid urban growth in Mexico City and Guatemala City shows us some of the characteristics of this process as it affects sex inequality. We have seen that both sexes suffer displacement and insecurity. While many men do not succeed in gaining jobs in the industrial proletariat, even within the marginal sector they enjoy certain advantages. Typically, they earn a higher income per hour or day of unskilled work than women. Although marginally employed men may be frustrated by periodic unemployment, given the probability that they will earn more in the occupations reserved for men, there are few attempts to compete for women's lower-paying service jobs during periods of unemployment. Examination of women's options shows that they are concentrated in the most marginal, least desirable jobs as servants or street venders, or at best running a small store from their homes. With the breakup of the household as a unit of production, women have had the least chance to join larger units of capitalist production which enjoy higher productivity and higher returns within the modern economy. They offer their services as individuals who are no longer integrated into the main productive processes of their society.

Another glimpse of sexual stratification can be derived from national statistics. Recent studies point out that since census reports are inconsistent in reporting male and female economic activity in the agricultural-subsistence economy, national statistics are most useful as a measure of sexual differences only when they refer to the nonagricultural economy, that is, the more urbanized sector of the national population (González Salazar 1976; Arizpe 1977; Bossen 1978). Thus, in Mexico, women were reported as 19.0 percent of the economically active population in 1969, with 89.2 percent of the active women in nonagricultural occupations (González Salazar 1976:185). In Guatemala, women were shown as only 14 percent of the economically active population, with 93 percent concentrated in the nonagricultural sector in 1973 (Guatemala 1974:27). In both countries, women occupy a more noticeable position within the nonagricultural labor force; women formed 27.1 percent of the nonagricultural, economically active population in Mexico in 1969, and 30.5 percent in Guatemala in 1973.

The type of occupational distribution found among the migrant and marginal populations of the two capital cities is a shared characteristic of the macroeconomic structure of both nations as shown in Table 3. More than two-thirds of the economically active women are concentrated in the services, and less than one-fourth in the industrial sector. Men's occupations are more evenly balanced between the industrial and service sectors, but in each country more than twice as many of the industrial sector jobs are held by men as women.

The case studies have shown that a large part of the economic activity of working-class and migrant women is in the realm of domestic service and petty trade. The national statistics reveal that this

is a general phenomenon. In Mexico, 19.0 percent of the economically active women in 1969 were domestic servants in private homes
(González Salazar 1976: 185) In Guatemala, where 64 percent of
all service workers are maids, domestic service accounts for 47 percent of the economically active women in the nonagricultural sector
(Guatemala 1974:27; Chinchilla 1977:53).

Table 3.   Occupational Distribution of Nonagricultural Economically Active
Populations of Mexico and Guatemala, by Sex

Economic	Mexico (1969)		Guatemala (1973)	
Sector*	Males %	Females %	Males %	Females %
Industry	43.5	21.8	50.1	23.3
Services	47.4	67.4	44.4	73.0
Other	9.1	10.8	5.5	3.7
Total	100.0	100.0	100.0	100.0

*Industry includes extractive, manufacturing, and construction. Services include
electrical, transportation, commerce, and other services.
Sources: Guatemala 1974: 26-27.
        González Salazar 1976:186.

The significance of this employment distribution and the concentration of women in domestic service is most evident when we consider the available data on wages. Domestic service is notoriously
poorly paid, falling well below the legal minimum wages that are
applied to other sectors. González reports that 87 percent of the Mexican women who work as domestic servants in private homes earn
less than 500 pesos per month (1976:195). The concentration of
women in poorer-paying jobs relative to men is shown by the census
data on monthly income for the nonagricultural population. Low
average earnings of women should not be attributed solely to their
lack of access to industrial jobs. A survey of selected industries in
Guatemala (Chinchilla 1977:50) shows that among skilled workers,
women's earnings average only 57 percent of male earnings, while
among unskilled workers they are closer to 86.8 percent.

Table 4.   Monthly Income for Nonagricultural Economically Active
            Population, Mexico, 1969

Income	Men (%)	Women (%)
1-499 pesos	18.9	45.1
500-999 pesos	35.0	27.1
More than 1,000 pesos	46.1	27.8
Total	100.0	100.0
No. of cases	(5,357,498)	(1,992,076)

Source: González Salazar 1976:194.

The studies of the place of women within the national economy thus support the finding that economic stratification by sex is a pronounced feature of the nonagricultural population. Nevertheless, reported rates of female economic activity well above those compiled for agricultural areas have often been taken as indications of greater equality between the sexes in the urban environment. Of course, such conclusions are based on an artifact of data collection rather than upon any discernible social reality. Further, many scholars have pointed out that the high rates of female activity in informal commerce and domestic service in fact disguise an extremely high level of female underemployment (González Salazar 1976, Arizpe 1977) and serve to justify "the government's unwillingness to do anything about it" (Arizpe 1977:34).

Conclusion

In this discussion of sexual stratifaction in Mesoamerica, I have concentrated upon the popular classes, the peasants, and the proletariat in rural and urban contexts. There are obviously a number of other major research topics of related interest that I have neglected. For example, the nature of sexual inequality within the middle and upper classes, or within different industries has not been considered. The research that we have examined, however, is sufficient to reveal the main outlines of the process of capitalist economic transformation that is affecting Mesoamerican peoples. In the peasant sector, we have observed the weakening of the household productive unit based upon sexual complementarity and mutual dependence. On the plantations, it was found that men are integrated into capitalist production as regular workers while women are marginally employed. Among the urban poor, both sexes suffer high levels of marginal employment and underemployment, but the nature of the occupational distribution and the rates of pay are more favorable to men and indicate that they are at least several steps closer to economic integration than women. In sum, the penetration and expansion of capitalist production has devalued, if not eliminated, women's traditional role in production. In return it has given them second-class status on the national labor market. In the face of massive unemployment, women's only recourse is the informal sector. In peasant, plantation, and urban contexts, women actively exploit local opportunities. Lacking capital, they are largely limited to petty trade or domestic service as a means of siphoning some cash out of the formal economy.

In general, as the capitalist market economy has expanded, the peasant, plantation, and urban divisions of Mesoamerican culture have been crosscut by a division between the more highly organized capitalist sectors and the myriad of small-scale subsistence producers who continue to fend for themselves without the benefit of organizational grandeur or economic monopolies. As different parts of the population are recruited into capitalist production, we find that females are consistently bypassed in favor of males and that the overall prospects for direct female participation are discouraging. Throughout Mesoamerica, then, we have observed a transformation of the sexual division of labor from one that simply divided the sexes by task to a more profound separation, channeling the sexes into two different economic sectors: the capitalist sector and the subsistence sector.

This transformation is consistent with the more general thesis of dependent capitalist development which holds that capitalism cannot really afford to dispense with or completely destroy the subsistence sectors of the economy, for it is from these sectors that it ultimately draws its cheap labor supply. It is by gaining access to labor that has been cheaply produced and maintained outside the capitalist system that capitalist enterprises are best able to pay the low wages upon which high profits are based. If this thesis is correct, then it should not surprise us that when rural populations are drawn into capitalist production, there are fractions of the population, or enclaves, that are "permitted" to persist at the margins of capitalism as a reserve. Circumscribed by expanding capitalist production, contemporary subsistence producers are certainly within the system, but not supported by it. The limited rewards that they receive trickle down through informally organized occupations and self-employment, as well as through emotional claims upon family members and kin. Hence, we find that while "integration" is proceeding for some sectors of the population, others are confined to informal self-employment in the subsistence sector, becoming increasingly dependent on those who have a lien on capitalist resources and rewards. Translating these trends into the realm of sex roles, females are disproportionately represented among the populations that are expected to maintain themselves and others outside the formal structure of the capitalist economy. Why women should so consistently serve this function in the different sectors of society is not entirely clear. At present, I can only suggest that this is an important area for further research and theoretical inquiry.

In sum, a wide-ranging body of research on sex roles in Mesoamerica indicates that national and macroeconomic changes do have a differential impact upon the sexes, and that they are creating a major schism between men and women that is conducive to increasing development of sexual stratification and inequality. As opposed to the attitudes held thirty years ago, I do not believe that current researchers regard sexual stratification casually, as a matter of domestic or family roles which lacks cause or consequences in the larger social and economic order. I can only hope that the recent awakening of interest in this serious problem of sexual stratification will be supported by further research and theoretical development by those who are concerned with Mesoamerican society.

NOTES

1. Equality of cash incomes is obviously greater if men and women coffee harvesters are paid at the same piece rates (data which Maynard did not provide), which seems to be the common practice in Guatemala.

2. Maynard (1963:281) states that "few Ladinos in the village earn a living through the farming of small properties."

3. Beyond Maynard's explanation in terms of machismo, I suggest that the Ladino male's "irresponsibility" and willingness to abandon his family merely reflect the opportunism that characterizes his economic position, and the fact that his best economic strategies are not in subsistence production but in successfully exploiting his favored position as a commercial intermediary and as a worker.

4. The suggestion that Zapotec men suffer greater underemployment than the women needs verification. It appears to be based on the observation that men may sometimes be totally inactive, while women are more continuously involved in service and selling activities. This may mask the fact that women's activities may be insufficiently productive or rewarding to support the women. It is possible that such disguised unemployment among women exceeds that among men. This would be consistent with women's lower earnings per hour of work.

5. The name of this community, T'oj Nam, is a pseudonym. Research in T'oj Nam and other Guatemalan communities was carried out in 1974-75 with the support of an Organization of American States Research Fellowship and the Department of Anthropology of the State University of New York at Albany.

6. If women contribute roughly half the labor power in household production by processing food, helping in the fields, and maintaining the labor of husband and children, their returns are obviously better ($.60-$2.00) than the returns from weaving.

7. Cosminsky and Scrimshaw state that in five years, 20 girls, with a mean age of 17, have left the plantation for work. Their Table 4 of comparative age composition shows 32 girls aged 15 to 19. The data given do not indicate whether the 20 females who went to work outside but regularly send money home are still counted as residents of the plantation. If the migrants have been subtracted, then only 38 percent are out migrants, but if they have not been subtracted, then 62 percent of this age group leave to work elsewhere.

8. A temporary exception to this policy is described and analyzed in Bossen (1978).

9. As many as 50 percent of the women in the central barrio, where commercial opportunities are best, are economically active. In the more remote sections of worker housing, female commercial activity drops for lack of demand.

10. While the schoolteachers are women, they are not recruited from the resident worker population, but from the urbanized middle class.

11. A recent article by Rothstein (1979) reports similar findings in a Mexican town with the introduction of industrial employment. In San Cosme, the proletarianization of the males through wage labor in textile factories increases male cash income, while women's nondomestic productive activities decline and their domesticity (nonremunerated housebound family service activities) increases.

12. June Nash (1976:9) has criticized the use of the term marginal to describe women's roles under dependent development, since it could be interpreted to mean that women are not producing essential services for the capitalist system. She emphasizes that women continue to make a crucial but unmeasured economic contribution to society through their unpaid reproduction and maintenance of the labor force within the home. By using the term marginal, I do not mean to imply that women are unimportant to the continued functioning of the capitalist economy, but that they are obligated to perform their functions outside of its formal structure and reward system.

13. Unfortunately, Arizpe does not offer specific examples of nonmarginal or nondomestic jobs obtained by the female migrants from this town. She only notes that they have become dispersed within the urban population. It would be interesting to learn exactly what percentage gain access to industrial jobs or other formal employment.

14. Lomnitz uses the label head of household in two different ways. First, it means senior male, and includes females only when senior male partners are absent, as in Table 4.1 with 22 out of 177 households headed by women. A later sample of 142 female heads of households seems to refer to any senior female, female parent, or wife. Elsewhere (Bossen 1976), I have discussed the disadvantages of using the former definition due to the inadequacies and distortions it fosters in economic data.

15. San Lorenzo is a pseudonym originally applied to this settlement by Roberts (1973). I have retained the same name in my own research (Bossen 1978) which includes a restudy of the same population.

REFERENCES

Adams, Richard N.
1960   "An Inquiry Into the Nature of the Family," in *Essays in the Science of Culture: In Honor of Leslie A. White,* ed. Gertrude Dole and R. Carneiro (New York: Crowell).
Arizpe, Lourdes
1975   *Indígenas en la ciudad de México: El caso de las "Marías"* (Mexico: Sep/Setentas).

1977   "Women in the Informal Labor Sector: The Case of Mexico City," *Signs* 3:25-37.

Boserup, Ester
1970   *Women's Role in Economic Development* (London: George Allen and Unwin).

Bossen, Laurel H.
1976   "Household Work Patterns in an Urban Shantytown in Guatemala," *Western Canadian Journal of Anthropology* 6:270-76.
1978   "Women and Dependent Development: A Comparison of Women's Economic and Social Roles in Guatemala" (Ph.D. diss., State University of New York at Albany).
1979   Plantations and Labor Force Discrimination in Guatemala," *Peasant Studies* 8(3):31-44.

Chiñas, Beverly L.
1971   "Women as Ethnographic Subjects," in *Women in Cross-Cultural Perspective*, ed. Sue-Ellen Jacobs (University of Illinois: Department of Urban and Regional Planning).
1973   *The Isthmus Zapotecs: Women's Roles in Cultural Context* (New York: Holt, Rinehart & Winston).

Chinchilla, Norma S.
1977   "Industrialization, Monopoly Capitalism, and Women's Work in Guatemala," *Signs*, pp. 38–56.

Cosminsky, Sheila, and Mary Scrimshaw
1976   *"Sex Roles and Subsistence: A Comparative Analysis of Three Central American Communities,"* paper presented at the Seventy-fifth Annual Meeting of the American Anthropological Association, Washington, D.C.

Gillin, John
1952   "Ethos and Cultural Aspects of Personality," in *Heritage of Conquest: The Ethnology of Middle America*, ed. Sol Tax (Glencoe, Ill.: Free Press).

González Salazar, Gloria
1976   "Participation of Women in the Mexican Labor Force," in *Sex and Class in Latin America*, ed. June Nash and Helen Safa (New York: Praeger).

Guatemala
1974   *Anuario estadístico*, Ministerio de Economía, Dirección General de Estadística.

Hellbom, Anna-Britta
1967   *La participación cultural de las mujeres: indias y mestizas en el México precortesiano y postrevolucionario* (Stockholm: Etnografisk Museet).

Lomnitz, Larissa Adler
1977   *Network and Marginality: Life in a Mexican Shantytown* (New York: Academic Press).

Maynard, Eileen
1963   "The Women of Palín: A Comparative Study of Indian and Ladino Women in a Guatemalan Village" (Ph.D. diss., Cornell University).
1974   "Guatemalan Women: Life under Two Types of Patriarchy," in *Many Sisters,* ed. Carolyn Matthiasson (New York: Free Press).

Nash, June
1976   "A Critique of Social Science Roles in Latin America," in *Sex and Class in Latin America,* ed. June Nash and Helen Safa (New York: Praeger).

Nash, Manning, ed.
1967   *Social Anthropology.* Vol. 6 of *Handbook of Middle American Indians,* ed. R. Wauchope (Austin: University of Texas Press).

Peltier, R., and Ana Galvan
1971   "Estudio socioeconomico de vendedores ambulantes," unpublished manuscript.

Roberts, Brian
1973   *Organizing Strangers: Poor Families in Guatemala City* (Austin: University of Texas Press).

Rothstein, Frances
1979   "Two Different Worlds: Gender and Industrialization in Rural Mexico," in *New Directions in Political Economy,* ed. M. Barbara Leóns and Frances Rothstein (Westport, Conn.: Greenwood Press).

Slade, Doren
1975   "Marital Status and Sexual Identity: The Position of Women in a Mexican Peasant Society," in *Women Cross-Culturally: Change and Challenge,* ed. Ruby Rohrlich-Leavitt (The Hague: Mouton).

Tax, Sol
1952   "Economy and Technology," in *Heritage of Conquest: The Ethnology of Middle America,* ed. Sol Tax (Glencoe, Ill.: Free Press).

Vogt, Evon, ed.
1969   *Ethnology.* Vols. 7 and 8 of *Handbook of Middle American Indians,* ed. R. Wauchope and G. R. Willey (Austin: University of Texas Press).

3

A Demographic Survey of Contemporary Guatemalan Maya: Some Methodological Implications for Anthropological Research

John D. Early
Florida Atlantic University

In the original *Heritage of Conquest* volume, the ethnography of the Guatemalan Maya played an important part in the discussion of the structure of Mesoamerican Indian society. Since that time, Guatemala has continued to be an important area for these studies. Several questions can be raised, however, about the uncoordinated tradition of Mayan ethnography in Guatemala. The first concerns its sampling accuracy (Nash 1967:9). How representative is the research of all the Maya in the country? Does it show the sociocultural conditions of the majority or is it biased in terms of a few atypical types? Another question concerns the use of the ethnographic method to study contemporary Mayan culture. Since it is a small-group methodology, is it adequate for the sizes of Mayan groups and their webs of interaction? Finally, the information generated to answer these methodological questions gives some indication of the direction of change of the Mayan culture—whether it is disappearing or whether the cultural definition is being altered.

To date these questions have been unanswerable because they require survey data providing an overview of the number, location, and types of Mayan groups. Survey materials are scarce in peasant systems such as Guatemala with their high rates of illiteracy. To overcome this obstacle, demographers frequently extrapolate peasant structures from industrial systems. However, peasant and industrial systems are distinct in structure and dynamics. Therefore any simple extrapolation from one to the other is invalid. When survey data are available in peasant systems, their poor quality frequently makes them useless for analytical research. Verification tests can be run to determine what parts are of acceptable quality, however, and sometimes these tests can be used to revise the unacceptable portions. I have completed such a study for the Guatemalan data base employing ethnographic insights to develop the methodology. Revisions were made of the 1950, 1964, and 1973 national censuses using criteria developed in earlier studies.[1] Among the revised variables are the Indian and Ladino populations at the departmental and municipio levels. These data provide for the first time an overview of the number, location, and types of Mayan groups.

Survey of Contemporary Guatemalan Maya

HOW MANY?

The revised Indian population figures are presented in Table 1. In 1973 (the most recent available census, with another one being enumerated in 1981), there were 2,680,178 Maya in Guatemala (according to the revision of departmental populations), constituting 48 percent of the national population. The municipio revision gives a total of 2,826,376 Maya. The two sums are not in agreement because of different methodologies employed for adjusting the two levels of data. Using as an average the 2.7 percent Mayan rate of population increase for 1970-72, there are between 3,230,393 and 3,406,604 Maya in Guatemala in 1980, or 47.3 percent of the national population. The revision gives a greater absolute number and relative proportion of Maya in the national population than do the census figures. The revisions also indicate that the proportion of the Maya in the national population is declining.

Table 1. Mayan Population of Guatemala

YEAR	Author's Revision of Censuses		Indian % of National Population In National Census
	Mayan Population	% of National Population	
1950	1,611,928	56.2	53.6
1964	2,185,679	50.3	42.2
1973	2,680,178	48.0	43.8
1980	3,230,393	47.3	—

BASIC MAYAN SOCIAL UNIT

The social unit of analysis needs to be determined before decomposing the Mayan national population. Tax (1937) established the municipio as the unit. Many since have reaffirmed its importance. Hunt and Nash claim, "The Indian is conscious of the unity and uniqueness of his municipio" (1967:272). Like any such principle, it should be used with caution, as indicated by the following reservations. Cámara (1952:153), in the original *Heritage* volume, noted that when acculturation takes place, the cabecera becomes the focal point of change. Wagley (1969:55) mentions cases where the municipios have been reformulated by the national government but the Maya continue to use the older formation as the basis of social interaction. Hunt and Nash (1967:273) point out that in some cases the strongest sentiment of belonging may be focused on one of the subunits of the municipio. I would emphasize that no municipio is an isolate unto itself. All have important economic, political, and church links to the wider society, as is characteristic of peasant structures (Redfield 1956; Adams 1957; Wolf 1966). Thus, although the municipio is the basic social unit for the Maya, there is no municipio whose sociocultural interaction can be understood without reference to the surrounding regional and national structures. The converse is also indicated. If the Indian is not free of the Ladino, neither is the Ladino free of the Indian. In this regard, the revised census figures show that every municipio has some Indian population. Although in some municipios the percentage of Indians is quite small, the presence of some Indians in every municipio refutes the impression sometimes given in the literature of the complete disappearance of the Maya from some parts of the country.

DEMOGRAPHIC DENSITY OF THE MAYAN GROUPS

Simmel (1950:87-180) has shown the importance of group size for a number of social processes. There is a rather wide range of sizes of Mayan groups in the municipios. Table 2 presents this information in two sections. The first part employs a scale with units of 500 up to 5,000. The second part summarizes this information and continues using a scale with units of 5,000. As seen in the last column, the Maya have both small and large groups regardless of what definition one wishes to use for this classification. Fourteen percent of the municipios have Indian populations of less than 500, while 7.1 percent have populations over 25,000. San Pedro Carchá, in Alta Verapaz, and Guatemala City have the two largest absolute populations. The Maya comprise only 10 percent of Guatemala City population.

REGIONAL DENSITY

Guatemala is a country of diverse regions. Table 2 employs a fivefold regional classification which is the first to use municipio data. It yields greater ecological and social discrimination than departmental data. The divisions are as follows: (1) The metropolitan area consists of the municipios in the department of Guatemala. They are influenced by their proximity to Guatemala City and for this reason have been separately classified. (2) The south coast area contains the municipios in the departments of Escuintla, Suchitepéquez, and Retalhuleu along with the municipios of Ayutla, Ocós, and Pajapita in San Marcos; Coatepeque and Genova in Quezaltenango; Chiquimulilla, Taxisco, and Guazacapan in Santa Rosa; Moyuta and Pasaco in Jutiapa. (3) The western highlands consist of the departments of Sacatepéquez, Chimaltenango, Sololá, Totonicapán, Huehuetenango, Quiché, Alta Verapaz, Baja Verapaz, and the remaining municipios in Quezaltenango and San Marcos. (4) The eastern highlands include the departments of Progresso, Zacapa, Chiquimula, Jalapa, and the remaining municipios in Santa Rosa and Jutiapa. (5) The northern region consists of the departments of Peten and Izabal. Table 2 shows regional variation in the density of the Mayan groups. The highest density is in the western highlands with 67 percent of the municipios having Indian populations of more than 5,000. The area of lowest density is the eastern highlands with 52 percent of the municipios containing Indian populations of less than 500 and 79 percent with less than 5,000. The northern sector resembles the eastern highlands with 75 percent of its municipios having Indian populations of less than 5,000. The South Coast and the metropolitan areas are intermediate.

CULTURAL CHANGE AMONG THE MAYA

The more than three million Maya in Guatemala are not a homogeneous group. There is variation of Mayan customs between different municipios. But more importantly, Mayan groups are changing by adapting themselves to the national culture. Two to six of every 1,000 Maya each year cease to identify themselves as Indian and become Ladino (Early 1975:266). Many other Maya adopt some Ladino traits while retaining Indian identification. The process frequently is due to the economic adaptation of a land-short peasantry in order to survive. Wage labor in agriculture, transportation, or services gradually sets up pressures for further adaptation and more acculturation. As a result, important changes are taking place in the traditional Mayan culture. The process is gradual and can be marked by stages. Recently (Early 1982), I have developed and validated a fourfold classification: traditional municipios, adaptative municipios, modified municipios, and ladinoized municipios.[2]

The traditional municipios include two subtypes. Some are still very traditional as indicated by over 90 percent of both men and women using Indian dress (Wagley 1941, 1949; Bunzel 1959). Other traditional communities are feeling greater change pressures as indicated by a low percentage of men retaining Indian dress. These communities are usually involved in wage labor outside the municipios. Five to ten percent of the Indian population over seven may be literate. Pluralism begins in these communities. Protestant and Catholic Action organizations make their appearance as small groups. The *principales* are still important, but they now represent the dominant traditional faction rather than the whole community (Colby and van den Berghe 1969).

In the adaptive type, agriculture is still important, but about 50

Table 2. Municipios by Size of Indian Population, by Region, 1973

	Region												
	Metropolitan Municipios		South Coast Municipios		Western Highlands Municipios		Eastern Highlands Municipios		Northern Sector Municipios		Totals		
Indian Population	#	%	#	%	#	%	#	%	#	%	#	%	Cumulative
1 - 499	3	23.1	4	7.8	1	.6	32	51.6	5	31.2	45	14.1	14.1
500 - 999	3	23.1			7	3.9	6	9.7	2	12.5	18	5.6	19.7
1,000 - 1,499	1	7.7	4	7.8	7	3.9	4	6.5			16	5.0	24.7
1,500 - 1,999			4	7.8	6	3.4	2	3.2			14	4.4	29.1
2,000 - 2,499			7	13.7	7	3.9	2	3.2	2	12.5	18	5.6	34.7
2,500 - 2,999			3	5.9	9	5.0	1	1.6	2	12.5	13	4.1	38.8
3,000 - 3,499			2	3.9	7	3.9					9	2.8	41.6
3,500 - 3,999			2	3.9	6	3.4					8	2.5	44.1
4,000 - 4,499			1	2.0	5	2.8	1	1.6			7	2.2	46.3
4,500 - 4,999					3	1.7	1	1.6	1	6.3	5	1.6	47.8
1 - 4,999	7	53.8	27	52.9	58	32.6	49	79.0	12	75.0	153	47.8	47.8
5,000 - 9,999	3	23.1	12	23.5	53	29.8	5	8.1	1	6.3	74	23.1	71.0
10,000 - 14,999	1	7.7	8	15.7	18	10.1	3	4.8	3	18.8	33	10.3	81.3
15,000 - 19,999			2	3.9	24	13.5	3	4.8			29	9.1	90.4
20,000 - 24,999			2	3.9	5	2.8	1	1.6			8	2.5	92.9
25,000 - 29,999					7	3.9					7	2.2	95.1
30,000 - 34,999					7	3.9	1	1.6			8	2.5	97.6
35,000 - 39,999					1	.6					1	.3	97.9
40,000 - 44,999					1	.6					2	.6	98.5
45,000 - 49,999					2	1.1					2	.6	99.1
50,000 - 54,999					1	.6					1	.3	99.4
55,000 +	1	7.7			1	.6					2	.6	100.0
TOTAL	13	100.0	51	100.0	178	100.0	62	100.0	16	100.0	320	100.0	

percent of it is cash crop rather than subsistence. Hinshaw's (1975) research in Panajachel is an excellent study of this type. The literacy rate rises to 50 percent. The civil offices as designated by the national law are the town authority. The Protestant and/or Catholic Action groups have become important segments of the community. Many appear to be semisecularized in their world view. The *principales* and the religious hierarchy are still present, but now represent a minority view. Warren's (1978) study of San Andres Semetabaj details the change in world view from the traditional to the adaptive type. Brintnall's (1979) ethnography of Aguacatán analyzes and stresses the systemic nature of the change process.

In type three, or the modified community, the above tendencies continue to develop. Unfortunately, there are no ethnographic studies of these communities since 1950. San Luis Jilotepeque (Gillin 1951; Tumin 1952) falls in this classification, but the field work dates from the 1940s. Since there were fewer possibilities at that time for Indian involvement in the national culture, the picture presented by San Luis no longer appears applicable.

In type four, or the ladinoized type, acculturation is well advanced. W. R. Smith's (1977) study of the town of San Pedro Sacatepéquez in San Marcos appears to represent this type. (The municipio falls in type three, but Smith (1977:103) stresses the contrast between the cabecera and outlying areas.) Here agriculture lags far behind commerce in importance. Protestantism, national Catholicism, and secularism are the predominant world views, with little left of the traditional Mayan. The *principales* and the civil-religious hierarchy disappeared a number of years ago. There is a high degree of literacy and interest in education. A distinction is now made by the Maya themselves between the *"naturales"* or traditional Mayan corn farmers of type one and the *"civilizados"* or the acculturated, educated Maya of type four. Acculturation to Ladino and national culture is well advanced, but strong ethnic identity is retained. Most of the communities of this type are in the eastern highlands and have not been studied. It is not clear how representative San Pedro Sacatepéquez is of this type, since it is in the western highlands. The high degree of ethnic identity may be influenced by the historical rivalry with the neighboring Ladino town of San Marcos.

The last columns of Table 3 show the distribution of the Indian

populations in each municipio according to the four types, during
the last three national censuses. There is an inversion of some expected values between 1950 and 1964, reflecting the ethnic problems of the 1964 census (see Early 1982). Nevertheless the overall
trend is evident. By 1973 there had been a substantial decline in the
number of traditional municipios and a significant increase in the
modified and ladinoized types. The traditional type dominates in
the western highlands in all three periods even though there was a
substantial decline in 1973. This is the heartland of traditional Mayan
culture. The table clearly shows the result of closer Mayan involvement in the national economy and the impact it is having on traditional culture. Most of the Maya of the eastern highlands had
substantially changed before 1950. The tables show that even with
this change, however, a number of Indians in this region still retain
Indian identity. The ladinoized type also predominates in the northern sector. The south coast shifted from a predominance of the adaptive type to the modified type in 1973. The area around Guatemala
City is marked by the predominance of the ladinoized type, although
San Juan and San Pedro Sacatepéquez (Department of Guatemala)
have retained many traditional elements in spite of their proximity
to the capital.

Table 4 is essentially the same as Table 3, but population figures
are used instead of the number of municipios. Only a third of the
Indian population of the country belongs to the traditional type from
over one-half at the two previous census periods. In the eastern highlands the large Chortí municipios centered on Jocotán are responsible for some important shifts in the percentages. The metropolis and
the northern sector have some large variations because of the small
number of municipios. The survey data presented in Tables 2, 3,
and 4 show for the first time the distribution of the Mayan population in Guatemala by size of the group, region, and degree of acculturation.

Sampling Accuracy of the Ethnographic Tradition

The previous survey of the types of acculturating Maya reveals a
striking imbalance in the coverage of the ethnographic tradition.
Most of it has been done in the traditional municipios of the western

highlands. There was some work in the eastern highlands in the 1940s, but since then little has been done. Approximately three-fourths of the Guatemalan Maya live in the western highlands where the traditional type predominates. This concentration undoubtedly has influenced the selection of the area and type for ethnographic work. But the almost exclusive concentration on this type and in this sector has led to an imbalance. Table 4 shows that in 1973 about two-thirds of the country's Mayan population no longer live in traditional municipios. If the exclusive aim of the ethnographic tradition has been to record the traditional culture before it radically changes, then the imbalance is understandable. To this writer, however, such a focus appears too narrow. One of the principal aims of social science is to understand sociocultural patterns. In any science, patterns are understood by their performance in variable and discriminate situations. If the research tradition only concentrates on one type and one sector, then the opportunity for comparative research and discriminate analysis is lost. In other words, it is more than likely that elements of the traditional culture can be fully appreciated only by understanding what happens to them in the process of change. This has been the methodological loss from the failure to study significantly changed Mayan groups.

Adequacy of Ethnography for Studying the Contemporary Maya

As shown by the demographic survey, there are relatively few small groups of Maya in Guatemala. As shown by the unanimous consent of the literature about their peasant status, the Mayan groups are involved in webs of social interaction that are regional, national, and even international. Therefore the exclusive use of ethnography, a small-group methodology, cannot attain the goals of social science analysis for any type. The implication is not that the ethnography should be discontinued—quite the contrary. But it must be combined with survey methodologies in order to understand the sociocultural structures and dynamics of groups of the sizes seen in the tables. The ethnographic tradition has had a semiconscious realization of this difficulty. The usual solution has been to piece together disparate ethnographic studies and extrapolate from them, as in the *Handbook of Middle American Indians*. Since the various ethnographies were not

Table 3. Acculturation Typology by Number of Municipios by Region; 1950, 1964, 1973

Acculturation Types	Metropolis No.	%	South Coast No.	%	Western H. No.	%	Eastern H. No.	%	North C. No.	%	Total No.	%
1950 Census												
1. Traditional	3	23	7	14	106	60	1	1	1	6	118	38
2. Adaptive	3	23	24	47	54	31	2	3	4	24	87	28
3. Modified	1	8	7	14	10	6	6	9	4	24	28	9
4. Ladinoized	6	46	12	25	2	4	52	85	6	47	78	25
TOTAL	13	100	50	100	172	100	61	100	15	100	311*	100
1964 Census												
1. Traditional	5	38	11	22	122	69	1	2	2	12	141	44
2. Adaptive	1	8	24	47	30	17	4	6	2	12	61	19
3. Modified	1	8	9	18	22	12	2	3	5	29	39	12
4. Ladinoized	6	46	6	12	3	2	55	89	7	47	77	24
5. Unclassifiable											1	
TOTAL	13	100	51	100	177	100	62	100	16	100	319*	100
1973 Census												
1. Traditional	3	23	3	6	75	42	—	—	1	6	82	26
2. Adaptive	2	15	14	27	59	33	2	3	3	18	80	25
3. Modified	1	8	19	37	30	17	4	6	5	29	59	18
4. Ladinoized	7	54	15	29	13	7	56	90	8	47	99	31
TOTAL	13	100	51	100	177	100	62	100	17	100	320*	100

*See note 3.

Table 4.   Acculturation Typology by Indian Population by Region; 1950, 1964, 1973

Acculturation Types	Metropolis Pop.	%	South Coast Pop.	%	Western H. Pop.	%	Eastern H. Pop.	%	North C. Pop.	%	Total Pop.	%
1950 Census												
1. Traditional	35,892	43	35,284	18	815,946	68	16,408	10	2,671	18	906,201	55
2. Adaptive	44,240	53	129,852	65	342,048	29	18,177	11	8,827	60	543,144	33
3. Modified	646	1	15,802	8	28,965	2	49,646	30	1,075	7	96,134	6
4. Ladinoized	2,744	3	17,153	9	12,985	1	82,633	50	2,158	15	107,698	7
TOTAL	83,522	100	198,091	100	1,199,944	100	166,864	100	14,731	100	1,653,177	100
		5		12		72		10		1		100
1964 Census												
1. Traditional	63,826	50	63,049	24	1,269,088	76	41	0	15,441	45	1,411,445	62
2. Adaptive	61,113	48	141,772	54	226,469	14	45,566	24	8,685	22	485,605	21
3. Modified	1,095	1	46,154	18	157,636	9	17,353	9	3,070	9	225,308	10
4. Ladinoized	2,049	2	9,857	4	16,089	1	130,623	67	7,262	25	165,880	7
5. Unclassifiable			815								815	
TOTAL	128,083	100	261,647	100	1,669,282	100	193,583	100	34,458	100	2,287,053	100
		6		11		73		8		2		100
1973 Census												
1. Traditional	62,904	36	11,268	3	946,061	46	—	0	12,353	19	1,032,586	36
2. Adaptive	15,738	9	104,039	31	728,749	35	10,117	4	29,968	47	888,611	31
3. Modified	90,308	52	157,539	47	285,289	14	42,755	19	7,579	12	583,470	21
4. Ladinoized	4,159	2	59,842	18	93,998		172,931	77	14,137	22	345,067	12
TOTAL	173,109	100	332,688	100	2,054,097	100	225,803	100	64,037	100	2,849,734	100
		6		12		72		8		2		100

83

conceived with a common research design in mind, since they were undertaken in different time periods, and since they were never coordinated in any manner, extrapolations have not been satisfactory. This is noted in the reviews of the *Handbook* articles by Bunzel (1969: 949) and Siverts (1970:872).

Ethnography and National Population Censuses

The demographic survey and the critique of the ethnographic tradition indicate some methodological directions for anthropological research. Combining ethnographic and survey methodologies is a difficult undertaking. The administration of survey instruments in peasant villages is risky and questionable because of high rates of illiteracy, suspicion of people asking questions, and lack of knowledge about the nature of such studies. For this reason, the most extensive of all survey instruments, the national censuses, take on a significance different from that in industrial systems. In spite of their deficiencies, they are often the only source of survey data. They have a scope that never could be duplicated by private resources. Therefore the need of a marriage between ethnography and survey methodologies frequently means a marriage of ethnography and national censuses, especially the population censuses. For anthropologists, this is an extension of their interest in village censuses which has a long tradition—back to Rivers and Malinowski. Without it, the significance of much ethnography remains unknown because of the sampling problem. On the other hand, the national censuses, both past and future, need ethnographic input for their validity and analytical usefulness.

With regard to past censuses, the main problem is salvaging poor data arising from faulty questionnaire construction or enumeration problems. Some questions and their coding are designed within a framework applicable to Ladino and elite society. Among the less acculturated Mayan types, these questions yield poor data. For example, the marital status question in the Guatemalan census is coded by the usual international categories of single, married, divorced, and widowed. The consensual union category is also added. It is defined by the lack of a civil ceremony. Guatemala has one of the highest rates in the world for consensual unions; however, this high rate is caused by listing most Mayan unions as consensual. The Pauls (1963) have described the three types of marriages in Mayan villages—traditional *pedido,* elopement, and modern. All three are marriages in terms of commitment and kin support. Only the modern type, which is infrequent in many areas, includes a civil ceremony. Therefore the census coding yields apparently useless data by this ethnographic evaluation. But at the same time the ethnographic imagination can see its analytical value. The decline in consensual unions among the Maya can be used as an index of the extending influence of the legal system and the national government into the Mayan groups, as discussed by Adams (1967). This is an example of salvaging data from past censuses and obtaining important analytical information from it.

Developing quantitative correction factors is another important aspect of salvaging data from past censuses. My ethnographic work revealed the reasons for the ethnic misclassification of the Maya in the censuses, and at the same time suggested the quantitative relationships whereby it could be corrected (Early 1974). As a result, revised Indian population figures for both departments and municipios were obtained for three national censuses. These revisions have allowed numerous ratios and percentages to be derived for further analytical work.

With regard to future censuses, ethnography has an important role to play in their construction at the national level—in much the same way that the ethnographer formulates his own village census. Usually a national census develops a tradition around its census questionnaire. Ethnographic insight can be used to evaluate the analytical and administrative importance of questions presently in use. Anthropologists will be in a much better position to perform this function, however, if they have used the census for analytical purposes. In the 1950 Guatemalan population census, several items were included to identify Mayan culture. These included consumption of wheat bread, use of Indian clothing, type of Indian language spoken, and type of footwear worn. In the 1964 census only the clothing and footwear items were retained. "Type" of Indian language was changed to use of Indian language, and the wheat bread question dropped entirely. In the 1973 census the clothing, language, and footwear questions were transferred to the housing census on the assumption that all in the household would have the same response. Any ethnographer knows this is not the case, and that important information was lost. To this writer's knowledge, however, none of these census items had been used by social scientists. Therefore their usefulness began to be doubted by census officials (who have little time to do analytical work). If anthropologists had shown the analytical importance of this survey data, the relevant questions might have been preserved on the questionnaire of the population census.

Another example is an item on religion, which was included in 1950 and 1964, but dropped in 1973. However, in the 1950 and 1964 censuses the coding categories were inadequate. No distinction was made between various types of "Catholic," that is, traditional Maya or Catholic Action. Furthermore, in the 1950 and 1964 analyses of the censuses, no tabulation was made for that item below the department level. Anthropological analysis could have stressed the vital importance of the question for analysis of change, and assisted with developing a coding system to characterize adequately village situations.

Another common problem in questionnaire formulation is the use of questions and coding categories that assume an industrial system and have no relevance in peasant areas. They provide useless and non-discriminating information. Examples are occupation and unemployment questions. Ethnographic analysis could develop the pertinent questions and coding categories required to obtain knowledge about peasant economies.

The administration stage is another area where ethnography can assist the national censuses. Here translation problems for the Indian who does not speak Spanish must be investigated. The use of interpreters may help, but only if the categories exist in both languages. Census domains need cognitive mapping to clarify communication problems.

The importance of anthropological participation in the national census as outlined here has some precedents. Kingsley Davis (1951: 55), in his famous population study of India and Pakistan, noted that the first census officials in India were men of anthropological interests rather than census statisticians. Davis thought this was fortunate as cultural knowledge was much more important at that time. Such a perspective is needed if the Guatemalan censuses are properly to enumerate a group that comprises almost one-half of the national population.

The Future Direction of Mayan Culture

Although this essay has been primarily concerned with the use of survey methodology, the census results provide some clues for the dynamics of acculturation and the future of the Mayan heritage. For example, there has been a decrease of the Mayan population living in traditional municipios from over one-half in 1950 to slightly over a third in 1973. Moreover, the greatest number of municipios undergoing acculturation are in the western highlands, and on the south coast. These two regions exist in symbiotic relationship to each other. The south coast is an area of latifundia, the large commercial plantations oriented toward agricultural production for export. Agricultural labor is an absolute necessity for the success of this effort. The western highlands are an area of extreme minifundia, with the Indian population forced to seek wage labor on the south coast in order to survive. This symbiosis underlines the importance of understanding the national and international economic structures and their impact on the current changes in Mayan heritage. The differing interpretations of these larger economic structures by Adams (1970), Guzmán Böckler and Herbert (1970), and C. A. Smith (1972) need expansion to give greater understanding of this process.

This demographic survey has shown that there are over three million Maya in the national population of Guatemala. They are a slight minority of the national population and their proportion is decreasing because of acculturation and the higher Ladino rate of natural increase (Early 1975). There is no indication, however, that the Maya will disappear from Guatemala. The changes indicated in this paper suggest that Mayan culture is in a process of reformulating itself as it moves from the traditional form. The decline in the number of Maya living in traditional municipios will probably accelerate. It is highly probable that there will be increased penetration by national and international economic structures into Mayan culture. Therefore it appears that in the long run the Mayas will become an ethnic group within the national culture except for isolated pockets of the traditional culture remaining in the western highlands.

NOTES

1. Details on the methodology of revision are contained in Early (1974) and of municipio data in Early (1982). Because of space limitations, they are not repeated here.

2. The methodological details of this typology are contained in Early (1982). An operational criterion was needed to mark the stages of acculturation. A search was made of the ethnographic literature which indicated that the percentage of Indian women in a municipio who retain Indian dress (either a specific municipio form or the generalized form) provides such a criterion. This percentage was calculated for every municipio in the country in the years 1950, 1964, and 1973. Municipios with a score of 90 percent or more of women using Indian dress were called the traditional type. The remainder of the scale could be cut by 10 percent intervals yielding ten types; however, a statistical small-number problem would arise. It was decided to use 30 percent intervals over the remainder of the scale giving three more types. Usage of 89 percent to 60 percent was called the adaptative type; 59 percent to 30 percent usage was called the modified type, and 29 percent to zero was called the ladinoized type. The ethnographic literature of the municipios falling in each category was then searched to identify the structural characteristics of each type.

The typology was then validated by showing that it discriminated four variables in a predictable manner: Mayan fertility, Mayan mortality, the Indian percentage of a municipio population, and intratype ethnic misclassification in the last three censuses. The validation shows the classification has analytical utility.

3. The total number of municipios in the tables is different from the actual number of each census year because of the collapsing together of some municipios in the data base. Guatemala City is rapidly expanding and spilling beyond its traditional boundaries into the neighboring municipios. Its vital registration has been confounded with theirs. Consequently Chiantla, Mixco, Villa Nueva, and Petapa have been combined with Guatemala City and treated as a single municipio. In the department of Totonicapán there is a bitter land dispute between San Bartolo and

Momostenango which has led to inconsistent enumeration. They have been collapsed and treated as a single municipio. The number of municipios differs for each census year because of the creation of new municipios in the intervening years.

REFERENCES

Adams, Richard N.
1957   *Political Changes in Guatemalan Indian Communities* (New Orleans: Tulane University Press).
1967   "Nationalization," in *Social Anthropology,* ed. M. Nash. Vol. 6 of *Handbook of Middle American Indians,* ed. R. Wauchope. (Austin: University of Texas Press).
1970   *Crucifixion by Power: Essay on Guatemalan National Social Structure, 1944-66* (Austin: University of Texas Press).
Brintnall, Douglas E.
1979   *Revolt Against the Dead* (New York: Gordon and Breach).
Bunzel, Ruth
1959   *Chichicastenango* (Seattle: University of Washington Press).
1969   "Review of *Social Anthropology, Handbook of Middle American Indians,* vol. 6," *American Anthropologist* 71:949-51.
Cámara, Fernando
1952   "Religious and Political Organization," in *Heritage of Conquest: the Ethnology of Middle America,* ed. Sol Tax (Glencoe, Ill: Free Press).
Colby, B. N., and P. L. van den Berghe
1969   *Ixil Country: A Plural Society in Highland Guatemala* (Berkeley and Los Angeles: University of California Press).
David, Kingsley
1951   *The Population of India and Pakistan* (New York: Russell & Russell).
Early, John D.
1974   "Revision of Ladino and Maya Census Populations of Guatemala, 1950 and 1964," *Demography* 11:105-17.
1975   "The Changing Proportion of Maya Indian and Ladino in the Population of Guatemala, 1945-69," *American Ethnologist* 2: 261-69.
1982   *The Demographic Structure and Evolution of a Peasant System: The Guatemalan Population* (Boca Raton: University Presses of Florida).

Gillin, John
1951   *The Culture of Security in San Carlos,* Middle American Research
        Institute, Publication 16 (New Orleans: Tulane University).
Guzmán Böckler, Carlos, and Jean-Loup Herbert
1970   *Guatemala: Una interpretación histórico-social* (Mexico: Siglo Vein-
        tiuno Editores).
Hinshaw, Robert
1975   *Panajachel: A Guatemalan Town in Thirty Year Perspective* (Pitts-
        burgh: University of Pittsburgh Press).
Hunt, Eva, and J. Nash
1967   "Local and Territorial Units," in *Social Anthropology,* ed. M. Nash.
        Vol. 6 of *Handbook of Middle American Indians,* ed. R. Wau-
        chope (Austin: University of Texas Press).
Nash, Manning
1967   "Introduction," in *Social Anthropology,* ed. M. Nash. Vol. 6 of *Hand-
        book of Middle American Indians,* ed. R. Wauchope (Austin:
        University of Texas Press).
Paul, Lois, and D. Benjamin
1963   "Changing Marriage Patterns in a Highland Guatemalan Com-
        munity," *Southwestern Journal of Anthropology* 19:131-48.
Redfield, Robert
1956   *Peasant Society and Culture* (Chicago: University of Chicago Press).
Simmel, Georg
1950   *The Sociology of Georg Simmel,* trans. Kurt Wolf (Glencoe, Ill.:
        Free Press).
Siverts, Henning
1970   "Review of vols. 7 and 8 of the *Handbook of Middle American
        Indians ,*" *American Anthropologist* 72:872-76.
Smith, Carol Ann
1972   "The Domestic Marketing System in Western Guatemala" (Ph.D.
        diss., Stanford University).
Smith, Waldemar R.
1977   *The Fiesta System and Economic Change* (New York: Columbia
        University Press).
Tax, Sol
1937   "The Municipios of the Midwestern Highlands of Guatemala,"
        American Anthropologist 39:423-44.
Tumin, Melvin M.
1952   *Caste in a Peasant Society* (Princeton: Princeton University Press).

Wagley, Charles
1941   *Economics of a Guatemala Village,* American Anthropological Association Memoir, no. 58 (Washington, D. C.).
1949   *The Social and Religious Life of a Guatemalan Village,* American Anthropological Association Memoir, no. 71 (Washington, D.C.).
1969   "The Maya of Northwestern Guatemala," in *Ethnology,* ed. E. Vogt. Vol. 7 of *Handbook of Middle American Indians,* ed. R. Wauchope (Austin: University of Texas Press).
Warren, Kay B.
1978   *The Symbolism of Subordination* (Austin: University of Texas Press).
Wolf, Eric
1966   *Peasants* (Englewood Cliffs, N.J.: Prentice-Hall).

4

Urbanization in Mexico: Beyond the Heritage of Conquest

Robert V. Kemper
Southern Methodist University
and
Anya Peterson Royce
Indiana University

Introduction

The first Heritage of Conquest symposium began with the follow-ing statement: "We have all seen different parts of the elephant—different parts of Middle America or different kinds of people; . . . That all of us together may reveal the elephant that none of us has seen, to put our special information into the perspective of the whole—that is the idea of the Seminar" (Tax 1952:8). This paper began with the same goal: to bring together the diverse writings of anthropologists, historians, and other social scientists who have treated distinctive aspects of Mexican urbanization. This synthesis attempts to blend a wide range of scholarship and to do so without abusing the special interests of different disciplines or the particular strengths of competing methodologies. At the same time, we hope that this review of Mexican urbanization reveals something new about the "elephant" and how it has changed since that first Heritage of Conquest symposium three decades ago. If we have been successful, this synthesis tells us not only how urbanization has been linked to broader transformations of Mexican society, especially the waves of external domination throughout the pre-Columbian, Colonial, and National periods, but also how our interest in urban problems reflects important changes in social scientific theories and methodologies in the last thirty years.

The Problem of Urbanization

Urbanization is one of the great themes in the transformation of the region of Mesoamerica into contemporary Mexico. Thus, it is not surprising that anthropologists, historians, and other social scientists have devoted considerable efforts to understanding its many facets during the three decades since the original Heritage of Conquest symposium. In this paper we approach urbanization from two perspectives: on the one hand, we describe the process in terms of its demographic, ecological, economic, political, and sociocultural dimensions; on the other, we discuss the theoretical perspectives, methodologies, and data sources with which scholars try to comprehend the process.

In contrast to those who define urbanization narrowly, we believe that it is best understood as a multidimensional process within a society's overall historical-structural transformation. In the case of Mexico, this process is understood only partially. The gaps in our knowledge result not only from a lack of key data, but also from distinctive disciplinary orientations. For example, the division of Mexican urbanization into numerous temporal and spatial categories tends to force scholars into describing only fragments of the overall process. Given this emphasis on different periods and different regions among different disciplines, our assessment of similarities and differences in the urbanization process is necessarily synthetic. It is appropriate, then, to begin by outlining the periods and regions which combine to form the framework within which urbanization occurs.

Following standard practice, we divide Mexican history into pre-Columbian and post-Conquest periods at the point of the fall of

Tenochtitlán in 1521. The former is divided further into three phases—pre-Classic (before A.D. 1), Classic (A.D. 1 to 900), and post-Classic (900 to 1521)[1]—which correspond to the rise and fall of great urban centers and their empires. The post-Conquest period may be divided into Colonial (1521-1821) and National (1821-present) phases at the point of Mexican independence from Spain. A further subdivision of the National phase into Early (1821-1940) and Contemporary (1940-present) eras not only reflects the transition of the urban system from a "traditional" to a "modern" demographic pattern, but also marks the transition from historical to social scientific research styles. While this temporal scheme is somewhat arbitrary, perhaps obscuring the finer points of debate among archaeologists, historians, and other social scientists, it does provide a useful framework for synthesizing the historical dimensions of Mexican urbanization.

Regarding the spatial aspects of urbanization, one immediately confronts the question of the appropriate boundaries of the region. There is considerable geographical variation—from Mesoamerica as a cultural area defined retrospectively by archaeologists and ethnohistorians, to New Spain as a political territory created by Spain, to Mexico as a nation-state created and sustained by internal revolutions. Perhaps equally important, however, is the regional and local variation within these spatial-temporal units of analysis. Although the major city-hinterland systems shift over the centuries, the preeminent region of urbanization over time has been the Valley of México, followed by the Valley of Oaxaca, the Mayan lowlands and highlands,[2] the western Mexico-Tarascan area, the Bajío, and the northern borderlands.[3]

The interaction of these regions and the periods described earlier provides a matrix within which scholars from several disciplines investigate urbanization. What we know that pre-Columbian urbanization derives primarily from archaeological and (to a lesser extent) historical-ethnohistorical investigations. Research on Colonial urbanization has been mainly in the hands of historians, with a few important contributions from archaeologists, ethnohistorians, and geographers. Urbanization during the early National period has yielded to techniques used by historians and ethnohistorians, while the contemporary National period has been examined by anthropologists as well as by demographers, economists, geographers, political scientists, and sociologists. In all of these fields, the bulk of the literature has been composed of case studies rather than comparative research, whether across time periods or geographical regions. Moreover, few scholars have tried to deal with the urbanization process throughout Mexican history and prehistory. As a result, what we present here has been pieced together from our examination of a variety of analytical units studied by scholars of diverse disciplines in a wide range of temporal-spatial contexts.

Pre-Columbian Period

The study of urbanization has been a major aspect of the archaeological and historical investigations of pre-Columbian Mexico for more than half a century (e.g., Gamio 1922). Despite this long tradition of research, many of the basic features of pre-Columbian culture and society are still veiled in mystery.

One of the major elements of the research on pre-Columbian urbanization involves the determination of what types of settlements can be classified as "cities" or as "urban."[4] The long-standing debates regarding the nature of Maya ceremonial centers is a prime example of the problems inherent in treating urbanization archaeologically. Moreover, the emphasis on major sites and spectacular finds has tended to orient research toward specific places and their internal features rather than toward an appreciation of the broader process of city-hinterlands interactions. Only in recent years have scholars given greater attention to the larger regional aspects of urbanization.

Archaeologists and historians have elaborated several temporal-spatial schemes for understanding the pre-Columbian period of Mesoamerican history. Although many of these schemes are much too detailed to be discussed here (see volumes in the *Handbook of Middle American Indians* and a number of recent textbooks and essay collections), there is general agreement that the division of the pre-Columbian period into pre-Classic, Classic, and post-Classic phases is directly related to the rise and fall of urban centers and their empires in different regions of Mesoamerica.

The pre-Classic (or Formative) period ranges from about 2500 B.C.

at its earliest manifestations to A.D. 250 at its latest, with a terminal date of A.D. 1 used for the region focused on Teotihuacán in the Valley of Mexico. This period of agricultural innovation was marked by the emergence of permanent, nucleated settlements dominated by local elites. Moreover, interregional trade became common throughout much of Mesoamerica during the latter part of the pre-Classic. In all regions of Mesoamerica the rise of ceremonial centers during this period reflected long-term trends in population growth and wider use of natural resources and/or agricultural potential (Helms 1975:34).

With the Classic period comes the full blossoming of urbanization in Mesoamerica. Although the term *classic* is often used in a technical sense to refer to styles of workmanship in stone, painting, cloth, clay, mosaics, and even architecture, it also refers to "related sociocultural developments including the rise of urbanism and of states, the elaboration of more intensive agricultural techniques, particularly irrigation, to support a steadily increasing population, and the growth of interregional trade" (Helms 1975:51). These characteristics of the Classic were manifested in different ways in several of the important regional urban centers which evolved during this period. The linkages among these urban systems, in both the highlands and lowlands, reflect the centripetal and centrifugal aspects of urbanization in the Classic era.

Although a number of reasons have been suggested for the decline of the major Classic urban centers, we still lack definitive explanations for the end of this era between A.D. 700 (the destruction by fire of Teotihuacán) and A.D. 900-1000 (the abandonment of Monte Albán and many of the Mayan ceremonial centers). A variable combination of population pressures, agricultural-subsistence base problems, trading difficulties, political-institutional rigidity, and cultural stagnation were likely involved in the demise of the urban infrastructure and way of life associated with the Classic period.

The post-Classic period, which involved centrifugal urbanization trends in most regions of Mesoamerica, is often characterized as being more militaristic and secular than the earlier periods. These tendencies may reflect the emergence of "states" and alliances. These highly stratified societies were aggressive in military, political, and economic affairs. With some regional variation, the urban network in Mesoamerica expanded to previously marginal or peripheral areas, settlement patterns (nuclear and dispersed) became more complex, irrigation agriculture more common, and population growth was fostered. The northern domination—first by the Toltecs of Tula and later by the Aztecs (Culhua Mexico) of Tenochtitlán—of the rest of Mesoamerica was well established by the latter part of the post-Classic era. This domination is reflected in the military conquests and subsequent political control of the Triple Alliance as well as by the expansion of economic interchanges through a series of ports of trade in southern Mesoamerica (Helms 1975:98-104). Although a number of peoples—the Tarascans and the Zapotec, for example—resisted the encroachment of the Aztecs throughout the post-Classic, one can only speculate on what might have been the future of urbanization in Mesoamerica if the Spaniards had not intervened so abruptly in its history in the early sixteenth century.

Colonial Period

The fall of Tenochtitlán ushered in a new era in Mexican urbanization. Between 1521 and 1820, the Spaniards created hundreds of cities and towns, both on or near established indigenous sites and in newly conquered lands beyond the limits of the former Aztec empire. This considerable urban expansion was not carried out just to assure military and political control of the vast region which came to be known as New Spain, but to create a system for exploiting its human, mineral, and agricultural resources for the benefit of the home country (Bassols Batalla 1979:95-98). The settlement policy of the crown and its representatives reflected therefore what Morse has rightly called the "centrifugalism of the Latin American town as a point of assault on the land and its minerals" (1971:5). In this context, the hegemony of Mexico City reflects an urban system designed to expedite the flow of goods between the hinterlands and the capital and thence through Veracruz to Spain—as well as the reciprocal counterflow of goods and immigrants from Spain to Mexico.

The key to understanding Colonial urbanization is the Spaniards' imposition of the hierarchical urban system of Castile (i.e., the ciudad, the villa, and the pueblo in descending order) and a parallel administrative hierarchy (i.e., the cabecera, the *sujeto,* and the barrio or estancia) upon the remnants of the Aztec system of tribal city-states. The urban system of New Spain during the early Colonial period "fitted into a larger imperial calculus of political and fiscal privilege" (Morse 1971:6). The Hapsburg bureaucratic procedures fostered separatism, isolationism, and provincialism within the colony in a misguided effort to strengthen the role of the crown and its representatives.

The political-administrative system was headed by the viceroyalty of New Spain, which had jurisdiction over the audiencias (headed by captain-generals) established in Mexico City (1527), Guatemala (1543), and New Galicia (1548), as well as those of the Antilles and the Philippine Islands. This system was mirrored in the religious-administrative system: the archbishopric was established (1546) in Mexico City and a series of bishoprics were created in provincial cities. As Hardoy and Aranovich (1978:85) have pointed out, "The seats of the archbishops and bishoprics were thus determined by a clear hierarchical concept which corresponded to the relative importance of the political and commercial functions of various cities." This dual political and religious hierarchy prevailed in New Spain until the Bourbon Reforms of the mid-eighteenth century. Under the rule of Charles III, a new system of thirteen intendencias and internal provinces was created out of the archdiocese and the other nine dioceses, plus three new zones corresponding to Zacatecas, Guanajuato, and Veracruz (Unikel et al., 1976:19).

Within this administrative structure, colonial urbanization also had to respond to a variety of local demographic, ecological, economic, and military forces. The Conquest brought in its wake a demographic disaster; the population of the lowlands was reduced to a small proportion of what had existed in those zones and even the highland populations suffered great losses from the effects of diseases and continuing epidemics. While scholars continue to debate the magnitude of population decline in the sixteenth century (see Cook and Borah 1971), there can be little doubt that the fragility of the urban system in New Spain was due in part to the problems of establishing a system which depended on a different ecological strategy than had existed in pre-Conquest times. As a result, the sixteenth-century urban system laid the foundation for what Borah (1951) has called New Spain's "century of depression" in the seventeenth century (for a contrasting view, see Boyer 1977). The extended transportation and communication networks needed to service a colony of some 4.2 million square kilometers was simply too much for the viceroy, located in Mexico City, to control and maintain. Especially along the frontiers, the urban system reflected the necessity to establish military forts (presidios) to keep local indigenous populations from revolting or harassing the Spaniards' efforts to establish mining or agriculture in these regions (e.g., the Pueblo Indians of northern New Mexico successfully revolted in 1680 and held the Spaniards at bay until the "reconquest" in 1692 (Cámara 1979:104)).

The Colonial urban system consisted of a variety of settlement types. According to Unikel et al. (1976:18), we can distinguish three major urban forms: the administrative-military cities such as Mexico City, Guadalajara, and Mérida; the port towns such as Veracruz, Acapulco, and Mazatlán; and the mining centers such as Guanajuato, Pachuca, Zacatecas, San Luís Potosí, and Taxco. In addition, the urban network of towns in the rich agricultural region of the Bajío stands out as a distinctive component of the urban system, including as it did such cities as Querétaro, Guanajuato, and Zamora, and the subordinate towns of Acambaro, Celaya, León, Silao, Irapuato, Salamanca, and Salvatierra.[5]

In addition to the three urban towns outlined by Unikel, we can define at least three types of city-hinterland relationships for the colonial period: the major urban centers which dominated their respective hinterlands without effective competition from secondary towns (e.g., Mexico City, Guadalajara, Puebla, and Oaxaca City); the development of parallel cities in specific regions (e.g., the symbiotic relationship between Orizaba as a transport, processing and manufacturing center and Córdoba as a commercial and agricultural storage center); and the case of the Bajío region, which combined agricultural and mining activities among a network of interdependent cities and towns (see Moreno Toscano 1978a; Unikel et al. 1976).

Although Mexico City appears as the dominant point of the Colonial urban system, the available demographic data suggest that a rank-size hierarchy existed during the late Colonial period. For instance, in 1970, Mexico City had 113,000 inhabitants, while the second city (Puebla) had 57,000, and the third city (Guanajuato) had 32,000 (Wibel and de la Cruz 1971:95). Of course, this demographic hierarchy was flexible: Guanajuato's population shot up to 71,000 in 1803 and reached 90,000 in 1809 before falling off rapidly during the revolution to just 36,000 in 1822, while Querétaro's population swelled to 90,000 by the end of the revolution, more than twice its former size. In sum, population trends were greatly affected by the impact of political events and by the rural and urban dislocations (and epidemics) which followed in their wake.

By the middle of the eighteenth century the urban network of Colonial New Spain was completed. It spread from the hamlet of San Francisco in Alta California to the city of Mérida, with the focus always on Mexico City and thence to Spain. The exploitative, dependent character of Mexican urbanization during the colonial era reflected the institutions—economic, political, religious, and social—that were responsible for building and maintaining the hierarchy of towns, cities, and villages.

The Colonial period was brought to a close by *el grito*. This shout for freedom spread from the geographically and politically remote frontier until it closed the vital trade routes which linked New Spain to Spain. The war for independence lasted from 1810 to 1821. Just as the Conquest profoundly affected the Aztec-dominated urban system in central Mexico, so the fierce fighting between the loyalists and the *independentistas* had significant consequences for the Colonial urban system. Mining and agricultural productivity declined sharply, throwing the entire economic system into disarray. Many mestizos and Indians abandoned the villages and towns as unsafe; their massive migrations temporarily swelled the populations of Mexico City, Querétaro, and Guadalajara. New port cities blossomed temporarily along the Gulf Coast and along the Pacific as the loyalists struggled to keep their ties with Spain and the revolutionaries sought to get clandestine supplies from abroad. Although the decade of violence involved great economic disorganization and considerable cityward migration, it did not result in the precipitous population decline associated with the Conquest. The colony had 6,122,000 inhabitants in 1810 and actually grew to 6,800,000 citizens by 1823 (Wibel and de la Cruz 1971:95). Ultimately, independence simply pushed the Bourbon administrative and economic reforms one step further, thus breaking the restrictive chain between Mexico and Spain and creating the possibility for reorganizing the Colonial urban system and the hierarchy of power which it represented.

This survey of Colonial urbanization reflects our dependence on the historical and ethnohistorical research that has blossomed in recent years. While most studies have focused on the local level (i.e., specific cities or towns), an increasing number of scholars are concerned with regional, colony-wide, or even international analyses of Colonial socioeconomic transformations. Whatever the level of investigation, we are dependent upon surviving archival records (located in Spain, Mexico, and elsewhere), church and civil registers (especially those dealing with births, deaths, and marriages), contemporary travelers' and scholarly reports (e.g., Humboldt, Lopez de Velasco, and Vazquez de Espinosa), and data on spatial forms and their distributions (e.g., maps, plans, architectural remains) as a data base for describing and analyzing Colonial urbanization. These kinds of data are distributed very unevenly for the different cities and regions of New Spain. This unevenness makes it difficult to construct longitudinal time-series analyses for specific cities and to carry out comparative synchronic analyses of cities and towns (see Wibel and de la Cruz 1971; Borah and Cook 1978).

Not surprisingly, research on Colonial urbanization is dominated by historians. Within that discipline, it is possible to distinguish several approaches to the problem of understanding Colonial developments. First the work of Sherburne Cook and Woodrow Borah (1971) has provided important insights into the processes of population change in Mexico in the post-Conquest period. Their demographic orientation has been complemented by a growing interest in the economic dimensions of Colonial urbanism, which is reflected in the studies of Alejandra Moreno Toscano (1968) and her students in the Seminario de Historia Urbana at El Colegio de México. The regional focus on colonial life, and its concomitant urban dimensions, is illustrated by the definitive studies by Charles Gibson (1964) on the continuities and changes in Aztec society during the Colonial period. And, finally, the emphasis on case studies is well represented by the works of scholars like Richard Boyer (1977) on Mexico City, David Brading (1971) on the mining and Bajío towns, Brian R. Hamnett (1971) on Oaxaca and Puebla, Philip W. Powell (1944) on frontier silver mining towns, P. J. Bakewell (1971) on Zacatecas, and John Super (1973) on Querétaro.

In contrast to the historians' interests in the Colonial period, relatively few anthropologists have dealt with that phase of Mexican history and even fewer have concentrated their attention on urban problems. Aside from Gamio's (1922) global analysis of developments in the Teotihuacán Valley, and Othón de Mendizabal's (1946-47) and Aguirre Beltrán's (1946, 1967) studies of various aspects of pre- and post-Conquest Mexico, the urban focus is a recent interest, perhaps partly stimulated by the first Heritage of Conquest symposium. In contemplating the anthropological contributions to Colonial urbanization studies, one is struck by the broad temporal-spatial framework adopted. Since all of these scholars also have done archaeological or ethnographic fieldwork to complement their colonial researches, the results tend to illuminate not only the Colonial period but also its linkages with the pre-Columbian and National periods of Mexican history. Among the most outstanding ethnohistorical studies are those by Eric Wolf (1955) on cultural integration of the Bajío in the eighteenth century, by Thomas Charlton (1972) on changes in population and settlement patterns in the Teotihuacán Valley, by Grant Jones and his collaborators (1977) on the situation of the Maya in the Colonial period, and by Fernando Cámara (1979) on patterns of migration into the northern frontier territories. Typically, none of these studies focuses on urbanization per se, but rather discusses urban problems in conjunction with broader socioeconomic developments. Perhaps the only anthropologist to deal primarily with Colonial urbanism is John Chance (1975, 1978), who has analyzed problems of race and class in the city of Antequera (Oaxaca) as well as the broader question of whether Colonial cities were "precapitalist" or "industrial."

In addition to the investigations of the historians and the anthropologists, a few studies have been carried out by scholars in other social science disciplines. For example, geographers Robert West (1949) and Donald Brand (1958) made early contributions to our understanding of northern mining communities such as Parral and developments along the Pacific Coast; art historians George Kubler (1948) and Sidney Markman (1975) have made important studies of Mexican Colonial architecture and townscapes; architect-planner

Jorge Hardoy (1978) has authored a number of studies which place New Spain in the broader context of Colonial Latin American urban patterns; and demographer Kingsley Davis (1960) has described the process of Colonial urban expansion in Latin America in which Mexico played such a significant role.

National Period

Independence from Spain did not usher in an era of rapid urban growth. On the contrary, the haciendas—which Eric Wolf (1959: 245) has called "the ramparts of power in the countryside"—assumed a central place in the economic and political struggles between the new nation's liberal and conservative forces. Not until the "Porfirian peace" was established in 1880 did industrial and urban development receive significant encouragement from the government. The overthrow of Díaz in the Revolution (1910-21) was marked by a call for "land and liberty," while the Cárdenas presidency (1934-40) represented the apogee of agrarian reform schemes. Then, beginning in 1940 and continuing to the 1970s, industrialization and urbanization have been the dominant features of the Mexican "miracle" of economic development.

This continuing dialectic between city and countryside can only be understood in the context of international capitalist expansion in the nineteenth and twentieth centuries. The United States has played an important role both as protagonist and partner in establishing the conditions within which the urban system of modern Mexico has developed. Throughout the period 1821-80, which we may consider an era of "revolution and reform," Mexico and the United States were in confrontation. The war with Anglo settlers in Texas (1836), the conflicts in California and in the heart of Mexico (1848), and the Gadsden Purchase of La Mesilla in Arizona (1853) fundamentally transformed the national territory. From 4.2 million square kilometers at the time of independence, the nation shrank to less than 2.0 million square kilometers.

Mexico's urban system changed little between 1921 and the period marked internally by the Reform Laws and externally by the Civil War in the United States. The national population was 8.4 million in 1862 and it was growing at a rate of just one percent per annum. The hegemony of Mexico City (population 210,000 in 1862) was a persistent feature of the urban system, but it was not until this point in Mexico's urban development that the rank-size hierarchy began to give way to a pattern of primacy (Unikel et al. 1976:22). This transformation can be partially traced to the promulgation of the Reform Laws, especially the disentailing of the holdings of large civil and religious corporations after 1859.

By 1870, Puebla finally fell from its traditional second place in the urban hierarchy, as Guadalajara (with a population of 65,000) prospered as a regional center in the western highlands. Meanwhile, Guanajuato and other cities in the Bajío began to suffer a gradual decline in their relative importance. Although British capital helped to finance the redevelopment of mining in many areas after independence, by the 1860s Guanajuato—located in isolated, mountainous country, its silver mines exhausted, and its population down to 37,000—was a dying city (Wibel and de la Cruz 1971:98-99). Another important development was the effort to spread trade to ports other than Veracruz. Tampico became Mexico's second major port and prospered through the efforts of foreign merchants who serviced the interior as far west as Zacatecas and San Luís Potosí (Wibel and de la Cruz 1971:100).

Thus, as Mexico entered the final two decades of the nineteenth century, it was saddled with a highly regionalized, weakly articulated urban system in which the cities were consumers rather than producers. The urban and overall population growth rates were low, with the cities rarely outpacing the national trends. Mexico City was emerging as a primate city, not so much because of its own dynamism as by default.

Into this power vacuum came Porfirio Díaz, who ruled from 1877 to 1911 with lofty disregard for the harsh realities of Mexican life as experienced by 90 percent of the nation's population. Díaz established a stable environment which attracted considerable foreign investment capital. In this period of dependent capitalism, the government granted numerous concessions to encourage industrialization and to shift the economy away from its agricultural subsistence orientation. The combination of peace, rising exports, growing mining exploitation, industrialization, and development of a national railroad system gave a sharp boost to urbanization (Wibel and de la Cruz 1971:100-101).

The expansion of the railroad network had diverse consequences for the urban system. The construction of rail lines benefited the cities that were thereby connected to Mexico City and the major ports, but it also marked the demise of many towns that were by-passed. With the completion of the Mexico City-Veracruz line in 1872, and expansion of the rail network to other cities in the core region by 1880, Veracruz reaffirmed its position as the major port city on the Gulf Coast. While Mexico City, Guadalajara, Toluca, and Aguascalientes grew rapidly as diversified centers of commerce and manufacturing, Puebla, Morelia, Tlaxcala, León, and Guanajuato were reduced to cities commanding only limited regional markets. Perhaps the clearest example of the impact of railroad is that of Tor-reón, Coahuila: "it blossomed overnight as a thriving center of cotton production for the national market; from a rancho of 200 inhabitants in 1892 it became a city of over 34,000 by 1910" (Wibel and de la Cruz 1971:102).

In such circumstances, the largest cities began to assert their dominance—growing at twice the national rate—during the 1880-1910 period. For instance, in 1884 Mexico City had 300,000 in-habitants; Guadalajara 80,000; Puebla 75,000; and Monterrey 42,00. In 1910, these four cities were still the largest in Mexico, with 470,000, 119,000, 96,000, and 79,000 inhabitants, respec-tively (Boyer 1972:157-58; Unikel et al. 1976:377-80). What is surprising—in the light of the twentieth-century primacy of the capital—is that during the early years of the Porfirian regime Guadalajara, as well as Mérida, Monterrey, San Luís Potosí, and Ve-racruz, grew more rapidly than did Mexico City. Indeed, as late as the end of the century, Nuevo León (i.e., Monterrey) was a more important industrial center than the capital.

By the first decade of the twentieth century, the orientation of the railroad system, the strict governmental control of public fi-nances, and the free access of foreign capital combined to concentrate national affairs in Mexico City. The impact of foreign and local in-vestments in urban and industrial projects created an urban system which began to differ significantly from that of fifty years earlier. By the end of the Porfirian regime, certain tendencies of twentieth-century urbanization were already established: the high primacy of Mexico City; the importance of Veracruz as the principal foreign port; the political and economic dependence on foreign countries; the configuration of the multifunctional system of cities in the Bajío; and the isolation of the ports along the west coast (Unikel et al. 1976: 23-24, 36).

If the "Porfirian peace" had encouraged industrialization and urbanization through dependence on foreign investments, then the Revolution and its aftermath reversed priorities by attempting to resolve long-standing rural problems and by discouraging U.S. and other foreign intervention in Mexican affairs. Unlike the War for Independence a century earlier, the Revolution had a dramatic impact on the nation's population structure and urban system. The total population fell from 15.2 million in 1910 to 14.3 million in 1921. The destruction of many small communities and the general insecurity in the countryside created a great wave of migration toward the cities. During the Revolution the number of localities with 5,000 or fewer residents dropped from 70,738 to 62,671, with most of the loss accounted for by the complete depopulation of the small ranchos (Unikel et al. 1976:30). The rural violence and consequent disruption of economic activities in the central region had a debilitating effect on several cities and towns in the Bajío. León had been the nation's fourth largest city in 1900, but dropped to seventh in 1910 and eighth in 1921; Guanajuato had been eighth in 1900, fourteenth in 1910, and then fell to twenty-seventh in 1921; and Querétaro had been thirteenth in 1900, eighteenth in 1910, and nineteenth in 1921. The flow of refugees from the countryside increasing the proportion of urban dwellers from 11.7 percent to 14.7 percent of the total national population and, more significantly, firmly established the capital's predominance in the urban hierarchy: Mexico City grew from 345,000 inhabitants in 1900 to 471,000 in 1910, to 662,000 in 1921 (Unikel et al. 1976:377).

The end of the Revolution may be marked with the ascension of Alvaro Obregón to the presidency in 1921, but "the turning point of Mexico's Revolution" (J. Wilkie 1967:37) came with the election of Lázaro Cárdenas in 1934. Whereas earlier "Revolutionary" governments had adopted a passive role in social and economic affairs, Cárdenas—from rural Michoacán—was determined to use state funds to achieve social justice, especially in the rural sector. He increased social and economic expenditures to a new high and firmly established what Wilkie (1967:37) has called "the active state." The worldwide depression of the 1930s provided Cárdenas the opportunity to turn the political revolution of 1910 into a true social revolution. His actions to nationalize petroleum properties (1938) and his efforts to develop agrarian reform programs that would break up latifundios and would create communal ejidos demonstrated his determination to lessen Mexico's dependence on the United States and other foreign powers. In the process, he turned his administration away from urban and industrial challenges and reaffirmed his concern for the countryside where the bulk of the population lived.

The Revolution's lingering effects on the national demographic structure and the peasants' new hopes for economic prosperity through agrarian reform lowered the rate of cityward migration during the 1930s. The depression disrupted urban life more than it hurt the villages. In addition, large-scale governmental irrigation projects in the northwest created alternative destinations for many potential urban migrants.

In sum, the 1910-40 period, an era of "revolution and rural reform," was characterized by relatively slow rates of population growth and urbanization, with considerable variation among different regions. Mexico City continued as the nation's primary city as its population reached the 1.5-million mark in 1940.

The decade of the 1940s represents a critical inflection point in the process of Mexican urbanization. The end of the depression, the creation of a migrant labor (bracero) program with the United States during World War II, the development of several major hydroelectric river-basin projects, the spread of government-sponsored health and education programs, and the continuation of agrarian reform schemes combined with new governmental policies oriented to industrial development to boost urbanization to new heights. The period since 1940 has been characterized by relatively rapid urban growth in contrast to that of the revolutionary era.

The total population of Mexico grew from 20 million in 1940 to 49 million in 1970, and is projected at 69 million for 1980. This rapid population growth, reflecting steady declines in mortality (and especially infant death) rates while fertility rates have remained high, is without parallel for a nation of this size. The overall high natural growth has combined with substantial cityward migration to force the urban population growth rate even higher. The population in localities with 15,000 inhabitants or more grew from 3.9 million in 1940 to 22.0 million in 1970, and is projected at 36 million for 1980. The imbalance between the growth of urban and rural localities was greatest in the 1940s when the government shifted its focus away from agrarian reform to industrialization and urban infrastructure development. Cityward migration has been a major force for urban growth since 1940, accounting for perhaps half of all urban expansion during this period.

These demographic changes have not occurred in isolation from the broader transformations of Mexican society since 1940. The concentration of population and industries in a few metropolitan centers has occurred as a result of deliberate policies followed by governmental and private sector forces. Mexico City has been the primary beneficiary (or victim) of these centralization policies. In commerce, education, labor, banking, telecommunications, housing, and so on, the forces of centralization have created a pattern of "primacy" even more powerful than that evidenced by mere population growth.

The development of the present urban system is dependent not only on internal population trends and governmental policies favoring centralization, but also on transnational economic and political forces. For example, the correlation between urban growth and governmental policies of import-substitution industrialization in the 1940s and 1950s is obvious. Similarly, the expansion of large-scale irrigation agriculture in the north, the continuing problems of small-scale seasonal agriculture in the central and southern highlands, the participation of millions of men in the bracero program between 1942 and 1964, and the proliferation of investments in urban infrastructure and services all reflect the role of foreign investments in contemporary Mexico.

The results of this "dependent urbanization" (see Castells 1977) are everywhere apparent. Vast "backward" regions conjoin islands of wealth; huge cities grow inexorably at incredible rates; poverty is a way of life for all but a small minority of the population; environmental problems of air pollution, traffic, open space, and water and sewage are aggravated in cities and in the hinterlands; the flood of legal migrants and undocumented workers to the United States exacerbates conditions in the border cities; and tourism and petroleum exports seem to be the only means of generating sufficient foreign exchange revenues to keep the system going.

The landscape of contemporary Mexico reflects a process of slowly filling in the urban structure of the nation (R. Wilkie 1976). Perhaps the most radical efforts to change the settlement pattern were the agrarian reform programs for establishing small ejidos. After an initial burst of activity in the late 1930s, the government has continued to create ejidos throughout the underdeveloped countryside, with the most recent programs involving colonization in Quintana Roo and Chiapas. Despite these policies to encourage peasants to stay in rural areas, it appears that urban growth has been fueled by the abandonment of small settle ments.

In contrast to the ejido programs, the government has done much less to develop "new towns" within the urban sector. With the exception of suburban developments (e.g., Cuautitlán-Izcalli) in the Mexico City metropolitan area and a single significant case of an industrial development (i.e., Ciudad Sahagún in the state of Hidalgo), urban creativity has been oriented primarily to the tourist sector. The development of Cancún, Ixtapa, and a series of other coastal resort towns represents a very specialized kind of urbanization. Recently, the success of petroleum exploration-refining activities in the Gulf Coast area has led to the creation of petro-towns (e.g., Ciudad Pemex) which have their historical parallels in the specialized mining towns of the seventeenth and eighteenth centuries.

In the absence of serious governmental or private sector efforts to reduce the centralization of the urban structure on Mexico City in the four decades since 1940, it is especially noteworthy that the "filling in" of the settlement pattern has involved a historically significant shift of population away from the core region and toward the northern frontier (as well as to the west and east coasts). The shift in population to the northern borderlands is of special importance because it corresponds to a parallel movement toward the southern Sun Belt within the United States. The large size and high growth rates of the border cities make it unlikely that the interdependence between the two nations is likely to diminish in the near future.

These transformations of the urban system and their attendant problems (e.g., housing, jobs, education, transportation, services) are the subject of the recent National Plan for Urban Development, issued in mid-1978. The purpose of the urban development plan is to coordinate governmental and private sector actions to establish a better balance in the nation's urban growth than would occur through laissez-faire policies. The major aim of the plan is the decentralization of industries and population toward areas beyond the Valley of Mexico. To this end, a number of "parastate" enterprises are to be moved from the capital to other regions of the country and several hundred industries (especially those responsible for high levels of air contamination) will be transferred out of the metropolitan area beginning in early 1980. The plan also calls for shifting federal government budget priorities away from the Federal District and toward other, less well developed regions, with special attention to the problems of the northern borderlands.

This recent focus on decentralization as a solution to the problems of Mexican cities does not directly address the conditions of life in Mexico City itself. Estimates of what it will cost the government to expand necessary services just to keep pace with projected population growth run into the billions of pesos. Since the budget for the Department of the Federal District already is larger than those of all the states taken together, it is questionable whether enough funds will be available to cope with Mexico City's problems and also foment decentralization and regional urban-industrial development for the coming two decades and beyond. It is also problematic whether sufficient revenues (foreign exchange) can be generated by the oil boom and the tourist industry to subvent such impressive urban development plans at a time when the countryside suffers declining agricultural productivity and continuing population emigration.

Scholarship on Mexican Urbanization in the National Period

Research on urbanization in the period since 1821 involves a combination of historical, ethnohistorical, and social scientific efforts. As a highly visible component of Mexican development since 1940, urbaniza tion has received considerable attention from more and more social scientists. In contrast, very few social scientists and relatively few historians or ethnohistorians have examined urbanization for the 1821-1940 period. To be sure, the power of the haciendas made nineteenth-century cities less important in the urban system than they are today. Also, the century of conflicts from independence to the Revolution destroyed many kinds of historical documents. Considerable information about general economic and political developments in the Reform era has been assembled and analyzed by Franciso López Cámara (1967). Similarly, Daniel Cosío Villegas and his collaborators (1957-65) have analyzed at great length the social, economic, and political issues of the Porfirian epoch. In neither case, however, is the focus of research on urbanization per se. In contrast, the members of the Seminario de Historia Urbana at El Colegio de México (Moreno Toscano 1978b) offer some tantalizing analyses of local-level urbanization, at least for cities with good archives and commercial records. Even somewhat fragmentary records can yield useful results. For instance, by examining available baptismal, burial, and marriage registers for León (Guanajuato) for the period 1720-1860, David Brading and Celia Wu (1973) were able to relate population transformations in the region to broader socioeconomic indicators such as epidemics, famines, and *mestizaje*. Their work, like that of Wibel and de la Cruz (1971) and Moreno Toscano (1978b), also benefits from crossing the colonial-national boundary that demarcates so much historical scholarship on Mexico. In this context, the early National period is still relatively understudied compared to the Colonial period or the period since 1940 (Margolies 1979:9). The nineteenth century thus offers an arena in which historians and ethnohistorians could make major contributions to our knowledge of Mexican urbanization.

More research has been done on the early twentieth century. The demographic aspects of urbanization have received particular attention since data are available for each decade through the decennial censuses begun in 1900. This emphasis on population and locality data marks the entry of demographers and geographers into the circle of urban specialists (e.g., Bassols Batalla 1979; Gutierrez and Valverde 1975; R. Wilkie 1976; Unikel et al. 1976). Given the quantity and quality of data available for analysis, these studies tend to deal with national and regional urbanization patterns rather than with local trends.

Most social scientists who deal with the early twentieth century treat it merely as prelude to their main focus on contemporary Mexican cities. An important recent exception to this orientation is found in the work of two anthropologists—Larissa Lomnitz and Marisol

Pérez (1978)—who have traced the evolution of an urban elite family from the 1860s to the 1970s. They give as much attention to the early phases of the family's entrepreneurial career as to its recent confrontation with transnational enterprises. Their analysis of this family and its social networks presents a microcosm of Mexican urbanization during the past one hundred years. As such, it illustrates the advantages of combining ethnographic interviewing with examination of broader economic and political trends.

Since 1940, studies of Mexican urbanization by social scientists have multiplied to the extent that it is now exceedingly difficult for an individual to keep abreast of the wave of publications by Mexican and foreign scholars. We can speak of this research in terms of three main categories: that based in cities, that conducted in the hinterlands, and that concerned with the urban system.

We may distinguish two general types of city-based research. On the one hand, many studies have examined some aspect of Mexican life in cities, with the city serving merely as the location rather than the focus of research. Such studies usually tell us little about the urbanization process.[6] On the other hand, studies of cities emphasize the ways in which the urban context influences behavior and beliefs. This orientation to "the city as context" (Rollwagen 1972) treats the urban setting as an independent variable within the urbanization process, especially in city-hinterland comparisons.

A second major category of urban research begins from a rural base. Numerous scholars, especially anthropologists and geographers, have examined the "diffusion" of city traits to the hinterlands. The other face of these diffusionist studies is represented by the hundreds of reports on rural-urban migration. There are very few studies of the "diffusion" of rural traits to cities and there are even fewer studies of urban to rural migration.

The third major category of urban studies deals with urban systems. These "systems" range from narrowly defined regions (e.g., regional market systems), to the entire nation, and even to the international structures within which Mexican urbanization develops.

These diverse contexts for urban research are, in turn, linked to different kinds of analytical units, each of which reflects certain theoretical and methodological assumptions about Mexican urbanization.[7]

First, there is a tradition of research on individuals or families caught up in the urbanization process. This ethnographic approach, much favored by anthropologists, was made famous by Lewis's (1959, 1961) fieldwork among Tepoztecan migrants to Mexico City and among Mexico City slum dwellers in general.

Second, many researchers have emphasized the analysis of residential units, ranging from central-city slums to peripheral squatter settlements. This focus on the "community" dimensions of urban environments is especially clear in case studies (e.g., Lomnitz 1977), but also influences the character of comparative studies (e.g., Cornelius 1975; Eckstein 1977).

Third, a number of scholars have chosen to focus on socioeconomic groups in Mexican cities, especially the poorest "marginal" groups. Such studies have ranged from small-scale ethnographic inquiries, as with Lewis's studies of the "culture of poverty," to the extensive sociological surveys exemplified by the Monterrey Mobility Project (Balán, Browning, and Jelín 1973) and its Mexico City counterpart (Muñóz de Oliveira, and Stern 1977).

Fourth, some social scientists have focused on specific populations, especially ethnic groups. Such research is well represented by Butterworth's (1962) studies of Mixtec migrants from Tilantongo (Oaxaca) in Mexico City.

A fifth and final approach to the analysis of Mexican urbanization emphasizes political-administrative units. These can include whole cities (or their subunits), regions (e.g., municipios, states), or even the entire country. This "macro" approach depends heavily on census and survey data and thus tends to focus on the structure of the urban system, at whatever level, rather than on the behavior and beliefs of individuals. The work of Unikel and his colleagues (1976) at El Colegio de México demonstrates the value and significance of this approach.

A review of the literature shows that, despite this diversity of approaches to the study of Mexican urbanization, from the 1940s through the 1960s most social scientists shared a number of assumptions about the relationship between city and countryside. Urbanization was linked with industrialization as a major feature of modernization, which was evidenced by the Mexican economic development "miracle" in the postwar era. Even such divergent thinkers as Robert Redfield and Oscar Lewis were in accord regarding the critical role of the city as the "motor" for societal modernization. The "folk-urban continuum" (Redfield 1941) is thus of a piece with the later ideas of "urbanization without breakdown" (Lewis 1952) and the "culture of poverty" (Lewis 1959).

By the late 1960s, however, a number of social scientists began to question the scenario and benefits of urban development implicit in the modernization perspective. As the First United Nations Development Decade came to a close, economists and other social scientists realized that the "gap" between developing and developed regions was not closing as predicted. In Mexico, the critique of modernization theory and policy was heightened by the efforts of President Luís Echevarría to be recognized as a leader of those Third World countries that sought to establish a new international economic order. The economic crisis of the early 1970s, reflected in the 1976 peso devaluation and the continuing flow of "undocumented workers" to the United States, demonstrated the need to shift the attention of social scientists away from the internal problems of Mexican society and toward the international economic-political structure within which Mexico's "underdevelopment" persisted.

The focus of criticism was not urbanization, but rather the broader setting of "modernization" in which urban development was only one of several interrelated components. The magnitude of Mexico's metropolitan problems meant that the generalized attack on modernization theory was quickly joined by a more specific critique of prevailing concepts about urbanization. The city, on the one hand, became viewed as a center for domination over a dependent periphery while on the other, as an extension of the foreign "metropole"— for example, the United States, Western Europe, and Japan—into the arena of Mexican society. The city assumed the role of intermediary in a process of surplus capital extraction and cultural exploitation. This process of "dependent urbanization" did not reveal itself through more studies of "individuals or aggregates of individuals, their values, attitudes, and beliefs," but through analysis of "the mode of production, patterns of international trade, political and economic linkages between elites in peripheral and central countries, group and class alliances and conflicts, and so on" (Valenzuela and Valenzuela 1978:550).

The new "dependency" perspective emphasizes relationships of inequality within and beyond Mexican society. This revolution in social scientific world view reflects a broader trend away from a philosophy of democratic consensus through gradual modernization and toward radical (Marxist or neo-Marxist) theories of class struggle and revolution. The optimism of an earlier generation of scholars has been overwhelmed by this preoccupation with the inequalities built into the structure of Mexican society.

Whereas the modernization paradigm stressed the key role of culture and community in the development process, the dependency perspective emphasizes an ecological-societal (Schwartz 1978) or political-economic (Walton 1979) approach to urbanization. As a result, neither city nor countryside provides a necessary and sufficient context for research. As Alejandro Portes and Harley Browning have commented, "It is perhaps ironic that the proper course of future urban research be defined as lying beyond the city itself" (1976:4).

Redefinition of context also forces reconsideration of the appropriate units of analysis. Urban studies conducted under the banner of modernization tended to be highly empiricist and oriented to specific disciplinary problem-sets. The urban research of the 1970s demonstrates a multidisciplinary character. As John Walton pointed out in a timely review article, what is "beginning to emerge . . . is a new unit of analysis based on distinctive *vertically integrated processes* passing through a network from the international level to the urban hinterland" (1979:164). A number of scholars, from a variety of disciplines, are now attempting to treat individuals and institutions, squatter settlements and corporations, ethnic groups and political-administrative units—in effect, everything studied under the rubric of urbanization—within a single overarching analytical framework. The new directions in urbanization research in Mexico are blurring the boundaries of the field, although, as Portes and Browning have argued, "this seems a small price to pay for a growing understanding of the realities faced by urban and rural populations . . . and the lines along which their present situation is likely to evolve" (1976:14).

This emphasis on "process" rather than "place" opens new horizons for the study of Mexican urbanization. City and countryside cease to be arbitrarily separated by simple demographic criteria and come to be seen as integrated social processes (Leeds 1976). For anthropologists, especially, this transformation in research paradigm has had the effect of amalgamating their traditional "village" orientation with their recent fieldwork in urban settings (see Chambers and Young 1979:63).

Conclusion

"As anthropologists we have not paid much attention to the cities . . ."; this was George Foster's (1952:66) comment about the status of anthropological studies on urban Mexico at the first Heritage of Conquest symposium. The evidence presented in this paper demonstrates that thirty years have made a great difference in the dedication of anthropologists, historians, and other social scientists to the study of urbanization of pre-Columbian Mesoamerica, Colonial New Spain, and the nation of Mexico. We can mark this progress by a comment that appeared in the editor's introduction to a recent volume with the theme "Anthropological Perspectives on Latin American Urbanization." The editor, a political scientist, praised our work in these words: "Anthropologists have . . . been responsible for some of the highest quality work in the interdisciplinary field of Latin American urban studies in recent years" (Cornelius 1974:9). This revolution in the anthropological orientation toward research on urbanization bids well for the future, and thus, perhaps, is as important as the results achieved so far.

In examining Mexican urbanization across a time span of some 2,000 years (see Hardoy 1975), we must concur with Nancy Farriss that the division of Mexican culture history into "pre-hispanic, colonial and modern periods, each allotted to different disciplines, can obscure some of the basic continuities in that history" (1978:187). Although the character of the available scholarly research makes it impossible to abandon these chronological divisions, we have tried to stress the continuities as well as the disruptions in urban development through the entire time span under consideration. In this regard, one of the important results of this paper is how scholars in different disciplines use distinctive methodologies, techniques, and data to describe urban phenomena. From the archaeologists with their focus on material remains, to the historians with their emphasis on archives and documents, to the social scientists dedicated to interviewing, participant observation, and survey research, the concern is the same—to analyze Mexican urbanization in all of its diversity.

One of the advantages of the longitudinal approach taken in this paper is that patterns in Mexican urbanization reveal themselves that otherwise are obscured by narrower temporal and spatial concerns. In this regard, a major finding of our study is that urban development in Mexico has not been a uniform process. To the contrary, urbanization has demonstrated dramatic cyclical fluctuations over time and through space. There has been a constant dialectic between city and countryside, with the balance of power and control swinging from one to another depending on current conditions. These centripetal and centrifugal aspects of the urbanization process have corresponded not only to internal events but also, and especially in the post-Conquest era, to external events beyond the boundaries of Mexico.

The pre-Columbian era involved a series of distinctive urban developments in different regions which flourished and then collapsed. The tension was always between dispersed settlements and the urban ceremonial-administrative centers. In times of agricultural prosperity and population growth, the balance swung in favor of the cities. The period between the Classic urban sites and the later rise of Tenochtitlán and the Aztec empire was a downturn in urbanization in most of Mesoamerica. The success of the Aztecs in dominating the central highlands and in extending their control over vast reaches of Mesoamerica brought urban forces once again to the fore.

The Spanish Conquest brought a great decline in population, a restructuring of the countryside, and the creation of many new towns and cities. The sixteenth century was thus a period of contradictions. A much wider urban network was established, but it was weakly integrated within New Spain, since most ties were focused on Spain through Mexico City and Veracruz. During this period, urbanization corresponded with externally based exploitation of the natural and human resources of the region.

In the seventeenth century, New Spain suffered economic problems in the face of the accumulated problems (especially population decline) of the previous century. The urban network was extended farther to the north for purposes of mining and ranching activities, but the urban system was still internally weak. The colonial population began to grow again, although slowly, and the urban system was still strongly linked to Spain.

The eighteenth century was a period of revival, especially during the period of the Bourbon economic-administrative reforms favoring "free" trade and local development. The Bajío and the mining areas prospered again and the internal population growth created a market for New Spain's production. The Colonial area expanded to the far north, but these lands were sparsely populated by colonists and very weakly integrated with the central zone. The latter part of the eighteenth century, taken as a whole, was a period of positive urbanization linked to externally generated economic stimuli.

The nineteenth century brought an end to the Colonial regime. Independence brought a period of violence and turmoil that caused economic reverses for the new nation of Mexico. The new ruling class was composed mainly of conservative criollos who were more interested in their landed estates than in urban commerce or industry. The conflicts with Texas and the United States resulted in drastic reduction of the northern frontier area, but had the positive effect of eliminating a vast zone that had, in any case, been weakly linked to the rest of the country. The wars of the 1830s and 1840s, and the subsequent involvement with the U.S. Civil War, brought Mexico into direct and constant confrontation with its northern neighbor. During the first part of the nineteenth century, urbanization was slow and population and economic growth unspectacular. The Reform Laws brought a major impetus to change in the urban system with the expropriation of church and corporate lands and urban properties. Then, during the last two decades of the century, the Porfirian dictatorship turned Mexican affairs toward industrial and urban development. The creation of a national railroad network was critical in centralizing the urban hierarchy on Mexico City, with Veracruz as the key port for exports and imports. The role of foreign capital increased and dependent industrialization began in earnest. Related activities in large-scale mining, agriculture, and ranching provided the rural dimension to a major spurt in urban development.

The twentieth century brought with it the overthrow of the Porfirian regime. The countryside was swept with fighting and the cities emerged as places of refuge for peasants and aristocracy alike.

Mexico's leaders turned their attention inward, and especially in the Cárdenas era, were concerned with reforming land and labor laws. Although there were considerable differences in regional population and economic growth in the period between 1910 and 1940, the general pattern was a slowing of the pace of urban development and the emergence of Mexico City as even more dominant than before. The emergence of an activist state prepared the way for a greater role of the federal government in future urban and industrial growth.

The period since 1940 has generated an explosion of industrial and urban development. Cities have grown rapidly and the entire nation's population has expanded as a result of lower mortality rates and continuing high fertility. Cityward migration has reached very high levels, providing a base for high natural urban growth rates. During this period the urban structure of Mexico has been filling in the gaps, with notable urban development in the areas to the north and west of the central highlands. The linkages with the United States have been strengthened as a result of the flow of migrant workers (both legal and illegal) and the spectacular growth of Mexico's northern border cities in the 1970s. Throughout this period, Mexico City tightened its grip on the national urban system. It emerged as one of the great metropolises of the world—with a population of perhaps fifteen million in 1980 and an inordinate share of the nation's economic, political, social, and cultural activities. This centralization of the urban system has been widely observed by social scientists interested in urbanization in recent decades, but until the end of the 1970s little effective governmental action had been taken to shift the balance of power. The new efforts to counteract policies that encouraged urban and industrial concentration will not result in immediate decentralization. The historical and structural aspects of Mexican urbanization cannot be so easily altered by mere legislative measures. It remains to be seen whether the most recent period of urban centralization, spurred on by intensive investments by multinational corporations and international monetary agencies, can be counterbalanced during the remaining two decades of this century.

In summary, Mexican urbanization is a multidimensional process within the society's overall historical-structural transformation. This review article shows, we hope, that its demographic, economic, ecological, political, and sociocultural components must be examined jointly within a framework that reflects the temporal and spatial diversity of the Mexican experience.

NOTES

1. These periods vary somewhat for different regions within Mesoamerica and scholars have divergent opinions regarding which events should mark the boundary points of this threefold scheme (see Helms 1975:28-110).

2. We reluctantly exclude the urban developments in the Maya highlands of Guatemala from our discussion because of space limitations. The shift in boundaries from Mesoamerica to the Spanish Colonial and later National periods presents analytical problems that are difficult to resolve in this brief treatment of urbanization.

3. The changing northern frontier of Mesoamerica, New Spain, and Mexico presents problems similar to those of the separation of Guatemala from Mexico. Given the importance of the modern nation-state for urbanization, our analysis will include discussion of cities in the northern borderlands.

4. Hardoy (1973) offers a set of ten criteria for determining the urban status of a society. They are useful for our purposes because they are based on pre-Columbian data which do not presuppose a high-level technology. Societies lacking draft animals and the wheel such as characterized Mesoamerica simply cannot be evaluated in the same terms as those that do have such facilitators of urban planning. The criteria are also flexible enough that they can be applied to the three areas of Mesoamerican urban development without masking regional differences. The criteria are as follows: (1) large and highly populated for the time and place; (2) a permanent settlement; (3) having a minimum density for its time and place; (4) having urban structures and layout, as indicated by recognizably urban streets and spaces; (5) a place where people lived and worked; (6) having a minimum of specifically urban functions, such as a market and/or a political and administrative center and/or a military center and/or a religious center and/or a center of intellectual activity with the corresponding institutions; (7) a hierarchical heterogeneity and differentiation of society including residence of the ruling classes; (8) a center of urban economy for its time and place, having a population which depended to some extent on the agricultural production of people who lived partially or totally outside the city proper. Part of the labor force was involved in processing raw materials for a market larger than the city itself; (9) a

center for services for neighboring areas and the nucleus of a progressive pattern of urbanization and diffusion of technical advances; and (10) having an urban way of life, as opposed to a rural or semi-rural life, for its time and place (1973:xxi-xxii).

5. Hugo Nutini (1972:93) offers an alternative typology of colonial cities: (1) administrative-bureaucratic cities; (2) mining-manufacturing cities; (3) trading-agricultural cities; and (4) military-religious cities. He notes that "these are not always functionally exclusive categories, since there were a number of cities which fulfilled two or more functions."

6. The historian Richard Boyer has noted a similar problem in historical studies. He refers to these as the "episodic stream of history": they are "accounts of an individual, an institution, or the social and cultural life of the viceregal capital" (1977:457). He goes on to say that such studies are concerned simply with the city as the place where the "dramatic, the bizarre, the celebrated, the gifted" occurred and lived, and that they shed little light on the process of urbanization or on the city as a phenomenon (1977:458).

7. The archaeologist Barbara Price (1978:58) has made an interesting comparison of the approach of archaeologists and ethnologists to Mexican urbanization: "The overall methodological implications of the nature of the urbanism process for anthropological research strategy are considerable. The very physical and sociological prominence of urban communities has distinctly affected the course of research history. Their dominant position as the peaks of regional site stratification pyramids has been a double-edged sword and, paradoxically, has not favored the holistic view advocated above. In archaeology, . . . work has often concentrated on urban or urban-like sites, first, because of their striking visibility as ruins, and, second, because they are the settlements most likely to yield the remains of the kind of elite culture so favored by art historians and museums. . . . the traditional archaeological approach to urban research has tended to lack even a functional concept of the city as a whole. If the sustaining areas have been scanted, so, too, has most of the city itself, with the exception of the most elaborate tombs, and elite residences.

"The impact of urban dominance has been very different in ethnology. As in archaeology, the traditional approach has been one-sided, but it has come from the opposite side. Traditional ethnographic community studies have tended to emphasize the most primitive, isolated, "exotic" groups in any area. . . . When urban studies have been undertaken, they have tended to focus on the poorest, most disadvantaged urban dwellers. As in archaeological work, parts are intensively studied without relating them to the whole."

REFERENCES

Aguirre Beltrán, Gonzalo
1946   *La población negra de México* (México, D.F.: Fondo de Cultural Económica).
1967   *Regiones de refugio: El desarrollo de la comunidad y el proceso domini-cal en mestizo América* (México, D.F.: Instituto Indigenista Interamericano).

Bakewell, P. J.
1971   *Silver Mining and Society in Colonial Mexico: Zacatecas, 1546-1700* (Cambridge: Cambridge University Press).

Balán, Jorge, Harley L. Browning, and Elizabeth Jelín
1973   *Men in a Developing Society: Geographic and Social Mobility in Monterrey, Mexico* (Austin: University of Texas Press).

Bassols Batalla, Angel
1979   *México: Formación de regiones económicas* (México, D.F.: Universidad Nacional Autónoma de México).

Borah, Woodrow
1951   *New Spain's Century of Depression*, Ibero-Americana, no. 35 (Berkeley and Los Angeles: University of California Press).

Borah, Woodrow, and S. F. Cook
1978   "The Urban Center as a Focus of Migration in the Colonial Period: New Spain," in *Urbanization in the Americas from its Beginnings to the Present*, ed. Richard P. Shaidel, Jorge E. Hardoy, and Nora Scott Kinzer (The Hague: Mouton).

Boyer, Richard E.
1972   "Las ciudades mexicanas: perspectivas de estudio en el siglo XIX," *Historia Mexicana* 86:142-59.
1977   "Mexico in the Seventeenth Century: Transition of a Colonial Society," *Hispanic American Historical Review* 57:455-78.

Brading, David A.
1971   *Miners and Merchants in Bourbon Mexico, 1763-1810* (Cambridge: Cambridge University Press).

Brading, David A., and Celia Wu
1973   "Population Growth and Crisis: León, 1720-1860," *Journal of Latin American Studies* 5:1-36.

Brand, Donald D.
1958   *The Development of the Pacific Coast During the Spanish Colonial Period in Mexico* (Berkeley and Los Angeles: University of California Press).

Butterworth, Douglas S.
1962   "A Study of the Urbanization Process Among Mixtec Migrants from Tilantongo in Mexico City," *America Indígena* 22:257-74.

Cámara, Fernando
1979   "Differential Migration Streams, Economic Growth, and Socio-Cultural Changes in Mexican Border Cities," in *Migration Across Frontiers: Mexico and the United States,* ed. Fernando Cámara and Robert V. Kemper (Albany: State University of New York, Institute for Mesoamerican Studies).

Castells, Manuel
1977   *The Urban Question* (London: Edward Arnold).

Chambers, Erve, and P. Young
1979   "Mesoamerican Community Studies," *Annual Review of Anthropology* 8:45-69.

Chance, J. K.
1975   "The Colonial Latin American City: Preindustrial or Capitalist?" *Urban Anthropology* 4:211-28.

1978   *Race and Class in Colonial Oaxaca* (Stanford: Stanford University Press).

Charlton, Thomas Henry
1972   "Population Trends in the Teotihuacán Valley, AD 1400-1969," *World Archaeology* 4:106-23.

Cook, Sherburne F., and Woodrow Borah
1971   *Essays in Population History: Mexico and the Caribbean, I* (Berkeley and Los Angeles: University of California Press).

Cornelius, Wayne A.
1974   "Introduction," in *Anthropological Perspectives on Latin American Urbanization,* ed. Wayne A. Cornelius and Felicity M. Trueblood, Latin American Urban Research, vol. 4 (Beverly Hills, Cal.: Sage Publishers).

1975   *Politics and the Migrant Poor in Mexico City* (Stanford: Stanford University Press).

Cosío Villegas, Daniel (author, vols. I, V, VI; ed. et al., remaining vols.)
1957-65 *Historia moderna de México,* 7 vols. (México, D.F.: El Colegio de México).

Davis, Kingsley
1960   "Colonial Expansion and Urban Diffusion in the Americas," *International Journal of Comparative Sociology* 1:43-66.

Eckstein, Susan
1977   *The Poverty of Revolution: The State and the Urban Poor in Mexico* (Princeton: Princeton University Press).

Farriss, Nancy M.
1978   "Nucleation versus Dispersal: the Dynamics of Population Move-

ment in Colonial Yucatán," *Hispanic American Historical Review* 58:187-216.

Foster, George
1952   "Comment on Sol Tax's paper on 'Economy and Technology'," in *Heritage of Conquest: The Ethnology of Middle America,* ed. Sol Tax (Glencoe, Ill.: Free Press).

Gamio, Manuel
1922   *La población del valle de Teotihuacán* (México, D.F.: Dirección de Talleres Gráficos de la Secretaría de Educación Pública).

Gibson, Charles
1964   *The Aztecs under Spanish Rule: A History of the Indians of the Valley of Mexico, 1519-1810* (Stanford: Stanford University Press).

Gutierrez de MacGregor, Maria Teresa, and Carmen V. Valverde
1975   "Evolution of the Urban Population in the Arid Zones of Mexico, 1900-1970," *Geographical Review* 65:214-28.

Hamnett, Brian R.
1971   *Politics and Trade in Southern Mexico, 1750-1821* (Cambridge: Cambridge University Press).

Hardoy, Jorge E.
1973   *Pre-Columbian Cities* (New York: Walker).
1975   "Two Thousand Years of Latin American Urbanization," in *Urbanization in Latin America: Approaches and Issues,* ed. Jorge E. Hardoy (Garden City, N.Y.: Doubleday, Anchor Press).
1978   "La cartografía urbana en América Latina durante el período colonial. Un análisis de fuentes," in *Ensayos histórico-sociales sobre la urbanización en América Latina,* ed. Jorge E. Hardoy, Richard M. Morse, and Richard P. Schaedel (Buenos Aires: Comisión de Desarrollo Urbano y Regional, Ediciones Siap).

Hardoy, Jorge E., and Carmen Aranovich
1978   "The Scale and Functions of Spanish American Cities Around 1600: An Essay on Methodology," in *Urbanization in the Americas from its Beginnings to the Present,* ed. Richard P. Schaedel, Jorge E. Hardoy, and Nora Scott Kinzer (The Hague: Mouton).

Helms, Mary W.
1975   *Middle America: A Culture History of Heartland and Frontiers* (Englewood Cliffs, N.J.: Prentice-Hall).

Jones, Grant D.
1977   *Anthropology and History in Yucatán* (Austin: University of Texas Press).

Kubler, George
1948   *Mexican Architecture of the Sixteenth Century*, vol. 1 (New Haven: Yale University Press).
Leeds, Anthony E.
1976   "Urban Society Subsumes Rural: Specialties, Nucleations, Countryside, and Networks—Metatheory, Theory, and Method," *Atti del XL Congresso Internazionale Degli Americanisti* 4:171–82. (Genoa).
Lewis, Oscar
1952   "Urbanization Without Breakdown: A Case Study," *Scientific Monthly* 75:31-41.
1959   *Five Families* (New York: John Wiley & Sons).
1961   *The Children of Sanchez* (New York: Random House).
Lomnitz, Larissa Adler
1977   *Networks and Marginality: Life in a Mexican Shantytown* (New York: Academic Press).
Lomnitz, Larissa, and Marisol Perez
1978   "The History of a Mexican Urban Family," *Journal of Family History* 3:392-409.
Lopez Cámara, Francisco
1967   *La estructura economica y social de México en la época de la Reforma* (México: Universidad Nacional Autónoma de México).
Margolies, Luise
1979   "The Process of Social Urbanization in Latin America," paper presented at the Seventy-eighth Annual Meeting of the American Anthropological Association, Cincinnati.
Markman, Sidney D.
1975   "The Dominican Townscape for 'Pueblos de Indios' in Colonial Chiapas," *Atti del XL Congresso Internazionale Degli Americanisti*, vol. 4 (Genoa).
Mendizabal, Miguel Othón de
1946-47   *Obras completas*, 6 vols. (México: Talleres Gráficos de la Nación).
Moreno Toscano, Alejandra
1968   *Geografía economica de México (siglo XVI)* (Guanajuato: El Colegio de México).
1978a   "Regional Economy and Urbanization: Three Examples of the Relationship Between Cities and Regions in New Spain at the End of the Eighteenth Century," in *Urbanization in the Americas from its Beginnings to the Present*, ed. Richard P. Schaedel, Jorge E. Hardoy, and Nora Scott Kinzer (The Hague: Mouton).
1978b   *Ciudad de México: ensayo de construcción de una historia* (México,

D.F.: Instituto Nacional de Antropología e Historia, Colección Scientífica no. 61).

Morse, Richard
1971   "Trends and Issues in Latin American Urban Research, 1965-1970 (Part I)," *Latin American Research Review* 6:3-52.

Muñóz, Humberto, Orlandina de Oliveira, and Claudio Stern
1977   *Migración y desigualdad social en la ciudad de México* (México, D.F.: Instituto de Investigaciones Sociales, Universidad Nacional Autónoma de México).

Nutini, Hugo G.
1972   "The Latin American City: A Cultural-Historical Approach," in *The Anthropology of Urban Environments,* ed. Thomas Weaver and Douglas White, Society for Applied Anthropology, monograph no. 11 (Washington, D.C.).

Portes, Alejandro, and Harley L. Browning
1976   *Current Perspectives in Latin American Urban Research* (Austin: University of Texas, Institute of Latin American Studies).

Powell, Philip Wayne
1944   "Presidios and Towns on the Silver Frontier of New Spain, 1550-1580," *Hispanic American Historical Review* 24:179-200.

Price, Barbara J.
1978   "Cause, Effect, and the Anthropological Study of Urbanism," in *Urbanization in the Americas from its Beginnings to the Present,* ed. Richard P. Schaedel, Jorge Hardoy, and Nora S. Kinzer (The Hague: Mouton).

Redfield, Robert
1941   *The Folk Culture of Yucatán* (Chicago: University of Chicago Press).

Rollwagen, Jack R.
1972   "A Comparative Framework for the Investigation of the City-As-Context: A Discussion of the Mexican Case," *Urban Anthropology* 1:68-86.

Schwartz, Norman B.
1978   "Community Development and Cultural Change in Latin America," *Annual Review of Anthropology* 7:235-62.

Super, J.
1973   "Querétaro: Society and Economy in Early Provincial Mexico 1590-1630" (Ph.D. diss., University of California, Los Angeles).

Tax, Sol
1952   *Heritage of Conquest: The Ethnology of Middle America* (Glencoe, Ill.: Free Press).

Unikel, Luis, Crescendio Ruíz Chiapetto and Gustavo Garza Villareal
1976   *El desarrollo urbano de México: diagnóstico e implicaciones futuras*
        (México, D.F.: El Colegio de México, Centro de Estudios
        Económicos y Demográficos).
Valenzuela, J. Samuel, and Arturo Valenzuela
1978   "Modernization and Dependency: Alternative Perspectives in
        the Study of Latin American Underdevelopment," *Comparative
        Politics* 10:535-57.
Walton, John
1979   "From Cities to Systems: Recent Research on Latin American
        Urbanization," *Latin American Research Review* 14:159-69.
West, Robert C.
1949   *The Mining Community in Northern New Spain: The Parral Mining
        District,* Ibero Americana, no. 30 (Berkeley and Los Angeles:
        University of California Press).
Wibel, John, and Jesse de la Cruz
1971   "Mexico," in *The Urban Development of Latin America (1750-1920),*
        ed. R. M. Morse (Palo Alto: Stanford University, Center for
        Latin American Studies).
Wilkie, James W.
1967   *The Mexican Revolution: Federal Expenditure and Social Change Since
        1910* (Berkeley and Los Angeles: University of California Press).
Wilkie, Richard W.
1976   "Urban Growth and the Transformation of the Settlement Land-
        scape of Mexico: 1910-1970," in *Contemporary Mexico,* ed. J.
        Wilkie and M. Meyer (Berkeley and Los Angeles, Cal., and
        Mexico, D.F.: University of California Press and El Colegio de
        México).
Wolf, Eric
1955   *The Mexican Bajío in the Eighteenth Century,* Middle American
        Research Institute, Publication 17 (New Orleans: Tulane Uni-
        versity).
1959   *Sons of the Shaking Earth* (Chicago: University of Chicago Press).

II
Mesoamerican Institutions:
New Modes of Analysis

Introduction

In contrast to the first section, the papers in this section deal with traditional anthropological topics, topics which are also found in the original *Heritage* volume.

In the first Heritage conference, Beals discussed acculturation—the modernizing change of cultures—and the Pauls described life cycle data. In this volume Moore gains both greater breadth with the concept of enculturation and greater organization with the notion of life cycle as a career. Moore begins with an appraisal of the culture and personality literature in Mesoamerica, so closely tied to the work of John Gillin, a participant in the original Heritage symposium. Recognizing the role and interest of the state in defining the content of formal schooling, Moore then addresses the issue of cultural penetration, through both a review of the literature on rural education in Mexico and an appraisal of Illich's work on deschooling. As a result, he is able to gain new insights into the place of the school system in the culture and social structure.

Cosminsky's work addresses the changing context of health-seeking behavior by exploring access to "modern" medicine and "supernatural" curing in a framework of medical pluralism. She treats the pragmatic approach of householders to health care and their concurrent use of available health systems. The ability of many rural peoples to select from a number of health systems is the result of increasing cultural and institutional penetration, local syncretism, and other forms of response. Cosminsky's approach contrasts with cultural descriptions of Wisdom's sort, which focus almost exclusively on specialist-oriented traditional medical knowledge. Cosminsky reveals something of the options and alternatives available on-the-ground, a matter of disciplinary and applied interest.

The question of option and alternative is also primary in the articles by Gross and Kendall, and by Salovesh. Salovesh questions traditional geocultural divisions in the light of modern political boundaries and a broadly distributed Hispanic cultural heritage. He then details the importance of kinship and the strategies of kinship behavior that infuse the domains of politics and power, economics and wealth, and, even, religion. Indeed, in spite of the region's tendency toward loose, open bilaterality, a tendency that has apparently led some anthropologists to ignore Mesoamerican kinship as irrelevant, Salovesh persuasively argues that kinship is—if not the social structural backbone of every institution—at least the idiom in which strategies are carried out in most institutions.

Gross and Kendall detail the Tzutujil postmarital residence system. Their contribution is also "new" for Mesoamerica in that they combine a carefully wrought jural analysis of the normative system with a discussion of the complex circumstantial logic behind cases that on the surface seem to breach the norms.

Salovesh as well as Gross and Kendall enjoy several parallels, at least in their conclusions. For example, both papers agree on the significance of considering social action in light of alternatives available to actors.

More importantly, both papers point to a distinction of what may be described as essentialist and formalist studies of kinship. In this regard, many kinship studies appear to identify the essence of kinship as a concern for genealogical links, or as an analysis of jural-political kinship-based groups—kinship as it might be treated in a tribal setting. If kinship is not omnipresent or extensive or does not serve this jural-political role, if lineages and clans are not found (the argument goes), then kinship is not an important topic for analysis and kinship theory is of little use in contemporary anthropology. Alternatively, commitments to this perspective often force researchers to discover in their field sites such jural entities. A formalist argument, on the other hand, might identify elements in the debate on kinship analysis and apply them to new contexts. Kinship is then a valid topic because it defines epistemiological criteria for and shapes arguments in the analysis of many social institutions.

The two papers are complementary in their resolution of the issue. Although concerned to demonstrate the importance of kinship per se, Salovesh's broad view of the role of kinship includes ritual kinship, dyadic contracts, politics, economics, hierarchy, and other matters. By refusing to accept a preconceived notion of the essence of kinship, Salovesh shows more subtle and, for that reason, more powerful kinship infused into all domains of Mexican cultures.

The Gross and Kendall paper presents a test case for essentialist and formalist arguments: to what extent can the Maya be characterized as patrilineal? Residential mapping is often used as evidence that many Maya groups are unilineal. Exceptions to these arrangements are often attributed to local ecological circumstances, or to "loose structure." But what is the structure? And is spacial distribution a criterion of such structure? The Gross and Kendall paper attempts to demonstrate that a formalist approach to the data, through intensive field investigation, resolves the dilemma of the essentialist studies.

Of course, "new" as it is used in the title of this section of papers is certainly a misnomer. Nevertheless, we do have in these papers the first, or nearly first, application of several analytical techniques to these particular Mesoamerican institutions. The linkages sought by Moore between enculturation and schooling, and by Cosminsky among folk, traditional, and cosmopolitan medicine are new in recognizing the institutional penetration of the state and its agents. Equally, education and health have been important areas of planned structural and cultural penetration, as well as foci of applied research in anthropology. Salovesh's recognition of the important, if subtle, place of kinship in Mesoamerican regional social structure, and Gross and Kendall's detailed jural analysis and their careful case-in-context analysis of exceptions—the Manchester school in style if lacking in social dramas—are equally important and refreshingly different within the Mesoamerican region.

One can readily see that the papers in this section share a recognition of the penetration of politicojural, economic, and status considerations in the character (and therefore the explanation) of the particular institutions treated. And since politicojural, economic, and status matters are also regional phenomena, this section of papers also underlines the importance of the regional perspective in present-day Mesoamerican anthropology. The division of the papers is therefore somewhat artificial: the papers whose dominant emphasis is on the macroinstitutions themselves appear in the former section; the papers whose dominant emphasis is on the microanalysis of a particular institution in the light of the larger context appear here.

5
Anthropology and Education in Mesoamerica Today

G. Alexander Moore
University of Southern California

Anthropology has much to contribute to a discussion of formal education in Mesoamerica today. Some of our contribution stems from findings made generations ago; some of it derives from recent research, and much from conceptual advances made on the basis of old and new data. One of our central findings, not at all a new one, is that education, understood anthropologically, has relatively little to do with schooling. Education—or, as Wilbert (1976) terms it, "enculturation"—is a human universal; schooling is not. The proper direction of official policy toward schooling has been much debated lately by officials, educators, technocrats, Christian humanists, and radicals of every persuasion. They debate policies at the level of the nation-state, which for our cultural area, Mesoamerica, comprises at least two, Mexico and Guatemala. It is my belief that anthropological findings and conceptual advances can clarify the debate and help specify viable policy alternatives, as well as useful paths for future applied anthropological endeavors.

Anthropology, then, puts schooling into the whole context of enculturation and focuses on the several cultures of Mesoamerica, on those wholes which are going to be learned by new generations, with or without schooling. Anthropology focuses on informal learning, formal initiations by rites of passage into culture, on the ritual learning process, on master-apprentice relationships, and upon the interrelationships among the *whole* of these. This last category constitutes the study of culture and community, and within it, too, we are concerned with the effects—both desired and unintended—of formal, national, and bureaucratically organized schooling upon the local community.

In this paper we shall take up in turn several themes within the broader issue of enculturation within whole communities. First we shall explore the personality orientations of both Indian and non-Indian (Hispanic, Ladino, or mestizo, as all these terms have been used) cultures as these have been studied by anthropologists in the 1940s. Then we shall take up the question of the ritual learning process in Indian culture, and the nature of patron-client relations as a learning mechanism in the broader culture. We shall look at the nature of the formal schooling enterprise and judge it against its results, as well as the desire of educators and their critics.

Personality Formation in Mesoamerican Cultures

John Gillin (1947, 1951, 1955) has formulated the classic statements of personality in Indian and Latin cultures. These statements were won from fieldwork in San Luís Jilotepeque in eastern Guatemala and later from fieldwork in Moche, in coastal Peru. Although Gillin phrased his initial questions in terms of problems of individual "tension-management" as posed by contemporary psychologists, he ended up providing a portrait of the individual less in a "quest for security" than in the context of a total world view. Gillin thus reflected the concerns of American anthropology of the day, which was much interested in values and value orientations. In summarizing, Gillin examined each cultural view of the universe, the individual's relation to that universe, his relation to other individuals, and man's relation to man.

Gillin's view is explicitly cross-cultural and comparative. Thus his statements about Indians are in the light of an implicit contrast with Ladinos, and vice versa. Later his statements about Latin American culture are implicitly contrasted with North American culture as well.

Gillin found (1958:341-52) that Indians are passive, trying to be in harmony with a universe which is beyond human control, and within which one must practice cultural rules, by adhering to a rigid routine, in order to remain in harmony with the universe. The individual exists as a member of the group, which constitutes the supreme value. The uninterrupted practice of a cultural routine constitutes the highest satisfaction. His world view is centered on the local community, literally the navel of the universe, beyond whose bounds the world is frightening at worst and uninteresting at best.

In contrast, Gillin's Ladinos are active and aggressive, believing that man ought to dominate and control the universe. All natural and supernatural forces are personal and can be managed and manipulated on a personalistic basis. The individual personality constitutes the supreme value; the group existing to promote the individual. Routine is boring and unsatisfactory. The world is defined by modern geography, with an emphasis being given to an exalted notion of world metropolitan centers.

Later in a celebrated essay, "Ethos Components in Modern Latin American Culture" (1955), Gillin was to stress three themes: personalism, hierarchy, and the transcendental view of life. He departs from the earlier discussion by emphasizing the Latin acceptance of social class differences as being both inevitable and proper. Although the universe may be dominated and controlled by man on a material, superficial level, in the long run the more important universe is "beyond," *"más allá."* The greatest value, while individual, is also ethereal and spiritual. What Gillin was expounding was, in short, a quite intact sixteenth-century baroque world view of the transitory and ephemeral nature of human worldly existence, a world view surviving quite well in Latin America.

By and large Gillin's formulations, especially for Indian culture, have stood the test of time. Colby (1967) has updated the findings for Indian culture by including perspectives on pre-Conquest culture together with the rich data of the Harvard Chiapas project's fieldwork in Zinacantán. To Gillin's Indian ethos Colby adds a catalogue of traits: a concern with the face (literally a tendency to protect and shield the face and gaze, especially from outsiders); an elaborate etiquette for speaking; a preoccupation with relations between elder and younger siblings. Colby also adds several distinctions. Sixteenth-century pre-Conquest behavior is judged to have been much more assertive than contemporary Indian behavior; and the Nahuatl culture area is more egalitarian in its view of women than the Mayan area. (In addition, Colby attempts a bipolar distinction between those Indian cultures—classified by language group—which are "group supportive" versus those which are "self-protective." This discussion is singularly unclear; at the most one gets a notion of a continuum between two classificatory poles along which Indian groups may be placed.)

Gillin's formulation differed from others current at the time in anthropology by the absence of distinct correlation of personality orientation with child-rearing practices. In common with other later observers he notes that Indian parents were permissive, that suckling infants were fed on demand and weaned late; that children were trained at adult tasks as soon as they could undertake them. There were no dramatic customs, such as the swaddling of Great Russian children (Mead 1951, 1954) or abrupt toilet training practices as in Japan (Benedict 1946), upon which to direct attention and make correlations.[1] Rather, the data from Rorschach tests administered in Gillin's project disclosed that Indian adolescents tended to be imaginative and open toward the world until about age eighteen; then their personalities became "restricted," as they embarked on the rigid and "compulsive" pursuit of routine which was to mark the rest of their life.

I have shown that this sudden shift in personality orientation reflects a coming of age by ritual means. In my book on life cycles in one Mesoamerican community (1973a) I have shown that the marriage ceremony inducts the bride into new responsibilities, while it reconfirms these responsibilities to other married women attending the wedding. Likewise I show that the cargo system forms a lifelong career for its participants. Gillin had devoted much space in his book to describing that system, but as a series of discrete events, not a career. In a recent article (1979b) I have demonstrated that the recruit's first year in the cargo system (always on the civil side) is a rite of passage—a ritual initiation into manhood and the implacable routine Gillin emphasized. I draw my case from a particularly rich example, Atchalán, the Guatemalan community in which I did prolonged fieldwork. The very widespread reporting of such a year of civil-servant status at eighteen, however (see Cancian 1967), leads me to believe that the example is quite representative.

Redfield (1943) early believed that the Indian cargo ritual is "empty formalism," devoid of meaning to its participants, and therefore insignificant for enculturation.[2] My analysis and the burgeoning materials of new investigators in Chiapas (for example Rosaldo 1968, Vogt 1969—for Zinacantán; Nash 1970—for Tzo'ontohal) lay that notion to rest once and for all. The cargo system is pregnant with meaning, but relatively little of it is expounded in narrative form.

The cargo system may function as a rite of passage, but it differs markedly from the prototype of rites of initation as studied in, say, Africa or Oceania. There is no one-shot ordeal that is extreme, sudden, and relatively quick. Rather, to be initiated into manhood in Indian Mesoamerica takes a whole year, to begin with. My argument, as briefly as possible, is as follows. On the first New Year's day following his eighteenth birthday, the young Indian of Atchalán is separated from his home and thrown in with a company of his agemates who are lowly constables, servants at the beck and call of the mayor and his councilmen *(regidores)*. During his year of service he is indoctrinated in the civic culture by performing menial tasks and acting as a policeman to keep the peace. He must devote one week in six to twenty-four-hour duty. Two weeks in the year are devoted to sacred duty. All six weekly patrols are called upon to be the ritual servants of a saint, the accursed and ambivalent Judas—their patron—during Holy Week, and the town's patron San Juán Bautista, in June.

This year is a paradigm for the youth's next twenty years; in one year he learns the routine of his child-bearing years. Just as one week in six had to be contributed to the common good in civil or sacred duty, so in theory, must he give up one year of each three for continued service until he reaches his fortieth birthday. Service in a religious cargo is equivalent to service in the town civil corps at the same ranked level. In either case, civil or religious, he may discharge his obligations before his fortieth birthday by progressing up through the next two ranks above that of constable or its equivalent in a religious brotherhood.

About one-third of the men of Atchalán go on beyond this minimal service and climb the second and higher ladder of offices, culminating in full sponsorship of the fiesta of a saint, a very expensive proposition of two or three years' duration. The elite few who have done so are eligible, toward the end of their lives, to selection for the office of principal, or elder, who supervise the entire cargo system of the community.

I have also argued in another recent article (1979a) that this progression of serial offices, which are of two kinds, civil and religious, and which must be taken in a cross-cutting manner, is an implicit reflection of very ancient Mayan notion of time. The pre-Columbian Mayan calendar consisted of several calendar rounds. All were based on several counts of time, starting from a Day One, the initial day in counts of thirteen days, of twenty days, and of the solar year. The counts permuted around each other into rounds of 260 days, of 13 years, and of 52 years, each round coming to its end at the coincidence of two or more initial days in the several counts. A round of fifty-two years starts, for example, at the coincidence of initial days in all three counts. The cycles of service in the Atchaleño cargo system, one year, completed junior-level service, and the longer cycle of senior service, also resembled such permutations of time with civil and religious service permuted against each other, and all starting over on the coincidence of Day One's.

Indians are not the only Mesoamericans. Let us turn to customary ways of enculturation to Hispanic culture.

Patron-Client Relationships as Educational Devices in Hispanic Culture

There is a growing current of research coming out of the social anthropology of Spain and other Mediterranean countries which is proving useful for Latin Americanists. One of the most useful concepts has been that of patron-client relations, a concept which illuminates the oft-noted Latin personalism as no other concept does. The most egregious symbolic expression of both personalism and patronage is familiar to American anthropologists. In the custom of the penitential vow, or *promesa*, a Latin Catholic may beg a favor of a saint and in return promise to perform some penitential and self-abnegating feat, or make some sacrificial offering to the saint, whose honor is thereby extolled for all to see.

The first anthropologist to grasp the relevance of patron-client relations was Julian Pitt-Rivers with his study of an Andalusian village (1955).[3] Some of his findings are especially pertinent to Latin America. First, patronage as he found it is a dynamic adaptation to a basic social tension, the contradiction between an egalitarian personalistic ethic and the inequality inherent in a two-class social structure. In the idiom of patronage the individual finds the ideology for reconciling subservience with continued self-esteem. This is so because allegiance to a particular patron is supposed to be based on a spark of mutual empathy *(simpatiá)* and not self-interest. The contractual relationship, like that between the supplicant and the saint alluded to above, is personal, manipulative, and its content infinitely various. In essence it is a reciprocal tie, based on personal attraction, between unequal partners in an idiom of mutual respect. Being personal, the tie may also be quite intimate.

I have investigated the patron-client tie as an educational device at length in Chapter 6 of my book (1973a:95-120) and again as it applies to the enculturation of the Guatemalan landed upper class (1973b). I have concluded that patronage is an essential social glue in Latin America. By means of patronage, an individual—including the well-born—is able to validate the status to which he was born, and perhaps rise above; without it he may sink on the social scale. Briefly put, the ability to attract the beneficent attention of an older, more knowledgeable, and often richer and more powerful, individual, may be a quite unwitting individual gift. The sponsorship that ensues may be endlessly useful. The patron or sponsor may have the younger partner trained, may find him a job, get him contacts for his trade, profession, or business, even go so far as to provide introductions to suitable brides with the prospect of an inheritance. The relationship between a master tradesman and his apprentice is such a patron-client relationship. In Latin America it is quite likely to be embedded in more extensive networks of patronage; the master taking on an apprentice as a favor to a more powerful sponsor. The important thing is the personal factor. The relationship may be quite capricious in origin. But like romantic love in the institution of Western marriage, the element of whim or caprice may bring all sorts of useful things (as well as trouble) in its wake. There are ongoing, mutual, social debts, and a constant give-and-take of favors. In societies with long-term class inequalities the patron-client relations are also likely to be long term. Even the client who grows and prospers is not likely to grow to rival the stature of a patron many places above him in the social scale. For example, one case I discuss (1973a: 108-10) is that of an orphan who incurred the favor of a coffee planter. The youth has since gone on to become a prosperous local Ladino entrepreneur. Still his success in no way comes close to the aristocratic standing of the family of his now deceased patron.

Schooling in Mesoamerica

The problem of schooling in Latin America in general is that primary instruction is everywhere in law universal and compulsory and nowhere so in fact, not even in revolutionary Cuba.[4] Although anthropologists have long recognized the Latin tendency to issue law as statement of ideals rather than of feasible policy, the fact remains that this ideal remains short of realization.

Current information is hard to come by, but the general outlines of educational problems are clear. Six years of primary school are not within the reach of all. According to Lawrence Gale, "The average South American child in fact enjoys just over two years primary school, as against seven in Japan and nine in the U.S.A." (Gale 1969:29—based on 1964 statistics). There are great differences among countries, and most have been making tremendous strides since 1960 in increasing numbers of teachers, classrooms, and pupils enrolled. Even so, enrollments have usually not kept up with the birthrate. Moreover, most students who do start primary school do not finish the sixth grade. Gale cites UNESCO figures as of 1960 that some 80 percent of all primary pupils in Latin America drop out before reaching the sixth grade, and half of these in the first year (1969:30). In Guatemala, for example, only 18 percent of all those who enrolled once in the first grade actually graduated from the sixth grade in the decade between 1950 and 1960 (Moore 1973a:70). In Chiapas rural schools, according to Modiano (1973:91), only 1.5

percent of those enrolled were in the sixth grade. Nationally in Mexico the figure was 8 percent (rather than the 16.6 percent it would have been had all pupils been promoted through the grades without a high rate of repeating and dropping out).

All Latin American countries give education a high priority. However, none would expand the primary system to the detriment of the secondary school system. The latter by its nature is destined to serve a very small elite because it must draw upon a restricted population— primary school graduates, and not many of them. Still most countries have increased their secondary-school enrollments rapidly. Since growth rates usually start from small bases, they often conceal small absolute numbers enrolled and small proportions of the age-grade. Brazil, for example, almost tripled its enrollments in secondary schools in the decade before 1961, but that increase still represented only 12 percent of the age-grade—those from 12 to 18 years of age (Gale 1969:46). Even Argentina, long a model of educational achievement, had only 31 percent of the age-grade in high school (Gale 1969:46).

Secondary schools add a feature of cultural pluralism little explored by anthropologists in Latin America, the role and prestige of foreign schools: French, English and North American, German, Italian. These private schools enjoy links with the cultural missions of their mother countries, import foreign teachers, and offer much instruction in their mother tongue. They may cater to South Americans of the appropriate ethnic origin, but they also cater to urban elites. Their cosmopolitan influence is undeniable, even though they must follow the guidelines for secondary instruction laid down by the education ministries of the host countries.

Because of the deficiencies of the primary school system, there is a persistent problem with illiteracy in all Latin American countries (excepting Cuba, which claims to have virtually wiped out illiteracy— that is, reduced it to 3.8 percent—in its massive literacy campaign of 1961 (Fagen 1969:33-68). The illiteracy rate drops each decade in all countries, but because adult illiterates are joined by those new fourteen-year-olds not reached or reached unsuccessfully by the primary school system, the problem is perpetuated.

Even in those countries like Mexico and Cuba that have made a concerted effort to bring primary schooling within the reach of all potential pupils, the effort frequently lapses on the local level. Even Mexico has not quite met its goal. Modiano writes that the Eleven-Year Plan of 1959 had the goal of providing a classroom and a teacher for every 50 primary-age children in the republic. She estimates that in 1972 there were 223,000 primary teachers in the nation, but to meet the national goal of one teacher per fifty, among 12 million children, would have required a primary teaching corps of 240,000 (Modiano 1973:91). The shortfall, therefore, is somewhere around 17,000 teachers.

This lack indicates that the effort is strained at the local level, and it is precisely here that the problems of absenteeism, repeating, and dropping out are most visible. In Atchalán, the community in Guatemala that I studied, a sixth grade was instituted for the first time in 1968. This local school's decision thus destined a teacher and a classroom for all of 18 pupils, rather than to any of the several hundred enrolled in the first three grades.

Total school age population was estimated at 900; 450 were enrolled in the school (Moore 1973a:133, 149). The local authorities are responsible for dealing with truancy, but their efforts vary greatly. In Atchalán they were vigorous for a week or so at the start of the school year. Once the classrooms filled up, they laid off. Modiano, surveying schooling in the Indian communities of highland Chiapas, found great differences in enrollment from one to another. Proportions of those enrolled to those eligible varied from one-half in Chamula to four-fifths in Oxchuc (Modiano 1973:95-96).

After studying primary schooling in Atchalán, I have analyzed it in terms of pupil careers. The patterns I have discerned are quite obviously general in Latin America. Let us look at the age-grade of primary school-children, and classify them according to their status in schooling. (My analysis may be found in Moore 1973a:137). School-children legally comprise all children age seven to fourteen. Some of these are never inducted into the classroom; these are the out-of-school-children. Of those in school, each year's class is supposed to be comprised of age-mates born in the same year. Some few children do progress through the grades at the proper yearly rate. I call these the year-grade children. These are a relatively small elite, however. In every class there are those who are repeating the grade for the first or second time, the repeaters. Within each class there is a middling group, children the teacher recognizes as marginal, but who may be promoted to the next grade. In view of their marginal grasp of their lessons, they may join the future repeaters in the course of the next school year. Then there are the dropouts, who deplete the ranks of their grade group each year as they leave school for good, often after persistent absenteeism. Each grade is greatly reduced in numbers from the one that preceded it.

This pattern is by no means unique to Guatemala or Mexico. Rural Latin Americans, called to the primary schools, respond in much the same way, even in a revolutionary system with a large component of "work-study," as in Cuba. According to Nelson P. Valdés (1972:446), "Almost one out of every three children between the first and sixth grade (in Cuba) fails to be promoted at the end of the school year." He cites figures for 1967 showing there were 99,000 sixth-grade pupils enrolled versus 341,000 first-grade pupils in 1967, while for the same year only two-thirds, 66,000, of the sixth graders graduated from primary school (1972:435), and thus became eligible for consideration for recruitment into secondary schools.

In strict age-grading terms, then, the schools can be seen as a giant sieve which culls out a few schoolchildren who may then become the schoolteachers. In Guatemala, and in much of Latin America, an "empirical" or unlicensed schoolteacher need only have graduated from the fourth grade. Patronage did the rest. Today most are secondary school graduates, and have come a very long way from the sixth grade, let alone the fourth. Both Modiano and I have observed Indian teachers in the classroom. In Mexico, but not Guatemala, the government through the INI *(Instituto Nacional Indigenista)* has a policy of recruiting Indians to the teaching ranks, especially for the rural schools conducted by the INI, which are those responsible for the programs in bilingual instruction, that is, which start instruction in reading and writing in the mother tongue as a prelude for instruction in Spanish.

Channeling a few schoolchildren into teaching careers, then, is one social outcome of getting through the sixth grade. Most Indian parents, and in this Modiano and I concur, believe that the goal of schooling is to learn to read, write, and do sums. That, however, is by no means the whole agenda for the schools.

The schools in both Mexico and Guatemala are agents of national culture. Modiano calls them agents of acculturation to Mexican culture; they want to Mexicanize Indian children. I must add that they want to make national citizens of all children, Indian or Ladino. The school culture differs from that of the local Ladino or mestizo in exalting the value of the nation-state. This schooling is universalistic, bureaucratized, civic-minded. It seeks to make all citizens literate in the national language. It would have them bear the national documentation to prove their identities and show that they are voters in national elections (legally required of adult males in both republics), and responsible citizens who can enter in free contracts. (The civil marriage ceremony, the only legally valid one in Mexico, and so also in Guatemala until a few years ago, stresses that the parties are free adults acting of their own will.) Ideally such citizens are not only susceptible to recruitment into the teaching corps, but they are equipped for geographical mobility. They can move around and, with their schooling credentials, ideally find employment anywhere in the republic.

Such notions, or course, depart markedly from traditional Hispanic culture, let alone the Indian one. There is scant place for patronage and local particularism in this curriculum. This curriculum stresses hygiene and civic values just as much as the three R's traditional parents expect of it. The content of the lessons is almost entirely nationalistic. In Guatemala, for instance, third-grade children must memorize a list of the national rivers.

All instruction, however, is by rote and drill, and very little of it is by performing concrete tasks. Modiano contrasts this learning by memorization of verbal entities, spoken and written, with Indian learning of concrete tasks at home, by imitating adults. Ladinos, she holds, have in contrast always respected school learning as something of no immediate use or application, but of great value to have later in life. One suspects that the value is as much in the credential as in the learning, either in the information gained, or in the habits and skill of acquiring new knowledge.

In sum, schooling, from very limited sources, can be judged to be increasing in quantity in Mexico and Guatemala today. A very real problem remains in the inadequate covering of the primary school age-grade, especially in rural areas. Mexico, and now Guatemala too, is making a concerted effort to reach its Indian populations and to train teachers and devise bilingual materials especially for them. Modiano, who tested children for reading ability in Chiapas rural schools, judged the bilingual instruction to be considerably more effective in teaching Indian children to read (1973:129). From the viewpoint of both Indians and Ladinos, however, much of the goal of schooling must seem largely irrelevant, not only to getting through life, but getting through life according to both Indian and traditional Ladino values.

I could end the paper at this point, with the contrast between schooling and traditional enculturation, but this would deprive me of the subject of grass-roots alternatives to schooling, the phenomenon which interested me in this subject in the first place. To see alternatives to formal schooling in context, however, we must explore the radical critique of schooling coming from Ivan Illich.

Ivan Illich's Critique of Schooling

Ivan Illich is a radical Christian humanist. Vienna born, he is an ordained Roman Catholic priest and was once a monsignor. He came to Latin America by way of a Puerto Rican parish in New York, thence to Puerto Rico as vice-rector of the Catholic University. After a dispute over birth control he quit the practicing clergy to head an educational institute in Cuernavaca, whence he issues broadsides calling for heightened existential "awareness" in a variety of institutional settings, not merely schooling. These essays have been collected and issued in two popular books in the United States (1970, 1971).[5]

Illich is first and foremost a churchman. He is a latter-day pietist who calls for an existential Christian affirmation—a "celebration of awareness"—while living in and participating fully in the real, secular world. His theology is more than a theology of personal liberation, but is one of demystification and demythologization. In anthropological terms he seeks to take the "liminal" or "antistructural aspects" of existence, and in an act of will, make them part of ordinary, nonritual life.

Illich has issued a stirring moral indictment of schooling. The indictment is general, but the particulars of the case are drawn from both North and South America. His thought is not particularly systematic, but here are the main themes he covers.

Schooling as a universal or compulsory enterprise is to be understood as a specific outgrowth of post-World War I United States history. Only partially feasible in North America, it is an immensely expensive and wasteful enterprise when exported to Latin America, where it should be more properly regarded as "a harmless Victorian anachronism." In both North and South America, schooling is, increasingly, a liberal charade. Because the school system is in fact neither compulsory nor universal, nation-states perpetrate several injustices upon the pupils. They exclude many of the rural and the poor, but because they officially include them, and do in fact brush with many of them for brief periods, schooling labels them as inferior and rationalizes that label.

Moreover, the charade is a continuing one. School systems will never be equal to the task, simply because the task is so gargantuan and enormously expensive. Nation-states in Latin America may devote up to 30 percent of the national budget to education and still not provide enough schooling.

Further, Illich abhors the school as a gigantic ritual enterprise. He regards the school as set up by contemporary society, in a Durkheimian sense, as sacred ("a sacred cow," he derides). It is not only that the schools' mission is impossible and therefore false, but also, Illich believes, that the nation-state and the manipulative bureaucracy which represent it are false gods.

While Illich rejects schooling as an age-graded, compulsory, lockstep, bureaucratized enterprise, he does not reject education, the aim of which is ideally heightened consciousness or "awareness." His proposals, which are utopian, fall within what we could call informal education. At first he proposed that much training take place on the job. Factories, he said, should be turned into night schools and learning centers. Politics must become educational. In this vein, however, his specific suggestions were probably more designed to outrage and, therefore, heighten consciousness, than to be acted upon. He suggested that the guerrilla experience was highly educational.[6] Illich also called for special courses to train parents to teach their children how to read and write (1970:106-11).

Illich's later ideas (1971) are a bit more systematic, and call for using modern technology, especially computer memories, for a system of reciprocal tutoring, as well as a reference system for hardware systems of individualized instruction with machines, games, and other technologized learning. (Perhaps he is thinking of language labs, perhaps of "cybernetic" learning materials with instant feedback). One reference service, then, would be a "skill exchange" whereby individuals apprentice themselves to other individuals who had mastered some specific skill the apprentice wanted to learn. Another computer service would be "peer matching" which would link any two individuals who wanted to discuss some technique, book, or topic. (Small wonder that an earlier essay glorifies the coffeehouse as a place of spontaneous discussion!) The utopian vision that Illich extols is, in his terms, of a "left-centered" society, meaning one with plentiful one-to-one links and "learning networks" rather than hierarchical, bureaucratic structures, which are "right-centered." Finally, no person should be excluded from learning anything because of lack of prior credentials.

A Critique of the Critique

There is much that is refreshing, sympathetic, and to the point in Illich; however, he is a churchman and moralist. Our anthropological task is somewhat different from his. We must weigh his indictment against our data and our perspective. And we must judge his perceptions in the light of feasible policies and then ponder them in deciding the directions of research and action we might undertake in the future.

First, much in our data is in full accord with Illich's indictment. The failure of primary schooling in Mesoamerica can be seen, in our terms, to be a failure to create a feasible career for primary schoolchildren which leads all of them to graduation or "success" as defined by the schools. The magnitude of the failure in rural Latin America, amply confirmed by firsthand anthropological evidence, would boggle the mind of most educators in the United States; for that failure includes the very inadequate provision of teachers and classrooms for the primary-age population. However, and this is a major point in Illich's thinking, even when personnel and facilities are adequate, as they almost are in Mexico and seem to be in Cuba, they still alienate a large proportion of their target population, who join the ranks of the repeaters and the dropouts—the school-defined failures. This of course is a major problem with schooling in the United States.

Moreover, the anthropological study of schools in the United States has shown them to be bureaucratically organized enterprises indeed, which took their model from the nineteenth-century factory. Elizabeth Eddy has explicated the significance of the factory-model schools (1967, 1978). Like Illich she finds the model dehumanizing. In response to Illich's call for deschooling, however, we must add some specifically anthropological cautions and suggestions.

First, I must caution that it is very hard for this social scientist at least to believe that Latin America, or any other modern society, is going to "deschool." Once great complex institutions such as school systems are built it is very difficult to dismantle them.[7]

Nevertheless, there are institutions that successfully provide parallels to Illich's call for deschooling. The Catholic Church provides several such opportunities, most interestingly through movements of holy zealots living in the world. I have seen one such group in action in Atchalán, the Third Order of St. Francis, a Catholic lay brotherhood derivative of the Franciscan order. Its origins date from the Franciscan movement of the thirteenth century, but modern manifestations of the same sort of otherworldly religiosity in the midst of the world include Opus Dei, active among upper-class persons and professionals in general in Latin America, and the Cursillo movement, a Catholic revival by means of pietistic retreats. If the move to devolve clerical functions on married deacons in the Catholic Church gains impetus, or if indeed some of the clergy in the future does not have to embrace celibacy, some of Illich's vision may come true as one more movement contained within the Holy Mother church.

Likewise I believe that the vast ersatz universal and compulsory schooling establishments shall continue in Latin America, but then certain deschooling movements shall coexist right alongside them.

Fortunately schooling, for all that it might indeed be a Durkheimian sacred cow, is not really that central an enterprise in the rural villages of Mesoamerica. Its capacities to harm, while they may be felt burningly by Illich, are still largely symbolic. Much economic, social, and human development can and does get done without much schooling.

Thus, it is interesting to note that a developmental economist's restudy (Avila 1969) of four Mexican villages studied by anthropologists from the late twenties through the early forties, these dates providing baselines for measurement. Avila concludes that the four villages (Tepoztlán, Chan Kom, Mitla, and Soteapan) had made tremendous strides toward economic development and personal prosperity. All four stood on the "threshold of self-sustained growth." Moreover, all four had done so with minimal schooling development. The school system had expanded, but it was far from reaching everybody, imparting universal literacy, or indoctrinating most of the citizens in the national culture. Avila did stress, however, that emigration from the villages to the cities could have devastating effects on national, if not local, development.

Likewise, when Henry Dobyns (1971) wrote about the educational aspects of Cornell University's applied anthropology project to develop the community of Indian ex-serfs on the Hacienda of Vicos in Peru, schooling is one of the last educational devices he discusses. First in the list of "enlightenment and skills" which reached the Indians of Vicos was patient instruction in how to increase their potato harvest on the same lands. The spread of "potato power" came first. Second were the subsequent direct relationships with regional marketing centers and middlemen, and a resulting spread of skills, such as trucking, and seamstressing with newly acquired sewing machines. At the same time Allen Holmberg, in the role of the patrón of the Hacienda (which was leased by the project during its life until the peasants finally got the wherewithal, including official permission, to buy the estate for themselves) obliged the Indians to meet in assemblies which he turned into seminars on parliamentary procedures, the election of officers, and the assumption of joint responsibility for decisions. The importation of journeymen to train peasants in certain trades followed. It was only at this point that the school began to play a role. Even when Dobyns wrote, the school, finally locally controlled and responsive to the Indians, only enrolled some 18 percent of the potential pupils. That percentage was sufficient, however, to have enough literate young men in key posts to carry on with not only economic development, but the assumption of more and more autonomy relative to the rest of the society. Universal literacy is far from a prerequisite for the devolution of power upon a responsible peasant population, nor for its economic development. It is only necessary to have some literate individuals among the local leadership.

Moreover, when deschooling does arise, it is likely to do so in a spontaneous, grass-roots manner, quite unnoticed by reformers and educators. I have written at length about such spontaneous attempts at alternative instruction in Atchalán (1973a:156-93, reprinted 1976). One attempt derives from the church, though not from the clergy but from lay zealots. These are "chantry classes" which teach the Roman Catholic catechism and other sacred texts by heart; pupils being called upon to chant texts in unison from appropriate cues from the doctrine master. Such classes were the dominant mode of instruction in Europe during the Middle Ages, and are still the traditional way children are taught in Islamic primary schools in much of the village Middle East to this day. The mechanism is essential to the newly militant Roman Catholic Church in Latin America which is making a concerted effort to bring its flock to the church, not just by means of a one-shot sacrament—baptism (a life-crisis rite)—but by means of regular participation in Holy Communion (a weekly rite of intensification). To gain entry to the Lord's Supper, first communicants must show they have reached both understanding and reason by their grasp of sacred texts. These very loosely organized classes, conducted by their masters from devotion more than from material need, are models of how to get particular useful skills across, if in a ritualized fashion.

A more significant effort, perhaps, is the appearance of a grassroots peasant schoolmaster who imparts literacy instruction in his house in the evening. To my surprise I discovered that this man, although officially co-opted into the several national literacy campaigns in Guatemala, had long antedated them in his efforts. His model is important for both classroom techniques and the social context. In the class, he trains Indian pupils at their own pace, face to face and individually (if in small groups), in ways that are rather like their learning adult tasks by imitation at home. Socially, he is related in reciprocal fashion to the fathers of the pupils as if he were their godfather. He is accorded a godfather's respect and showered with gifts of food on the local feast days. The model is transferable, for I discovered and studied another much younger peasant free schoolmaster who had been recruited to the role by the official literacy campaigns, but who had stayed on teaching after their demise because of the pressures of the parents of prospective pupils (Moore 1969).

Conclusions

Human beings get through their life cycles with or without formal schooling but never without educational devices that induct them into their own culture. As anthropologists we have long been intimately acquainted with the Indian peasant cultures of Mesoamerica. We have both admired that culture for its integrity, but deplored its modal personality for being too "restricted," "passive," and inwardly defensive. We are newly becoming aware of the importance of the ritual learning process, of the cargo system as an ongoing rite of initiation as well as of intensification, in keeping that modal personality quite literally "ritualistic." We are also becoming newly aware of the importance of patterns of patronage and clientage for Hispanic Mesoamericans. We have long been aware of the role of playful imitative learning within the home, an importance recently restated forcefully by Modiano for Chiapas Indians (1973:26-86). We bring all this awareness to any consideration of formal schooling, anywhere. The first thing we ask is how does schooling fit into the culture.

Thus, together with the linguists, we have long had a special responsibility for helping to elaborate and assess programs of bilingual education. Mexico has shown the way in these programs by fostering them at the highest official level and by utilizing talented Mexican academicians in their implementation (Heath 1972). Guatemala, too, in more modest ways is following suit.

Anthropologists also have a responsibility to aid in conceiving and propagating education that is fully bicultural and fully developmental for the groups it touches. Here we must join Illich's critique of schooling with our own data and our own perspectives. We must agree that schooling generally is too bureaucratized, expensive, and even when formally provided may still be resisted and dropped out of by its clients as alienating and degrading. (By "grading," says Illich, schooling automatically also "degrades.") I have attempted to provide some anthropological perspective to the radical critique by studying and describing spontaneous alternatives to formal schooling in one Mesoamerican community. We must continue this inspection in other, and diverse, settings.

The directions of future research into the educational potential of alternatives to schooling are likely to be many. Some shall crop up in unforeseen places and ways. But some likely settings suggest themselves. In particular we might look at national rituals: rallies, political parties and their meetings and committee structures; elections, even pilgrimages. We need to explore many models of dyadic "skill exchanges," being mindful of the widespread model of patron-client relations in Latin America and its use as a vehicle of the stratified class structure. Any skill exchange is going to create reciprocal obligations. These may resolve themselves in the relatively egalitarian quasi godfatherhood granted the voluntary peasant schoolmasters I studied in Atchalán, or they may resolve themselves in other humanly enriching ways. To understand these mechanisms more fully we need to study the full range of master-apprentice relationships in Mesoamerica. Arensberg and Kimball (1968:332-60) have shown how, in the Irish case, the debt an apprentice incurred to his master was resolved by devoting his journeyman years to the master's service before setting up his own shop. Reciprocal obligations may be a mutually enriching learning experience, but in a society marked by sharp class and ethnic division they may also lead to stereotyped subservience. We need information on how to avoid such outcomes.

It is fashionable to be pessimistic about Latin America today. I for one see grounds for optimism precisely in the magnitude of social processes and in our still immense ignorance of them. Human beings and social groups have ways of finding their own ways out. As Mexico and Guatemala and other Latin American nations increasingly take charge of their own destinies, it behooves anthropologists of whatever nationality to be there illuminating the ways of the little people, and to continue telling academicians, moralists, and policy makers of the diverse cultures that make up any great national society.

NOTES

1. The most memorable paper touching on child rearing in the literature from these years is Benjamin Paul's on symbolic sibling rivalry in an Indian village (1950). Here the malady of a newborn child is taken to

reflect the older child's jealousy. The older sibling's soul is believed to be devouring the soul of the younger rival, and his cannibalistic desires are ritually deflected upon a chicken tied to the baby's body. The drama is remarkable; it ties in neatly with the theme of "institutionalized fear of envy" noted by so many observers of these villages. It reflects the deflection of internal tensions upon the spirit world, outside the village. And, I would add, it reflects the belief that outsiders may be cannibals; as in times of the pre-Columbian invasion of Guatemala from central Mexico, they certainly were.

2. Redfield based his assertion on such evidence as the Indian's performing verse dramas, for example, the "Moors and Christians," by reciting Spanish they ill understood and never explicating the spectacle in speech to the spectators. It is true that Mesoamerican Indians have not been a rich source of narrative lore. Comparatively few anthropologists have collected much narrative. Notable ones who have are Mendelson (1956) and Gossen (1974). Gossen's narratives are carefully located in the cultural view of time and space of one community, Chamula, whose locale is seen to be a cosmology complete unto itself.

3. Another especially good treatment is in Kenny (1960).

4. Cuba has a dropout problem little different from that of Mexico. See Valdés (1972:446) for an estimate of 200,000 primary-age students not attending school. Cuba also has a high rate of failure, grade repeating, and a low rate of primary school graduations—all standard problems in Latin America.

5. *Deschooling Society* (1971) is perhaps better known than *Celebration of Awareness* (1970). I recommend the latter to anthropologists precisely because its two essays on schooling contain most of the ideas in the later book, and because it places those ideas in the context of Illich's thought on the church, the role of its clergy, North-South relations, and birth control.

6. For one Latin response, the demythologization of guerrillas, see Rangel, 1977. I must note that both the political party and the mass really have been used to great educational effect by Fidel Castro.

7. The nearest thing that comes to mind is the fate of the Christian churches in Europe after the Reformation; they were hardly dechurched. The analogy is apt, because Illich's more immediate vision is that of a transformed Catholic Church, outlined in his essay "The Vanishing Clergyman" (Chapter 6 of *Celebration of Awareness*). Here we have a vision of a Roman Catholic priesthood fully participant in the community, a priesthood of married men (he does not include women!), living and working in a secular existence, and celebrating communion in their homes with circles of communicants. I find it very unlikely that the Catholic hierarchy

is going to adopt this model in any thorough manner. Likewise it is unlikely that any national ministry of education is going to deschool its educational establishment.

REFERENCES

Arensberg, Conrad M., and Solon Kimball
1968   *Family and Community in Ireland,* 2d ed. (Cambridge, Mass.: Harvard University Press).
Avila, Manuel
1969   *Tradition and Growth: A Study of Four Mexican Villages* (Chicago: University of Chicago Press).
Benedict, Ruth
1946   *The Chrysanthemum and the Sword* (Boston: Houghton Mifflin).
Cancian, Frank
1967   "Political and Religious Organizations," in *Social Anthropology,* ed. M. Nash, Vol. 6 of *Handbook of Middle American Indians,* ed. R. Wauchope (Austin: University of Texas Press).
Colby, Benjamin N.
1967   "Psychological Orientations," in *Social Anthropology,* ed. M. Nash, Vol. 6 of *Handbook of Middle American Indians,* ed. R. Wauchope (Austin: University of Texas Press).
Dobyns, Henry F.
1971   "Enlightenment and Skill: Foundations of Power," in *Peasants, Power, and Applied Social Change: Vicos as a Model,* ed. H. F. Dobyns, Paul L. Doughty, and Harold D. Lasswell (Beverly Hills: Sage Publications).
Eddy, Elizabeth M.
1967   *Walk the White Line: A Profile of Urban Education* (Garden City, N.Y.: Doubleday, Anchor Press).
1978   "The Reorganization of Schooling: An Anthropological Challenge," in *Applied Anthropology in America,* ed. E. M. Eddy and William L. Partridge (New York: Columbia University Press).
Fagen, Richard R.
1969   *The Transformation of Political Culture of Cuba* (Stanford: Stanford University Press).
Gale, Lawrence
1969   *Education and Development in Latin America,* World Education Series (New York: Praeger).
Gillin, John
1947   *Moche: A Peruvian Coastal Community.* Institute of Social An-

thropology Publication 3 (Washington, D.C.: Smithsonian Institution).

1951   *The Culture of Security in San Carlos.* Middle American Research Institute Publication 16 (New Orleans: Tulane University). Translation: *San Luís Jilotepeque* (Guatemala: Seminario de Integración Social Guatemalteca, 1958).

1955   "Ethos Components in Modern Latin American Culture," *American Anthropologist* 57:488-500.

Gossen, Gary
1974   *Chamulas in the World of the Sun: Time and Space in a Maya Oral Tradition* (Cambridge, Mass.: Harvard University Press).

Heath, Shirley Brice
1972   *Telling Tongues: Language Policy in Mexico, Colony to Nation* (New York: Teachers College Press).

Illich, Ivan
1970   *Celebration of Awareness* (Garden City, N.Y.: Doubleday).
1971   *Deschooling Society* (New York: Harper & Row).

Kenny, Michael
1960   "Patterns of Patronage in Spain," *Anthropological Quarterly* 33: 14-23.

Lessa, William A., and Evon Z. Vogt
1972   *Reader in Comparative Religion: An Anthropological Approach,* 3d ed. (New York: Harper & Row).

Mead, Margaret
1951   *Soviet Attitudes Toward Authority* (New York: McGraw Hill, Rand Series).
1954   "The Swaddling Hypothesis: Its Reception," *American Anthropologist* 56:395-409.

Mendelson, E. Michael
1956   *Los escándalos de Maximón* (Guatemala: Seminario de Integración Social Guatemalteca).

Modiano, Nancy
1973   *Indian Education in the Chiapas Highlands* (New York: Holt, Rinehart & Winston).

Moore, Alexander
1969   "Las motivaciones de los maestros campesinos voluntarios en un pueblo guatemalteco," *Anuario Indigenista* 29:225-39.
1973a *Life Cycles in Atchalán: The Diverse Careers of Certain Guatemalans* (New York: Teachers College Press).
1973b *The Validation of Ascribed Status: Gentry Careers in Guatemala,* Proceedings of the American Ethnological Society (Seattle: University of Washington Press).

1976   "Alternative Attempts at Instruction in Atchalán," in *Schooling in the Cultural Context: Anthropological Studies of Education* (New York: McKay).

1979a   "Cunas y Mayas: Ensayo comparativo," *Revista Patrimonio Histórico* 2(1):73-114.

1979b   "Initiation Rites in a Mesoamerican Cargo System: Men and Boys, Judas and the Bull," *Journal of Latin American Lore* 5:55-81.

Nash, June

1970   *The Change of Officials in Tzo?ontohal, Chiapas, Mexico* (New Orleans: Tulane University, Middle American Research Institute).

Paul, Benjamin D.

1950   "Symbolic Sibling Rivalry in a Guatemalan Indian Village," *American Anthropologist* 52:205-18.

Pitt-Rivers, Julian A.

1955   *The People of the Sierra* (New York: Criterion Books, Chicago: Phoenix Books, 1961).

Rangel, Carlos

1977   *Del buen salvaje al buen revolucionario: Mitos y realidades de América Latina* (Caracas: Monte Avila Editores).

Redfield, Robert

1943   "Culture and Education in the Midwestern Guatemalan Highlands," *American Journal of Sociology* 48:640–48. (Reprinted in Roberts and Akinsanya 1976:57-64).

Roberts, Joan L., and Sherrie K. Akinsanya

1976   *Schooling in the Cultural Context: Anthropological Studies of Education* (New York: McKay).

Rosaldo, Renato I., Jr.

1968   "Metaphors of Hierarchy in a Mayan Ritual," *American Anthropologist* 70:524-36 (Reprinted in Lessa and Vogt 1972).

Valdés, Nelson P.

1972   "The Radical Transformation of Cuban Education," in *Cuba in Revolution,* ed. R. E. Bonadea and N. P. Valdes (Garden City, N.Y.: Doubleday, Anchor Press).

Vogt, Evon Z.

1969   *Zinacantán: A Maya Community in the Highlands of Chiapas* (Cambridge, Mass.: Harvard University Press).

Wilbert, Johannes, ed.

1976   *Enculturation in Latin America: An Anthology* (Los Angeles: University of California, Latin American Center Publications).

6

Medical Pluralism in Mesoamerica

Sheila Cosminsky
Rutgers University, Camden

One of the striking characteristics of medicine and health care in Mesoamerica today is its pluralistic and heterogenous nature. While some isolated villages remain, the spread of Western or modern medicine, especially in the form of patent remedies and injections, is rapidly increasing and few places remain untouched. This pluralism exists on at least two levels, including (1) the existence of parallel or alternative systems among which health seekers can choose—that is, pluralistic medical behavior on the part of the patient, and (2) the incorporation of elements from the different systems by practitioners or health providers, as well as by health seekers. These elements include disease categories, concepts of etiology, and treatment techniques (e.g., spiritists prescribing injections of penicillin or vitamins). The purpose of this paper is to examine this pluralistic situation, to review some of the approaches used to study this pluralism, and to point to some areas for future research. The paper focuses on rural rather than urban populations, and includes both Indians and mestizos or Ladinos.

Earlier studies, such as those reviewed in the *Heritage of Conquest* volume, stressed the supernatural aspects of curing, especially those attributed to the Indian cultures (Wisdom 1952). Although acculturative influences of Spanish culture were of interest, the influences of Western medicine were not of interest and went unmentioned. Also, empirical aspects of both the Indian and Spanish systems were scarcely mentioned in the *Heritage of Conquest*—such as the extensive pharmacopoeias, the concepts of hot and cold, and the importance of emotions in illness causation. There were some early ethnobotanical studies, such as Roys, *Ethnobotany of the Maya* (1932), but these were separate from other aspects of the healing systems and the overall sociocultural context. In general, there was a bias on the part of many anthropological studies toward overemphasizing the supernatural in curing, to the neglect of other aspects. In the 1950s and after, several studies were made and published that did consider these other aspects, including the empirical components and the impact of Western medicine, among them Adams (1952), Paul (1955), Aguirre Beltrán (1963), and Foster (1958, 1967). Some of those studies were spurred by interest from international health agencies and national ministries of health in promoting public health programs. The findings of many of these studies have been synthesized and analyzed in the excellent article by Adams and Rubel and in other articles in the *Handbook of Middle American Indians* (1967).

The separation of the "natural" or empirical and the "supernatural" aspects of the indigenous healing systems goes back to the Spanish Conquest. The Spaniards recorded the herbal knowledge of the Indians, which they considered in the domain of "medicine," and separated it from that of the ritual aspects, which they considered "religion" or rather "paganism," because it differed from the Catholic religious doctrine. While they collected and respected the herbal knowledge, they tried to eliminate the indigenous practitioners and curers and their ritual practices as being contrary to Catholicism, which was viewed as the only true faith. They did not understand the "holism" of the indigenous system, and applied their own model of medicine and religion. Much of what is regarded as "traditional" medicine today is the amalgam and syncretism of this earlier pluralism of indigenous and sixteenth-century Spanish medicine and religion. This process did not take place at one time, but was and is a gradually dynamic and dialectical process (Tedlock, this volume), that continues into the present.

The separation of medicine and religion is reinforced by the domination of Western medicine, with its biomedical model, and dualism of mind and body, and as Collado has stated, the conquest of the countryside by the city imposing an urban rather than a rural paradigm of healing (1978). The process is reinforced by the present religious doctrines, especially those supported by the Catholic Action (or orthodox Catholicism) movement and Evangelical Protestantism, which forbid their members to use traditional curers and spiritists, and whose missionaries provide clinics for Western medicine (as well as the Evangelical faith healing). I would suggest that at least in some areas of Mesoamerica the reported decline of shamans and traditional curers is due to the activities of these religious missions rather than to the spread or success of Western medicine. To many people, there is no conflict or competition between Western medicine, which may be used to treat symptoms, and traditional or alternative forms of healing which may be used to treat the causes, especially problems of ultimate causation. The spreading of Western medicine is supported by the political and legal system, since it is the only type of medicine officially recognized by the government, supported by the Ministry of Health and promoted through the medical schools and the pharmaceutical companies. In Guatemala, traditional healers are officially prohibited to practice, although they are active in both urban and rural areas (Velimirovic 1978:181). Some indigenous curers in Guatemala said that performing rituals that involved burning incense was forbidden in the capital.

The earlier studies of indigenous medicine were based on an assumption of homogeneity and uniformity of belief and behavior. The descriptions of these systems were often ideal models. For example, food taboos during illness were described as beliefs that everyone shared, but few studies considered the extent to which people actually followed these proscriptions. Some recent studies have stressed diversity and intracultural variation (Pelto and Jerome 1978). Logan (1977), Foster (1979), and Messer (1978, 1981) discuss some of the methodological problems inherent in trying to study this variation as pertaining to the hot-cold classification of foods and medicines. While intracultural diversity has probably always existed to some degree, the increasing pluralism and availability of other alternatives has resulted in a remarkable heterogeneity of Mesoamerican medical behavior and beliefs. Moreover, while several approaches and paradigms are being used to study such phenomena, others need to be developed for further insight.

The medical facilities and resources differ in their availability and accessibility in different parts of Mesoamerica, but in general include self-treatment with home remedies, and treatment by such practitioners as folk healers (shamans, herbalists, curanderos, bonesetters, and midwives), spiritists, injectionists, pharmacies, traveling vendors, public and private clinics, hospitals, and physicians. The concepts and components which guide such treatment derive from the different Indian, folk Ladino (Woods 1977) or mestizo, spiritism (Kearney 1978), homeopathic (DeWalt 1977), and Western (also referred to as modern, scientific, biomedical, or cosmopolitan) medical traditions. Individual practitioners combine elements from these different traditions in various proportions and styles. The diversity of resources indicates the oversimplification of the traditional-modern dichotomy. Some traditions do not fit into this classification scheme, such as spiritism, which is derived from a European tradition, neither modern nor traditional, yet uses and integrates elements from both. In addition to the varieties of "traditional" healers, there are a variety of forms of modern medicine, which are represented differently by the pharmacies, lay "doctors," public health clinics, hospitals, and physicians.

The most common approach used to study this medical pluralism and its patterns of interaction is a correlation approach. One type of study correlates the characteristics of the patient, as the independent variable, with resource utilization or treatment strategy. The characteristics of the patients include such factors as age, sex, number of children, income, religion, ethnicity, and level of acculturation as measured by various indices such as travel, work outside home, and education. McClain (1977) provides an example. Using a correlational approach, she concludes that in the mestizo community of Ajijic, Mexico, traditional-oriented women use both traditional and modern resources, whereas modern-oriented women use only modern resources. Modern-oriented women tend to experience modern diseases more than traditional diseases. Traditional-oriented women, however, tend to experience traditional and modern disease to the same extent, although they experience the former more often. On the other hand, modern women are just as likely as traditional women to impute traditional causes to illnesses for which they or members of their families were hospitalized. McClain suggests this is true because the cognitive features of modern medicine are not available to them.

Other studies report correlations of characteristics of the illness with those of the patient and the type of treatment. Fabrega has correlated several such factors in a study done in San Cristobal, Chiapas. In one report, Fabrega and Manning (1979) analyze the form of medical treatment and the prevalence of illness with ethnicity as the independent variable. They show that Ladina housewives are more likely to visit a physician or drugstore than *indigenas,* and do so in 75 percent of cases, whereas *indigenas* are more likely to visit the curer. Ladinas sought help from the pharmacy in 65 percent of cases and *indigenas* in 42 percent. Another report from the same study (Fabrega and Zucker 1979) concentrates on the role of the type of symptoms in the choice of medical practitioner, correlated with ethnicity, and shows that the kinds of symptoms women take to practitioners is similar regardless of what type of medicine he practices, although each group tends to have their preferred practitioners (as stated above). Ladinos, however, tend to judge illness as less serious than *indigenas* during each segment of the illness (precontact segment, contact day, and postcontact segment). The authors state they deliberately do not analyze illness treated by both types of practitioners or by neither (e.g., self-treatment or pharmacies) in this report. This omission may oversimplify their result.

Another commonly reported pattern is the compartmentalization of diseases and their corresponding treatments—that is, "folk" illnesses such as *susto* or "evil eye" are cured by traditional curers, while other illnesses, such as bronchitis or diarrhea (usually diseases that have been successfully treated with antibiotics), are treated with modern medicine.

Several of these correlation studies have been summarized and reviewed by Foster and Anderson (1978) and Young (1981). More recent studies, however, have indicated a more complex situation, and suggest that such adversary or dichotomy models are oversimplified and thus possibly distorted. Multiple usage is common, especially sequentially, but even simultaneously. For example, an infant who is being given medicine prescribed by a physician for diarrhea may be taken concurrently to a local curer for the evil eye. Although certain "folk" illnesses are thought to be cured only by folk curers, this belief does not preclude the use of modern medicine to treat some of the symptoms. In other cases, the symptoms are treated with modern medicine, while the cause of the illness (e.g. witchcraft, transgression) is treated by a folk specialist (Gonzales 1966, Nash 1967). Other studies have found that the persistence and increasing severity of an illness makes traditional treatments and etiologies relevant, often after home remedies, patent remedies, and clinic or physician consultations (Cosminsky 1972a, 1972b, 1977).

Such correlation studies indicate the "whats" involved in the interaction of the different medical systems and factors associated with medical choices, but not the "whys" and "how." That is, they are not explanatory. They tend to present a synchronic and static analysis of medical behavior rather than a dynamic and processual one. Furthermore, the types of questions and surveys often used in these studies tend to encourage simplified answers and either-or categories, such as monocausal illness etiologies or single treatments. Other studies, using different approaches, such as decision-making models (sometimes in addition to the correlational approach), indicate a more complex picture with informants giving multifactorial etiologies of their illnesses, multiple resource usage for the same illness, and changing disease categories as the illness progresses. Traditional or folk theories of illness etiology are often multifactorial and multilevel (e.g. immediate and ultimate levels of causation), which permits the use of different treatment resources for the same illness (Adams 1952; Adams and Rubel 1967; Douglas 1969; DeWalt 1977; Woods 1977; Cosminsky 1972b, 1977).

The emphasis in these studies is on the strategies used in coping with illness. These decision-making models are actor oriented, and seek to answer why the actor does or does not choose a specific type of treatment, under what situations each strategy is used, and what are the determining factors of these choices (Cosminsky 1972b,

Young 1978). Some of the important factors that have been found to influence these decisions are the perceived effectiveness of the treatment, perceived severity of the illness, distance, time, faith in the treatment or practitioner, accessibility, social costs (e.g. both gain and loss of status), household composition, economic resources, financial cost (including fees, transportation, wages and time lost from work, medicines, etc.), the social context, and the cultural beliefs and orientations of the actor. One of the difficulties of the decision-making approach is to devise a means of weighting these variables and determining their interaction. Nevertheless, this approach tends to present a more complex and hopefully more accurate view of illness behavior. It enables one to view illness as a social process by focusing on the alternative treatments and strategies a person employs and under what conditions he makes these therapeutic choices.

Although a variety of strategies are used, one trend reported by Cosminsky and Scrimshaw (1980) for a lowland Guatemalan population is to begin with low-cost or home remedies and move to more expensive resources as the course of the illness proceeds and becomes more serious. There is also a back and forth movement between resources, or a shot-gun approach, however, often based on referrals and advice from relatives and neighbors and other practitioners, which seems to be associated with increased desperation over the perceived increasing severity and persistence of an illness.

This pluralistic behavior is pragmatic, often based on trial and error, perceived effectiveness, the uncertainty of illness causation, and expectation of quick results. For example, if a child has diarrhea, it could be the evil eye, so he is taken to a curer. If the diarrhea continues, then maybe the cause is some other factor, so he is taken to a different resource. This process of multiple therapies continues until the patient is cured or feels relief. In addition to this empirical and pragmatic behavior, however, faith in the supernatural or spiritual aspects of curing plays a role, as reflected in the persistence of traditional curers and the increasing spread of spiritism.

Pluralistic medicine is manifested not only in the coexistence of several traditions, each with its own specialists, ideology, and practices, which are used by the client population, but also in the integration of elements from each of these traditions by the folk practitioners (except for the physician). Many folk practitioners and specialists use pharmaceutical medicines in their treatments (antibiotic and vitamin injections, medicated plasters, pomades, purgatives, and tonics), as well as herbal remedies. They are eclectic and adopt whatever is useful and available to them from various systems, but increasingly turn to Western medicine. They use both "material" medicine and spiritual means to cure illness. Spiritists write prescriptions, they use invisible X-rays, invisible operations, and spirits of dead doctors. They use certain aspects of the doctor's role as their model, and thus acknowledge and reinforce the doctor's prestige. They have adopted primarily the technology and pharmaceuticals, however, reflecting both their own and their client's faith in these aspects of Western medicine. At the same time, this role adaptation increases the practitioner's chances of successful practice. Although the overwhelming direction of influence is that of Western medicine, there are some Indian influences, such as Indian spirits appearing to the spiritists or referring to the spirits as naguales (an Indian concept of a companion spirit that traditionally was an animal).

Pluralism occurs not only on the level of therapeutic techniques and remedies, but also in terms of concepts and disease categories. Studies in highland and lowland Guatemala (Cosminsky 1975; Cosminsky and Scrimshaw 1980) show that people believe that vitamins, as well as calcium and iron, are substances that help cure by giving one strength, is in accordance with the folk belief that strong blood will give one resistance against illness and evil influences, and conversely, weak blood increases one's susceptibility to illness. Vitamins, iron, calcium, and liver extract have been integrated into the folk system as inherent strength givers through this strong-weak principle. They are taken in the form of medicines, usually injections and tonics. Vitamin injections are especially valued as it is felt they are more effective and work faster than pills, are easier to give children, and are thought to provide the strength needed for the patient to recover. Vitamins are not conceived of as an important ingredient of food. The emphasis on these injections and tonics is supported by the physicians, pharmacists, and folk practitioners who increasingly prescribe them. The concept of vitamins is accepted by the people, but incompletely understood or misunderstood.

Patent remedies, including vitamins, minerals, and antibiotics, have also been classified into hot, cold, and fresh categories in accordance with the folk hot-cold principle of opposition, depending on the disease for which they are used and their bodily effects. For example, penicillin is hot because it is used for pneumonia, a cold illness (Harwood 1971; Cosminsky 1975; Logan 1973, 1977).

Disease terms and categories from Western medicine are increasingly used, but not necessarily understood. Some people from a Guatemalan lowland plantation were given diagnoses of *infección* (infection) by doctors in the nearest town, but without any explanation of what the term means. Some patients thought infection referred to something blocking the stomach, a parallel diagnostic category to the folk illness of *empacho*. One informant said she was confused because one doctor told her that her baby had bad parasites and another said that he had *infección*. She had no idea that these might refer to the illness (Cosminsky and Scrimshaw 1980).

The existing pluralism provides flexibility and fulfills different needs of the population. The folk systems are open ones, as manifested by the eclecticism of both the clients and practitioners, who adopt and adapt aspects from the array of coexisting medical traditions. This openness of folk systems, as Press (1978) points out, is manifested by the acceptance of inputs from other alternative health systems, including Western medicine, and also inputs from other institutional sectors, such as religion and the family. According to Landy (1974) the "traditional" healer role stands at the interstices of religion, magic, and the social system, and gains his power from this position. This contrasts sharply with the closedness of Western medicine which is discontinuous from ordinary social processes (Press 1978) and is nonaccommodating to alternative systems. Just as in the earlier Spanish Conquest, Catholicism was seen as the only true religion, and in today's conquest, Western medicine is viewed by many of its practitioners as the only true medical system.

One of the characteristics of the pluralistic system as presently practiced in much of Mesoamerica is the increasing prevalence of "technologized" medicine or what has been referred to as "pharmaceutical medicine" (Leslie 1976). Studies in both highland and lowland Guatemala (Cosminsky 1972b; Cosminsky and Scrimshaw 1980) found the major resource of Western medicine is the pharmacy or store, and patent medicines are the most frequently chosen medical alternative (Marshall 1980). Although the pharmacy is the initial resort in many cases, including self-treatment, it is also the end of the pathway for almost all other resources, since many practitioners of parallel or alternative and Western medicine give prescriptions for patent medicines which are usually filled at a pharmacy. Pharmacists prescribe drugs and give injections on their own, according to the symptoms described by the clients. The pharmacist thus acts as a lay doctor, diagnosing and recommending medicines, as well as filling prescriptions. Some pharmacists also have knowledge of folk medicine and sell various oils and concoctions such as *Agua Florida* and *Esencia Maravillosa*. They can serve as cultural brokers articulating the different systems, although representing predominantly one component of the Western medical system. Ferguson (1980) has reported similar findings in the town of Asunción, El Salvador. Despite the increasingly frequent use of the pharmacies, the role of the pharmacist or of the pharmacies as a medical resource has received little attention by anthropologists and is an important area for future research.

The choice of Western medicine, especially antibiotic and vitamin injections, frequently results in inappropriate usage with consequent ineffective treatment. While research is needed on evaluating the efficacy of various types of traditional and folk healing, evaluation is also needed on the effectiveness of this type of pharmaceutical medicine. One type of inappropriate usage is the underuse of medicines, especially antibiotics, characterized by short-term treatments and small quantities. This underuse is promoted by several factors: (1) practitioners sometimes prescribe short-term treatments, (2) the economic constraints mean people can often only afford to buy a small quantity at one time, and (3) people expect unrealistically quick results. The observed rapid effects of antibiotic injections have now been generalized to other patent remedies.

The expectation of quick results also leads to multiple usage. If people do not obtain rapid relief, they change physicians or curers. The patients thus may not stay long enough with the practitioner or physician to be cured. Since the patients tend to change practitioners if dissatisfied, they cannot follow the outcome or know the effectiveness of the treatment. If a practitioner or resource gives credit, then the patient may switch to one with whom he does not have a debt from one where he has used up his cash or credit. Possible drug interactions may be a problem resulting from this switching.

There is overuse and abuse of antibiotics and injections of all kinds, given and prescribed freely by almost all practitioners, folk and Western, spiritual and material. This overuse exists throughout Guatemala where it has been reported that in 1976, Guatemalans spent $40 million in buying medicines (not including institutional or physician sales) (U.S. Agency for International Development 1977). One obvious danger of this overuse is the potential buildup of antibiotic resistance. Misuse of pharmaceuticals is especially evident in the prevalence of vitamin and calcium injections. Their popularity partly stems from a misunderstanding of the concept of vitamins and from their possible rapid effect. This effect is often a short, temporary one, however, and these injections are overcharged for by the pharmacists, resulting in a waste of money for many patients.

This "commercialization of health" is spreading through the promotion of pharmaceuticals, which is carried out by both multinational and local drug companies, and through salesmen and mass media, especially radio advertisements. Most practitioners are dependent on the pharmacists for their knowledge of pharmaceuticals, who in turn are dependent on the salesmen or detail men from the pharmaceutical companies for knowledge of the effects of new drugs (as are the physicians). Recent studies show that in many Latin American countries, drug companies emphasize the benefits and indications of drugs to physicians but minimize the hazards and adverse effects (Silverman 1976).

Although some areas in Mesoamerica remain which have not yet felt the impact of this pharmaceutical medicine, and are still relatively independent in terms of their own indigenous health care systems, these are relatively few. In many places, inappropriate treatment, miscommunication, extensive promotion and overcharging of pharmaceuticals, the prestige of modern medicines (especially injections), and other factors have resulted in an overinvestment of medicine relative to people's resources. Ironically, the amount spent and allocated for medicines may detract from that spent in other areas that would increase the standard of living (better housing, sanitation, food, etc.), expenditures which have a greater overall impact on health. Similar results and concerns have been reported by Ferguson (1980) in a study of the pharmacies in Asunción, El Salvador.

Another possible effect of the inappropriate usage of Western medicine is increased utilization of resources in the spiritual domain, contributing to the persistence and increase of folk practitioners and spiritists. At the same time the adaptability and success of these practitioners in filling the needs of their clients points out weaknesses and inadequacies in the delivery and practice of Western medical care, another area in which more anthropological research is needed.

One can safely conclude that today's anthropology of Mesoamerican medicine must deal with a plethora of complexities, whether the intent is theoretical understanding, or applied intervention, or, we hope, an effort to achieve both.

REFERENCES

Adams, Richard

1952   *Un analisis de las creencias y prácticas médicas en un pueblo indígena de Guatemala.* Instituto Indigenista Nacional Publicación 17 (Guatemala).

Adams, Richard, and Arthur Rubel

1967   "Sickness and Social Relations," in *Social Anthropology,* ed. M. Nash. Vol. 6 of *Handbook of Middle American Indians,* ed. R. Wauchope and G. R. Willey (Austin: University of Texas Press).

Aguirre Beltrán, Gonzalo

1963   *Mágia y Medicina* (Mexico: Instituto Nacional Indigenista).

Collado Ardon, Rolando

1978   "Rural Medical Care or Rural Organization for Health," in *Modern Medicine and Medical Anthropology in the United States-Mexico Border Population,* ed. Boris Velimirovic. Pan American Health Organization, Scientific Publication 359 (Washington, D.C.).

Cosminsky, Sheila

1972a   *Utilization of a Health Clinic in a Guatemalan Community,* Atti del XL Congreso Internazionale degli Americanisti, Roma-Genova (Genoa: Tilgher).

1972b   "Decision Making and Medical Care in a Guatemalan Indian Community" (Ph.D. diss., Brandeis University).

1975   "Changing Food and Medical Beliefs and Practices in a Guatemalan Community," *Ecology of Food and Nutrition* 4:183-91.

1977   "The Impact of Methods on the Analysis of Illness Concepts in a Guatemalan Community," *Social Science and Medicine* 11:325-32.

Cosminsky, Sheila, and Mary Scrimshaw
1980   "Medical Pluralism on a Guatemalan Plantation," *Social Science and Medicine* 14:267-78.

DeWalt, K.
1977   "The Illnesses No Longer Understand: Changing Concepts of Health and Curing in a Rural Mexican Community," *Medical Anthropology Newsletter* 8:5-11.

Douglas, Bill
1969   "Illness and Curing in Santiago Atitlán" (Ph.D. diss., Stanford University).

Fabrega, Horacio, Jr., and Peter Manning
1979   "Illness Episodes, Illness Severity and Treatment Options in a Pluralistic Setting," *Social Science and Medicine* 13:41-52.

Fabrega, Horacio, Jr., and Martine Zucker
1979   "Components of Illness and Type of Medical Practitioner: A Comparative Study," *Social Science and Medicine* 13:13-23.

Ferguson, Anne
1980   "The Role of Pharmaceuticals in the Process of Medicalization in Asunción, El Salvador," paper presented at the Seventy-ninth Annual Meeting of the American Anthropological Association, Washington, D.C.

Foster, George
1958   *Problems in Intercultural Health Practice,* Social Science Research Coucil, Pamphlet no. 12 (New York).

1967   *Tzintzuntz án: Mexican Peasants in a Changing World* (Boston: Little Brown).

1979   "Methodological Problems in the Study of Intracultural Variation: The Hot/Cold Dichotomy in Tzintzuntzán," *Human Organization* 38:179-83.

Foster, George, and Barbara Gallatin Anderson
1978   *Medical Anthropology* (New York: John Wiley & Sons).

Gonzales, Nancy
1966   "Health Behavior in Cross-Cultural Perspective: A Guatemalan Example," *Human Organization* 25:122-25.

Harwood, Alan
1971   "The Hot Cold Theory of Disease," *Journal of the American Medical Association* 216:1153-58.

Kearney, Michael
1978   "Espiritualismo as an Alternative Tradition in the Border Area," in *Modern Medicine and Medical Anthropology in the U.S.-Mexican Border Area,* ed. Boris Velimirovic. Pan American Health Organization, Scientific Publication 359 (Washington, D.C.).

Landy, David
1974   Role Adaptation: Traditional Curers Under the Impact of Western Medicine, *American Ethnologist* 1:103-27.
Leslie, Charles
1976   *Asian Medical Systems* (Berkeley and Los Angeles: University of California Press).
Logan, Michael
1973   "Humoral Medicine in Guatemala and Peasant Acceptance of Modern Medicine," *Human Organization* 32:385-95.
1977   "Anthropological Research on the Hot/Cold Theory of Disease: Some Methodological Considerations," *Medical Anthropology* 4:87-112.
Marshall, Mary
        "Illness in a Guatemalan Maya Community." Ph.D. diss., Yale University.
Messer, Ellen
1978   *Zapotec Plant Knowledge: Classification, Uses, and Communication about Plants in Mitla, Oaxaca,* Memoirs of the Museum of Anthropology, no. 10, part 2 (Ann Arbor).
1981   "Hot-Cold Classification: Theoretical and Practical Implications of a Mexican Study," *Social Science and Medicine* 15(B):133-45.
McClain, Carol
1977   "Adaptation in Health Behavior: Modern and Traditional Medicine in a West Mexican Community," *Social Science and Medicine* 11:341-47.
Nash, June
1967   "The Logic of Curing Behavior: Curing in a Maya Indian Town," *Human Organization* 26:132-40.
Paul, Benjamin
1955   *Health, Culture, and Community* (New York: Russell Sage Foundation).
Pelto, Gretel, and Jerome Norge
1978   "Intracultural Diversity and Nutritional Anthropology," in *Health and the Human Condition,* ed. Michael Logan and Edward Hunt (Boston: Duxbury Press).
Press, Irwin
1978   "Urban Folk Medicine," *American Anthropologist* 80:71-84.
Roys, Ralph
1932   *The Ethnobotany of the Maya,* Middle American Research Series, no. 3 (New Orleans: Tulane University Press). (Reprint, Philadelphia: Institute for the Study of Human Issues, 1976).

Ryesky, D.
1976   "Conceptos tradicionales de la medicina en un pueblo Mexicano: un analisis antropológico," *Sep/Setentas* 309 (Mexico City: Secretaria de Educación Publica).

Silverman, Milton
1976   *The Drugging of the Americas* (Berkeley and Los Angeles: University of California Press).

U.S. Agency for International Development
1977   *Analisis del sector salud Guatemala,* vol. 1 (Guatemala City: La Agencia de los Estados Unidos en Guatemala para el Desarollo Internacional a Guatemala).

Velimirovic, Boris, and Helga Velimirovic
1978   "The Utilization of Traditional Medicine and its Practitioners in Health Services: A Global Interview," in *Modern Medicine and Medical Anthropology in the United States-Mexico Border Population,* ed. Boris Velimirovic. Pan American Health Organization, Scientific Publication 359 (Washington D.C.).

Wisdom, Charles
1952   "The Supernatural World and Change," in *Heritage of Conquest,* ed. Sol Tax (Glencoe: Free Press).

Woods, Clyde, and Theodore Graves
1973   *The Process of Medical Change in a Highland Guatemalan Town,* Latin American Studies Series, vol. 21 (Los Angeles: University of California Latin American Center).

Woods, Clyde
1977   "Alternative Curing Strategies in a Changing Medical Situation," *Medical Anthropology* 1:25-54.

Young, James
1978   "Illness Categories and Action Strategies in a Tarascan Town," *American Ethnologist* 5:81-97.

1981   *Medical Choice in a Mexican Village* (New Brunswick: Rutgers University Press).

which we are to draw our empirical data. I will consider three usual alternatives, all of which have presented major difficulties. I believe that the data we consider should come from a variety of cultures whose geographic and cultural epicenter lies somewhere within Mexico, but whose outer limits go well beyond the borders of that nation. These are the so-called Mexican cultures to be considered here.

The second issue, central to this paper, concerns why the study of kinship in Mexican cultures has been neglected when kinship considerations permeate all phases of social interaction in these cultures. Nutini is quite right in saying that "Mesoamerican anthropologists in general have not been interested in kinship studies" (1976a:4). There are both good and bad reasons for this lack of interest, and it is useless to cry that we should develop the interest because that's what anthropologists are supposed to do. One source of difficulty has been that our ideas about studying kinship often are based on formal structures and jural forms, but the cultures of Mexico do not emphasize the kinds of kinship structures and forms which anthropological theory is equipped to handle. A concern with the forms of kinship ultimately must lead to considerations of the content carried by those forms, and that content easily may go beyond jural rules. Questions about kinship are most meaningful when they are part of larger questions about a way of life.

Once the ethnographic focus is identified and there has been some initial consideration of possible uses of kinship materials in understanding the selected cultures, we can turn to the data of kinship as such. But what data are we to consider? There have not been enough serious studies of kinship systems and kinship behavior in Mexican cultures to support orderly comparisons of differing patterns. Systems of kinship terminology are a typical example. Romney claims, "Of the several hundred terminologies published on Middle American groups, the majority are so incomplete and so internally inconsistent as to preclude any meaningful analysis" (Romney 1967:207). There are equivalent gaps in materials dealing with the structure of kin groups, marriage and residence patterns, and most other aspects of kinship. A regional survey, in the face of such shortages of data, would clearly be out of place. This is not to say that we know nothing about kinship in Mexican cultures—quite the contrary is true. What it means is that a general study must necessarily concentrate on extracting a series of patterns, based on widespread tendencies and widely accepted principles, in the organization of the ways of kinship in Mexican cultures. It is still too soon to deal with detailed specifics.

My examination of the ways of kinship begins with questions of how kinship ties are established and maintained. To begin with, this means the use of names and kinship terms in the establishment of consanguineal kin groups. The next series of principles and tendencies deals with marriage practices and residential rules. All these factors, in combination, have major consequences in the structure of coresidential kinship groups. Except for trivial or residual cases, however, there is no such thing as a pattern of purely consanguinel residence groups, and there are significant kinds of kinship groups that are not coresidential. To understand both kinds of groups, we must look at ideas about the distribution of authority and power and their transmission along various kinds of kinship lines. Furthermore, in the cultures we are studying, kinship is not limited to consanguinity and affinity: compadrazgo, in both formal and informal manifestations, functions as a valid form of kinship in its own right. In examining all these matters, we want to know, I think, how kinship statuses may be affirmed and achieved, and what differences those ties may make.

Toward Defining an Ethnographic Focus

Anthropologists who have studied peoples living in the territory ranging, more or less, from the Great Basin in the United States to the Isthmus of Panama have long faced problems in defining the larger cultural entity their studies may illuminate. I consider here the three most widely used "solutions" to these problems: units called "Mesoamerica," "Middle America," and "Mexican culture." Discussion of the three kinds of units leads me to reject them all for current purposes. I propose the adoption of a different kind of ethnographic unit here.

The classic definition of the Mesoamerican culture area appears in Kirchhoff (1943). His definition of the Mesoamerican culture area depends, above all, on an implicitly evolutionary classification of cultures at the time of the Conquest. He wants to define an area occupied by "superior cultivators" or "High Cultures" as a contiguous whole. (Kirchhoff accepts the inclusion of hunter-gatherers and others within the "High Culture" zone because these lesser included groups share membership in the same language families as the area's superior cultivators, and they share many other cultural traits with them as well.) Kirchhoff clearly establishes the uniqueness and importance of a Mesoamerican culture area at the time of the Conquest, and for several centuries before. The traits on the list he uses to establish the area, however, are no longer relevant. Some are dying practices, such as pulque making, the special digging stick called a *coa*, the ceremonial use of turbans, and a few others. But most of the once-diagnostic traits are now known only to ethnohistory and archaeology. Nobody makes clay bullets for blowguns in what once was the heart of Mesoamerica, or wooden swords with obsidian chips along their edges, or step pyramids, or new hieroglyphic texts. Several pre-Conquest languages have become extinct, many areas have no remaining speakers of Native American languages, and every town has at least some Spanish speakers. Most culture traits characteristic of the entire area—and much of the rest of the world—appear nowhere in Kirchhoff's lists. These traits include matches and machetes, radios and radial tires, magazines for reading and other magazines—for rifles. In view of these facts, it is best to limit the use of the term "Mesoamerica" for studies that concentrate on the pre-Conquest epoch for which the definition was framed. Contemporary social anthropology needs something different, not limited to the time of the Conquest.

"Middle America" has gained a great deal of currency among those seeking an alternative to Kirchhoff's Mesoamerica. Somehow it seems to be assumed that everyone knows what and where Middle America is, so specific definitions are not given in most of the literature of the last thirty or forty years. Even the *Handbook of Middle American Indians* eschews a general definition. So shall I. But whatever else the term may mean, in the hands of anthropologists its use almost always shows a strong bias toward defining the universe of study as if Indians were the only actors on the cultural stage. That bias permeates the original Heritage of Conquest symposium. It is the conscious organizing principle of the *Handbook.* I have argued elsewhere (Salovesh 1979) that the time is long past for studying Middle American Indians as if they lived in cultural isolation. Even those who want to focus exclusively on Indians cannot understand their subject matter without looking beyond the localized municipio. Those who want to compare communities with each other, or understand processes of culture change, or use such generalizing concepts as "peasantry," must from the outset deal with events and processes whose very nature transcends the bounds of both *indigenismo* and localism. In such a context, the term "Middle America" has accumulated too many limitations for continued usefulness.

Some workers have given up on both "Mesoamerica" and "Middle America" to concentrate on what they call "the culture of Mexico." Edmonson (1957) both follows and makes valuable contributions to this line of thought. I will let his article stand for the entire class because Edmonson is very clear about what he is doing and why he does so, and because, unlike some others, he openly recognizes the shortcomings inherent in the approach. Edmonson's triangulation on the culture of Mexico is built out of a collection of regional, class, factional, and ethnic (including Indian) cultures. His clear implication is that all of these varying cultures are interesting because and to the extent that they are variations on a single, unifying pattern. He even argues (1957:228) that most of the Mexicans traditionally studied by anthropologists are essentially marginal to Mexican culture as an integrating whole. Thus he seems to say that the only way to define a single pattern for the culture of Mexico is to exclude those parts of Mexico's cultural diversity that do not fit comfortably. This exclusion alone calls the entire approach into question.

In this paper, I want to emphasize both cultural diversity and tendencies toward unity, with both a geographic focus and some outward extensions of that focus. Saying that our ethnographic data come from "Mexican cultures" provides a starting point. To use the word *cultures* in a plural form is not to say that there is no overarching pattern that unites the diversities of variation. It is to say, instead, that the question of unity is to be resolved out of the data, rather than by an a priori assumption. What remains to be asked is which cultures, out of the many found in Mexico and its neighbors, are to be included among those whose diversities and possible unities are to be studied.

There is good reason to be flexible in drawing a boundary to the southeast of Mexico proper. The cultures of speakers of Yucatec, Tzeltal, and other Maya languages of Mexico cannot be understood completely without reference to those who live in Guatemala and speak Quiché, Mam, and related languages. Any reluctance to focus exclusively on Middle American Indians should not be taken to mean that there are any Middle American Indians who should not be considered in our kinds of studies. All Middle American Indians must be considered, on an equal footing, regardless of whether their home territories are in Mexico, Guatemala, Belize, or other countries.

It is harder to know what to do with non-Indians living in nations to the southeast of Mexico. Mexicans, Guatemalans, and Hondurans show many cultural similarities; some of these point to a commonality of Hispanic influence shared with all of Latin America, while others are specifically regional. The problem of supranational Hispanic cultural similarities considerably challenges any attempt to restrict the basic definition of a culture area. *Mexican cultures* is, however, broad enough in scope and extension to imply more than Mexico alone.

Still speaking of geographic extension, Mexico's northern border is clearly not the same as its northern cultural frontier. In part, this discrepancy is an artifact of North American conquest of territory that once belonged to Mexico. Thus many people whose beliefs and practices fit well within the range of cultures located in Mexico never have been citizens of Mexico, although their ancestors may once have been. Furthermore, on any given day millions of Mexican citizens are to be found in the United States and Canada. Their presence elsewhere does not make them any the less Mexican in culture. For me, and for the purposes of this paper, these culturally Mexican peoples must be considered an integral part of the range of variation when we try to understand the cultures of Mexico. In fact, their contact with the quite different cultural patterns of the English-speaking north may make invaluable contributions to our understanding of cultures located completely within Mexican territory.

The "Mexican cultures" providing the ethnographic data of this paper, then, are cultures whose heartland is clear but whose northern and southeastern boundaries are fuzzy. Thus the range of cultures to be considered includes both the whole cultural diversity contained within Mexico and many cultures physically based outside Mexico. I think this is a proper reflection of ethnographic reality. It is, furthermore, a reality of very long standing, seen also in the bounds of the Royal Audience of New Spain and the captaincy-general of Guatemala, not to mention ancient Mesoamerica and its affinities with, say, Hopewellian cultures far to the northeast.

Studying Kinship in Mexican Cultures

Any attempt to review what we know about kinship and social organization in the cultures of Mexico and its political neighbors must begin with the question of why so little has been done in this field when there have been so many ethnographic studies by such a large number of social anthropologists. That question can also be posed in inverted form: is there any reason to suppose that it might be useful to concentrate on kinship studies in Mexican cultures?

One explanation of the neglect of kinship studies in our area may be found in accidental history. Redfield, Wolf, and Foster, each for his own reasons, chose to emphasize factors other than kinship, and their influences have had a kind of founder's effect on those who came later. Redfield's model of a folk-urban continuum, operationalized in his studies of Yucatán (1941), sees kinship as a major organizing principle at the folk end of the continuum. At the same time, he views the cultures of Mexico as stages in movement away from folk-type organization. Hence kinship should be less and less important in such cultures—thus less and less interesting to the anthropologist. Wolf (1955 and elsewhere) views communities and their constituent parts as territorial units in the complex politicoeconomic interactions that condition types of peasantry. In his analyses, kinship plays a secondary role at best. Foster (1961 and elsewhere) emphasizes the achieved status inherent in dyadic contracts. The implicit, sometimes even explicit, contrast is with an alleged ascription of status in kinship systems. In all of these studies, a downgrading of interest in kinlike interactions was part of an argument for studying other factors *in addition to* kinship rather than in place of kinship. In our recognition of the cogency of those arguments, we have gone to the extreme of concentrating almost exclusively on those other factors while forgetting about kinship. Nonetheless, kinship and families exist and are important even in the conceptual extreme of "pure" urbanism in Redfield's continuum; kinship itself provides a mechanism tending to perpetuate peasantry as a social condition as well as a politicoeconomic form; and in Mexican cultures, at least, dyadic contracts are systematically biased in favor of those perceived as kin (or, through marriage or compadrazgo, those made into kin). The accident of anthropological tradition in these matters is not dictated by the facts on the ground. Unfortunately, the tradition has all but achieved the status of an ideological belief that kinship "has to be" unimportant in Mexican cultures.

Another reason for the neglect of kinship studies in this area is inherent in the state of the analytic art in anthropology, and in the ethnographic facts themselves. Our theories and analyses are most highly developed in two kinds of studies: those of unilineal descent and intergroup marital alliance. In Mexican cultures, unilineal descent groups are rare—some would say extinct. Systematic intergroup alliance through prescribed or preferential marriage is not the way things are done here—at least not in the ways characteristic of southeast Asia. On the other hand, anthropological studies of bilateral kinship systems have always lagged behind studies of other types. And Mexican cultures are overwhelmingly bilateral.[1] Similarly, our theories are strongly developed for the understanding of formal structures and jural norms. Optative structures, where many partially independent factors combine as vectors in determining outcomes, are more characteristic of Mexican cultures than are jural norms. The analysis of such forms of social organization is inherently complex, necessarily leaning on statistical as well as structural models. Because we, as anthropologists, tend to feel uncomfortable with statistical models, we have also tended to avoid studying those kinds of kinship materials whose analysis demands such models.

Whatever the causes of the relative neglect of kinship studies in the past, recent work seems to be reversing this trend. Early works in this new wave include Diebold 1966; Nutini 1968; Hunt 1969; and Nutini, Carrasco, and Taggart 1976, based on a 1969 symposium. A realization that kinship is more worthy of intensive study than once was thought comes from independent work on many facets of life in Mexican cultures. Kinship and residence rules turn out to be the skeleton and muscles giving shape to the structure of local groups, rural-urban migrations, patterns of deviance and the control of deviants, political interactions, economic interchange, ritual recruitment, and the adjudication of disputes in study after study. The all-pervading *personalismo* and interindividual dyadic contract make sense only when seen against a background of kinship-based rules. These kinds of facts make kinship studies not only useful but essential to the understanding of Mexican cultures.

Some General Principles in Mexican Kinship Terminologies

The most widespread system of kinship terminology in Mexican cultures is provided by standard Spanish. Some local systems consistently substitute slightly nonstandard terms (*abuelito, mamacita* instead of *abuelo, madre*) but follow the same terminological patterning found in standard Spanish. In this pattern, siblings in ego's generation and lineal relatives in other generations are distinguished from collateral relatives. The system is bilateral in the sense that relatives on the mother's side are not disinguished from relatives on the father's side in basic terminology. (Compound descriptive terms can be used when more specificity is called for: e.g., "es mi abuelo, papá de mi mamá"—he is my grandfather, father of my mother.) First ascending, first descending, and ego's own generation are clearly distinguished from each other for both lineal and collateral relatives. Generational distinctions tend to break down in more distant generations. (Thus FaFaBr and other collaterals of the second ascending generation are frequently called *tío,* the same term used for FaBr and MoBr.) First cousins (*primos hermanos*) are frequently, but not always, distinguished from other collaterals (*primos*) in ego's generation. There is disagreement and inconsistency in the terms used for collaterals more distant than parent's sibling or sibling's child in adjacent generations, and there are no commonly used terms for similarly distant relatives more than a generation removed from ego. Sex of the relative is usually specified by a standard grammatical ending (*-o,* male or sex not specified; *-a,* female; for plurals, *-os,* males or both males and females; *-as,* females). Special terms (*padre, madre,* plural *los padres*) are used in place of grammatical devices for distinguishing sex of parents. Sex of the speaker is not marked for the basic terms of standard Spanish kinship. Affinal terms are used for spouse's parents and siblings, for parent's spouse, and (less frequently, usually expressing negative affect) for parent's spouse's child. Other affinal relatives are sometimes addressed by metaphoric extensions of terms for consanguineals, particularly as an expression of positive affect.

Standard Spanish kinship terminology provides a base for three kinds of systematic departures where Spanish is a language of communication: term substitution, nonstandard regional systems used by monolingual Spanish speakers, and glosses for different kinds of terms and statuses among those using Spanish as a second language.

"Term substitution" is used here to cover cases where a nonstandard word is used in place of the standard one, but both the standard and nonstandard words are applied to exactly the same range of relatives. The most widespread example is a general reluctance to use the word *madre* in any but the most formal of settings. Typical substitutes include *mamá, mamacita,* and the less frequent *madrecita.* *Papá* in many places regularly appears in place of *padre,* and rural areas show a preference for *abuelito* as a grandparental term. Other substitutions (e.g., *tata* for father) are confined to areas with large Indian populations, while some substitute terms have only limited regional or subcultural currency.

Regional departures in which Spanish speakers use Spanish words for classes of relatives other than those delimited by the standard Spanish kinship system have not been widely studied. In the hopes of stimulating others to investigate alternate systems in Mexican Spanish, I adduce one example known to me from fieldwork among regional Ladino elites in Chiapas, but also encountered in Mexico City and among migrant workers in the United States. In this variant system, ego merges one set of grandparents with parents by calling them *papá* and *mamá,* while the other grandparents are kept distinct by the terms *abuelito* and *abuelita.*[2] My original data seemed to show this as a merging of *father* and *father's father,* separating them from *mother's father.* Additional work turned up cases where *father* regularly merged with *mother's father,* while *father's father* was the one called *abuelito,* among individuals who otherwise followed the same cultural patterns as the ones merging patrilineal ancestors. Additional data in these cases both explains the difference and shows how I received the misimpression of patrilineality. This usage, it turns out, is the systematic reflection of power distribution in localized extended families and their nonlocalized equivalents. The grandfather called *papá* is always the dominant figure in such a

multigeneration kinship group; conversely, where one of the grandparents is clearly dominant in the lives of his married children, his
grandchildren call him *papá*. Since there is a bias toward patrilineality
in extended families, but not a rule specifying patrilineality as the
exclusive basis for such groups, it is easy to see why I first though
this was a patrilineal skewing of the kinship system—and why, and
to what extent, I was wrong.

The third class of departures from standard Spanish kinship is quite
different from the two just described. In the first two kinds of cases,
we are justified in taking the standard Spanish system as a base and
the differing systems as variants. But when the informant usually
speaks another language, and Spanish is simply the language of contact, it can be quite inaccurate to say that the kinship system elicited in Spanish using Spanish words as kinship labels is merely a
variant of the Standard Spanish system. Some of my informants, for
example, have been quite consistent in applying the label *hermano* to
brother, father's brother, mother's brother, and *first cousin* alike. Others
inconsistently refer to the same individual as *hermano, tío,* and *primo.*
These Spanish usages all make sense when it is recognized that these
same informants, speaking Tzotzil, use the single term *bankil* for a
man's older, nonlineal male relative. Distinctions between *brother,
uncle,* and *cousin* are not operationally significant in the culture of
these informants, but the distinction of older male collateral relative
from younger male collateral relative clearly is. Their opposition of
*bankil and 'it'in i*s reflected in the way they use the Spanish words
tío-hermano versus *sobrino-hermanito,* and it is unfair to regard the words
as having any necessary connection with a Spanish terminological
system. They are, instead, Spanish glosses for words and statuses in
a different language and culture.

There are many distinctive systems of kinship terminology among
Middle American Indian cultures. Attempts to classify these systems
in terms that have standard applications elsewhere (e.g., Lowie's or
Murdoch's categories of kinship systems) have proved uniformly
disappointing. The Omaha-like system of Chalchihuitán is systematically quite different from the Omaha-like system of Cancuc.
Moreover, the differences between them cannot be attributed to geographic separation (for both communities are in highland Chiapas),
or to great linguistic difference (for while one community is Tzeltal

speaking, the other Tzotzil speaking, the glottochronological separation between the two is not appreciably greater than separations known within either language), or to interobserver bias (for our best data on both communities comes from the same worker, Calixta Guiteras Holmes). Similarly, the "lineal" system of the Sierra Totonac is quite different from the "lineal" terminology of the Yalalag Zapotec: witness the fact that siblings are distinguished from cousins in the former, but not in the latter. Useful classification of whole systems is probably fruitless in the present state of our knowledge.

Some general observations on Indian kinship systems are nonetheless possible. First of all, most present-day systems are bilateral rather than unilineal, with the most notable exceptions occurring among the Maya, particularly in Chiapas. Second, there is a widespread tendency to place great importance on distinctions of relative age within a generation. In some systems, relative age distinctions cut across generation lines. We see this in the Tzotzil example I cited above, where the relatives we would class as *brother, uncle, cousin,* and *nephew* are lumped into two classes: older, *bankil,* and younger, *'it'in.* Thus, uncle younger than ego is classed with younger brother, while nephew older than ego is classed with older brother. The use of this cross-generation relative age criterion in many systems has led to confusing or misleading descriptions in the literature when the analyst, following genealogical mapping, considered one generation at a time. In many systems, sex of the relative is distinguished only for relatives older than ego. Third, some systems have different, or partly different, terms according to the sex of the speaker. In a few cases men make different classifications of the kinship universe than those made by women, in addition to using different words marking sex of the speaker. To continue my examples from San Bartolo Tzotzil, men call older male collateral relatives *bankil* while women use the word *šibel* for what is otherwise the same class of relatives. On the other hand, men have two words—*'it'in,* younger male, and *išlel,* younger female—where women have only one, *muk,* younger relative. Fourth, where systems exhibit any tendency to unilineality in kinship terms, it is always in the direction of patrilineality, never matrilineality. In the few systems where parallel cousins are distinguished from cross cousins, siblings are merged with the parallel cousins. Systems in which the two kinds of cross cousins are distinguished from each other are rare but not unknown. There is some evidence, both comparative in the ethnographic present and historic from early Colonial times, that patrilineal systems were once more widespread among Middle American Indians, and that these systems have moved toward different types of bilateral systems in the present.

Individual and Family Names

The choice of an individual's name usually rests with the parents. The use of Spanish personal names from the calendar of saints is typical, but the saint chosen is not necessarily one whose feast day coincides with the actual date of birth. Those born within a few days of the date dedicated to a saint regarded as particularly propitious, or those born even within some weeks of a saint's day providing occasion for a major local fiesta tend to be given that prominent saint's name despite the technical difference in dates. In such cases, the saint's day rather than the birth anniversary is used for subsequent "birthday" celebrations. Moreover, individual names traditional within a particular family may be assigned in place of, or in addition to, calendrically appropriate saints' names. Some family traditions among speakers of Indian languages preserve the use of pre-Conquest day names; in at least some cases, certain pre-Conquest day names are assigned appropriately according to a continuation of a pre-Conquest calendar. This practice has been observed, for example, among the Lacandon.

The assignment of family names is not usually a matter of choice. The standard naming system, typical of most Mexican cultures, is binominal. A child's family name consists of father's patronymic followed by mother's patronymic. This family name is retained for life, and transmitted to children by the same rules. Women add the word *de* and the husband's patronymic to their birth names at marriage; they may substitute *viuda de* (widow of) for the simpler *de* at the husband's death. For most purposes, a man is known by his personal name followed by his father's patronymic; signatures tend to add the initial of the mother's patronymic. On formal occasions, and in normal reference to such highly prominent figures as the president of Mexico, the full binominal name is used. Unmarried women are spoken of the same way, but married women are most frequently referred to as *la señora de* (husband's patronymic) and sign their names as personal name, father's patronymic, *de,* husband's patronymic.

I know of two fairly common variants of the standard system for deriving surnames. In the first, father's patronymic and mother's patronymic are linked by a connective *y* (English *and*). This practice is particularly common in settings where the individual so named is in frequent contact with English speakers in the United States. It serves to emphasize, to the Anglo outsider, that the father's patronymic is a surname, rather than a "middle" name. The same usage also occurs within Mexico, but I have not yet learned the rules governing its use. Another regular, but less frequent, variant gives mother's patronymic first, followed by the word *de (of)* and the father's patronymic. The late Marcelo Diaz de Salas, in explaining his own surname to me, claimed that such a combination arises when the mother's family is regarded as so prominent that her descendants (or her husband) want to emphasize their connection in following generations. Once created, the new combination is transmitted patrilineally as a single unit and combined with maternal surnames in the usual way.

The preceding discussion of standard practices for establishing an individual's surname is a necessary background to the presentation of alternate naming systems followed in many Indian communities. Instead of presenting all the known ways of assigning Indian surnames, I shall limit myself here to presenting the outline of the systems best known to me, those of highland Chiapas Tzeltal and Tzotzil speakers.

Among the Tzeltal and Tzotzil, every individual carries a Spanish surname. In written records, the standard Mexican binominal system is followed, but the "standard name" is normally used only for or by outsiders. Within the community, the single Spanish name is the same as the father's Spanish surname. Each individual's name is nevertheless binominal in form; the second surname (usually in the Indian language, but occasionally derived from Spanish) is transmitted with the Spanish surname as a single unit. Thus the children of Juan Pérez Jolote (Pozas 1952) would also be called Pérez Jolote regardless of their mother's surname. Each second surname is linked with a single Spanish surname exclusively, but there may be many different second surnames associated with one Spanish first surname. Thus, in Chamula anyone named Jolote would also be named Pérez, but some named Pérez might also be named Zopilote rather than Jolote.

Second, Indian surnames sometimes are survivals of sixteenth-century Maya day names, as, in San Bartolo, names whose modern standardized spellings are *Im, Chawin, Mol,* and *Chiquin.* Sometimes the names of animals, plants, or natural objects *(Bolom,* jaguar, *Chenek,* bean; *Ukum,* river) are used as surnames. Finally, kinship terms *(Ni* son-in-law; *Yol,* child); and even fossilized nicknames *(Kantsikan,* he wants his woman) occur.

Some authors, following Villa Rojas (1947), have seen in the Indian surname system clear evidence for patrilineal clans either in the present or in the post-Conquest past. Villa Rojas himself sees the first, or Spanish, surname as a clan marker while he takes the second, Indian surname to be a label for a lineage. He argues that Oxchuc is divided into six patrilineal exogamous clans, each divided into several lineages. He claims that all members of a single clan recognize kinship, on the basis of their shared Spanish surname, and extend incest taboos to all members of the clan. Members of a single lineage are said to regard themselves as particularly closely related, and a shared Indian surname is sufficient evidence to establish that closeness, even in the absence of known genealogical links. Other authors working in neighboring communities consistently report that those sharing the second, or Indian, surname form an exogamous group but they are unable to demonstrate Spanish-surname exogamy. In fact, marriages between two individuals sharing the same Spanish surname are common throughout the area, and not unknown even in Oxchuc where Villa Rojas studied. Moreover, there is no solid evidence for the regular delegation of authority over an entire name-group for either Spanish or Indian surnames and no strict localization of patrilines. Thus, if clans exist among any Middle American Indian groups today, it will take better evidence than that adduced by Villa Rojas to demonstrate the fact. Nevertheless, as we shall see below, name-group exogamy and a tendency to patrilocal-virilocal postmarital residence clearly introduce a patrilineal bias into systems that are formally bilateral.

Marriage Practices and Postmarital Residence

For the purposes of this paper, *marriage practices* will be used as a cover term for complex sets of beliefs and behaviors regarding the choice of marital partners and the nature of marriage itself. For simplicity, *postmarital residence* will be limited to cases where both bride and groom marry for the first time.

Marriage in Mexican cultures is seen as an institution providing for both the sexual cohabitation of a man and a woman and the social position of their children. Sexual cohabitation alone, particularly when it is clandestine, is not regarded as equivalent to marriage. In many Mexican cultures, however, a man and a woman are regarded as married if they overtly form a single household without benefit of any marriage ceremony. In such cases, particularly where open cohabitation has been continuous for a number of years, legal systems may grant jural rights to both partners just as if they were married. Offspring of such unions may achieve recognition of inheritance rights in the estates of both parents. Children of these unions normally take their surnames from both parents exactly as they would had there been a formal marriage. Under civil law within Mexico, marriage is a simple contract whose execution requires little more than appearance before an appropriate official and inscription of the fact of marriage in the local civil register. Upon valid civil marriage, both parties automatically acquire jural rights with respect to each other, and their ensuing children have automatic inheritance rights. Marriage in the Catholic Church, under Mexican law, is conditional upon prior marriage of the partners under civil law. In many local cultures, therefore, civil marriage is called "marriage under one law" while Church marriage is called "marriage under the two laws." Open unions, civil marriage, and Church marriage are not regarded as marriages until and unless sexual and residential cohabitation takes place.

In some Indian cultures, there is an alternative kind of marriage ceremony that does not necessarily lead to physical cohabitation. These forms of traditional marriage involve complex series of exchanges and rituals in which the parents of the prospective couple are primary participants. Once the ceremonial series is completed, the couple is regarded as married, and appropriate affinal terms begin to be used between the two families. Cohabitation of the married couple, however, need not take place immediately after the ceremony; in some cases, the couple is still regarded as husband and wife even though cohabitation never occurs. (Salovesh 1976 contains a fuller description of one such system.) Ordinarily, however, cohabitation is the normal result of a traditional marriage, and such marriages are frequently followed by civil or both civil and religious marriage.

Monogamy is the rule in traditional, civil, and religious marriage but open unions, often taken as equivalent to marriage, are not quite so exclusive. Where the equivalent of polygamy occurs, it takes the form of polygyny; polyandry is not practised. The termination of marital relationship, once cohabitation has taken place, is possible under any of the four forms of marriage. In open unions and traditional marriage, physical separation is sufficient to terminate the relationship. Civil divorce is somewhat more complicated, but easy and inexpensive to obtain. Church marriages may be dissolved only through highly complicated and expensive procedures, and to all intents and purposes divorce as such is impossible. But if there has been a church marriage and a valid civil divorce, the fact that the Church regards the marriage as still valid is not a bar to remarriage under civil law. Divorce or its equivalent, followed by remarriage to another partner, is almost as common for civil marriages as it is for free unions. Indeed, the incidence of remarriage under civil law after one or the other partner has abandoned a church marriage may not be significantly less frequent than remarriage after civil divorce when there was no church marriage. At any rate, divorce and its equivalents are so common in some Mexican cultures that they are structural regularities. In my long fieldwork in San Bartolo, I have yet to meet a married person over the age of forty who could not name at least one prior spouse as the parent of some of the informant's children.

The first set of rules to be considered in the choice of marriage partners is those dealing with whom one may not marry. Primary relatives are universally excluded as potential spouses; so are parents' siblings and siblings' children. Marriage with parallel cousins does not occur. Isolated cases of cross-cousin marriage with first cousins have been reported, but all contemporary Mexican cultures formally prohibit marriage with any first cousin. (Some evidence suggests that cross-cousin marriage may have been encouraged among the pre-Conquest Maya, but this still remains unproven.) Name-group exogamy is frequently the rule where an Indian system of binominal surnames occurs. Except for Oxchuc, where, according to Villa Rojas, there is Spanish name-group exogamy, the prohibition is against marriage with a person bearing the same second, or Indian, surname and does not exclude marriage with one sharing the same first, or Spanish surname. Moreover, Villa Rojas's data regarding what he calls "clan" exogamy have been questioned by other authors who have worked in Oxchuc. Thus, even the exception is questionable. In some communities, territorial groups partially based on kinship considerations through the operation of residence rules are reported to follow rules of exogamy. These rules of barrio or calpul exogamy, however, are weak and can be transcended through formal petition or informally evaded without fear of strong sanctions.

Except for the exclusions laid down by incest rules and rules of exogamy, there are few formal rules specifying the choice of marriage partners in Mexican cultures. Of course, religious beliefs promote endogamy among Catholics, but since the overwhelming majority of the population is at least nominally Catholic (and since only a minority of marriages take place under Church auspices) such beliefs have little operational significance. Barrio or calpul endogamy is said to be the norm in many communities, particularly among Indians. Some communities (especially, but not exclusively, in the Maya area) are reported to be divided into endogamous moieties, primarily along territorial but partially on kinship lines. Even these rules of endogamy leave a wide field of potential spouses for any given individual.

The actual choice of a marriage partner is subject to two opposing sets of expectations in nearly all Mexican cultures. First of these is the widespread belief that the individual should be in control of this decision: spouses should choose each other. Opposed to this belief is the expectation that the extended families of both bride and groom are deeply involved in the marital relationship, and thus should have a controlling voice in the selection. For example, it is often the case that the respective parents of the bride and the groom are regarded as compadres to each other as a result of the marriage. Compadrazgo is always regarded as a voluntary relationship; hence the parents have veto power over their children's marriage. Neither of these beliefs is absolute or exclusive in its application. The outcomes for individual marriages range from marriages arranged by the family to elopement to avoid family wishes.

There are some patterns of marital choice which regularly occur but are not the subject of strict rules. Among Indians, community endogamy is common. In all Mexican cultures, marriages are most frequent within groups of roughly equivalent status. There is thus a strong tendency to endogamy within ethnic groups, social classes, groups characterized by differential access to power or prestige, and even in occupational groups. Wide status disparities between husband and wife or between their families are quite rare. Within these limits, individuals seek to marry up rather than down; that is, in the abstract they express preference for marriage with someone of slightly higher status over marriage with someone of slightly lower status. Comparative social position is always a factor in choosing a marriage partner but it is not the only controlling factor.

Once a marriage has been entered into, the married couple must go somewhere to live. Unfortunately, there have been few studies of the details of postmarital residence. Most ethnographies simply report either the presence of a rule of patrilocal-virilocal residence or the practice of neolocal residence. Both are statements about ideal norms rather than descriptions of actual practice; even as ideal norms, these statements are not a reflection of the full ethnographic reality. In the comments that follow, I offer generalizations that go beyond the data available in published sources. They are put forward with the intent of stimulating discussion and further research rather than as summaries of what we know now.

In Mexican cultures, there is a strong belief that a newly married couple should live with or near some close relatives of either the bride or the groom. All other things being equal, the groom's parents are the relatives of choice. Help in obtaining a place for newly married children to live is regarded as a parental obligation, more binding in the case of sons than daughters. A common result is the formation of extended family households, particularly in a patrilineal form. Other expectations crosscut the expressed preference for patrilocal residence. Aging parents trying to provide for their old age regularly offer special advantages to induce the husband of one of their younger daughters into matrilocal residence. When the groom's parents do not approve of the marriage but the bride's parents do, residence with the bride's parents is preferred. When neither set of parents is able or willing to help in providing a place to live, residence with (or with the assistance of) any other relative is preferred over neolocal residence. Finally, residence with relatives who are better off financially or better placed politically is preferred to residence with those who are less well off or less powerful. This preference for what I have elsewhere called "luxurilocal residence" may take priority over either the normally preferred patrilocal residence or the matrilocal alternative, even when the parents are willing and able to provide a place to live.

Whatever the location and form of initial residence after marriage, living with or with the assistance of already-married relatives means, to a large extent, living under the control of those relatives. There is thus a second belief in Mexican cultures regarding where a married couple should live: that after an initial period of residence with or near some close relative, a couple should establish an independent household away from the control of others. At any given time, then, most couples are in neolocal residence. The residential life cycle of a marriage goes from participation in an extended-family household (or its close equivalent) to operation as a nuclear family. If the marriage lasts long enough, the third stage in this cycle is a return to the extended family, this time as the senior and controlling generation.

The foregoing rules of residence, especially in combination with rules of barrio or *calpul* endogamy, tend to tie family lines to specific localities within a community. Even though there are usually no rules calling for the localization of patrilineal groups, there is a clear tilt to social arrangements that makes the actual distribution of people on the ground resemble localized patrilineages. This tilt begins in the choice of marriage partners. Although marriage across wide differences of social status is discouraged, when status differences exist they are in the direction of female hypergamy more often than not. When women marry up, patrilocal residence is the likely outcome because of the preference for luxurilocality. Even in the absence of the effects of female hypergamy, the preference for initial patrilocal residence leads to the same end. Choice of place of residence in the usually later stage of neolocality is conditioned by the initial patrilocal bias. The "new" location of neolocality tends to be close to the place of initial residence, and such neolocality by itself does not operate so as to break up the localization of patrilines. Thus it is fair to conclude that kinship in Mexican cultures shows a consistent bias toward patrilineality, despite the surface forms of bilaterality.

Compadrazgo

This is not the place to attempt a complete explanation of the nature and role of compadrazgo in Mexican cultures. That task has been undertaken more times than the limited published data justify. (Good overviews may be found in Ravicz 1967 and Gudeman 1971; the most extensive and detailed data for a single area are in Nutini 1976b. See also Kendall 1974, for Guatemala.) The comments that follow are an attempt to place compadrazgo in the context of kinship studies.

Compadrazgo is a voluntary relationship growing out of ritual sponsorship. The type case for this relationship is seen at baptism. In this rite, two new dyadic relationships are added to those that link the baptized child to its birth parents: the relation of godchild to godparent, or *ahijado* to *padrino-madrina;* and the relation of child's parent to sponsor, or *compadre-comadre* to *compadre-comadre.* The essence of compadrazgo as an institution is found in the continuing relationship between compadres; only baptism among the many rites that may establish compadrazgo sets up continuing rights and obligations between sponsor and person sponsored. The primacy of compadre to compadre links is seen most clearly when the place of the baptized child is taken by an object, ceremony, or institution sponsored by the padrino. Compadrazgo may be established, according to local custom, by a myriad of alternative acts of sponsorship: of a new car or house, a new business venture, or even special ceremonies whose primary function seems precisely to be one of affording occasion for establishing compadrazgo.

Compadrazgo is not regarded as fictive or imitation kinship in Mexican cultures. The bonds between compadres are as real, as important, and as lasting as any other form of kinship. In many kinship systems, compadrazgo is fully integrated into the rest of the kinship system; compadrazgo relationship can even be mapped into a componential analysis of the total kinship system without analytic difficulty. The major difference between compadrazgo and consanguineality, in the eyes of many analysts, is its voluntary aspect. Even this distinction is only a surface difference. Only the relationship between parent and child is fully ascribed in Mexican cultures. The fact of birth to a particular pair of parents only serves to define a group of potential relatives. Reaffirmation and achievement of kinship by voluntary interaction as an adult is a prerequisite to the maintenance of kinship with all relatives other than parents and children.

Optative Structures in Mexican Kinship

Many observers of Mexican cultures have commented on the lack of rigid rules in the systems of kinship, marriage, and residence. They seem to mean by this perceived lack that behavior and belief are consonant with nonpatterned personal choice, rather than with a single, internally consistent model of social organization. To put it bluntly, that observation is simply wrong.

The rules of kinship interaction in these cultures are much more complex than those of simple unilineal systems, but there definitely are rules. On one level, nearly every kind of kinship status and kinship interaction takes place in a field where alternative rules seem to apply. Where rules specifying two or more opposing outcomes all seem relevant to the same choice, it is easy to conclude that the rules don't mean much. But where such situations apply, deeper analysis reveals that the same system includes sets of metarules about which rules shall take priority in given circumstances. When observation shows, for example, that upon marriage some couples go to live with the groom's parents, some to live with the bride's parents, some to live with other relatives, and some to establish independent households of their own, it is easy to conclude that there is no regular rule of residence. But a closer look at why each couple chooses a particular place of residence can show that each "choice" was, in fact, obligatory in the specific circumstances. The rules for choosing which set of rules to follow are themselves discoverable, but only if they are sought.

This discussion, though much-condensed and descriptive, outlines some general principles of social organization in Mexican cultures, and offers occasional comments on the anthropological study of such matters. I would like to conclude with some general observations about the interdigitation of kinship considerations with other kinds of activities in Mexican cultures. Perhaps the best place to look for relevant information is in the interaction of individuals with groups and official bureaucracies.

In Mexican cultures, individuals interacting with formal institutions and groups usually approach that interaction through personal intermediaries. "Do you have to go the hospital? Let us talk to Tío Pepe; I think he has a compadre who is on the staff." "No, we can't go to the Banco de Comercio for this loan; we don't know anyone there." "Compadre, would you pardon me for the trouble I am causing you, could you speak to the principales so that I may become mayordomo for the next fiesta?" The ideal intermediary outside the nuclear family is a compadre, because the implied equality of the relationship makes it easier to ask for favors without simultaneously confessing inferiority. Lacking an appropriately placed compadre, consanguineal relatives are preferred over affinal ones when intermediaries are sought. When no relative has appropriate contacts, desperation leads to the choice of a politically powerful or rich acquaintance to intercede. If no intermediary can be found, the typical response is to avoid interaction with the external institution if at all possible. If repeated contact with an institution or a group is unavoidable, then reasonable and prudent behavior dictates the establishment of compadrazgo or affinal kinship links with someone who does have good connections in that institution. Again and again, the behavioral expectation is that the individual interacts with groups and institutions through networks of interpersonal ties of kinship.

The role of kinship outside the structure of families and residential groups, then, is that it provides the interface between the individual person and the group polity. In this sense, kinship pervades nearly all public interactions in Mexican cultures. Close understanding of the mechanisms of kinship in those cultures is thus a prerequisite to understanding all other social interactions.

NOTES

1. This doesn't mean that all these bilateral systems are the same, or even amenable to one-to-one mapping correspondence. The conceptual and systematic differences between two bilateral systems can be much greater than those between a typical Crow and a typical Omaha system.

2. In my experience, the most frequent usage links *papá* with the *grandparent's given name: Papá Augusto,* that grandfather whose name is Augusto, as opposed to the other grandfather or ego's father. The two terms act as a linked pair of bound morphemes.

REFERENCES

Diebold, Richard A.
1966   "The Reflection of Coresidence in Mareño Kinship Terminology," *Ethnology* 5:37-79.
Edmonson, Munro S.
1957   "A Triangulation on the Culture of Mexico," in *Synoptic Studies of Mexican Culture,* ed. Robert Wauchope, Middle American Research Institute, Publication 17 (New Orleans: Tulane University).
Foster, George M.
1961   "The Dyadic Contract: A Model for the Social Structure of a Mexican Peasant Village," *American Anthropologist* 63:1173-92.
Gudeman, Stephen
1971   *The Compadrazgo as a Reflection of the Natural and Spiritual Person,* Proceedings of the Royal Anthropological Institute 1971:45-71.
Hunt, M. Eva
1969   "The Meaning of Kinship in San Juan: Genealogical and Social Models," *Ethnology* 8:37-53.
Kirchhoff, Paul
1943   "Mesoamérica: sus límites geográficos, composición étnica y caracteres culturales," *Acta Americana* 1:92-107.
Kendall, Carl
1974   "Filiation and Brotherhood: Compadrazgo in Esquipulas, Guatemala" (Ph.D. diss., University of Rochester).
Nutini, Hugo G.
1968   *San Bernardino Contla: Marriage and Family Structure in a Tlaxcalan municipio* (Pittsburgh: University of Pittsburgh Press).
1976a   "Introduction: The Nature and Treatment of Kinship in Mesoamerica," in *Essays on Mexican Kinship,* ed. Hugo Nutini, Pedro Carrasco, and James Taggart (Pittsburgh: University of Pittsburgh Press).
1976b   *Ritual Kinship* (Austin: University of Texas Press).
Nutini, Hugo G., Pedro Carrasco, and James M. Taggart
1976   *Essays on Mexican Kinship* (Pittsburgh: University of Pittsburgh Press).

Pozas, Ricardo A.
1952   *Juan Pérez Jolote: biografía de un Tzotzil* (México, D.F.: Fondo de Cultura Económica).
Ravicz, Robert
1967   "Compadrinazgo," in *Social Anthropology,* ed. M. Nash. Vol. 6 of *Handbook of Middle American Indians,* ed. R. Wauchope (Austin: University of Texas Press).'
Redfield, Robert
1941   *The Folk Culture of Yucatán* (Chicago: University of Chicago Press).
Romney, A. Kimball
1967   "Kinship and Family," in *Social Anthropology,* ed. M. Nash, Vol. 6 of *Handbook of Middle American Indians,* ed. R. Wauchope (Austin: University of Texas Press).
Salovesh, Michael
1976   "Postmarital residence in San Bartolome de los Llanos, Chiapas," in *Essays on Mexican Kinship,* ed. Hugo G. Nutini, Pedro Carrasco, and James M. Taggart (Pittsburgh: University of Pittsburgh Press).
1979   "Looking Beyond the Municipio in Chiapas: Problems and Prospects in Studying Up," in *Essays in Honor of Sol Tax,* ed. Robert Hinshaw (The Hague: Mouton).
Villa Rojas, Alfonso
1947   "Kinship and Nagualism in a Tzeltal Community, Southern Mexico," *American Anthropologist* 49:578-87.
Wolf, Eric
1955   "Types of Latin American Peasantry: A Preliminary Discussion," *American Anthropologist* 57:452-71.

8

The Analysis of Domestic Organization in Mesoamerica: The Case of Postmarital Residence in Santiago Atitlán, Guatemala

Joseph J. Gross
University of Alaska
and
Carl Kendall
Stanford University

A single chapter in the original *Heritage of Conquest* volume was devoted to the topic of social organization. In it, Calixta Guiteras Holmes sought to uncover the articulation between kinship terminologies, marriage rules, postmarital residence, and lineages and clans as distributed in Mesoamerica. In part, this effort may have reflected some degree of acceptance among the organizers and participants of a common system of kinship categories and criteria for inclusion. At very least, they were familiar with the different kinship systems current. In contrast, the contemporary literature on Mesoamerican social organization does not reflect any such unity. Recent reviews of Mesoamerican social organization by Nutini (1967, 1976), Romney (1967), and Selby (1976) demonstrate the diversity of approaches, and the felt inadequacy of analyses.

Among the issues singled out by Nutini is that of postmarital residential arrangements. Nutini remarks that anthropologists in

Mesoamerica have failed to explore "the possibilities for redefining residence rules beyond the standard definitions provided by Murdock (1949) and others, in order to apply them to essentially cognatic societies or societies which are no longer tribal but which have a significant modicum of organizational similarities to tribal societies" (1976:8). His reference to tribal societies in this context perhaps contrasts the supposedly rigid kinship and jural-rule-bound tribal society with cognatic systems that present greater morphological diversity. And this assumption is supported by his next sentence: "Under these conditions, generalizations in terms of traditionally defined rules of residence, which are essentially mechanical (emic and normative) devices, cannot be applied at face value to situations in which a significantly statistical (etic) approach would be in order" (1976:8). In one sense this criticism is directed toward the structuralist and idealist commitments of the research program that Guiteras Holmes's report represented. Currently, inductivist and materialist commitments have come to play a larger role in anthropologists' work on Mesoamerican social organization (see Collier 1975; Nutini 1976; Selby 1976). These commitments are not new, though. They can be found, for example, in Tax's *Penny Capitalism* (1953). But integrating statistical and normative orders of data as called for by Selby (1976:32), or, to put it differently, mixing quantitative and qualitative paradigms for research is difficult today as it was when the first *Heritage* volume was published.

In spite of the difficulty, postmarital residence is an ideal topic for attempting the integration of statistical and normative orders of data. On the one hand, residence is, for the most part, an easily verifiable event. On the other hand, residence is hedged up by normative rules. An integrative opportunity for theory exists since explanations in terms of residence rules that follow from considerations of kinship have generally failed. The exemplar that follows attempts to discover the relationship between the "logical configuration of kinship and behavior" (Selby 1976:33-34) in light of actual postmarital residence in Santiago Atitlán.

To begin with, the problem of describing residence choices is complicated by the need to operationalize these choices in a spatio-temporal frame. Terms proliferate to describe residential arrangements: household, houseful, premises, compound, and other terms.

As devices for censuses, these concepts are often useful, but they may not be valid entities to the natives described. Next, the questions of available alternatives, length of stay, coincident or necessary property transfers or property exclusions, and other factors may complicate the interpretation of apparently straightforward census results (see Godelier 1975). The difference between statistical descriptions of events and elicited normative rules concerning those same events leads some researchers to claim a "loose-structure" (see Gudeman 1976) for some societies, thus confounding inductivist and structuralist commitments. Worse yet, researchers depending on census or survey evidence may posit such structures as unilineal descent groups, lineages, patrilineal compounds, or other social structural features, when, in fact, the people described do not incorporate in their cultures the jural-political criteria that underlie the social theory of such corporate groups. This latter objection we will address in more detail.

The domestic environment becomes crucial to the examination of these issues because it is both a locale for the ongoing struggles of consumption and production, and a context in which reproduction and socialization take place. Precisely because of the absence of lineages and other kin-based units of jural status, the household becomes an important mediator of individual participation in the community at large.

In another sense the domestic activities of people are often the very stuff of fieldnotes: especially in Mesoamerica where the Catholic trinity, ritual kinship, and political and economic paternalism all so explicitly share the idiom of family. With all this interest it is indeed surprising, as Nutini notes, that domestic organization has been so diversely and incompletely treated.

An ideal experimental situation or case study which would elucidate the problems in Maya residence patterns would be one where the incidence of patrilocality or virilocality is high, similar "agnatic" sentiments and preferences are recorded, but the kinship system is bilateral. Santiago Atitlán, a Maya community located in the southwestern highlands of Guatemala, provides such a case. This town was intensively investigated by one of the authors (Gross) from June 1971 to November 1972 and the summer of 1973. At the time of the field study, Santiago boasted a population of approximately

13,000 persons, 95 percent of which were native Tzutujil speakers (to be referred to henceforth as "Atitecos"). Data collected on 266 residential alignments at marriage show that 67 percent were virilocal and the remaining 33 percent were uxorilocal. These frequencies are comparable to those communities argued to have patrilineal descent systems (see e.g., Villa 1945; Vogt and Ruz 1965; and Collier 1975). The Atiteco kinship system is strictly bilateral, however, and together with the statistical pattern of postmarital residence it is consonant with social forms of other non-Tzutujil-speaking populations in the western Guatemalan highlands (see e.g., Tax 1953; Hinshaw 1975; Warren 1978).

Atitecos' recorded sentiments, in addition to their explicitly stated preferences, are very similar to those argued to be indicative of patrilineal kinship. Unmarried males often cite numerous cases and situations that are attempts to underscore their rationale for avoiding uxorilocal *(pjay)* residence even though the expenses of such a union are less than half the cost of virilocality. These episodes generally depict the difficult relations one would have with the parents-in-law, such as hostility of the father-in-law toward the son-in-law, stinginess, spitefulness, jealousy, unreasonable demands, and the like. The prospect of uxorilocal residence is looked upon by most single Atiteco males as undesirable, if not horrendous. In fact, they suggest that this form of marital residence is practiced by either the poor, the unfortunate, or the orphaned. Similar observations have been made for neighboring communities (Bunzel 1952; Hinshaw 1975). Therefore, the examination of Atiteco postmarital residence patterns should be valuable in elucidating the issues discussed above.

The critical problem for most studies, rule based or otherwise, of residential alignments is to demonstrate a link between the observed frequencies and the underlying configuration of constraints and incentives that are hypothesized to generate them. The strength of the presumed links are then assessed mainly through the examination of the numerical data and by resort to notions of consistency. On both these tests the notion that residence patterns in Maya communities are the outcome of a particular type of kinship system or that they arise from particular economic or environmental pressures fails. Although there is a definite "agnatic" bias and no single Maya community, where numerical information is available, exhibits a frequency of virilocality under 55 percent (for example, Redfield and Rojas 1934; Villa 1945; Miller 1964; Vogt 1969; Nash 1970; Thompson 1974; Collier 1975), it is nevertheless true that the frequency of uxorilocality rarely falls below 20 percent. (We have never found an exception based on the material available to us. There may be such a community but it makes little difference.) The essential problem is that the same observations have been recorded on preferences, sentiments, and frequencies of postmarital residence choices found in communities suggested to have patrilineal kinship ideology (Villa 1945; Collier 1968, 1975; Vogt 1969) as in those communities shown to have bilateral kinship systems (see Nash 1970; Gross 1974; Hinshaw 1975). This point is crucial to the argument on kinship and residence for it calls into question the consistent relationship between the observed patterns of residence found among the Maya and the presumed effects of kinship or ecology for the pattern.

The subsequent analysis has three parts: first, the structural frameworks within which postmarital residence choices are made will be described. It is necessary to outline a number of critical features of Atiteco domestic group structure, kinship relations, and world view that taken compositely directly affect residence choices; secondly, we show how these structural frameworks produce residence choices; finally, we demonstrate how this analysis permits one to give a more adequate account of residence choices, of the subordinate uxorilocal element as well as of the dominant patrilocal pattern.

Although uxorilocal *(pjay)* residence is looked on by most Atiteco males with a good deal of distaste, this does not imply that it is necessarily either a social aberration or a recent by-product of economic or ecological pressures. A critical feature to note at the onset is that the practice of uxorilocal residence in Santiago is an institutionalized alternative to virilocality and, hence, a cultural norm (for a similar, but not identical, argument see Collier 1975:79 and elsewhere). This argument is supported by the observation that the last-born child *(ch'ip),* male or female, remains in the natal household at marriage and, thus, brings into it a spouse. Important to note is that this pattern is followed by the last-born child and not necessarily by the last surviving or remaining child, who may select from different options. Genealogical data reveal that the the male-to-female ratio of last born is about the same. There is no selective infanticide, nor do parents seem to have a sexual preference in their offspring. The ideal family, according to numerous informants, consists of two sons and two daughters, and the birth orders appear unimportant. Finally, uxorilocal residence is named and contrasted with virilocality as in the anthropologist's census question: "did you petition your wife or did you go into her house (hold)" *(ak'utun awxqayil o pjay at bnaqwa'?")*. In the context of marriage discussion, *pjay* indicates uxorilocality. (In other contexts it can refer to the household or to the community in general.) The evidence, then, is strong that uxorilocal residence is an institutionalized practice among the Atitecos, and there is much evidence to suggest that it is a widespread Maya phenomenon (Hunt and Nash 1967) which appears to have a good deal of antiquity at least among the Quiché (Miles 1957) and the Yucatan Maya (Scholes and Roys 1948). There is additional evidence for its existence among the Chortí (Wisdom 1940) and the contiguous rural Ladinos of eastern Guatemala (Kendall 1974).

It should also be noted at this point that the immediate postmarital choice on residence is limited to one of at most two possibilities: either the groom or the bride secedes from his or her household and joins that of the other spouse. Depending on birth order, (e.g., last born) residence choice may be even more restricted. Because marriage is only the first of a series of steps to full jural adulthood, residence in one set of parents' household does not end the couple's jural minority (for a greater elaboration of this point see Gross 1974). Why is it, then, that uxorilocal residence is regarded as highly undesirable by Atiteco males in light of the fact that it is permissible for all and may be required for one member of every sibling set? The subsequent analysis in attempting to explicate this question will show the pertinence of both an emic and an etic approach.

Structural Frameworks

DOMESTIC GROUP STRUCTURE

The domestic group or household *(-choch* or *-jay* depending on context, see Gross 1974) is the smallest political unit in Santiago. Each person's formal politicolegal position in the community is initially determined by reference to the household in which membership is held. A person can hold membership in only one household at any one time. The principal jural authority in this social unit is the male head *(ttixel)* who, along with his wife, established it. Each household is established by a conjugal pair following partition from a parental household. The mean time for partition falls between two and three years after marriage. Gross found that the vast majority of couples separated from the parental household after the birth of the first child. Through the act of formal partition, jural citizenship is accorded the couple and they, then, become the legal representatives of their own unit and its members (including themselves) in respect to the community. Although no ritual or ceremony was observed to indicate the change in status, it appears that parental consent to partition in the presence of their compadres is all that is publically required. There is no succession to household headship and, hence, the duration of a household is for the life of its founding conjugal pair. Married or unmarried members are jural minors and subject to the founding couple's authority for as long as they remain in the household.

Newly established households are viewed as economically independent and politically autonomous. Viewed from the political system, they are a new and independent source of personnel for community offices, the census, or for various ritual or community services. They are also economically independent in that they produce their own food and cook and eat it separately from that of the natal household. Thus, the new household is an independent production and consumption unit. There is a common labor force and a common purse that are controlled by the male and female heads of each household. All wages earned by members are put into the common fund for expenses such as marriage, baptisms, medical care, and the like. Finally, all members share a common hearth.

A critical feature of domestic group structure in regard to postmarital residence is that the parents in the household in which the couple is resident after marriage have the obligation and, as we shall see, the privilege, to help set up the independent household. A house site and dwelling, housewares, and some arable land are usually furnished the new household. This obligation is explicitly referred to several times in the marriage ceremony (Gross 1974:105 and elsewhere). A regular pattern observed is for a house to be built by the son's household before he becomes engaged or, at least, before the bride comes to reside in her new household. In the case of the uxorilocal pattern, nothing is quite so explicit or prepared so well in advance. Whatever the case may be, the dwelling, site, arable land, and furnishings are given the couple in usufruct *(-sip)* and not as inheritance *(-coch)*. Although the general pattern is for these possessions to become part of the offspring's inheritance at the parent's death, they may also be taken back if filial duties are not fulfilled. At this juncture, it is important to note that after partition has taken place the couple is no longer subject to the obligations attendant on membership in the parental household; rather, the obligations owed are based upon kinship or a "dyadic" relation structured by other factors, for example, holder-heir relationship (see Gross 1974).

KINSHIP AND INHERITANCE

Even though household membership may change, kinship and its associated sentiments, obligations, and expectations remain intact. This point is reflected by the prestations of food and other goods that are sent to parents on particular days of celebration such as Holy Week, Corpus Christi, All Souls, and others. In the early years of marriage, the parents expect only token gestures from their children. That is, the food that is sent may be only enough for one meal, if that. Whatever the prestation, it is symbolic of the offspring's continuing filial duties toward parents after household partition. Parents, in turn, are expected to offer counsel and provide some forms of assistance for children when required. As time progresses and the parents get older, however, more is expected from the children until the day is reached for *psman:* ideally, the parents receive food from each of their children on a regular daily basis (each child should supply the food for one week on a rotating basis among the siblings). It is common for at least one or more children to neglect this duty, especially daughters living virilocally and sons uxorilocally. Parents, on the other hand, are extremely important for their children's children, especially in the area of religious rituals and socialization. For example, it is the grandparents who organize and take the lead in the various "rites of passage" the grandchildren must observe; for example, they prepare for the occasion of the child's baptism by soliciting a *madrina* and provide the food and drink for the fiesta.

The important point concerning kinship for this inquiry is that the transmission of scarce resources (land, cattle, chattel, etc.) is from parent to child irrespective of residential propinquity or household membership (see Nash 1971; Collier 1975). Thus, the kinship relation and not household membership determines eligibility for inheritance. It should be remarked here, which is usually not mentioned in most studies (see Collier 1975), that inheritance is only one way to acquire such possessions. In fact, a number of gifts and settlements, both tied and untied, are transmitted to offspring (see Davis 1977: 182-85 for an explication of property transfer terminology). Other forms of dispersal of resources are renting land, sharecropping, purchasing land. Such arrangements may also be made in the lowlands with either Ladinos or other Indians. All involve a number of different property transfers and settlements, and all are closely controlled through inheritance and other settlements by virtue of kinship ties. Receiving and using ancestral land are, as noted by others (Bunzel 1952), however, extremely important to the Atitecos. As among other Maya, both males and females gain access to residential and arable land, chattel, and other heirlooms. Inheritance, then, is bilateral in Santiago, but property is not always evenly distributed among children or between the sexes. In fact, whether a child receives an inheritance at all depends to a large extent on whether the filial obligations have been fulfilled during the parents' lifetime. In the course of this study it was observed that daughters who went to live virilocally at marriage are often, though not always, disinherited of land and cattle. But it is not simply the case that giving a dowry, however small, disinherits the daughters. The reasons generally given for disinheritance were that the daughters had "forgotten their parents" or that "their husbands were hostile" or "disrespectful." Most studies have accepted these reasons and/or suggested spatial distance as the cause of daughters' disinheritance. If our analysis is correct, the reason, as we will show later, lies not only in fulfilling obligations of filial responsibilities but knowing who, in fact, controls the household resources necessary to fulfill such obligations. This point will be examined later in the analysis.

A very important point for our inquiry concerning inheritance is that spouses do not inherit each other's property. A spouse may hold, rent, farm, or exploit the possessions of a deceased spouse only until the legitimate offspring of the deceased holder are socially mature. There are cases where this does not obtain but they do not weaken the argument; they merely point out the complexity of property transfers in Santiago. Consequently, the estates of a husband and wife remain distinct for purposes of inheritance and legal control, although the land may be farmed jointly, and the products harvested are shared commonly.

WORLD VIEW

Male-Female Relations. A man without a wife, in Atiteco society, is never socially complete. Thus, widowers tend to remarry quickly (Vogt 1969) and male youths are generally married for the first time before twenty-one years of age. Without a wife, a man cannot hold political or ritual offices of any prestige. This includes widowers as well as single youths. In order to complete service in the cofradia system, for example, it is necessary to have a living, resident wife. The important role of the wife in complementing her husband has great antiquity among the Maya, and is not a recent development (see e.g., Gross 1978). Yet, given the central role of the wife in Maya society, women are considered to be inferior to men and they are not always regarded as fulfilling equal but separate roles. Male superiority is expressed in numerous ways, especially by association of man with the superior right side and woman, created from man's left side, according to Atiteco myth, associated with the more sinister elements in culture. Examples of this hierarchical differentiation include the facts that in church women sit to the left of the cross and men to the right and that women walk three or four paces behind their husbands. Women should never place themselves in a higher physical position in respect to their husbands, especially in the sexual act, for fear that it may weaken him and make him vulnerable to the attack of malevolent forces. Thus, a wife should never step over her husband while he is sleeping or lying down nor step over his clothing, tools, bed, and the like (see also Hinshaw 1975). The ideological separation of the sexes is further manifest in the person of the witch (*q'som*) who is often characterized in stories as a female who is out to destroy her husband. In such stories, women, as witches, place themselves in a physically superior position to their sleeping husbands by walking back and forth over his body twelve times, thereby weakening the husband and making him susceptible to misfortune. Witches appear to be the symbols of aggressiveness and express through their acts the converse of the ideal woman.

In the sphere of public affairs, the male head is in charge of the household, represents the members to the larger community, and has final decision over the members' activities. Although the female head *(teej)* directs the other females of the household and may be found to be the *de facto* head of the unit, it is still the *ttixel*, (male household head) who represents the household in the political community. It is the male who holds political or ritual offices in the community and in the role of household head has a voice in community affairs. Women hold ritual offices only as a complement to their husbands serving a cargo in a cofradia (there are some exceptions to this). Civil offices have no such complementary role for women. Important here for the problem of residence is that the ideal situation for an Atiteco male is to be in a clear and unambiguous position of control and authority over wife and family. A strong incentive for a male would be to establish a relationship with a woman that was clearly consistent with the ideological and symbolic order.

Land and the Ancestors. The transmission of land from one person to another in agricultural societies has long been viewed as a crucial factor affecting residential alignments as well as constituting a reflection, if not a determinant, of the kinship system (e.g., Morgan 1871, and more recently Goody 1976). The importance of the inheritance of land for the structure of the domestic field of social relations is rarely disputed by Mesoamerican scholars. In Maya communities, where one usually finds that the predominant statistical pattern of land inheritance is from father to sons or other male relatives coupled with an explicit preference for 'ancestral' lands and where the residential alignments seem to favor, statistically if not ideally, a 'patrilocal' pattern, the conclusions reached by anthropologists are usually one of the following: (1) the 'cause' of such a pattern is a 'patrilineal descent' ideology or (2) the 'outcome' or 'result' of such a pattern is a 'patrilineal descent' ideology (for Mesoamerican examples on the former view see Vogt and Ruz 1965, and for the latter see Collier 1975). Although it is not our intention to enter

into a debate on the primacy of the chicken or the egg, it is worth
noting that a logical or functional connection between inheritance,
residence, and some sort of value placed on 'ancestors,' on the one
hand, and unilineal kinship system, on the other (see Evans-Pritchard
1965; Fortes 1969:276 and elsewhere) has never been shown. The
confusion or problem seems to rest, as Fortes (1969:277) suggests
on a "failure to discriminate between the observer's construct and
concepts, on the one hand, and the actor's rules and procedures, on
the other. . . ." The anthropological issue is this: under what circumstances is it appropriate or not appropriate to apply such concepts as "descent," "unilineal" group, or others especially when such
usage carries the full implication of comparability to the African or
other specified models (Fortes 1969:277-78).

A good deal of ambiguity has arisen in the Mesoamerican literature from a failure to employ such concepts consistently. For example, one finds the term *patrilineal group* used to designate an aggregate
of persons related to each other not only as father and sons but also
father-in-law and sons-in-law or daughters-in-law or mother's brother
and sister's son and the like. Moreover, while the term *patrilineal
inheritance* is usually employed to designate the transmission of property between father and sons, in reading Mesoamerican studies more
closely one discovers that daughters also inherit, as well as others
such as adoptees, though sons and adoptees are found to inherit most
arable land, but not exclusively so (see Bunzel 1952; Vogt 1969;
Collier 1975). Thus, we find that the Mesoamerican uses of these
concepts are not only questionable conceptually but wrong empirically. The analysis in this section should help elucidate the relation
between the observed pan-Maya pattern of emphasizing "ancestral"
land and kinship.

In Santiago, as in many Maya communities in Chiapas, Mexico
and Guatemala, there are both communal lands and privately held
or "owned" land. Consequently, there are a number of ways by which
a person may acquire land *(-uleu)*. As a jural adult (i.e. the head of a
household) one is eligible to rent *(-kaj)* communal land *(pbaldi)* at
the annual cost of ten cents per *cuerda* (approximately one-fifth of
an acre). The yet remaining arable, communal lands that are not in
production are located on the upper reaches of the volcanoes San Pedro

and Toliman. These particular lands are not very productive or would not be good agricultural lands owing to the steepness of the terrain, thinness of the soil, and the problem of erosion from runoff during the rainy season. These lands have remained forested although some trees are harvested, primarily for firewood. Some land on the higher slopes of San Pedro was cleared for maize farming during the period of field work. Normal swidden techniques were employed: trees were felled, and the undergrowth was burned. Most people, however, simply use these higher areas to collect firewood, herbs, and to hunt birds and opossum.

In addition to communal lands, a householder can rent land from another Atiteco. In such cases, the cost is usually a share of the harvest. Widows without able male children and spinsters living alone have no other recourse but to rent out their lands for a share of the harvest because of a strict sexual division of labor with regard to agriculture. Finally, land may be rented from Ladino landlords in the southern lowlands. Such land, located primarily in the municipio of Chicacao, Department of Suchitepequez, is highly productive, yielding two maize harvests annually. *Sacate* (a grass or hay) is planted with the first corn crop, and constitutes the only rent for the use of the land over the entire year. Generally, kinsmen or friends will rent contiguous plots (size depending on need and availability), thus ensuring friendly neighbors, traveling companions along "dangerous" roads, and persons to rely upon for assistance during the planting and harvesting seasons.

Since land can be individually owned in Santiago, it can also be sold *(-k'ayixic)* to any other person, Atiteco or Ladino. More commonly, however, land sales are restricted to Atitecos and most frequently to kinsmen *(ch'alal)*. Depending on the type of land (garden, bean and/or maize fields, orchard, etc.) and its location, prices vary from a few quetzales (dollars) to over a thousand quetzales per *cuerda*. The more expensive land is residential *(-rlgar)* and lakeshore property; the latter may be used either for truck gardens or chalets (lots purchased by Ladinos on which to build summer homes). The least expensive land is located on the higher northeast reaches of the volcano Toliman which is found at some distance (9 km.) from the community.

The selling and buying *(-loq')* of land among the Atitecos is a very common practice for both the rich and the poor. Any excess capital is often used to purchase additional land. On the other hand, if cash is needed to offset some unanticipated expense, land is the only asset or commodity that an Atiteco can turn into cash quickly either as collateral for a loan or by direct sale. Thus, if a major illness should befall a family and specialists with special medicines are required, land would be sold, preferably to a kinsman, if cash were not available in the household purse to pay for such expenses. Cases have been recorded of elderly persons who have divided their land among the offspring, yet retained a parcel of land that was to be sold at their death to pay for the funeral expenses. A proper burial, including all the rituals at home, church, and cemetery is of critical importance to Atitecos even though it is expensive. Although one of the offspring would more than likely purchase such land, there have been cases and situations where such land has been sold to another Atiteco.

Thus, transactions involving land are a regular feature of Atiteco life. Land is both an investment and an insurance against future needs. We have found that the amount of purchased land as a share of a family's estate varies from 0 to 90 percent and the percentage appearsto vary with the phase of the developmental cycle. Thus, all household heads from the sample with at least one married child had acquired some land through a commercial transaction, but a couple who had just partitioned from a parental household would have only the land and dwelling given to them by one set of parents. It is reasonable to expect, then, that at some point in the life of an Atiteco, land will be purchased or sold, or both by that person. What is the role of the "ancestors" *(erelaj)* in such a pattern?

In the past, at least, the Atiteco and other highland Maya of Guatemala had a strong identification with their ancestors and with particular regions. This facet of Maya life is clearly expressed in the *Popol Vuh* and the *Annals of the Cakchiquels* which lay claim to lands based upon ancestral titles. This sentiment and view is still quite evident in communities of this region. Santiago's participation in this system reflected in the shrines that serve as boundary markers at major crossroads. These markers delineate the town's land base, which is protected by the ancestors who live in the shrines as well as in the various *cerros* (hills) that line the border of the region. Although membership in the Atiteco community and access to land were based in the past on showing descent from an ancestor, it did not matter which line of descent a person used or how many times descent lines were crossed. The political community was, in effect, recruited through bilateral or cumulative filiation (Gross 1978).

Today, the boundaries and mode of recruitment are not so clear-cut, but, in respect to land, there are still strong sentiments and preferences for ancestral land. Such land, if sold, should only be sold or given to close kinsmen, that is, a descendant or one who shares a common great grandfather or great grandmother. Although, at a very general level, all Atitecos claim to be kinsmen in respect to the outside world (their common expression to denote this is the phrase *qch'alalqi* ["we are brothers" or "kinsmen"]), within the community, only those persons who can detail their kinship to a common, specifiable ancestor, if descent is not apparent, are felt to be eligible to buy, sell, rent, or trade ancestral land. If land is purchased or sold to a "nonkinsman" a ritual is usually performed, in addition to the legal ceremony, which informs and propitiates the ancestors. Otherwise, Atitecos say, misfortune may befall both buyer and seller. It would seem then, that only land that can be claimed through filiation, or land that has been ritually released, is actually farmable, from an individual's viewpoint. Consequently, land given to a wife at inheritance or household partition might not be looked upon as a real windfall from the husband's point of view. In fact, neglect of wife's property is quite common in Santiago and elsewhere in the highlands (see Bunzel 1952; Hinshaw 1975; Warren 1978).

We mentioned above that a wife residing virilocally has little chance of inheriting land or chattel unless she fulfills her filial obligations. If our analysis is correct, the reason for some daughters not inheriting their share of the parental estate is not merely a function of distance from their natal household. Rather, it appears to be a function of who controls the household resources. In the case of virilocality, the husband controls the household resources and he determines if they shall be used for fulfilling his spouse's filial obligations. This would seem to hold true for the reverse case of uxorilocal residence as well. If the essential conflict in a family is over the rights to control the productive and reproductive resources, as many social theorists suggest (see Fortes 1958:3), then the husband, in a virilo-cal situation, would not necessarily welcome the wife's potential source for independence particularly in such a system where he would have no authority over it and cultural reasons for not using it. This point will become clearer in the following section.

How Structural Frameworks Produce Residence Choices

To begin with, it may be observed that the requirements placed upon the last-born child *(ch'ip)* are institutionalized ways of ensur-ing each married couple (household heads) of some assistance in old age and a proper ritual passage at death. Gross did not find a single case where the last born seceded from the natal household at marriage. The last born is well socialized into his or her responsibilities by the time he is ready to marry. The reward for fulfilling these expecta-tions is that the last-born child will inherit the site and dwelling of his parents and often the chattel property such as money, cattle, jewel-ry, and the like. In theory, all such land and chattel should be di-vided equally among all the surviving offspring, but the parents often save choice land from division to ensure their own maintenance and proper funeral which would devolve to *ch'ip,* if surviving.

The position of the last born in the social structure appears to be a neat structural way of handling the problem of status and security in old age. This practice, however, is affected by demographic variables. First, there is a high mortality rate in Santiago among children up to age 6 and especially between birth and one year where mortality rates of 40 percent are not exceptional (see Hinshaw, Pyeatt, and Habicht 1972 for rates in other towns around Lake Atitlán). As a consequence of this mortality rate among children, not all last-born children will survive, implying that the institutionalized mechanism of ensuring some security in old age does not operate for all couples nor even in a majority of cases.

An additional demographic factor is that not all couples will suc-ceed in having children. In the event of a barren union, divorce and remarriage are options that are usually followed until offspring are produced or a single person with children (previously divorced) is married. In cases where a couple have no surviving offspring, they will adopt an heir who will fulfill the obligations of the last born. The quest for an heir can also be interpreted as the result of pressure from the political-ritual community. It appears that only persons who have children, real or adopted, hold offices. Additionally, only couples who have assisted children in establishing independent households have sufficient public stature for serious consideration of their arguments in public gatherings. The Atiteco expression is that such peoples' "words have meaning." As a consequence, one would expect to find each married couple ensuring that at least one of their offspring or adopted children will remain in the household at marriage. This hypothesis is borne out by both the statistical and normative data on marriage and residence (see Gross 1974). Finally, in cases where there are only daughters, difficulties sometimes arise given the normative and statistical preference for virilocality. This preference will be discussed below.

In the majority of the cases, there are a number of surviving offspring who will marry, and postmarital residence becomes problematic for both parents and children. Ideally, all Atitecos would like to have their sons bring wives into the household, and their daughters bring husbands (see discussion in Wisdom 1940 for the Chortí). Owing to economic factors, however, very few are able to achieve the ideal. Indeed, setting up a couple in an independent household is very expensive. Even for couples who reside uxorilocally, the capital and material outlay by the bride's father is far greater than the benefits received from the son-in-law as an additional labor resource or even as a potential wage earner (see Gross 1974 for a detailed discussion). Indeed, some parents find it difficult to set up one child and almost impossible to assist more than one. In general, parents will attempt to assist as many children as possible in establishing an independent household. Aside from statistical support for this finding, additional confirmation is found in observations that rich families tend not to intermarry with other rich families. Among the Atitecos, as elsewhere around the lake (see Hinshaw 1975), there is a general sentiment often expressed that one should seek a poor husband or wife. Atitecos argue that they work harder, expect less, and are more grateful for that which they receive. Gross found that marriage negotiations with poorer families involved fewer visits before permission for marriage was granted, meaning less expense.

An important point concerning marriage negotiations is that the central issue is where the couple will live after marriage and not necessarily if they should marry. Marriage negotiations among relative equals in the economic and political sense can be long and grueling where the father of the bride may find the prospective son-in-law acceptable only if he would reside *pjay,* or uxorilocally. This is particularly true of families with only daughters, where there is an explicit attempt to bring in at least one son-in-law. Where there is resistance to an uxorilocal arrangement, elopement is the institutionalized way out of the stalemate (see Gross 1974). Elopement can only take place if the parents of the boy agree, since it will be they who are legally responsible and must pay any fines or spend time in jail. From this discussion a testable hypothesis emerges: the incidence of elopement should increase as the distribution of wealth becomes more even as a result of more widely available wage labor and other sources of income. On the surface, Paul's study of elopement (1963) appears to support the above hypothesis.

Finally, male resistance to uxorilocal residence helps explain why last-born daughters find it difficult to marry, which is reflected in the average age of engagement: last born—22 years; others—16 years (Gross 1974). Additionally, there appears to be a high rate of spinsterhood among the last born. In fact, the only spinsters in the sample were last-born females.

A direct consequence of setting up one's married child with a house site, dwelling, housewares, arable land, and perhaps more, is that the child and spouse will be under the jural control of the parents, since lands are tied and the child is given only rights in usufruct which may be rescinded if filial obligations are not fulfilled. The implication is that the larger the number of children assisted in establishing their own independent households the greater the security in old age. The jural relationships established between parents and children through such prestations are binding even though household partition has occurred, thereby ending the jural minority of the children and the obligations of household membership. Thus, postmarital residence, where bilateral kinship is the rule, provides a way for parents to maintain control over the children even though group or lineage bonds are nonexistent.

Residence Choices Analyzed

It is clear from the preceding description that a couple's decision on postmarital residence is not one of choice or the weighing of advantages strictly from their perceived needs. More accurately, the decision on postmarital residence is, first of all, not arbitrary but an option between two alternatives. Furthermore, the last-born child has no alternatives. Beyond these constraints, the persons who make the decision are not the newly marrying couple but, rather, the heads of their households. The latter have the jural authority, pay for the various engagement and wedding expenses, and provide for the couple's support after the marriage; that is, one of the families must be willing to provide such support. Crucially, it is the household head's position in the community as well as security in old age that are most directly affected by the postmarital residence patterns of their offspring. For a clear understanding of postmarital residence in Santiago, then, there are two major areas of interest which are crucial—that of the prospective groom and bride, and that of their respective household heads.

In general, Atiteco males find uxorilocal residence undesirable. Those particular males who in fact reside uxorilocally have mixed feelings, with negative ones predominating. Those interviewed described their situation as difficult and filled with tension, especially between them and their fathers-in-law. For example, one young groom related that he awoke one morning with his father-in-law's hands around his throat screaming that the son-in-law was too arrogant and should get out. According to the groom, the fact that the son-in-law was making one quetzal per day and the father-in-law was earning nothing apparently caused much conflict within the household. A nephew of the father-in-law also supported this view.

In many cases, however, young men have had parallel encounters with their parents; relations are filled with strife and tension, which appears to make the possibility of uxorilocal residence more palatable. Yet, the actual cause of such tension may be the result of parental pressure on the child to seek a *pjay* (uxorilocal) marriage because they are either unable to meet the expenses or do not feel obligated to expend the household resources for a *k'ut* (petition) marriage. There are a number of reasons for not feeling obligated, all of which center on the son's cash earnings history (see Gross 1974 for a discussion). Whatever the actual cause for uxorilocal residence may be, it remains clear that Atiteco males, in general, find such an arrangement less than ideal and, at best, a second choice, although for some it may be the only choice open to them.

Considered in the light of the social structure and its institututions, the bases of these negative sentiments can be clearly perceived. First, the house site, dwelling, arable land, housewares, and other items given to the couple at household partition remain, in the case of uxorilocality, under the authority, if not control, of the bride's father. The son-in-law remains under the thumb, so to speak, even after household partition. At the death of the father-in-law, the son-in-law does not finally succeed to the former's position of authority, rather, it is the daughter (wife) who is the heir and the one who will succeed to the jural authority over the property. In a real sense, the wife will be the household head rather than the husband, at least in terms of property relations. Although sufficient data are not available to make any definitive conclusions, it has been observed in Santiago that a wife's inherited arable land was often neglected until offspring were old enough to work it. This practice appears to hold irrespective of whether residence is virilocal or uxorilocal. Additionally, husbands who reside uxorilocally immediately after marriage, and not at some later date, rarely were found to farm their wife's land even when otherwise landless. Their economic input was derived largely from wages earned through craft specialization, agricultural labor, and/or trade. To what extent the reluctance to exploit the wife's property is related to Atiteco ideas about ancestors and land use is not clear. Many Atitecos say that such beliefs and practices are no longer critical. Yet, the reluctance to exploit such land is present although economic gains are obvious. Whatever the case may be, the husband is in the position of a tenant in respect to his wife's property. The wife is in a *de facto* position of authority because of the property relations established. The husband, then, must accept her potential authority and her ascendency over him. This position of inferiority is not consistent with the ideal objective for Atiteco males. He is not the clear and unambiguous head of his household.

Finally, when residing uxorilocally, a man's right to remain on the land in the event that his wife predeceases him is contingent on their producing children. This also holds for women residing virilocally. A man living on his wife's land will not, as a rule, gain jural control over it nor over the children through it. On the other hand, the children will gain control over the mother's property and, thus, they gain a kind of ascendancy over their father. The following account will clearly illustrate the point.

Axwan, at the time of the field study, was a man about 54 years old. By 1972, he had resided uxorilocally for about 35 years. In 1962, after his parents-in-law had died and his wife had received her inheritance, Axwan opened up a small cantina selling both legal and illegal rum. Before this, he was a trader purchasing fruits and vegetables in Santiago and selling them in the fincas on the south coast. In early 1972, his wife died unexpectedly. The cantina was closed for mourning, as was the wife's compound upon which the cantina rested. Although Axwan was very reluctant to give up the cantina to his son, he had no choice in the matter when the son began to push his claim. Even though settled out of court by kinsmen, Axwan refused to talk to the son after the transfer. Moreover, the son's action forced his father (Axwan) to take up the trade business again, since he had no other source of income. His children did not appear ready to support him at that point.

This case aptly illustrates the problems that a male can encounter in uxorilocal residence. After household partition, the wife has a *de facto* ascendency over the husband in terms of control over property. In addition, his children will have ascendency over him should his wife predecease him as in the case of Axwan. It should now be clear why Atiteco males argue that only the poor, the landless, or the orphaned would tolerate a situation where the father-household head is in a subordinate position. Symbolically, ideologically, and sociologically, the relationships between husband and wife and between father and children are skewed. Virilocality is preferred by men because they are in a clear position of control and authority over the land and household, which is more consistent with the structural incentives outlined above.

If the decision about postmarital residence were made strictly by the groom, virilocality would no doubt be the choice with only a

few exceptions. If the bride had a choice, uxorilocality would predominate. Neither the bride nor the groom has that much choice,
however, because they must reside in one or the other parental household. The actual choice of postmarital residence is a negotiated decision made by the respective household heads. The groom's parents
will always inform their son well in advance of his courting if they
are willing to support his petitioning a wife, or whether he should
plan on finding a wife and father-in-law who will take him in. Thus,
each son knows before he begins to court whether postmarital residence will be virilocal or uxorilocal. Elopement points this out clearly. Before the boy can elope it is necessary that he have, minimally,
his father's approval, for it is the latter who will suffer any legal
reprisal.

   Parents, in general, would like to assist each of their children to
establish an independent household, but the probability of this hap-
pening is slight, given the economic constraints outlined above. All
things being equal (if they ever are), sons are preferred over sons-in-
law. However, a son-in-law who comes from a poor family is considered to be very attractive for a daughter when uxorilocality is at
stake. From the standpoint of the social structure, a son is the ideal
recipient. The relationships between the son and the parents is structured first and foremost by the bonds of kinship, implying particular and filial obligations. The prestations of property, real and chattel,
given at household partition perpetuates a certain degree of economic
and political subordination which is normally lost with secession from
the household. Thus, the kinship tie is reinforced with a property
relationship which anchors the bonds more firmly. On the other
hand, the relationship with the son-in-law is primarily contractual
in nature and primarily between the spouses, although respect should
always be shown toward the parents of the spouse. The son-in-law
has no vested interest in the property given at partition since he will
never "own" it or control it. Thus, the relationships between the
son-in-law and the wife's parents have little moral content, and not
a lot of advantage for either in real economic terms.

   Another concern is for a respected adult career, and a man's power
and prestige are largely dependent upon the number of persons he
can rely upon for political, economic and/or moral support. For example, a man, as he gets older, would like to sponsor a saint into his

house or some ritual event, or the like. The cost is high and, if assumed alone, often prohibitive. But if he can call upon a number of persons for money or assistance through labor or some other contribution, then his ability to sponsor such an occasion is more likely. The ties and obligations established through kinship but reinforced by prestations of property provide the core of a man's personal following or support group. This core consists largely of offspring and their spouses, although some collaterals may be included, especially in cases when a sibling's children are adopted. The binding of such kinsmen early on through the prestations of property at household partition provides the actual core of a man's personal network that he can and will call upon for support not only in old age but also to fulfill a political-ritual ambition or for economic assistance. Controlling postmarital residence is an important way to ensure a core of supporters and control over them after household partition. During the period when children are members in the parental household, the parents' jural and economic authority over them is clear. This authority is maintained in the absence of lineage and other corporate kin-group ties through assisting children to establish independent households. Ironically, by providing the means to become independent, the parents continue their jurally dominant position. This analysis explains more clearly the nature of the compound. It is neither an extended family nor a corporate descent group as is often suggested. Obligations are only owed to the natal household heads and not to other members.

The predominance of virilocality, then, is the outcome of a number of features of Atiteco life. The factors which influence postmarital residence include ideology, economics, kinship, and politicolegal relations. The outcome revolves around the attempt by Atiteco household heads to maintain the domestic dependence of children when marriage, partition, and daily economic independence create new structural relations and imply a new locale.

The implications of this study for monocausal or rule-based theories should be clear. Although economic considerations and affective and jural relations are important determinants of residential alignment, they are not the only factors. It is necessary to examine such basic societal features as kinship, marriage, and citizenship which give rise to such surface manifestations. It is misleading and wrong to analyze residence patterns in terms of discrete rules or types that come into effect at marriage (Fortes 1958:3). Residence patterns are the result of choices based upon a number of incentives as well as of structural constraints that are past, present, and future. A single rule or a single incentive, such as economic greed, would presuppose too rigid a system to be able to respond to varied conditions. The question that must be addressed is what is the structural context in terms of which choices on residence arise and are made, and, importantly, by whom are they made?" The latter point of the question—who makes the choice—is rarely addressed, not only in the Maya literature on residence but elsewhere. The general approach is to assume, often mistakenly, that the groom or the couple makes the choice, as it is assumed to be in the U.S.—which, it should be noted, though the U.S. process is not all that clear. (For an example from the Maya literature, see Collier 1975).

The present analysis offers a more complete approach to the examination of residence. Rather than resting the analysis on either a rule of residence that somehow comes into effect at marriage, or describing the choices of individuals attempting to maximize their economic position in the marketplace, or their mechanistic responses to factors in the environment, our approach attempts to analyze in detail the constraints and incentives that set the conditions and determine the options available. By narrowing the field of choices to a manageable few, they become more predictable. By focusing exclusively on amount of land available or other economic variables, we would have missed essential factors in Atiteco residential alignments. The key was to determine who controls both productive and reproductive resources at various phases. This goal led to a focus on the interests of fathers who in fact make the final decision regarding postmarital residence. The household heads, the fathers and mothers, will bear the expenses of a marriage including assisting the couple to independence, but the parents, and the fathers in particular, have a vested interest in determining that at least one of their children brings in a spouse at marriage. Preferably, as many children as possible should bring in spouses because it adds to the potential power and authority of an Atiteco father in the community. It thereby becomes possible for a man to pass through the cofradia or other positions of prestige and authority within the community.

In conclusion, this approach to the analysis of residential alignments is more powerful than previous models in that it explains more
material. It draws together data that seem to be disparate and un-
connected. The approach not only accounts for uxorilocal residence
as well as the predominant virilocal pattern. It also explains such
phenomena as spinsterhood, and by implication bachelorhood, late
marriage of last-born women, a function of the witch, intergen-
erational and husband-wife relations, ancestors, land-tenure issues,
and more. Finally, elopement is more clearly understood as an institutional mechanism, rather than as an anomalous event, that has
become more prevalent due to a break with tradition, as some scholars have suggested (e.g. Woods and Graves 1973).

REFERENCES

Bunzel, R.
1952   *Chichicastenango: A Guatemalan Village* (Seattle: University of
        Washington Press).
Collier, G.
1968   "Land Inheritance and Land Use in a Modern Maya Communi-
        ty" (Ph.D. diss., Harvard University).
1975   *Fields of the Tzotzil* (Austin: University of Texas Press).
Davis, J.
1977   *People of the Mediterranean: An Essay in Comparative Social Anthro-
        pology* (London: Routledge & Kegan Paul).
Evans-Pritchard, E. E.
1965   *The Position of Women in Primitive Society and Other Essays in Social
        Anthropology* (New York: Free Press).
Fortes, M.
1958   "Introduction," in *The Developmental Cycle of Domestic Groups*,
        ed. Jack Goody (Cambridge: University Press).
1969   *Kinship and the Social Order* (Chicago: Aldine Press).
Godelier, M.
1975   "Modes of Production, Kinship and Demographic Structures,"
        in *Marxist Analyses and Social Anthropology*, ed. M. Bloch (New
        York: John Wiley & Sons).
Goodenough, W.
1956   "Residence Rules," *Southwestern Journal of Anthropology* 12:22-37.

Goody, J.
1976   *Production and Reproduction: A Comparative Study of the Domestic Domain* (Cambridge: University Press).
Gross, J. J.
1974   "Domestic Group Structure in a Mayan Community of Guatemala" (Ph.D. diss., University of Rochester).
1978   "Marriage and Family among the Maya," in *Family and Kinship in Middle America and the Caribbean,* ed. A. Marks and R. Romer (Leiden: Royal Institute of Linguistics and Anthropology).
Gudeman, S.
1976   *Relationships, Residence and the Individual: A Rural Panamanian Community* (Minneapolis: University of Minnesota Press).
Hinshaw, R. E.
1975   *Panajachel: A Guatemalan Town in Thirty Year Perspective* (Pittsburgh: University of Pittsburgh Press).
Hinshaw, Robert, Patrick Pyeatt, and Jean-Pierre Habicht
1972   "Environmental Effects on Child-Spacing and Population Increase in Highland Guatemala," *Current Anthropology* 13:216-30.
Hunt, E. and Nash, J.
1967   "Local and Territorial Units," in *Social Anthropology,* ed. M. Nash. Vol. 6 of *The Handbook of Middle American Indians,* ed. R. Wauchope (Austin: University of Texas Press).
Kendall, C.
1974   "Filiation and Brotherhood: Compadrazgo in Esquipulas Guatemala" (Ph.D. diss., University of Rochester).
LaFarge, O.
1974   *Santa Eulalia: The Religion of a Cuchumatan town* (Chicago: University of Chicago Press).
Miles, S. W.
1957   "The Sixteenth-century Polkom-Maya: A Documentary Analysis of Social Structure and Archaeological Setting," *Transactions of the American Philosophical Society* 47:4.
Miller, F.
1964   "Tzotzil Domestic Groups," *Journal of the Royal Anthropological Institute* 94:172-82.
Morgan, L. H.
1871   *Systems of Consanguinity and Affinity of the Human Family.* Vol. 17 of *Smithsonian Contributions to Knowledge* (Washington, D.C.: Smithsonian Institution).
Murdock, G.
1949   *Social Structure* (New York: Macmillan & Co.).

Nash, J.
1970   *In the Eyes of the Ancestors: Belief and Behavior in a Mayan Commu-*
         nity (New Haven: Yale University Press).
Nutini, H.
1967   "A Synoptic Comparison of Mesoamerican Marriage and Family
         Structure," *Southwestern Journal of Anthropology* 23:383-404.
1976   "Introduction: The Nature and Treatment of Kinship in Meso-
         america," in *Essays on Mexican Kinship,* ed. Hugo G. Nutini,
         Pedro Carrasco, and James M. Taggart (Pittsburgh: University
         of Pittsburgh Press).
Paul, B. D.
1963   "Changing Marriage Patterns in a Highland Guatemalan Com-
         munity," *Southwestern Journal of Anthropology* 19:131-48.
Redfield, R., and A. Villa Rojas
1934   *Chan Kom: A Maya Village* (Washington, D.C.: Carnegie Insti-
         tution).
Romney, A. Kimball
1967   "Kinship and Family," in *Social Anthropology,* ed. M. Nash.
         Vol. 6 of *Handbook of Middle American Indians,* ed. R. Wau-
         chope (Austin: University of Texas Press).
Scholes, France V., and Ralph L. Roys
1948   *The Maya Chontal Indians of Acalan-Tixchel: A Contribution to the*
         History and Ethnography of the Yucatan Peninsula. Carnegie Insti-
         tution of Washington, Publication 560 (Washington, D.C.).
Selby, H.
1976   "The Study of Social Organization in Traditional Mesoamerica,"
         in *Essays on Mexican Kinship,* ed. Hugo G. Nutini, Pedro Car-
         rasco, and James M. Taggart (Pittsburgh: University of Pitts-
         burgh Press).
Stern, L.
1973   "Intra-household Movement in a Ladino village of Southern
         Mexico," *Man* (new series) 83:393-415.
Tax, S.
1952   *Heritage of Conquest: The Ethnology of Middle America* (Glencoe,
         Ill: Free Press).
1953   *Penny Capitalism: A Guatemalan Indian Economy.* Carnegie Insti-
         tution of Washington, Publication 128 (Washington, D.C.).
Thompson, Richard A.
1974   *The Winds of Tomorrow* (Chicago: University of Chicago Press).
Villa, R. A.
1945   *The Maya of East Central Quintana Roo.* Carnegie Institution of
         Washington, Publication 559 (Washington, D.C.).

Vogt, E. Z.
1965   "Structural and Conceptual Replication in a Zinacantán Culture," *American Anthropologist* 67:342-53.
1969   *Zinacantán: A Maya Community in the Highlands of Chiapas* (Cambridge, Mass.: Belknap Press of Harvard University).
Vogt, E. Z. and A. Ruz
1965   *Desarrollo cultural de los Mayas* (Mexico: Universidad Nacional Autónoma de México).
Wagley, C.
1949   *The Social and Religious Life of a Guatemalan Village,* Memoirs of the American Anthropological Association, no. 58 (Menasha, Wis.).
Warren, Kay B.
1978   *The Symbolism of Subordination* (Austin: University of Texas Press).
Wisdom, C.
1940   *The Chorti Indians of Guatemala* (Chicago: University of Chicago Press).
Woods, C. M. and T. D. Graves
1973   *The Process of Medical Changes in a Highland Guatemalan Town* (Los Angeles: University of California, Latin American Center).

Section III

Symbolism and Ideology
Some Recent Approaches

Introduction

The papers in this section all deal with symbols, a battered word, to be sure, the overuse of which demonstrates the anthropologist's incessant quest for meaning. The anthropologists represented in this volume pursue meaning in symbol and structure in ideology. They do so in a more direct sense than the anthropologists at the first Heritage of Conquest symposium. In that earlier time period, religious matters were described (as beliefs and practices) rather than analyzed (as symbols and ideologies). But a foreign context makes the search for and discovery of meanings difficult. Indeed, important symbols are most often inscrutable to the casual observer. This then, is the contribution of long-term intensive fieldwork: to provide an insider's view of the security and special knowledge of the cultural traditions that attract hordes of tourists to Mexico and Guatemala.

But success in such studies is often elusive. Scholars may fall into the trap of the survival theory of ideas, or use a simple diffusion model to account for their presence. More successful efforts seek linguistic models of cognition or careful descriptions of social discourse to explain the myths and tales, the ideas of good and ill fortune, as well as the everyday and also the more esoteric life worlds constructed by these cultures. In one sense we come closest to touching the peoples of Mesoamerica in this section, for here we can try on their ideas for size.

Tedlock's paper demonstrates how many anthropologists had been insensitive to the richness of a foreign tradition. The apartness and distinctiveness, the logic of community and ethnic distinctiveness are woven into the play of the diverse traditions found in Momostenango. The phenomenologists that Tedlock cites have helped a generation of sociologists and social philosophers "suspend" disbelief long enough to discover the numerous life worlds that surrounded them in their own cultures. Perhaps Tedlock's novel usage will aid anthropologists working in Mesoamerica as well. Tedlock points out that the symbols of Momostenango are not blended or syncretized. Rather, they are compartmentalized into distinctive, dialectically interactive categories. They comprise, in fact, the models for indigenous action (to borrow from Geertz) that maintain Indian identity.

Crumrine's paper on the Mayo applies the symbolic analytical techniques of Victor Turner to this Sonoran people. The paper addresses the question of alternative interpretations of ritual acts and demonstrates how, through careful analysis, single, more convincing interpretations can be found. This is important since the problem of multiple interpretations has been a stumbling block for symbolic studies.

To be sure, the Mayo live outside the traditional boundaries of Kirchoff's Mesoamerica, although they are within the ethnographic area of Middle America. Nevertheless, the root metaphor that Crumrine explicates, the Holy Family, is certainly found throughout Mexico and Guatemala, and in much of the region down to and including Panama. These cultural parallels tend to confirm Salovesh's unease with rigidly drawn geocultural boundaries. As in Tedlock's paper, Crumrine shows that the local meaning of events is not just borrowed from Catholic church theology. It has an indigenous meaning that is validated and verified through its structural isomorphisms with family and communal organization.

Méndez Domínguez's paper steps back from this intensive local ethnographic approach and attempts a comparative ethnology of folk medical beliefs and practices for Guatemala. The ethnological tradition—culture mapping, if you will—never reached fruition in Guatemala. Community studies, as Méndez Domínguez points out, left many sections of Guatemala uncharted. Méndez Domínguez brings to this renewed trait mapping the formal logic of French structuralist thought, which he applies to the rapidly growing area of medical anthropology.

While the semiotic tradition is present in Méndez Domínguez's article, it is the key to the analysis Hawkins offers. Hawkins's contribution discusses Ladino and Indian cultures as a single linked entity. This position is intimated at the social level via notions of state penetration (Section I), but Hawkins discusses how the distinctive ethnic premises are forged into a cultural whole that nevertheless maintains ethnic diversity.

In Section II, the essentialist-formalist distinction was applied to theories of kinship. The distinction can also be applied to ethnic identity. Is there an essence, unique to an ethnic group? Or do formal operators such as opposition or complementarity at the micro- and macrolevels determine apparently unique group characteristics? Couched this way many would opt for Hawkins's formalist position, but Hawkins demonstrates how the definition of culture framed by Redfield has resulted in anthropologists having seen Mesoamerica in essentialist terms and that it impeded their ability to see Mesoamerica in formalist terms. In the conclusion of his paper, Hawkins captures a feeling widely shared among the participants in the second Heritage of Conquest symposium: a desire to break out of old interpretations, while maintaining a shared disciplinary context for research.

9

A Phenomenological Approach to Religious Change in Highland Guatemala

Barbara Tedlock
School of American Research
and
Tufts University

Today, anthropologists in highland Guatemalan communities may easily observe the indigenous people entering the local Roman Catholic church, or perhaps carrying saints around in processions. If they are aware of what day it is on the 260-day pre-Hispanic calendar, they may find that people are visiting the church not because it is a saint's day, but because it is (for example) Eight Quej, and that the visits to the church were preceded by visits to an outdoor shrine where copal incense and liquor were offered before a stone idol. Those who stop to listen to what is said may hear them reciting the Lord's Prayer while they stand before the stone idol, on the one hand, and directly addressing pagan deities within the church, on the other.

Around 1700, observations similar to these were made by the Dominican friar Francisco Ximénez, who had served in several highland Guatemalan communities. He complained, for example, that "the Indians attend church more on days that they celebrate" than according to the church calendar, and that although public parts of their rituals may appear to have Christian content, "there in secret they commemorate their paganism well enough." Summarizing his views, he wrote that "to me it seems that the most accurate way to understand who the Indians are, . . . and to define them with adequate definition, is to define them by contradictions" (Ximénez 1967:6, 34).

To date, the favored anthropological explanation for religious actions like the ones described above is rooted in what La Farge called his "purely tentative" and "extremely doubtful historical reconstruction "of five distinct periods in the rhythm of acculturation. These five periods as described by La Farge in 1940 were (1) *Conquest,* 1524-1600, when violence shattered the Indian cultural structure; (2) *Colonial Indian,* 1600-1720, when Spanish and Christian elements were absorbed wholesale and many Mayan elements were destroyed or mutilated; (3) *First Transition,* 1720-1800, when suppressed Mayan elements emerged and were integrated with Spanish-Christian elements into a new pattern; (4) *Recent Indian I,* 1800-80, when the integration became a smooth blend, well stabilized with the individuality and roundness that mark any culture; and finally (5) *Recent Indian II,* beginning in 1880, when the machine age and the Spanish-American cultures invade Recent Indian institutions, bringing conflict and acculturation (La Farge 1940:290-91).

During the Wenner-Gren seminar that led to the original *Heritage of Conquest* volume, Ralph Beals extended La Farge's scheme into Mexico and he renamed the Conquest and Colonial Indian periods *Early Colonial* noting that at this time most of the European "medieval" characteristics in contemporary Indian cultures were absorbed. In the next stage—*Second Colonial* (La Farge's First Transition)—he noted that there was a conscious effort to revive native cultures; the remainder of the Second Colonial period and two *Republican* periods (La Farge's Recent Indian I and II) involved the integration of mixed culture and the reinforcement of rejection patterns; finally he added the *Modern Republican* period dating from the Mexican Revolution of 1910 when the medieval character of society was profoundly modified and in some cases destroyed (Beals 1952:227-30).

During one of the sessions that followed Beals's presentation, Fernando Cámara Barbachano and Alfonso Villa Rojas found his modification of the La Farge scheme to be applicable to the Chiapas highlands, and Villa asserted that "the importance of the scheme is that it shows the process of acculturation" (Tax 1952:250). In fact, La Farge and Beals do not deal with "process," but rather, they present static, nonprocessual schemes which treat acculturation—and its opposite, revivalism—as diagnostic traits that may be present or absent during particular episodes of history. These episodes have a curious resemblance to archaeological strata; La Farge even titled his article, "Maya Ethnology: The Sequence of Cultures."

Charles Wisdom, in a paper prepared for the same Wenner-Gren conference at which Beals presented his scheme, followed a much simpler path to arrive at an account of "present-day Middle American supernaturalism," saying that it was "an end product of the combination of Spanish Roman Catholicism (especially that of the 16th, 17th, and 18th centuries) and the indigenous religion and magic." He adds that "what we have is not a mere combining of two elements, a grafting of one upon another, but rather what might be called a complete fusion, to the extent that the Indians themselves are unaware that any such historical process has taken place" (Wisdom 1952:119-20). Sol Tax, in the discussion following Wisdom's paper, took the supposed lack of Indian self-consciousness a step further, denying even that the natives might rationalize this fused religion after the fact. When Nathan C. Whetten asked Tax whether the people of Chichicastenango position the saints within a hierarchy of authority, he replied, "Theologians may rationalize, but simple people neither rationalize individually nor do they have a cultural rationalization" (Tax 1952:136).

More recent scholarship on Mesoamerican religion has followed Wisdom's simplified scheme, in which the focus is on an "end product," rather than the contrasting stages of the La Farge and Beals schemes. Manning Nash (1958), Donald E. Thompson (1960), William Madsen (1960), and Ruben E. Reina (1966), among others, argue that after the Spanish Conquest the indigenous religion or religions of Mesoamerica underwent a process of change involving the loss of many native elements and the wholesale addition of many foreign Catholic elements. These foreign elements were accepted only insofar as they were compatible with or even directly resembled the existing native cultural configuration, framework, ethical system, or world view. Then these new elements and old patterns "fused," "welded," or "blended" together and underwent a process of reinterpretation or secondary elaboration which produced a stable though syncretistic religion. Wisdom's assertion that the natives are unaware of the heterogeneity of the cultural sources of this "fused" religion has been repeated many times. On the other hand, Tax's denial that the natives engage in "rationalization" of this religion has clearly been contradicted, at the individual level, by such recent works as Calixta Guiteras-Holmes's *Perils of the Soul* (1961), and at the cultural level by such works as Gary Gossen's *Chamulas in the World of the Sun* (1974).

My own fieldwork in Mesoamerican religion was conducted in Momostenango, a Quiché Maya community in the midwestern highlands of Guatemala, during a total of about twenty months in 1975-76 and 1979.[1] In order to see and describe with new eyes the meaning of what was occurring in the religious life of this community during that period, I found it necessary to suspend what Husserl called the "natural attitude" and set aside, or "bracket," the raw data of immediate sense experience—for example, the observation of persons burning copal incense at a mountaintop altar dedicated to a saint. For as Schutz and other sociological phenomenologists have argued, naive empiricism leads only too quickly to "common sense" explanations for these actions.[2] In this case the easy way out is to conclude that these people are either Catholics, but "folk" Catholics, or else that they are part of a grand syncretistic Christo-pagan religion that has an existence all its own. This kind of explanation for social action avoids the difficult question of the intentionality of the action, the question of its meaning, for the actors.

In order not to move quite so rapidly from simple empiricism to "common sense" explanations of the empirical data, I found it necessary also to "bracket" the vast anthropological literature on religious syncretism, with its mechanical and organic metaphors of "welding," "blending," and "hybridization." This "bracketing" then enabled me to observe that, contrary to the expectations of many social anthropologists, the norms and activities in the religious, as well as other areas of life in Momostenango, were far from united. Indeed, ideas about what is or should be done and what is actually done are often quite incongruent.

The apparent religious groupings within this midwestern highland Guatemalan community of more than 40,000 people consist of five Protestant missions, the Roman Catholic Church (which is involved in the lay Catholic Action program), twenty confraternities (cofradías), four brotherhoods (hermandades), and a scattering of spiritualists. In addition, there is a triple-tiered hierarchy of priest-shamans that actively perpetuates both the Quiché 365-day solar and 260-day divinatory calendars, an intricate system for the interpretation of dreams and of internal body sensations, and a complex cosmology. On the bottom tier are the "mother-fathers of the patrilineages" *(chuchkajawib rech alaxic),* who are the priest-shamans for the more than three hundred landholding patrilineages in this community. Above these men are the canton priest-shamans *(chuchkajawib rech canton)* for the fourteen rural cantons of the municipality, selected through divination by the group of priest-shamans residing in each canton. On the top of the hierarchy are two "priest-shamans of the town" *(chuchkajawib rech tinimit),* who are also chosen through divination, this time by the fourteen canton priest-shamans. Surrounding this hierarchy is a large group of more than ten thousand men and women known as daykeepers *(ajk'ij),* who are carefully taught calendrics and divination by the priest-shamans. From this large population the patrilineage priest-shamans and a majority of the leadership personnel in the confraternities are recruited.[3]

The twenty confraternities in Momostenango, unlike those in many other highland Guatemalan communities, are not directly united with the civil hierarchy. In other words, there is no overt pattern of alternation between civil and confraternity service that leads to the status of elder.[4] Instead, the elders are respected older men who are usually members of the priest-shaman hierarchy or else merchants and military officers who employ daykeepers to divine and pray for them. Not only is service to a saint not obligatory for elder status, but two elders of my own acquaintance, both of whom are patrilineage heads and have served in high civil office, have not only never served a saint but consider the confraternities as secondary to the priestly duties they perform for their own patrilineages. In fact, these men as well as many other priest-shamans have insisted to me, in the context of discussions of their priestly duties and ideology, that they are not Catholics and that they never attend church. Since I myself, naively perhaps, observed both of them attending church, however, I directly questioned them about this clear contradiction. They replied that although they attend mass they abstain from receiving communion at the Roman Catholic priest's hand. Instead, they pray silently to their ancestors buried beneath the floor of the church and when the small bell rings at the end of communion they are blessed by these ancestors. Further, they attend church in order to remind the priest, by their presence but lack of participation at the communion rail, that it is their church and not his. From the viewpoint of the current priest, these priest-shamans should not be given communion anyway, since their names do not appear on church marriage rolls and they are thus (by his definition) living in concubinage; from their own viewpoint, the priest-shamans go on participating in communion in their own way without giving in to the Catholic priest's demands for church weddings.

The Catholic Action movement was introduced into the community in the early 1950s in order to make "real" Catholics out of people who were perceived by the Roman Catholic hierarchy in Guatemala as pagans. This is, in effect, the latest attempt to do something about problems of the sort Ximénez had observed two and one-half centuries earlier. Unlike anthropologists, who seem bemused by the syncretistic Christo-paganism prominently displayed in the confraternities of Guatemala, the established church is offended and has set out to separate and factionalize the indigenes dividing them into true Catholics and pagans (Wagley 1964:33-34; Warren 1978: 97). Their religious messages have been closely connected to agricultural and health benefits, which has helped to convert many indigenes to the new Catholic doctrine, greatly simplified and relatively saint-free. By 1954, the Ladino priest in Momostenango had converted so many pagans that when Eight Batz' (the initiation day for new daykeepers) arrived, he dared to lock the doors of the church. As a result hundreds of patrilineage priest-shamans and their initiates could not enter the church in order to visit Santiago, San Antonio Pologuá, and the Momostecan ancestors who are buried beneath the floor. That night the priest-shamans convened the elders, who decided to send a delegation to the church to confront the priest. The delegation, consisting primarily of patrilineage heads, informed the priest that he must leave Momostenango or be killed. He fled.

Soon thereafter, Momostenango was sent the current priest, who in the eyes of the elders, is just as bad as the previous one. One of the major complaints they have is that his catechism classes and prayer meetings keep young teenagers out late in the evening, setting up courting situations that undermine the traditional system of arranged marriages between men and women of neighboring patrilineages. They also openly disagree with him and his converts on religious doctrine. Instead of the standard trinity of Catholic doctrine, consisting of Father, Son, and Holy Ghost, they assert that the proper pantheon consists, at the highest level of generalization, of *tiox (dios)*, the *mundo*, and *nantat*. In this alternative trinity, Dios represents the entire Christian pantheon of dioses, including God, Jesus, ghosts, angels, saints, and virgins, together with their physical images in the local parish church and cemetery chapel. By *mundo*, they mean the earthly physical world as a whole, for which reason the *mundo* is sometimes addressed as *pachulum mundo*, "round World"; the plural form, *mundos*, covers the plurality of mountains and volcanoes of the world, in both their physical and spiritual aspects. By *nantat*, or "Mother-Father," they mean the ancestors in general, both as *uxlab*, "breath" or "spirit," and as *much'ulic bak, much'ulic ulew, much'ulic poklaj*, "powdered bone, powdered clay, powdered sand," referring to their physical remains.

Given this alternative trinity, the elders particularly oppose the Catholic priest's violent separation of God, as a purely spiritual entity and the ultimate source of all good, from the material world, a doctrine which leads, as they point out, to the confusion of the very earth itself with the devil. In their view, persons, gods, saints, their own ancestors, and the earth all possess mixtures of positive and negative qualities. For example, San Antonio Pologuá is a great causer of illness, and priest-shamans can cure disease because they know how to inflict it.

This profoundly dialectical view of man, nature, and religion, in which the two sides of a duality encompass or complete rather than oppose one another, finds itself confronted by the analytical view urged upon the *catequistas* (as Catholic Action converts are called by others), who have been taught that they must finally choose between being truly Christian, which is synonymous with all goodness and purity, and leaving themselves in the company of the priest-shamans, who are nothing but evil witches. When the priest-shamans assert that they do not attend church, they are responding to the push of this analytical dualism. Their statement is an idealized one, or what Schutz called a "project," a reflexive looking-forward-to or phantasying of a day when priest-shamans would in fact no longer attend church (Schutz 1967:59).

During the patron saint fiesta in 1976 the opposition between official Catholicism and the priest-shamans flared up in the open once again. On the twenty-fourth of July, when the religious leadership of the confraternity of the patron saint of Momostenango took the image of Santiago from the church, the second most important official in this group, the *teputado,* was drunk. That night he washed the face of the saint with hot water and as a result some eyelashes fell out. The next day everyone saw the unhappy result; it was considered a serious moral breech and the man was jailed. Citing his misconduct, the *catequistas* argued that since they themselves abstain from alcohol as a part of their religious duties, they should be allowed to staff the patron saint's confraternity rather than traditional Catholics.[5] After some debate, the elders decided to retain traditional Catholics in the first and third positions in the confraternity but to admit catequistas in the second- and fourth-ranking positions.

Why did the Catholic Action leadership wish to participate in an organization that involves public drinking during religious ritual and which the priest says is dominated by pagans? On the other hand, why did the traditionalists, who practice sexual abstinence on days of religious ritual, allow these unclean *catequistas,* who admittedly do not practice such abstinence, to enter this confraternity?

First of all, the dualism in these events moved from the external and analytical opposition between *catequistas* and pagans, to an internal and dialectical complementarity between different social actions taking place within a single religious institution. The priest-shamans say that they feel this new arrangement will work out well, given that both sides agreed that since the customs of the priest-shaman are older than those of the Roman Catholic Church, the first alcalde in the confraternity should always be a priest-shaman. He, as in the past, will be responsible for carrying out these ancient rituals at outdoor earth shrines on the proper days in the Quiché calendar. During the fiesta, the first- and third-ranking members of the confraternity would abstain from sex and give the saint and themselves the proper *traguitos* of liquor, while the two Catholic Action members would be trusted to abstain from alcohol and look out for the image so that no errors would be made because of drunkenness. Catholic Action members are pleased because now they can participate in part of the ancient customs of their native town without being totally under the religious authority of the hierarchy of priest-shamans.

Perhaps the elders are right and this grand dialectical scheme, with its complementarity of religious abstinences—sex and alcohol—will produce stability within this institution and perhaps even between *catequistas* and priest-shamans at large. One thing is for certain: since the relationship between man the producer of the social world and his product is dialectical (Berger and Luckmann 1966:61), we may expect that a chain of further contradictions and solutions will be set off, bringing vast changes to this confraternity.

By now it should be clear that the religion of highland Guatemala is hardly "fused," "welded," or "blended" into a stabilized, neatly balanced colonial syncretism, the frozen "end product" of processes of a type that occurred only in certain strata of past time. Such syncretism, or "Christo-paganism," is a typical positivistic structure-functional description which depends on mechanical and organic models of stable institutions. It should also be clear, from the Momostecan assertion that the customs of the priest-shaman are older than those of the church, that indigenous peoples are not necessarily unaware of historical processes. Further, in the example of the alternative trinity, it can be seen that indigenous peoples do indeed engage in the construction of rational schemes to account for the complexity of their religous heritage.

In a way, my own view of religous process in indigenous Guatemala is more in keeping with that of Ximénez, writing more than two centuries ago, than with that of anthropologists of the recent past. Where they saw a smooth blend, he saw contradictions. Arguments of the kind that took place recently in Momostenango began four and one-half centuries ago, and there is no reason to believe they have ever completely stopped.

NOTES

1. I gratefully acknowledge the financial support given to me during my research in Guatemala by the Graduate School of the State University of New York at Albany and by Tufts University. A Weatherhead Resident Fellowship at the School of American Research in Santa Fe, New

Mexico provided me the time, space, and environment in which to complete this paper.

2. For a good introduction to sociological phenomenology see Marvin Farber, *The Foundation of Phenomenology* (1962); Peter L. Berger and Thomas Luckmann, *The Social Construction of Reality* (1966); and Alfred Schutz, *The Phenomenology of the Social World* (1967).

3. For more detail on the religion of Momostenango see Barbara Tedlock, *Time and the Highland Maya* (1982).

4. The general pattern of Mesoamerican civil-religious hierarchies has been well defined and described by Sol Tax in "The Municipios of the Midwestern Highlands of Guatemala," (1937:442-44); and by Fernando Cámara Barbachano in "Religious and Political Organization," (1952: 142-73). Frank Cancian provides the most thorough discussion of the operation of the system within a single community in *Economics and Prestige in a Maya Community: The Religous Cargo System in Zinacantán* (1965). The reputedly pre-Columbian roots of the Mesoamerican civil-religious hierarchy have been explored by Pedro Carrasco, "The Civil-Religious Hierarchy in Mesoamerican Communities: Pre-Spanish Background and Colonial Development," (1961:483-97) and denied by Marvin Harris in *Patterns of Race in the Americas* (1964: 25-43).

5. The possible role of the current Ladino priest in encouraging the *catequistas* in their attempt to take over this symbolically important confraternity should be explored. Colby and van den Berghe report that a similar attempt in Chajul did indeed originate with the local priest (1969:286).

REFERENCES

Beals, Ralph
1952   "Notes on Acculturation," in *Heritage of Conquest: The Ethnology of Middle America,* ed. Sol Tax (Glencoe, Ill.: Free Press).
Berger, Peter L., and Thomas Luckmann
1966   *The Social Construction of Reality* (New York: Doubleday).
Cámara Barbachano, Fernando
1952   "Religious and Political Organization," in *Heritage of Conquest: The Ethnology of Middle America,* ed. Sol Tax (Glencoe, Ill.: Free Press).
Cancian, Frank
1965   *Economics and Prestige in a Maya Community: The Religious Cargo System in Zinacantán* (Palo Alto: Stanford University Press).
Carrasco, Pedro
1961   "The Civil-Religious Hierarchy in Mesoamerican Communities:

Pre-Spanish Background and Colonial Development," *American Anthropologist* 63:483-97.

Colby, Benjamin N., and Pierre L. van den Berghe

1969   *Ixil Country: A Plural Society in Highland Guatemala* (Berkeley and Los Angeles: University of California Press).

Farber, Marvin

1962   *The Foundation of Phenomenology* (New York: Paine-Whitman).

Gossen, Gary

1974   *Chamulas in the World of the Sun: Time and Space in a Maya Oral Tradition* (Cambridge, Mass.: Harvard University Press).

Guiteras-Holmes, Calixta

1961   *Perils of the Soul: The World View of a Tzotzil Indian* (Glencoe, Ill.: Free Press).

Harris, Marvin

1964   *Patterns of Race in the Americas* (New York: W. W. Norton).

La Farge, Oliver

1940   "Maya Ethnology: The Sequence of Cultures," in *The Maya and Their Neighbors*, ed. C. L. Hay, Ralph L. Linton, Samuel K. Lathrop, Harry L. Shapiro, and George C. Vaillant (New York: Appleton-Century).

Madsen, William

1960   "Cristo-Paganism: A Study of Mexican Religious Syncretism," in *Nativism and Syncretism,* Middle American Research Publication 19 (New Orleans: Tulane University).

Nash, Manning

1958   *Machine Age Maya,* American Anthropological Association Memoir, no. 87 (Menasha, Wis.).

Reina, Ruben E.

1966   *The Law of the Saints: A Pokomam Pueblo and Its Community Culture* (New York: Bobbs-Merrill).

Schutz, Alfred

1967   *The Phenomenology of the Social World* (Evanston: Northwestern University Press).

Tax, Sol

1937   "The Municipios of the Midwestern Highlands of Guatemala," *American Anthropologist* 39:423-44.

1952   *Heritage of Conquest: The Ethnology of Middle America* (Glencoe, Ill.: Free Press).

Tedlock, Barbara

1982   *Time and the Highland Maya* (Albuquerque: University of New Mexico Press).

Thompson, Donald E.
1960   "Maya Paganism and Christianity: A History of the Fusion of Two Religions," in *Nativism and Syncretism,* Middle American Research Institute, Publication 19 (New Orleans: Tulane University).
Wagley, Charles
1964   "The Peasant," in *Continuity and Change in Latin America,* ed. John J. Johnson (Palo Alto: Stanford University Press).
Warren, Kay B.
1978   *The Symbolism of Subordination: Indian Identity in a Guatemalan Town* (Austin: University of Texas Press).
Wisdom, Charles
1952   "The Supernatural and Curing," in *Heritage of Conquest: The Ethnology of Middle America,* ed. Sol Tax (Glencoe, Ill.: Free Press).
Ximénez, Fray Francisco
1967   *Escolios a las historias del origen de los indios.* Sociedad de Geografía e Historia de Guatemala, Publication 13 (Guatemala).

west Mexican symbolic structures are based upon the world of nature, conceived in terms of human social structure as a major root metaphor rather than upon the morphological structure and physiological functions of the human body.

Laura Makarius's paper, "The Mask and the Violation of Taboo," as presented in the symposium, "Masks and Masquerade in the Americas" (International Congress of Americanists, August 1979), brings up an extremely interesting analytical problem (1982). She quotes from a Mayo text (Crumrine 1973:1136-39). My Mayo friend was responding to the question, "But what do the *Chapakobam* signify and why the masks? Why do they have this form?" He answered, "They require it because they have paint. They paint themselves on their bodies with red paint which symbolizes the blood of Christ." Makarius argues that the relationship between the question and the response is based upon a universal fear of blood in primitive societies and especially in the Mayo case, the blood of Christ. The flow of blood is dangerous because if it is not checked it ultimately ends in death. The masks are worn as protection from the danger associated with blood. Violation of the blood taboos transmits the power of blood to the violator; thus the masks not only protect the individual masker from the power of blood but also take on this power of the blood because of their role in the crucifixion of Jesus. The Chapakobam *(Pariserom)* represent the soldiers in the army which captures and kills Jesus. In elaborating upon this argument Makarius draws heavily upon African examples as well as upon other American Indians ones. My understanding of the Mayo data leads me to question Makarius's interpretation not on the basis of her selection of this aspect of the text, because certainly the death of Jesus is a major symbol and event not only in the Mayo ritual but in northwest Mexican Easter ceremonialism in general. But her analysis lacks the broad emic base of (1) an approach which seeks to uncover the complexity of a set of ritual symbols as does Victor Turner or of (2) the organization, the ranking, of ritual symbols which Edward Spicer calls sets of orientations. The Mayo basic or root metaphors which act as mediators linking together separate rituals and symbols with cultural cognitive processes on one hand and with the physical world on the other, as discussed by James Fernandez (1974) and Brenda Beck (1978), are not found in physiological models, rooted for example in blood symbolism, but rather in social models based upon the family as a cultural as well as a biological phenomena. In this paper, I am not suggesting that Makarius is wrong, as Mayos do recognize blood as powerful, but that Mayo ritual emphasis would be placed elsewhere than upon the blood symbolism. Interestingly the African Ndembu ritual symbols as explicated by Turner also are based upon physiological models as root metaphors in contrast to the Mayo system. A combination of Turner's and Spicer's analytical methods when applied to the Mayo data clarify the Mayo system of ritual symbols and orientations and reveal a root metaphor, the Mayo Holy Family, which contrasts with that of the African Ndembu. This paper suggests that it makes more sense to typify northwest Mexican and perhaps also Mesoamerican root metaphors, which provide the organizing principle for sets of ritual symbols and orientations, as pointing to sociocultural phenomena rather than physiological processes. This insight provides a working hypothesis for the present paper. Thus Makarius applies a root metaphor which is characteristic of African cultures, to Middle American Indian ritual and symbolism. Certainly it will fit, but I question that it provides the best fit, especially in an emic sense.

The Method

In numerous publications, Victor Turner has developed and utilized the concept of ritual symbol:

> By "ritual" I mean prescribed formal behavior for occasions not given over to technological routine, having reference to beliefs in mystical beings or powers. The symbol is the smallest unit of ritual which still retains the specific properties of ritual behavior; it is the ultimate unit of specific structure in a ritual context . . . a "symbol" is a thing regarded by general consent as naturally typifying or representing or recalling something by possession of analogous qualities or by association in fact or thought. The symbols I observed in the field were, empirically, objects, activities, relationships, events, gestures, and spatial units in a ritual situation. (Turner, 1967:19)

How does the investigator go about isolating and analyzing ritual symbols? Turner (1967:20) suggests three classes of data which should be collected in the study of ritual symbols: "(1) external form and observable characteristics; (2) interpretations offered by specialists and by laymen; (3) significant contexts largely worked out by the anthropologist." Many of the ritual symbols that he isolates for Ndembu ritual involve specifically physiological referents, for example the *mudyi* symbol refers to a tree used in female initiation ritual, a tree which exudes a white milky latex or sap and stands for matrilineage, female solidarity, and the unique girl becoming a woman; or the *mukula* symbol refers to a second tree used in the male circumcision and female medicinal rituals which exudes a reddish sap and stands for the blood of childbirth, or menstruation, of animal game, of circumcision, and also for red medicines. The latter ritual symbol, the *mukula,* provides an excellent example for Makarius's analysis. Ndembu color symbolism also refers to a physiological metaphor (Turner 1967:80): "Blood, the main denotation of 'redness,' is even identified with 'power.' White, too, stands for life fluids; it represents milk and semen. Black, on the contrary, stands for body leavings, body dirt, and the fluids putrefaction, and for the products of catabolism." Ritual symbols contain three basic properties— "condensation," "unification of disparate significata," and "polarization of meaning" (Turner 1967:28). In condensation, "many things and actions are represented in a single formation." In the unification of disparate signifacata, "the disparate significata are interconnected by virtue of their common possession of analogous qualities or by association in fact or thought." As a result, symbols "bracket together the most diverse ideas and phenomena." In polarization of meaning, "dominant Ndembu symbols possess two clearly distinguishable poles of meaning," an "ideological pole" and a "sensory pole" (Turner 1967:28, italics removed).

Although Turner discusses dominant and instrumental symbols, his method provides no clear system of ranking the ritual's symbols. Edward H. Spicer, developing Linton's concept of "orientation," makes several most useful suggestions, ". . . those interests which are shared by all a society's members, together with the relative importance attached to them, give any culture configuration its orientations" (Linton 1936:443). The concept of "relative importance" of course is crucial here. Spicer presents several means of evaluating "importance"; "what do people talk about most; spend most time on; train their children; tell the anthropologist as outsider learning the culture; and choose when there is a conflict." For modern Sonoran Yaquis (northern neighbors of the Mayos) Spicer notes six ranked orientations: ceremonial labor or mutual cooperation with the supernatural; fiesta giving; paskola and deer dance arts; village self-government; agriculture (corn, beans); and wage labor, making money. Even though these orientations are somewhat more general than ritual symbols, their analysis embodies a useful approach as well as the concept of ranking. The rank order of orientations changes through time as the culture develops and adapts to internal and external changes.

Returning to Turner's analysis, one final point requires development before we turn to the Mayo and northwest Mexican materials. Turner's recent work has become more dynamic in his use of symbolism. In "Social Dramas and Ritual Metaphors" he (Turner 1974) has examined ritual in terms of the social drama of performance as well as of structure. He reexamines and applies Stephen Pepper's concept of "root metaphor" to social and ritual contexts. Pepper (1961), a philosopher, perceived that each philosophical system is based upon a metaphor or what he called the "root metaphor." It appears to me that a set or cluster of ritual symbols refers to or finds its basis in the "root metaphor," here developed by Pepper (1961:91-92):

> The method in principle seems to be this: A man desiring to understand the world looks about for a clue to its comprehension. He pitches upon some area of common sense fact and tries if he cannot understand other areas in terms of this one. This original area becomes then his basic analogy or root metaphor. He describes as best he can the characteristics of this area, or, if you will, discriminates its structure. A list of its structural characteristics becomes his basic concepts of explanation and description. We call them a set of categories. In terms of these categories he proceeds to study all other areas of fact whether uncriticized or previously criticized. He undertakes to interpret all facts in terms of these categories. As a result of the impact of these other facts upon his categories, he may qualify and readjust the categories, so that a set of categories commonly changes and develops. Since the basic analogy or root metaphor normally (and probably at least in part necessarily) arises out of common sense, a great deal of development

and refinement of a set of categories is required if they are to prove adequate for a hypothesis of unlimited scope. Some root metaphors prove more fertile than others, have greater powers of expansion and of adjustment. These survive in comparison with the others and generate the relatively adequate world theories.

At this point we shall turn to an examination of the Mayo and northwest Mexican materials in terms of these conceptual tools: the ritual symbol, the orientation, and the "root metaphor." The methods of analysis associated with these concepts prove very helpful in sorting out and analyzing these traditions in a more emic sense than many other approaches.

The Data

In this section, we shall examine the hypothesis that the family and its symbolic projection, The Holy Family, provide one of the modern Mayo root metaphors and at the symbolic level a meta-ritual symbol. The majority of Mayo Indian peoples live in southern Sonora and northern Sinaloa in the lower Mayo and Fuerte River valleys, on the flat coastal plain. Holding small parcels of land or memberships in ejidos, many Mayos engage in modern commercial irrigation agriculture, growing crops such as wheat, cartamo, corn, and cotton. Others, lacking lands, rely upon wage labor or upon fishing in the rich Gulf of California to gain a living. Shopping in the local mestizo markets and stores for clothing and staples and relying upon local banks for agricultural loans, Mayos are marginally integrated in the broader Mexican economic system. However, the Mayo belief and ritual systems stand apart from modern Mexican culture and from modern Catholicism.

A Mayo friend, whom I consider an expert on ritual matters although he chooses not to practice as a ritual specialist, and I shared the following experience. In Turner's sense this interpretation is one offered by a specialist. In Spicer's orientation analysis, it represents information which the individual himself decided would be an important aid in my understanding of Mayo traditions. In addition, his discussion was directed to the Mayo ritual hosts working in the church, which qualifies his little sermon as presenting content that was acceptable and of interest to other Mayos. When a special Holy

Cross ritual did not materialize, several of my Mayo friends took me to a local church to pay our respects to the Santa Cruz there. The *Paskome* (hosts) who were decorating the altar and the Santa Cruz image (a wooden cross wrapped in blue ribbon) ran out for chairs and coffee. Growing out of some words of explanation, one of my friends drifted into a Mayo *hinabaka* (sermon). Talking about some of the images, he placed emphasis on the image of the Holy Family *(Sagrada Familia)* and pointed to a picture of God, Mary, and the Christ Child. Since this "Holy Family" concept was acting as an integrating symbol in his sermon, it occurred to me that it might prove more generally applicable as a model and underlying structure tying together elements that had formerly appeared to me as contingent ones.

By the Holy Family, he explained he referred to God the Father and Joseph, *(Itom Achai O.?ola),* Jesus or the Son *(Itom Achai Usi),* and Our Mother, Mary *(Itom Aye).* These terms literally are identical to those of the nuclear family, *achai* or *in achai* (my father), *aye* or *in aye* (my mother), and *usi* or *in usi* (my child). On one hand, this metaphor is extended to the heavens. Any Mayo one might encounter would recognize the following statements as true. *Hu?u ta?a Itom Achai* (The sun is God, Our Father); *Hu?u mecha Itom Aye* (The moon is Our Mother). Many would accept the following although it is not as general a concept as the preceding; *hu?u chokim ili usim* (The stars are little children). Also the cycles of the moon and of nature are linked with Our Mother, especially *Itom Aye Eva* (Eve), and the menstrual cycle. On the other hand, the metaphor is extended to the world of the forest *(huya ania)* and to that of the sea *(bawe ania).* Many Mayo men are fishermen and call upon the protector of the fish for good luck as described in the following Mayo explanation (Crumrine 1973:1124):

> Fishermen, who either use a casting net or block a small bay and pick up the fish stranded by the receding tide, must work through the night. Because during the day time the fish will see them. It is dangerous at night especially near the ocean. Thus it takes a brave man to fish. When one fishes he calls out to the Old Woman of the Sea *(Bawe Hamyo?ola).* She is the protector of the fish, of the *Bawe Ania* (Ocean World). And if one wants luck at fishing, he must pray to her, *"Bawe Hamyo?ola kuchum ne mika;* give me fish."

The animals of the forest, *Huya Ania* (Forest World), also have a
protector, the Old Man of the Forest and His Wife *(Huya O?ola*
and *Huya Hamyo?ola)*. The animals are their children. When one
wishes luck at hunting he must call to the *Huya O?ola* .

When asked, fishermen will explain that there is a *bawe o?ola,* the
husband of the *bawe hamyo?ola,* although he seems to have little importance. Also the *huya hamyo?ola* seems unimportant. Thus the Old
Woman of the Sea and the Old Man of the Forest are the most important and are recognized as powerful by many Mayos. Some fishermen will recount experiences in which they saw the *Bawe Hamyo?ola*
and can describe her appearance. Señor Santiago is the supernatural
protector of domesticated animals:

> If one's animal is sick, he can make a promise to Señor Santiago.
> When the animal is cured, one pays by placing a ribbon for Señor
> Santiago on the altar or on the animal. Señor Santiago and his herd
> of domesticated animals live within a small mountain south of the
> Mayo River Valley. Here he herds his animals round and round
> within his mountain making winds (Crumrine 1973:1125).

Some Mayos conceive of the members of a church center as the *ili
usim* (little children) of the church saints; *Itom Achai* (generic term
for all male saints) and *Itom Aye* (generic term for all female saints).
Thus following Turner's suggestions of classes of data useful in the
study of ritual symbols, we may combine this information into a set
of "significant contexts largely worked out by the anthropologist."
These contexts unify the root metaphor, the modern Mayo family
(the physical aspect or sensory pole), with the meta-ritual symbol (the
ideological aspect or ideological pole), the Holy Family, and suggest the crucial and widespread nature of this root metaphor and
ritual symbol.

The modern settlement patterns and landholding system in the
Mayo River valley show a shift away from an extended family unit
to a nuclear family of father, mother, and children. Economic production, often the result of individual wage labor, also reveals family organization and regulation. The Mayo family provides the basic
concrete unit in both Mayo-mestizo consumption, distribution, and
exchange and also in Mayo-Mayo family visiting accompanied by
food exchange and in the production of Mayo ceremonials. Ceremo-

nials, symbolically coded in terms of the meeting of a male image *(Itom Achai,* God) and a female image *(Itom Aye,* Our Mother), include the families of the *Paskome* (hosts or *Ili Usim,* Little Children of the Saint) who provide the food and entertainment offered as a gift to the saint and the crowd. The *Bawe Hamyo?ola* and her husband protect their children, the fish of the sea, the *Huyo O?ola* and his wife *(Huya Hamyo?ola)* protect their children, the animals of the forest, and Señor Santiago, a manifestation of *Itom Achai* (God), protects the domesticated animals. Also, a contract exists between the earth, which sometimes is linked to *Itom Aye* (Our Mother), and humans who are nourished by and in turn nourish the earth.

> (I have heard, "bwiya bwa?anake," the earth will eat you. What does it mean? Is it correct?) Certainly it is truth, good words. We have made a commitment or an obligation with the earth. We move above the land, we make earthen pots, and plant the land. To Our Father (Itom Achai) we ask the favor, that we be able to easily till (break up) the land. Thus we eat from the body of the land. In exchange for this favor at the time of our death the earth will eat us. We have a commitment with the earth. We have an obligation to Itom Achai. We are baptized Christians and not animals. Thus we have this commitment to Itom Achai. When humans die the earth will eat us up, but God will restore us (Crumrine 1973:1143).

Thus the economic realms of the sea, the forest, the domesticated animals, and the productive earth, all represent transformations or elaborations on the ritual symbol and root metaphor of the Holy Family. Concerning social organization, the modern shifts in kinship terminology toward the Spanish system, the breakdown in large extended households, and the retention of the age-respect principle reveal the structure of the Holy Family model and take on meaning for Mayos in terms of this model. The extremely important ceremonial kinship system utilizes the family root metaphor and ritualizes the parent-child relationship yet makes practical use of the coparent relationship established through the ritual. The Mayo compadrazgo terms, *Bato Achai* (water father), *Bato Aye* (water mother), *Bato Usi* (water child), reflect the root metaphor. The pueblo and church organizations simply expand and transform the root metaphor into a sacred community with *Itom Achai* (God, Our Father) and *Itom Aye*

(Our Mother) (the male and female saints coded as parents) while the Mayo members of the community are the *Ili Usim* (little children of the Saints). Within the church sodalities the metaphor also exists; the three ranks of the *Paskome* (hosts) represent God the Father, God the Son, and the Holy Spirit often called *Itom Aye* (Our Mother). Discussions of the use and abuse of political power, as exemplified in Eastern rituals also are coded in terms of the Holy Family metaphor. Except for the Easter ceremonial, Mayo pueblo ceremonials generally involve exchanges with other church centers. These exchanges are ritualized in the encounter and embrace between the two saints, one from the host church and the other from the visiting church. The "embrace" unites two sets of oppositions both coded in terms of the Holy Family root metaphor: *Itom Achai* (Our Father, a male saint) versus *Itom Aye* (Our Mother, a female saint) and the Santos (the holy parents) versus the *Ili Usim* (Little Children, the human members of the pueblo). The church centers involved in these systems of saint exchanges reflect the recent local processes of village splintering, regrouping, and refocusing of Mayo religious cults around saints and churches further removed from mestizo centers. Thus the Holy Family metaphor provides a folk explanation of stability and change occurring within the environment, the Mayo family, and the broader sociocultural organizations. Most dramatically this underlying structure, based upon a folk model, proves sufficiently elastic to smooth out the irregularities of the recent contingent Mayo history and reorganize a ritual system which integrates Mayos across municipal boundaries without the mediation of a political organization, an organization which at present is controlled by mestizos (See Crumrine 1977).

Easter or Lenten ceremonialism tends to look inward upon each ceremonial center with similar rituals replicating each other in several centers. The following explanations would be typical and very common responses to questions concerning the meaning of the Easter ritual (Crumrine 1973:1127-29; 1978:232-33):

Joseph and Mary fled, out of shame it is said, because Mary was pregnant, and Joseph knew that he had nothing to do with it. But the angel appeared to Mary and told her not to be ashamed because she was going to give birth to Christ and he told her and Joseph not to be ashamed for it was the work of the Holy Spirit. He talked to Joseph alone, then, and told him not to leave Mary because of this. So Mary and Joseph came back to Belem, but there was no room for them anywhere so they had to go to a stable. And there the Child was born and the Three Kings came to see the Christ Child. The animals made special noises signaling his birth. The cock crowed, the donkey brayed, and the dog barked.

The Pontius Pilate started pursuing the Christ Child, it is said, because he was afraid. Since the Three Kings had visited Christ, Pilate thought the child must be pretty important. So the army of Pontius Pilate pursues the Christ Child every year, and kills him, but in the end He arises and He and the Three Kings triumph on the Saturday of Glory.

Christ, Itom Achai, taught, cured, was pursued, was crucified, and arose in the Mayo River Valley as he did in all parts of the earth. Itom Achai (Christ) traveled around the River Valley (the Mayo area) curing the sick and teaching. The Pariserom (the army of Pilate) finally chased him into the desert, the mesquite forest. They captured him there in the mesquite forest, and took him to the river to the abaso forest (cottonwood) where they crucified Itom Achai.

The Pariserom (Chapakobam or Judios, masked soldiers in the army of Pilate) followed and killed Christ because they wanted to command. They did not want him, Itom Achai, to command them. They wanted to command. But even though they won when they killed him, they did not win. Because due to their killing of Itom Achai Usi, they themselves had to die, had to die because of that. He arose and ascended into heaven. The army of Pontius Pilate is destroyed. Itom Achai's will is supreme and the Pariserom must die because they have disobeyed his will. The Pariserom took power and forgot that only Itom Achai commands.

Although most Mayos accept these myths as true, some of the members of the Parisero sodality suggest that they have God's permission and thus are not guilty for Christ's death. They explain that Jesus tired of this world and desired to return to his Father (see Crumrine 1974). The following much longer Lenten story represents the interpretation of a single individual, although the ideas embodied within the text are acceptable to Mayos generally. It also provides the full context of the materials which Makarius quotes. My questions and comments appear in parentheses (Crumrine 1973: 1136-39; 1978:233-35).

(The Easter ceremony is very interesting. How many Chapakobam were there?) The Chapakobam have permission to make the ceremony of Itom Achai (Our Father). (Why must the Chapakobam remain silent?) They must hold a cross in their mouth under the mask. (But on Wednesday, Tinieblas, they cry out?) They make the cry of the owl *(tecolote,* Sp.; *mu?u,* Mayo). (Why can they make sound only Wednesday night?) It is the custom. They also make the cry of the crow *(cuervo,* Sp.; *koni,* Mayo). (But the tecolote (owl) is a sign of the dead?) Yes! Yes! It is a bad sign. They aren't the dead. They just copy the song of the tecolote and the cuervo. (Where did the Chapakobam live? Aren't there stories about them?) It is a custom, they imitate what happened with Itom Achai. They imitate the time when Jesus appeared and the Pilatos killed him. (But what do the Chapakobam signify and why the masks? Why do they have this form?) They require it because they have paint. They paint themselves on their bodies with red paint which symbolizes the blood of Christ. (But I still do not understand why they need the masks?)

A long time ago in that time they were like Kaifas. And Kaifas was truly very hairy. Kaifas, when Our Lord was taken prisoner, when they took him prisoner in order to kill him, Kaifas was truly very bearded, very hairy. The masks are like this, are an imitation of this beardedness. (I do not know anything about Kaifas.) Kaifas is God's opposite, contrary (contra). He is God's enemy. (He isn't the Devil?) Exactly, he is the Devil. Kaifas is not baptized, not a Christian, he is the Devil, Lucifer. (And does he have soldiers?) Certainly, he has soldiers. (Are the Pariseros and the Chapakobam in his army?) Certainly. (Today where is Kaifas?)

Today Kaifas is ashamed because our Lord arose from the dead at Gloria in such a manner giving life to sinners. Kaifas has retreated to the forest. His soldiers have been killed, are dead, but Kaifas still lives. (It is possible to see Kaifas in the forest?) Of course. (Kaifas is not baptized?) No. Itom Achai contra hu?u. (This one is the opposite of Our Father.) Kaifas is the Devil, he is dangerous, bad. He does bad things. He tries to gain, to win, good men. It's diabolical. (Does Kaifas also have power?)

Certainly. Like God, Kaifas also has power. This is all written in the words of Itom Achai in white clay *(masilla blanca)*. These words have power. Here is permission from Itom Achai to do everything a Christian should do. With permission from Itom Achai's words one may act, without it one may not act. (And the witches are they friends of Kaifas?) Certainly. The witches make people sick and kill them. They are invisible, you cannot see them. They operate by bad thoughts through the mind. They are dangerous. (Do they have bad words?) Certainly. They have words which they use to make people sick, bad words. The Chapakobam imitate sorcery (as they do all kinds of Mayo behavior) but they do not have the power of a witch. They imitate the story of Itom Achai, of his death, burial, and resurrection. In the end they ask the pardon of Itom Achai. They make the ceremony of Itom Achai. They do the passion of Itom Achai.

II. (When I was here last year you told me about an enemy of God. His name was Kaifas. But I still do not know who Kaifas was?) There are two roads, a good one and a bad one. (The Paskolas (semiprofessional dancers and entertainers), what road do they take?) If they complete their promise and go to the altar asking forgiveness from God for their joking and bad talk, they are on the good road. But if they don't complete their promise and ask forgiveness, then they are promised to Kaifas. (A long time ago, were Itom Achai and Kaifas friends?)

In that time when this world commenced, Itom Achai began to make hens (gallinas) and all the things which exist. God made things correctly. The very close, very intimate friend of Itom Achai, Kaifas, began to imitate God. (Were they compadres?) No, only very intimate friends. Kaifas began to imitate God. When El Señor (God) made the hen, the hen saw the world and liked the world. The hen was happy, gay, because El Señor gave the hen breath. And Lucifer, this Kaifas, also began to make a hen. This hen he made of *(barro)* clay. In clay Kaifas began to make a hen. Instead of a good hen coming out a *tecolote* (Sp. owl) came out. Kaifas made an owl *(mu?u)*. Kaifas imitated El Señor. But this was not yet the sin which Kaifas was going to commit against El Señor. This wasn't much. Nothing much because Kaifas had equal power with El Señor. He controlled equal power to that of God. Kaifas was able to use the power, but he used it for bad purposes, for evil. And El Señor made the light of day and saw everything was good. In the light of day everything was good. People, men, he made. Because He foresaw them, saw that they were going to live in the world. Kaifas also made men, people. But the people Kaifas created were just like, were similar, to him. They were equal to Kaifas. When Kaifas made men, they came out equal to him, that is bad.

To turn to the understanding of The Good and The Bad. The Bad is to act in excess. Many, many of the men, especially those of Kaifas, wouldn't do because a man can sin with only a few words when they are about another. This danger converges in the tongue, the mouth, when a person talks of another. This is very bad, dangerous. Because to speak much about people who are not at fault, that is to say, to speak badly of a person, is a sin which God will not pardon. For those who speak badly, it is a means of falling. Well people should speak good words about others. This means our tongue can make us happy. One ought to respect others. One should give respect and tenderness to people, even those whom one doesn't know. In this form one should respect everyone, this is good. It is good to have respect for everyone. That is to say, many people go to sacred temples (churches). They go to the church, but they study other books, bad books. They aren't good Christians but bad, dangerous ones. They teach other bad things, dangerous things. The greatest good is to value, to appreciate, everybody. (Are some temples of the devil?) No! Itom Achai (God) made the temples.

And God gave permission for 6,000 years of trial. Nobody knows if the world will turn to God or to Kaifas. In these 6,000 years the devil will do what he can to gain it. But the wise men, even those of Rome, don't know what will happen. All this is according to the scriptures. But even the wise men don't know if there will be winds or perhaps nothing. (Where are we now?) We still lack 4,000 years. These things about the life and death of Our Señor are very sad. (Crumrine 1973:1136-39).

In summary, from "significant contexts largely worked out by the anthropologist" (Turner 1967:20) we may argue that these myths describe the creation of the world and of The Holy Family root metaphor (see the following figure). Two male gods with equal power interact on the basis of friendship and begin the creation of the world from clay. One imitates the other yet he fails to produce perfect imitations, and two groups of men as well as hens (domesticated animals) and owls (wild animals) are created. Also with the creation of men, speech, or at least the problem of speech, appears. It is intimated that the imitating god Kaifas speaks badly and refuses to respect the innovator God, Our Lord, *Itom Achai*. This sin *Itom Achai* cannot forgive, the friendship is broken, and Kaifas raises his army against *Itom Achai Usi* (The Son of Our Father). *Itom Achai* also creates woman from a rib of the already created man (see Crumrine 1973: 1139) and through the Holy Spirit impregnates Mary producing a Holy Child. When the Child matures, becoming a renowned curer and teacher, Kaifas's army captures and kills Him, thus introducing death. However, Christ triumphs over death and Kaifas, defeated, retreats to the mountains. Through the role of Kaifas which shifts from a friend, trickster, and imitator of God to that of an enemy, we see the appearance of fertility, the Holy Family, of death, and of language. This establishment of the Holy Family as a root metaphor provides a structure for other realms of nature; heavens, Father Sun, Mother Moon, their children the Stars; forest, Father, Mother of the forest and their children the Animals; the ocean, Father, Mother of the Fish, their children; the domesticated animals and their protector, Señor Santiago (a member of The Holy Family) who produces Winds.

The root metaphor and linked set of myths associated with the Holy Family members also discuss the types of relationships which tie members of the family to one another. *Itom Achai* is positively *Hue?ena* (dangerous). Like one's human father, one obeys *Itom Achai* or one is punished. The two following myths discuss the importance of respect for God (Crumrine 1973:1142; 1978:236).

I. A long time ago Our Lord came visiting his people in the Mayo River Valley. "What are you planting, my son?" he asked. Some people were not responsive, they did not believe in Itom Achai. They were ill-bred, unmannerly. When El Señor asked, "What are you planting?" they answered, "We are planting stones." God answered, "If you are planting stones then stones you will harvest." At this early time there were no mountains. God has not yet made the mountains. So all over the world, these people who answered, "stones!" lost their crops which turned into the mountains. Then God asked another man, "What are you planting, my son?" "I am planting pumpkins and corn," said the man. "Pumpkins and corn," replied God. "Then pumpkins and corn you will harvest." And God blessed the fields, they were fertile and a huge crop resulted. And the man harvested much corn and many pumpkins, because God had blessed the planting of the fields. The other man used bad words to God. But Itom Achai has power, (Machiria) light. The others were ill-bred (badly created), bad, and dangerous.

The Establishment of the Holy Family Model

God + Companion (Kaifas)

(creates)　　　(imitates)

Hen　　　　Owl

(domesticated)　　(wild)

(creates)　　　(imitates)

Man in his Image　　　Man (Capakoba) in his Image

Good Words, Respect　　Bad Words, Lack Respect,

Baptized　　　　Not-baptized

(creates)　　　(builds)

Woman from Man's Rib　　Army

(creates)　　　(pursues)

Child　　　　Child

(knowledge,　　　(captures, kills)
curing power)

Jesus　　　Jesus

(returns from　　(alone in shame and
the dead to His　　defeat retreats to
Mother and the　　the mountains)
Church)

Itom Achai—
Itom Aye
Itom Achai
Usi　　　　　　　　　　Kaifas

They did not believe in God. When God asked them a question they responded impolitely to Our Lord. Their words, their talk, was very bad. When Our Lord asked, "What are you planting?" they responded, "We are planting rocks." Thus rocks grew up in their fields. Thus they produced, grew, mountains, a crop of mountains. This was a long long time ago.

II. . . . God made all the world. . . . He is the creator of humanity just like the father is the creator of his son. But there is also death. . . . . God, El Señor, made (used) it in order to produce reformation. The woman who was watching El Señor opened the pot. She wanted to see inside. There was an old man, an ancient one. He was inside for the renewal of his body. From this old man the power of God was producing a child. This was the renovation through the power of El Señor. But because the woman looked, because she saw the meat of his body, the ancient one died forever. No human had the power to look into the pot.

On the other hand, Mayos characterize *Itom Aye* (Our Mother) as warm and loving, not *hue?ena* (dangerous). The following text illustrates this point (Crumrine 1973:1148):

> God made the world. It is powerful and beautiful. This world is a result of the powerful sacred hand of God. Some say there is no God. But if there was no God who would care for, look out for poor plain people like ourselves. No one would look out for us. We have to believe that God is protecting us. And that Itom Aye is caring for us. Because from whom are we born, if it isn't from Our Mother? Itom Aye is Our Mother from her we are born. Because Itom Aye is the only mother here. She is very beautiful because according to our beliefs She loves us. Itom Aye makes many miracles because She has power. She is a member of The Holy Family.

A final text (Crumrine 1979:108) describes the experience of a second Mayo during hurricane Liza which took place in October 1976. The experience is accepted as legitimate and as an actual occurrence by my friend who related it to me. This suggests that the root metaphor of The Holy Family is still effective among Mayos.

> Juan, a former paskome (ritual host) in Banari, saw Itom Achai and Itom Aye Guadelupe during the hurricane Liza. The wind was terrific and there were many clouds and much lightning but very little rain. Juan looked up in the sky and in the clouds he saw Itom Achai and Itom Aye. Itom Achai was trying to burn up the world and was throwing down lightning rays to ignite the world. Itom Aye was carrying a bucket of water. She was dumping the water on the fire and keeping the world from burning up.

Evidence of the continued strength of The Holy Family root metaphor is also found in modern Mayo revitalization movements (see Crumrine 1975, 1977; Erasmus 1961, 1967; and Spicer 1970). The ideology of these modern Mayo religious movements focuses upon an intense fear of the anger of *Itom Achai*, who has appeared to prophets and their followers and revealed that He intends to destroy humanity unless we return to traditional Mayo ceremonialism. The appearance of *Itom Achai* is not to be desired but represents a kind of punishment, an indication that *Itom Achai* is displeased with modern culture.

Conclusion

In summary, Mayo ritual and myth appear to be based not upon a physiological metaphor, but rather upon the Holy Family root metaphor. This ritual symbol and root metaphor consists of a sensory pole, the individual nuclear family, and an ideological pole, the Holy Family. Mayo rituals and myths manipulate and elaborate elements and aspects of this root metaphor and in so doing generate a complete world view dynamically adapted to recent historical events and present northwest Mexican culture and society. Beyond suggesting a new method of analysis, does this study contain useful insights for Middle American anthropology? In examining this question, we hypothesize that this root metaphor characterizes northwest and west Mexican ritual and belief systems. Spicer (1964) has developed the concept of a central Uto-Aztecan type of religious system and has isolated a dual seasonal pattern in Yaqui and Huichol ritual and symbolism. The dry, male, curing, danger, suffering-taboos season contrasts with the wet, female, fertility, benevolence, happiness-relaxation season. Although we do not have space here to develop the numerous parallels, I (Crumrine 1981) have shown how the Yaqui, Huichol, and Mayo ritual cycles converge, both structurally, based upon the concept of duality, and symbolically in terms of the family root metaphor. Even though the Huichol pantheon consists of a more diffuse set of supernaturals, the system is based upon the extended family, that is, upon the kinship system. Structurally, male and female provide a set of categories which reduce the numerous Huichol deities to a dual pattern. In the Mayo case male and female do not provide such neat categories; however, a second set of categories also drawn from the family root metaphor suggests interesting parallels. Mayo cold weather rituals treat the life, death, and resurrection of Christ that is the parent-child relationship and the authority of *Itom Achai*. On the other hand, Mayo warm weather ritual develops the encounter, the "embrace" of *Itom Achai* and *Itom Aye*, and involves interpueblo exchange and large festive ceremonials. The cold authoritarian "male" rituals of All Souls and All Saints and Lenten ceremonialism are replaced by the warm embraces of *Itom Achai* and *Itom Aye* characterizing the *Santisima Tiniran* and *Espiritu Santo* ceremonies. Thus a social root metaphor, that of the Holy Family, is more characteristic of northwest and west Mexican ritual and belief than one based upon human physiology. The examination of Middle American ritual symbolism in terms of this methodology should be interesting and productive.

REFERENCES

Beck, Brenda E.F.
1978   "The Metaphor as a Mediator Between Semantic and Analogic Modes of Thought," *Current Anthropology* 19:83-97.
Crumrine, N. Ross
1973   "La tierra te devorará: un análisis estructural de los mitos de los indígenas mayo," *América Indígena* 33:1119-50.
1974   "Anomalous Figures and Liminal Roles," *Anthropos* 69:858-73.
1975   "A New Mayo Indian Religious Movement in Northwest Mexico," *Journal of Latin American Lore* 1:127-45.
1977   *The Mayo Indians of Sonora, Mexico: A People Who Refuse to Die* (Tucson: University of Arizona Press).
1978   "A Transformational Analysis of Mayo Ceremonialism and Myth," *Journal of Latin American Lore* 4:231-42.
1979   "Mayo Indian Myth and Ceremonialism, Northwest Mexico: The Dual Ceremonial Cycle," in *Ritual Symbolism and Ceremonialism in the Americas,* ed. N. Ross Crumrine. Occasional Publications in Anthropology, Ethnology Series, no. 33 (Greeley, Colo.: Museum of Anthropology, University of Northern Colorado). (Also published in *Katunob* 10(2):44-66, 1977).
1981   "The Ritual of the Cultural Enclave Process: The Dramatization of Oppositions Among the Mayo Indians of Northwest Mexico," in *Persistent Peoples: Cultural Enclaves in Perspective,* ed. George P. Castile and Gilbert Kushner (Tucson: University of Arizona Press).
Erasmus, Charles J.
1961   *Man Takes Control: Cultural Development and American Aid* (Minneapolis: University of Minnesota Press).

1967   "Culture Change in Northwest Mexico," in *Mexican and Peruvian Communities, Contemporary Change in Traditional Societies,* vol. 3, ed. Julian H. Steward (Urbana: University of Illinois Press).

Fernandez, James W.

1974   "The Mission of Metaphor in Expressive Culture," *Current Anthropology* 15:119-45.

Linton, Ralph

1936   *The Study of Man* (New York: Appleton-Century).

Makarius, Laura

1982   "The Mask and the Violation of Taboo," in *The Power of Symbols:*
in press   *The Mask and Masquerade in the Americas,* ed. N. Ross Crumrine and Marjorie Halpin (Vancouver, B.C.: University of British Columbia Press).

Pepper, Stephen C.

1961   *World Hypotheses: A Study in Evidence* (Berkeley and Los Angeles: University of California Press, first published in 1942).

Spicer, Edward H.

1964   *Apuntes sobre el tipo de religión de los Yuto-Aztecas centrales,* Actas y Memorias del XXXV Congreso Internacional de Americanistas (Mexico).

1970   "Contrasting Forms of Nativism Among the Mayos and Yaquis of Sonora, Mexico," in *The Social Anthropology of Latin America,* ed. Walter Goldschmidt and Harry Hoijer (Los Angeles: Latin American Center, University of California).

Turner, Victor

1967   *The Forest of Symbols* (Ithaca, N.Y.: Cornell University Press).

1974   *Dramas, Fields, and Metaphors: Symbolic Action in Human Society* (Ithaca, N.Y.: Cornell University Press).

confined to a comparison between Western and non-Western beliefs and practices, the practical usefulness of this research is undeniable for public health programs where immediate, even though often palliative, results are desired.

The second trend, the anthropology of medicine, or ethnomedicine (see Hughes 1968:99) is based on the premise that not only states of health and illness, but also specific illnesses recognized in a particular society—including their etiology, prevention, symptomatology, and cure—are culturally defined (examples of this are Norge 1958; Frake 1961; Rubel 1964). In this type of research there is no need to take into consideration either the welfare of the people or matters of adequacy and efficiency of the beliefs and practices studied.

Both trends are present in Guatemalan studies. Anthropology for health has been mostly carried out by health and welfare organizations, such as the Institute of Nutrition of Central America and Panama (INCAP), the Family Welfare Association (APROFAM), the Academy of Medical and Natural Sciences (ACMN), and several religious organizations. Ethnomedical studies have mostly been carried out by anthropologists associated with either national or foreign universities. The contributions in this article fall within the context of the second trend.

Research in ethnomedicine in Guatemala reflects the stages anthropological research in general has gone through in this country. The work done by Germans (Stoll 1938; Schultz-Jena 1945; Termer 1957) at the end of the nineteenth century and the beginning of the twentieth was descriptive in nature, survey-like in extension, and lacking sociocultural depth. From a present-day perspective the research was methodologically archaic. The analytical unit was generally the large but poorly defined cultural area, within and outside of which few or no comparisons were attempted. If this tradition had continued for some decades more, however, an ethnological (comparative) approach might have eventually developed. But the tradition ended abruptly, giving way to the structural-functional approach.

American universities, influenced by Radcliffe-Brown's and Malinowski's teachings, introduced in the 1930s a more theoretically oriented research in which an in-depth understanding of society and culture was thought essential. Research was carried out in communities rather than in larger areas because the structural functionalists lacked interest in interchange and diffusion. They chose restricted areas of study, which cancelled the possibility of comparative studies in Guatemala. Compared to the U.S.A., where the ethnological phase was completed by Boas, Kroeber, Wissler, and others before the community studies developed, in Guatemala the area studies were developed too late and the community studies too early to produce a true ethnological understanding of the country. Consequently, at the end of the structural-functional phase, anthropological knowledge of Guatemala appears as a mosaic of scattered bits and pieces reflecting a variety of methods, interests, and theoretical orientations, but conforming to no particular pattern. As for ethnomedical studies, the lack of research with a widespread geographical coverage has led to overgeneralizations made on the basis of findings in restricted areas, and underestimations of the importance of differences found throughout the country.

This article reports a study which attempts to overcome some of the above limitations. The country was divided into fourteen regions on the basis of preliminary historical, geographical, and cultural criteria. Nineteen communities in eleven of the fourteen regions have already been studied during the last five years (see Map I). Each community was visited by professors and students of the Universidad del Valle de Guatemala for a period ranging from one to ten months in a single or in consecutive field sessions. This approach permits a deeper cultural understanding than that characterized by surveys, without forsaking an extensive geographical coverage. Key informants were used to clarify some issues, but the investigators relied on the bulk of the population to obtain data. The information was taped, usually in Spanish or in vernacular languages, and transcribed. The reader should be aware, however, that in spite of our efforts, there are differences in the quality and extensiveness of the data from one locality to another due to circumstantial issues. This variability, and the enormous lacunae in our present knowledge, obliges us to present the following description as a preliminary draft.

Distribution of Medical Beliefs and Practices

The frequency with which particular illnesses are mentioned in the written materials and tapes provides a first approximation to the distribution of medical beliefs and practices. The illnesses were arranged from the most frequently mentioned to the least frequently mentioned, and their relative importance was ascertained in each community. Greater facility in eliciting information regarding some diseases, as well as each interviewer's particular interests might have biased the information to a point that no serious statistical use of it should be made. However, a review of the data shows three important issues. First, folk medical beliefs and practices are still prevalent and widespread among the Indian population of Guatemala. Second, some of the most frequently mentioned illnesses like *ojo* and *susto* are recurrent in all the communities studied. Third, there are a number of illnesses like *hijillo, laele,* and *akwas,* which are also very frequently mentioned, but considerably more restricted geographically.

Simply using the name of illnesses would constitute a weak basis for drawing conclusions. First, it supposes that illnesses that share the same name in two or more communities have more in common than is the case. Another shortcoming is to overlook the similarities that may occur among illnesses of different names. Both of these assumptions have contributed to maintain a fragmentary and incoherent picture of folk medicine in Guatemala. Attempting to discover the patterns of variation and the geographical distribution of illnesses of the same name, and the common denominators between illnesses, constitutes the power of the comparative method here proposed. The following section exemplifies this procedure. The discussion begins using data on *hijillo, akwas, aire,* and *laele,* all of which are frequently mentioned illnesses restricted to some areas of the country. A discussion on two widespread illnesses, *ojo* and *susto* follows. Information on other illnesses is presented when needed to support the hypotheses that are forwarded.

Hijillo. For the people of Senahú, Chamelco, Purulhá, Chicaj, Tunucó and Pelillo Negro, in the eastern half of Gutatemala, *hijillo* is a serious medical hazard.[2] Swelling (Senahú, Purulhá, Chicaj), diarrhea (Chamelco, Chicaj, Purulhá), vomiting (Purulhá), hair loss (Senahú), in some cases marasmus (Chamelco, Chicaj), and stomachache and backache (Tunucó) are the common symptoms. The etiology of this illness is associated with sexual and reproductive processes and with substances and matters associated with these processes. The patient becomes ill by seeing a delivery or a coitus, usually between dogs (Chamelco, Purulhá, Chicaj); by touching a newborn animal or its mother or by touching a bitch not washed after having had

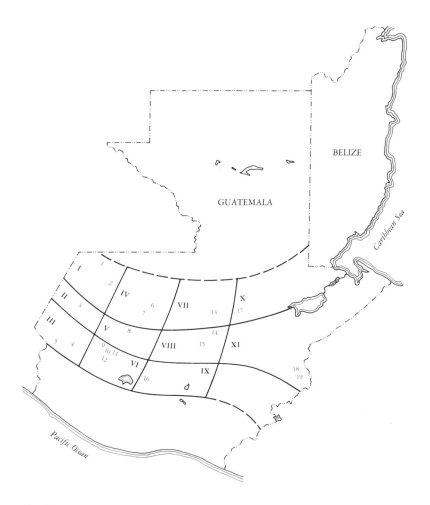

Map I

Region I	Region V	Region VIII
1 San Mateo Ixtahuacán	8 Scapulas	14 Purulhá
2 Soloma	Region VI	15 Chicaj
Region II	9 San Bartolo	Region IX
3 Todos Santos	10 Momostenango	16 Patzún
Region III	11 Santa María Chiquimula	Region X
4 Comitancillo incoming	12 San Francisco El Alto	17 Senahú
5 Tajumulco data	Region VII	Region XI
Region IV	13 Chamelco	18 Tunucó
6 Chajul		19 Pelillo Negro
7 Nebaj		

coitus (Senahú, Chamelco); by being exposed either to *vahos* (fumes, odors, emanations) of the placenta, to animals who recently have had sexual intercourse (Purulhá, Chicaj), or to the *vahos* of menstruation or the vaginal secretions of an animal in heat (Chamelco).

In the northern regions of Chamelco and Senahú only women are reported to "transmit" *hijillo,* hence the Kekchí name *chak ixk* ("woman's illness") given to it. In contrast, patients can be male or female adults as well as children, in both Senahú and Chamelco. In the south, in Purulhá and Chicaj, males who recently have had sexual intercourse can also produce *hijillo* in both males and females, but in these regions only infants and children are affected by it. Tunucó and Pelillo Negro (municipio of Jocotán) provide only fragmentary data that permits only preliminary statements; apparently most patients are male children.

Curing varies throughout the area. Covering and rubbing the patient's body with warm cow excrement to produce sweating precedes a cold bath at dawn in the Chamelco region. An addition or substitute for the previous procedure is drinking a beverage of wild pig sexual glands and taking dew baths. In the Purulhá region, cold baths early in the day and herb teas are the common procedure. In the Chicaj region warm water baths replace the cold baths of the two previous regions, but "cold"[3] elements, such as river pebbles, river plants, and *nixtamal* (corn dough) milk are added to the water to produce a cognitive coldness within a physical warmness. "Cold" foods, such as chicken, are included in the diet while hot ones, such as *caldos* (soups), are eliminated and considered very dangerous. In the Jocotán region curing is done with *horchata* (light gruel) made with ginger and drunk at dawn. The only case reported for Senahú mentions drinking laxatives.

A review of the etiology of this illness permits the differentiation of three kinds of agents: (1) those of a volitional character, as in the case of an intense desire typical of periods of rut, as in a bitch in heat; (2) *vahos,* as those produced by menstruation; and (3) those of a sensorial character, as when transmission occurs through sight or touch of filth.[4]

Considering all the regions studied, the most frequently mentioned agents of *hijillo* are of sensorial character. Up north, in the Chamelco region, "intense desire" is very important, while south, in Purulhá *vahos* are the usual cause. It is the contention of this article that these and similar etiological differences reflect the existence of several underlying "medical theories" with different levels of pervasiveness and systematization in the various regions. The distribution of geographically restricted illnesses and the ways people conceive other widely known illnesses correspond to the relative importance of these medical theories in the various regions. The following paragraphs describe the geographical variations in the conception of akwas and how these relate to the medical theories of "intense desire" and *vahos*.

Akwas. Akwas is another typical illness of eastern Guatemala.[5] It occurs frequently in Senahú, and Chamelco in the northeast, to a lesser degree in Purulhá, to the south, and probably is well known throughout the northwardly expanding Kekchí territory.

Akwas is not a set of symptoms, but a process which involves a pregnant woman or her mate, an unborn child, and an object, a thing, animal, person, or event, acting as a secondary or mediate agent. The mother or father is "impressed" by the "image" of the agent, which in due time affects the unborn child. The newborn child, any time after birth, has symptoms usually resembling the agent. Thus, symptoms vary greatly according to the characteristics of the agent, that is, a rash on the leg could be produced by a red *tamal,* funny tracheal sounds by a cow, green diarrhea by avocados, and scales on the head by fish. These are but a few examples of a very heterogeneous list.

Not only do symptoms and their agents vary, but also the manner in which an "impression" takes place. Very frequently an emotion mediates between the agent and the impression as in the following case. An *akwas* of squirrel's testicles occurred when a pregnant woman was astonished by the size of a squirrel's glands. Consequently, the child developed bumps on the head. An *akwas* of cracklings was caused by the mother's intense unsatisfied desire to eat fried pork lard when pregnant. Children with this *akwas* have pimples on the head and buttocks. A child was born with strangely formed ears because the mother ate mangoes with relish. Another child got thinner and thinner because his mother drank with disgust coffee unsanitarily prepared by her stepmother.

Sometimes, however, the "impression" occurs without mediation of an emotion. The "image" may just enter through the body's openings. The *akwas* of potato peels is produced by the pregnant woman having stepped over the peels. Girls suffering from this *akwas* are unstable and promiscuous. The mouth can also serve as a way for the image to get into the body. Eating spotted eggs produces pimples on the child's head. *Vahos* entering through nostrils and pores from ants accidently burned while the mother cooks, result in pimples all over the child's body. Simple sensorial contact, like touching, may also produce *akwas*.

In most cases the mother is impressed, but when an emotion mediates, the father may be the one "impressed." A father was astonished by another man who had a serious speech defect; consequently, he transmitted this defect to his child. These and similar variations are related to the pervasiveness of various ethnomedical beliefs in different regions.

Senahú and Chamelco are Kekchí-speaking regions, while Purulhá has an original Pokomchí population in which old and new Kekchí migrants from the north have settled. Among these three Kekchí populations one of the emotions more frequently reported in relation to *akwas* is an intense desire for something specific: 63 percent of the cases in Senahú, 37 percent in Chamelco, and 50 percent among the Kekchí of Purulhá. Other emotions and sensorial events are also important, but not even once are *vahos* mentioned in connection with *akwas* among the Kekchí Indians.[6] The situation sharply contrasts with the data of the native Pokomchí population in Purulhá among whom mention of them is very frequent.

Intense desire as an actual cause of illness during pregnancy is a belief widely spread throughout the country. Unsatisfied *antojos* (cravings) are a common source of illness south, west, and east of the Senahú and Chamelco regions, for instance in Chicaj, Patzún, Momostenango, Tunucó, and Pelillo Negro. But already in the neighboring Achí region of Chicaj, south of Purulhá, the name *akwas* seems not to be used, and unsatisfaction causes abortion rather than sickness. The same was found in the western Cakchiquel town of Patzún, in the Chortí region in the east, and is reported for Santa María Cauqué (García, Virrutia, and Béhar 1977), Chinautla (Reina 1966), and San Pedro La Laguna (Paul and Paul 1952; Rogoff 1977). Moreover, in Senahú and Chamelco the mother is the one who desires something specific while in the other regions the fetus is the one who wants to eat something; *el niño pide* (the child asks), it is said. When the desire is not satisfied in Patzún the children die and are "born with the tongue out in expectation of what was so cruelly denied." *Akwas* is an illness of "impression of images of things," while *antojos* in Patzún and also in the Chortí region concerns the desire for specific food, "real things."

"Impression" by images during pregnancy is common throughout Guatemala among Indians and Ladinos. But in Senahú, Chamelco, and Purulhá this process occupies a predominant place. The cases and kinds of impressions are more varied than in other parts of the country. Moreover, conceptions concerned with intense desires, *vahos*, and sensorial contact, which by themselves could be thought of as medical theories, seem to be embedded in a macro theory of "images and impressions."

Belief in *vahos*, very much restricted in the etiology of *akwas* in Purulhá, is prevalent in a larger geographical area when curing is considered. The most common cure for *akwas* includes *humar* (from Spanish *ahumar*, to smoke) the patient and its purpose seems to be to get the "image" of the thing and the "thing" back together. This is done by burning the agent or parts of it if the agent is an object, or a piece of cloth, hair, or nails if the agent is a person or living animal. Bones of dead animals can also be used. The sick child is placed face down to inhale the smoke. Since the "image" of the thing causing the "impression" is of an ethereal nature, the thing is also made ethereal by converting it into smoke, thus facilitating their reunion. Apparently, the fumes inhaled by the child "rescues" the "image." This interpretation made by some informants seems to be corroborated by the existence of an alternate cure when burning is impossible or inconvenient. This other cure consists of rubbing the part of the body affected by the "image" with the object, or part of it, responsible for the *akwas*, to get the image to stick to it.

After burning the object, the mother and child may taste the ashes, principally when an intense desire mediates in the etiology. This also helps to rescue the image. The image goes out of the patient to the remaining ashes. Consequently these ashes are dangerous; they contain a loose image corresponding to no actual "thing." They should be thrown away, or left on a street where the illness could be picked up by another pregnant woman or her husband.

Although *humar* is the most common curing method for *akwas* in these regions, those *akwas* produced by intense desire, north of Purulhá, emphasize mock satisfaction of an unsatisfied wish, that is, feigning to eat a crackling cures a child suffering of *akwas* of cracklings. It seems, therefore, that two theories coexist in this part of the country. The etiology of *akwas* in the northern regions is shaped by the theory of intense desire, while in Purulhá, in the south, it is shaped by the theory of *vahos*. The curing practices, however, exhibit a strong influence from the *vahos* theory throughout the *akwas* area. In general this geographical distribution corroborates the differences in interpretations found in *hijillo* to the north and south of this part of the country. Outside this area, intense desire is predominant in the etiology of *akwas*-like illnesses, but then it is usually not related to the macro theory of "impressions" and "images."

Aire and Laele. Unlike hijillo and akwas, *aire* (wind, air) is known in many parts of Guatemala (see Rodríguez Rouanet 1971:29-31), although its characteristics vary considerably from region to region. Some of these characteristics, and their geographical distribution are examined in the following paragraphs. The description begins with the Ixil town of Chajul, in the northwest. Here, the dominant theory concerns supernatural encounters, but there is also evidence of the hot-and-cold theory and the vahos theory, which gives the opportunity of tracing relationships to adjacent geographical areas.

Chajuleños distinguish two kinds of illnesses, those *con contenido* (with supernatural intervention), and those *sin contenido* (without supernatural intervention). *Culabi'* is an illness of the last type resulting from going into the cold air after being near the fire. Symptoms include convulsions, fever, and fainting fits. The blood *se engruma* (it becomes clotted), *se desarregla* (it spoils), *se corta* (it curdles), and sticks to the *nervios* (arteries) obstructing them. *Shwamal timvi'* (fever in my head) is another illness *sin contenido* in which *aire* intervenes. Symptoms develop also after going out into the cold air when one is warm, or has a cold. The "body gets cold and the blood looks for refuge in the head, the warmest place." Consequently, the brains become hot and full of blood making thinking difficult. Notice that in both illnesses body and environmental temperatures are involved. The complex body of ideas related to temperature clashes, mixtures and balance is here referred to as the hot-and-cold theory (see Foster 1953; Currier 1966; Adams and Rubel 1967; and Cosminsky 1977).

The conception of *aire* within the context of the hot-and-cold theory is further developed south of Chajul. In the Cachiquel town of Patzún, *qaq'iq* (air) is occasionally caused by *cólera* (anger), but usually by temperature clashes as when eating and drinking food (water, tortillas, etc.) served cold when the body is hot. A similar interpretation is held in San Francisco El Alto, a Quiché town west of Patzún, and southwest of Chajul. The importance of relative temperature is such that in Patzún and in San Francisco *aire* is displaced from the etiology, as in Chajul, to the symptomatology: patients suffer stomachaches and intestinal gases. This conceptual change is further exemplified by the belief that people who take cold baths may get *aire:* cold enters through the body's pores and "with time the coldness of the water becomes *aire* in the stomach." Some people in Patzún and San Francisco also believe that because the climate in these towns is cold, *aire* is a prevalent sickness. Bundling the lower part of a small child's body with warm covers in Santa María Chiquimula, northeast of San Francisco, but still south of Chajul, prevents cold air from entering the stomach through the body's natural openings.

But in addition to these conceptions embedded in the hot-and-cold theory, Chajuleños conceive another type of *aire*, one with *contenido*, and embedded in the theory of supernatural encounters. The distinction, as well as the relation between one and the other kind of illness can be appreciated in *chok'an* (cramps), also called San Pedro Vicario's illness[7] because this saint controls it. The cramps that characterize it result from going from warm quarters to cold air as in *aire sin contenido*. But sometimes these symptoms are due to a supernatural encounter occurring accidentally, or resulting from disrespect for ancestors, spirits, or gods. Differences in causation do not represent two levels of explanation (Foster and Anderson 1978: 68), one natural and immediate, the other supernatural and remote; instead they express two different sets of etiological ideas. When the first set is used, *chok'an* is an illness of the same kind as *qaq'iq'* (aire in Patzún). When the second set is used, it is an illness of the same kind as *laele,* the most typical illness in Chajul.

Laele (spiritual contact) or *lajvetzil* is a supernatural illness par excellence (see also *susto).* A spirit, or los muertos (the dead) touch a person for reasons similar to those mentioned for *chok'an,* and results in shaking, strong headaches, bodyaches, bruises, and strong twitching in the wrist. In extreme cases contact may occur because the spirit of the dead wants to single out someone for a death sentence, and therefore lashes the person's back, leaving it black and blue. The encounter may accidentally occur with any of "the spirits that roam the streets." It may also occur at the entrance of the hut where *Atnaj* Marcos and *Atnaj* Martín, of the *ronda* (sort of patrolling police among the supernatural), may be standing to make sure that the spirit of the night touches he who is at fault or any other member of his household. Curing requires the services of a *zahorin*. The patient is led to the family altar where incense is burned, and long prayers and apologies are offered to the ghost, or deity in question. Tobacco soaked in water and "containing prayers" is spat on the patient's face by the *zahorín* to remove the *tzini'* (what is wrong, the evil thing, the spirit). *Laele* relates to *aire* not only through sicknesses with double interpretations such as *chok'an,* but also through the association of air and wind with spirits and souls, because of their ethereal character and their common association with breathing. This relation is held and clearly expressed south of Chajul. In Patzún *qaq'iq'* (air) is caused by physical cold air, while *itzel qaq'iq'* (bad air) is associated with supernatural encounters.[8] These last lack, however, the social and cognitive prominence that *laele* reaches in Chajul.

Supernatural encounters and punishments are features usually combined in *laele,* a relatively well-defined illness. But outside the north-central region, these features recur usually in a separate form in the etiology of many illnesses. The data also suggest that their importance is considerably less than in the north-central region. Supernatural punishment is frequently an ultimate cause, and the encounter, the precipitating factor of sickness. The kind of beings encountered are usually not associated with a particular illness, but its characteristics are sometimes influenced by the dominant theory of the region. Around Lake Atitlán and towards the extreme west of the country, where cannibalism, envy, and wishful harm are important,[9] encounters with men with supernatural powers are very common. This is true of Santa Catarina Ixtahuacán, Patzún, and Todos Santos. In the Quiché region of Sacapulas there is even a specific illness for one particular kind of encounter. *Jurltzun* or *halacuero* (skin pullers) are men born on given days of the native calendar, endowed with supernatural powers, who suck small children at night. They cause *la caída de mollera* (fallen fontanel). La Farge (1947:151-155), Oakes (1951:170-177), Mendelson (1965:113-115), Woods (1968: 94-95), Douglas (1969:97-101), and Saler (1969:21-35) report on the importance of the *isom, characotel, win,* and other evil men with transformative powers, for Lake Atitlán and its environs, and for the extreme west. These regions contrast with the northeast. Thus, in Chamelco, encounters are most common with major deities, such as the *Tzultakas,* the owners of mountains and valleys.[10]

In *aire* the relationship between hot-and-cold theories and supernatural encounters also changes as one travels eastward from Chajul. The people of Chamelco combine a physical wind with the deification of air and supernatural punishment. The last feature is typical of *laele* and other illnesses caused by supernatural encounters. The first feature is typical of *culabi'* and other hot-and-cold illnesses. The second feature, a substitute for gods and the dead, is typical of the region. Notice it in the following expression: "People who do not think of God, but of evil things, are susceptible to become ill due to the *bad spirit of the air.*"

In Purulhá, south of Chamelco, *aire* is associated with materialized minor deities rather than with ethereal powerful ones as in Chajul, and is very much disassociated from the hot-and-cold conception, as the following example shows. A fifteen-year-old girl was washing in the river, "she probably was in love and was thinking evil things. A girl appeared to her. The other girl was the bad air. The fifteen-year-old girl became crazy." In Purulhá *aire* is also associated to the *shishimit,*[11] "a little animal-like being, similar to a little boy. Sometimes they appear in pairs, and are usually seen swinging from guava trees. They give bad air to those who see them. They give fever, and people may die." The cure consists of baths containing special leaves, the burning of *copal-pom* (type of incense), and the calling of the sick person's spirit (see also *susto*).

The *halacuero* and the *shishimit* dramatize some of the differences between east and west. The *halacuero* of Sacapulas is a man that crosses the natural-supernatural division to eat human bodies. The *shishimit* is a semigod that at times crosses the natural-supernatural lines to capture men's souls.

It is here in Purulhá, where *aire* is very much disassociated from the hot-and-cold theory, that the *vaho* conception of air gains ground.

It is said, for instance, that when curing is successful "one can see how he (the patient) expels fumes."

The association of *aire* with odors and fumes is stronger south of Purulhá. People of the Achí town of Chicaj believe that *aire* ambulates, coming from far away, "from other nations and volcanoes—air brings the blood of dead people and animals from other places. This blood is heated by the sun and emanates a bad smell." With the air also come "the *vahos* of those things sent by those who work with dirty things (the devil)."

As the last quotation makes clear, *aire* and *vahos* are related in this region because of their mutual association with the dead. *Vahos* emanate when passing from life to death, from being part of the living to becoming part of the world of inert objects. This world includes excrements, urine, sweat, placentas, meat, menstrual blood, corpses. Hence, the association of supernatural with *vahos* is a local variation of an association already present in Chajul's *laele: aosu ronda testas con un ánima,*[12] that is, sickness "because of encountering the spirit of the dead." In Chajul the ánima is, however, a personified entity while under the *vahos* theory it is diffused. In Chajul and Patzún the ánima is cold as the dead and the mountain wind. In eastern Guatemala the *vahos* are hot as the dying ones and also as the warm wind of the semiarid and jungle regions in which most people live. There is evidence of the association between *aire* and *vahos* in most of the curing practices. Burning cattle horns and aromatic plants near the sick are used to "counteract the stench of the dead."

Susto. The widespread distribution[13] of this illness makes it possible to weigh the relative importance of the various medical theories, without endangering comparability by changing from one illness to another. Let us return to eastern Guatemala where the distinction between thing and image, and also the process of impression are crucial. They constitute the bases for the competing theories of intense desire and *vahos.* The conception of *susto* in this area fits within these theories.

Lack of appetite, general apathy, fear, and fever are experienced after fright occurs. The *raniva* (the heart, or spirit) of those struck by fright leaves the body and remains in the place where the fright has occurred. At the same time, the image of the person, animal, or event causing the fright impresses the patient. Curing, therefore, consists of reestablishing the original order, inasmuch as this is possible. In doing thus, emphasis may be placed on one or another aspect of the etiological process: rescuing the spirit or expelling the image. In Chamelco both aspects of the etiological process are generally considered in the cure.

Fright may result from at least three situational settings: (1) when the person himself is the victim of a bad experience, for example when he falls in a well or in a river; (2) when another person or an animal is the cause of fright, for instance, when a bull pursues a person; (3) when a person, an animal, or an event interrupts or disturbs a relationship between two persons.

The procedures used to expell the image in the first two types stand in opposition. When only a patient is involved (type 1), there is no substantive thing acting as an agent to which the image can return. Consequently, the curing process requires the creation of a surrogate. For instance, a girl went to fetch water and fell into the river. She got frightened. A five-centimeter-tall clay doll was made. Thirty hairs from the top of the girl's head, some of her eyelashes, nails, and pieces of cloth were stuck on the doll. The doll and the girl were taken to the place where the fright occurred. The father whipped his daughter hard to oblige "the heart that scares" to leave the girl and stick to the doll. Then, the doll was buried to seal the association of the image and the thing—"Stay here, this is your place."

When the source of fright is another person or an animal (type 2), one might think that it would be sufficient to strike the patient so that the image could return to its source and the patient be cured. Instead, the thing, person, or animal is made ethereal like its image, to produce a reunion of both; for this purpose the person is *humado* (smoked) by burning hair, nails, cloth, and the like belonging to the source of sickness.

In type 1, the agent is not a tangible thing, and, therefore, it is necessary to create a tangible model of the patient to serve as a surrogate to the image. The association of the image with this surrogate is sealed by burying both in dirt. In type 2, where the agent is a tangible thing, an intangible model of the agent is made, and the association is sealed in the air, the invisible world. In both cases model and image are cast away from sight and from the world of the common living people.

Rescuing the patient's heart is, in most cases, a complementary part of curing. In type 1, the spirit may stay in the place where the fright occurred. Curing consists mostly of enticing it back by beating the place where it is supposed to be stuck to obtain its release. When an animal is involved as in type 2, the animal may also be beaten.

Some of the reported cases also suggest that *humar* might not only be the vehicle for the expulsion of the image but may provide for the return of the spirit. Burning the model of the agent forces the patient's image to return to its true owner. *Sustos* of the third type are discussed in the final section of this article.

In Purulhá, the symptoms of *susto* are similar to those of Chamelco, but curing emphasizes the calling of the spirit rather than the expulsion of the image. As in *akwas*, and consistent with the importance given to *vahos*, curing depends heavily on *soplar* (blowing) the wrist of the patient and, sometimes, the head and other parts of the body while calling the spirit. The few cases reported in Chicaj do not differ substantially from those in Chamelco.

In Chajul, where the theory of encounters is pervasive, fright usually takes place by encountering the supernatural as in *laele*. But sometimes *xobal (susto)* occurs due to "natural" events such as seeing a snake or taking a cold bath. In these cases, the hot-and-cold theory serves as a conceptual frame for the illness as in the case of *aire*.

The hands and face swell, the hair falls out, and the people become pale. Since the illness is *sin contenido* (that is, without supernatural intervention), calling of the spirit, so prevalent in Chamelco and more so in Purulhá, hardly takes place at all. Attention during the cure is placed on the expulsion processes and this has an entirely different interpretation from that given to it in the eastern regions. Sometimes the patient is made to drink a potion prepared with alcohol, *ruda* (Ruta graveolens), and other herbs that are considered hot. The person in charge of the cure takes this potion into his mouth and spits it on the patient's face and nude body making him sweat. After a while the patient, well covered, is left to relax. The purpose of the cure is to reestablish the heat in the body of the patient who is suffering from a "cold" illness. Sweating expells "something," probably the illness *(el mal)*, but nothing resembling an image, as in Chamelco.

South of Chajul, in the Momostenango region, *susto* is definitely a "cold" illness associated, as *aire* is in Patzún, with stomachaches, fever, and sometimes heartaches and nausea. Fright may follow an accident, an encounter with an animal, a fall, and in the case of children, it may occur after being beaten. But the consequences in Momostenango differ from the eastern region as well as from Chajul: *las lombrices se alborotan* (the intestinal parasites get excited and confused), coming out through the nostrils and mouth. Curing involves drinking hot beverages made with "hot" plants like *ruda,* which possess a strong smell, or *cruz de palo,* which is brought from the warm coastal area of the Pacific. They are considered to counteract the coldness of the disease.

Curing might also involve placing broiled meat on top of the patient's navel. The intestinal worms smell the food and settle down inside the worm bag that all of us have. There is neither calling of the spirit nor expulsion of an image or sickness. What is important is to restore the hot-and-cold balance or to "feed the worms."

In Patzún, to the southeast of Momostenango, and in Chajul, *kixawi'* or *ruwawneq* (fright) is a cold illness and is cured with hot herbs. But the hot-and-cold interpretation of *susto* is weaker than in Momostenango. This is unexpected since it is in this region where the hot-and-cold theory reaches its highest expression in *aire.* The data suggests some similarities with the Chamelco region and towns where impression is most important. But there are striking differences. In Patzún emphasis is placed solely on the rescuing of the spirit, while in Chamelco rescuing the spirit and expulsing the image are both important. These differences are dramatized by the curing practices. While in Chamelco a clay doll is buried with the image in the place where fright has occurred, in Patzún the spirit is brought back by placing some clay from the place where the fright occurred on the patient's forehead.

Our data for the extreme northwestern regions, although limited, suggest strong similarities with the Chajul regions. In the latter, the hot-and-cold theory is also dominant, although some attention is placed on calling the spirit. This is done in Soloma by whispering in the ear, on the back, and left side of the trunk every time that the *zahorín* spits the hot herb potion on the patient. The ceremony takes place at noon, inside a circle of nine white flowers. In Comitancillo (region III), in the extreme southwest, sweating practices also suggest a dominance of hot-and-cold theories, according to our incoming data. Just as the ideas presented for Chajul concerning the hot-and-cold theory reach the extreme west, so do the *laele*-like conceptions of Chajul, involving the supernatural, reach the extreme east. Among the Chortís there is mention of the "thieves of spirits that travel with the wind" associated with *susto*. Accordingly, the zahorín is not so sure, as in Chamelco, where the spirit may be, so to find it and rescue it are the important issues: *"palomita, palomita entra a tu cacaste, dónde te has metido?"* ("Little dove, where are you, come back to your cage.") The way the spirit is lost is a reminder of a supernatural encounter; the way the sickness is taken out from the patient is a reminder of the impression theory of nearby Purulhá and Chicaj. Not only is the spirit called, but a hen is rubbed over the nude patient's body to capture the illness.

Ojo. Like *susto,* this illness is well known throughout the country (Wisdom 1952:131; Gillin 1958; Paul 1959:14; Cosminsky 1976), and has a wide distribution, receiving many local interpretations. These interpretations seem to converge in Patzún, located about the center of the country, from where the description starts in an attempt to disentangle some of the complexities of this illness.

Just as *susto* is associated in Patzún with coldness and its cure usually involves heating, *ojo* is associated with "hotness" and its cure usually involves "cooling." "Cooling" is frequently done by rubbing an egg over the patient's body. The heat then passes to the egg and "cooks it." Heat may be thereafter dispersed or counteracted by submerging the egg in water with *ruda,* or by an equivalent procedure. The association with hotness is not exclusive to Patzún. In Chamelco, Purulhá, and Chicaj, curing may involve passing a live duck over the patient's body and then submerging it in water to avoid its death. Ducks, because of their association with water, are also associated with coldness. Among the Chortí, even farther east, "cold" substances such as lemon tree buds and "flowers of the dead" are spat over the patient's face.

In the western part of the country, *ojo* and hotness are also related, but the association is considerably weaker. It can be detected in Momostenango in the rubbing of the patient's body with a mixture of *ruda* leaves, and "cold" saliva. North of Patzún, in Chajul, the association of hotness in the etiology is remote. It may be present in the practice of making a cross with saliva on the child's forehead as a preventive measure and in the use of rose water in curing. On the contrary there is in most cases an association with coldnesss in the etiology. Thus, heating substitutes cooling in the curing practices. It is interesting to notice that this is achieved with some of the same herbs used in other areas to cool the body.

The relationship between ojo and hot-and-cold conceptions at a given cognitive level does not hinder relationships with other theories at other levels. This can be appreciated in the following analysis of "hot bloodedness."

In those towns, like Chicaj in the east, where the *vahos* theory is dominant, a large number of cases of *ojo* results from a child interacting or being in the proximity of a "hot-blooded" person. Hot bloodedness itself results from physical exertion, usually under a hot sun. Such a person is hot and sweaty. Two other beliefs are congruent with this one. On one hand, the people of Chicaj believe that the sun itself can produce *ojo de sol* (evil eye from the sun). On the other hand, and even more in accordance with the theory of *vahos, ojo* can be produced by people who smell of sweat even if they are not hot.

In Chamelco where the *vahos* theory is also strong, the word blood is usually substituted by the word *humor,* mostly meaning body odor. The *humor del cuerpo* covers an area of about a meter on each side of a person. When we walk we leave in our wake this *humor,* just as wild animals do. This attacks everything that is tender. Drunks, pregnant and menstruating women, and also horses and mules[14] can give *ojo.*

"Hot bloodedness" is also a cause of *ojo* in Patzún, but its meaning differs from that of eastern Guatemala. "Hot" and "strong" blood are terms used very much as synonyms in Patzún and they are frequently associated with cannibalism. This meaning becomes prominent as one travels westward to the department of Totonicapán.

In Momostenango, for instance, curing resorts to words of the kind "go away to the other side, leave me alone, go to your house," and "go away, go eat at my house, and stop eating (the patient)." It is also said that in the precise moment when the cure is successful, the eyes of the *ojeador* sting. These practices and ideas suggest a belief in "images" and "impressions" as in eastern Guatemala. There is at least one major difference, however. In Momostenango what is inside the patient is eating him up. This difference coincides with the fact that occasionally "bad blood" substitutes "hot blood."[15] Another substitution consists in replacing the circumstantial character of *ojo* by one dictated by nature and destiny. Men born with a mole in the eye are condemned to inflict damage on their fellowmen (Hurtado 1968). These ideas are very similar to those regarding the *halacueros* of the nearby town of Sacapulas. All of them are colored with cannibalism and witchcraft ideas.[16]

In Todos Santos at the extreme west, the Momostenango concept of "strong blood" is, to a great extent, substituted by the one of *ojos duros* (hard eyes). A "person with these eyes makes the other person's eyes fall." But the northwestern regions seem to escape from this association with negative forces. In Soloma (north of Todos Santos) and in Chajul (north of Momostenango) there is no prevalent association of *ojo* with cannibalism and witchcraft. Instead *ojo* is conceived within the hot-and-cold theory.

Intense desire is capable of producing "hot bloodedness." In Patzún it constitutes an inversion of certain kinds of *akwas* in eastern Guatemala. In *akwas* a pregnant woman intensively desires an object, the "image" of which impresses her own child in the uterus, making him sick. In *ojo* another person's child outside the uterus is desired, and his image is *halado* (pulled out) by the other person making the child, rather than the person who stole it, sick. A similar inversion is found in the cure. Just like the mother feigns to eat what was desired and not obtained in *akwas*, in *ojo* the child is caressed to avoid *ojo*.

Sexual connotations are present in this type of desire. A little baby boy's testicles may swell after being changed in front of strange women. Curing this type of *ojo* is said "to take away the shame that makes one love and desire *(querer)."*

In Momostenango, "shameful desire" is associated with "stealing away the little heart from the person." This loving and liking results in a sort of "spiritual cannibalism" consisting of subtracting something from the person. Cannibalism adds something to the person that eats him from inside. Cannibalism is based on negative or ambivalent feelings, spiritual cannibalism on liking and love.

Evidence of intense desire is found even in Soloma, in the extreme northwest. There *ojo* may be produced by the fact that one person likes another and curing may involve calling of the spirit while the curer blows in the child's mouth. But in Todos Santos, south of Soloma, cannibalism incipient in Patzún and stronger in Momostenango and Sacapulas, leaves little or no room for the stealing of the spirit. North of Patzún, in Chajul, where in most illnesses the supernatural encounters and the hot-and-cold theory are dominant, intense desire related to *ojo* is also found to have little importance.

A View Toward the Future

The previous discussion has dealt with some of the most common illnesses among Guatemalan Indians. The data suggest the convenience of distinguishing between the illnesses themselves and the more basic bodies of beliefs that underlie and may crosscut several illnesses. In terms of these bodies of beliefs, or ethnomedical theories, causative chains are formulated, states of health are interpreted, and curing practices are carried out. The importance of each of these bodies of beliefs varies from region to region determining the geographical distribution of some illnesses, and the local interpretation of others. These theories are not sharply defined bodies of beliefs. Transformational chains are produced by a combination of their features and by successive emphasis on some of the particular aspects of these theories.

The following ethnomedical theories are distinguished: *vahos;* intense desire and intense emotions which may be considered as modalities of a more embracing theory of impressions; the macrotheory of supernatural interventions with modalities of supernatural encounters, and supernatural punishment; the hot-and-cold theory which could eventually be considered part of a general theory of equilibrium (state balances), and the theory of cannibalism which may be paired with other theories of wishful harm.[16] This does not attempt to be an exhaustive statement on the number and kind of existent theories. Future studies may show the convenience of considering new theories and of sharpening the limit of the ones proposed here.

In a way, there are very few new formulations in this article. Wisdom (1952:129-32) several decades ago, recognized fright, evil air, contamination by the ritually unclean, and magical seizure by sorcery as the usual causes of sickness. Fright is caused by actual fear, hysteria, witnessing of violence, extreme upset, and the like. In addition he mentions two sets of body conditions: strong and weak, and hot and cold. The causes associated to the first set include abnormal body conditions due to overexertion, excessive sweating, childbirth, pregnancy, menstruation, and menopause, among others; disturbed emotional states, such as fear and anger; lack of full development; and possession of bland and appeasing qualities, such as beauty.

If something is novel in this article, it is the conceptual reorganization of the existing knowledge into two clear sets of cultural complexes, the illnesses, and the bodies of beliefs underlying them. Future studies should avoid confusing, for instance, *susto,* the illness, with *susto,* one of the intense emotions that is common in the etiology of many illnesses. This distinction is considerably helpful in systematically carrying out the characterization, and comparison of illnesses, and in understanding their geographical variations. Important question could be posed regarding origins, diffusion, and change concerning illnesses and medical theories. This, in turn, would be a step forward in the incorporation of medical data into a general ethnology of Guatemala, and for making ethnomedical research a powerful means for its development.

On the basis of the illnesses reviewed the following geographical distribution of theories is proposed (see Fig. 1). Future studies should constantly test it and improve it. *Vahos* is dominant in eastern Guatemala. Intense desire covers a large area starting in the northeast moving south and then to the northwest. In the western part of Guatemala intense desire, however, is contaminated by, or transformed into, a theory of cannibalism. Intense emotion, little discussed in this article, covers about the same area, but it also extends to the north-central region where it is entangled with the theory of supernatural encounters. Hot-and-cold dominates an area going north to south in the center of the country, but in the north this theory occupies a secondary position with respect to supernatural encounters. This theory is also important in some regions of the extreme west. Supernatural encountering is very strong in the north-central part of the country, but it is also prevalent in the northeast and, in a modified form, in the central and southeastern regions.

This geographical distribution also poses questions regarding the cognitive significance of the various theories: to what degreee these theories express differences in the ways reality is arranged. Since these theories shape the interpretation of illnesses, it would be convenient to begin the discussion on this topic with the definition of what an illness is.

An illness has a name. The name is applied to different aspects of the illness according to the user's knowledge, its pertinence as a social situation, and sometimes, to the characteristics of the particular illness. One may think of measles as red spots, a symptom. At times it is appropriate to think of malaria in terms of mosquitoes and swamps, two etiological aspects. Cancer may be synonymous with radiation and surgery, and tetanus with an injection; these are curing and preventive aspects of the particular illnesses. From a cultural viewpoint, these are all partial conceptions of relatively well-defined cultural units—the illnesses. These units involve actors in active and passive roles, behavior, events and circumstances, symbols, feelings, and instruments arranged in conceptions of states of being and causative chains.

The states of being are health and sickness. There are four causative chains: (1) those leading to health, (2) those leading to sickness, (3) those preventing sickness, and (4) those reestablishing health. Formal analysis could show the components in each chain, and how they relate to each other, thus revealing the structure of the illness. A statistical analysis of the frequency with which the various structural features recur in the ethnomedical theories and regions will constitute a major step in answering the question regarding different arrangements of reality. Neither the available knowledge nor the length of this article permits an in-depth exposition of this topic. But, we hope, some examples will reveal the potentialities of such an approach.

Curing may be focused on the agent, on the etiology, or on the symptoms. Modern Western medicine usually focuses on how to inhibit, expel, or destroy the agent. Occasionally, it focuses on the symptoms, but seldom on the etiology. Folk medicine in Guatemala frequently has its focus on the etiology. The illnesses described above share this quality and thus belong to the same class of illnesses. It would be a mistake, however, to think that all illnesses belong to this particular class in the Guatemalan Indian folk medicine.

In a medical system where the etiology is the main consideration,

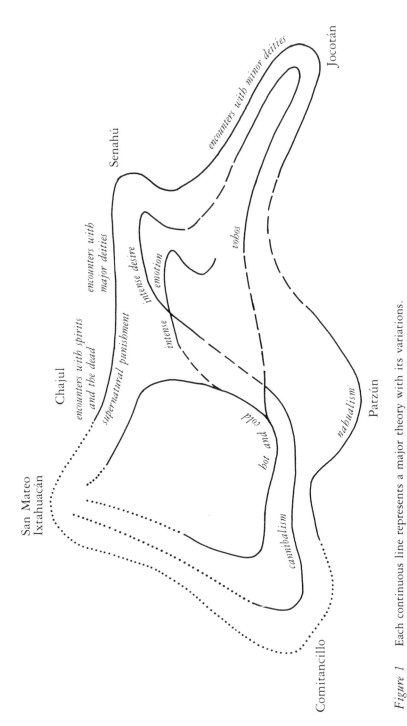

Figure 1 Each continuous line represents a major theory with its variations. Well-established and possible relations between theories are indicated by broken lines. Insufficient data and weak beliefs are indicated by dotted lines.

curing can be accomplished by inverting the behavioral components (the actions) while keeping relatively constant the substantive elements (persons, animals, things). This produces a functional inversion. A second alternative is to keep behavioral components relatively stable while semantically inverting the substantive components. This produces a nominal inversion. The third alternative is to create a complementary causative chain. In this case the majority of the components (persons, actions, instruments, feelings) of the curing chain would be identical, similar, or complementary to those of the etiological chain.

For an illness inspired in the theory of supernatural encounters, such as *laele* in Chajul, the first alternative is used. An individual (A) fails to act properly (-a) towards his ancestor (B). The ancestor gets angry, and talks (x) to the *anshels* (angels) and spirits, the owners of the illness, and the supernatural police (C, D, E, . . .), and God, or sends them word (x_1, x_2, x_3, . . .) of the need to capture (b) the individual's spirit (A_1). Curing is done by a patient's substitute, a specialist ($\approx$A) who approaches the ancestor or a deity in a correct way (a), sending word (-x_1, -x_2, -x_3, . . .) to the members of the same "supernatural bureaucracy," to obtain the spirit's release (-b) and the return of health:

etiology: $A \xrightarrow{-a} B \longrightarrow B \xrightarrow{x} C \xrightarrow{x1} D \xrightarrow{x2} E \xrightarrow{x3} H \xrightarrow{b} A_1$

cure: $\approx A \xrightarrow{a} B \longrightarrow B \xrightarrow{-x} C \xrightarrow{-x1} D \xrightarrow{-x2} E \xrightarrow{-x3} H \xrightarrow{-b} A_1$

For illnesses conceived within the hot-and-cold theory, such as *aire* in Patzún, the second alternative is used. Since cold wind (-A) gets inside (a) the patient (B) and produces (b) a cold (-X), the cure consists of taking hot things (A) to produce heat (X):

etiology: $-A \xrightarrow{a} B \xrightarrow{b} B \ -X$ $\left.\right\} \longrightarrow B$
cure: $A \xrightarrow{a} B \xrightarrow{b} B \ \ X$

In the following case of *akwas*, based on the theory of impression by strong emotions, a complementary causal chain serves as the cure. A pregnant woman (M) suffers a strong emotion (a) by seeing a crazy pig ($P_{1,2}$). As a consequence, the pig's image (-P_1), through the mother, impresses (c) the child (C), making him sick (C_{-P1}). The cure consists of using a pig substitute, for example its hair ($P_{1,2}$), and burning (x) it to produce an ethereal matter of the same kind, but complementary to the image ($-P_2$). One may assume that the child is impressed with the ethereal thing making it possible to release the "ethereal pig" ($-P_{1,2}$) from the child:

etiology: $\quad P_{1,2} \xrightarrow{a} M \longrightarrow -P_1 \xrightarrow{c} C_{-P1}$ ⟨ $\quad -P_{12}$

cure: $\quad M \xrightarrow{x} P_{1,2} \longrightarrow -P_2 \xrightarrow{c} (C_{-P2})$ ⟨ $\quad C$

Frequently, the combination of two of the three alternatives described creates complicated patterns when the illness is based on an intense desire. In an *akwas* of cracklings in Chamelco, a pregnant woman (M) has an intense desire (i) to eat cracklings, composed of image and thing ($x_{1,2}$), but inhibits herself (-a). Her child (C) is impressed with the crackling's image ($-X_1$). Curing consists in "editing the past." Cracklings are burned to produce an ethereal thing ($-X_2$) to complement the image. In this case, the mother feigns (b) to eat (a) the cracklings ashes, thus correcting the mistakes done in the past. In the past, the cracklings (in a material form) were in front of her face, in the future (f), they are considered as a desire. Now, after the illness takes places, they are in the past (-f), consequently she throws the ashes behind her back and avoids turning around. Hence the ethereal things—crackling ($-X_2$)—can travel to the past (-f) and get together with the crackling's image ($-X_1$). Were she to turn her back, they would remain in the present and the cure would not take place:

etiology: $\quad M^i \xrightarrow{-a} (f)X_{1,2} \rightarrow -X_1 \xrightarrow{f} C \rightarrow C_{-X1}$ ⟨ $\quad -X_{1,2}$

cure: $\quad M^b \xrightarrow{a} (-f)X_{1,2} \rightarrow -X_2 \xrightarrow{-f} C \rightarrow C_{-X2}$ ⟨ $\quad C$

Complicated patterns are also derived from the inclusion of chains other than the etiological and curing ones. In the following case of sexual fright of Chamelco inspired in the theory of strong emotions, the "normal" causative chain leading to health stands in a paradigmatic and complementary position with respect to the etiology and cure which also oppose and complement each other.

A man (A) and a woman (-A) were having sexual intercourse (a). Suddenly, a child (C_o) enters (-c). Sexual intercourse is interrupted. The semen (S), that normally is introduced (i) into the lower part of the woman's body (-U), does not flow (-i). Consequently, the normal result, the swelling (s) of the woman's abdomen ($-U_1$) does not occur. Also the normal expulsion (e) of a child (C_o) does not occur. Consequently the man becomes sick due to the strong emotion, his face (U_1) swells (s). To cure him the woman prepares water with her pubic hair ($\approx$S), as a substitute for semen. This is given to him to drink, that is, it is introduced (i) in the upper part (mouth) of the body (U). Swelling of the man's face disappears (-s):

chain
of normality: $\quad A \xleftarrow{a} -A: \quad S \xrightarrow{i} -A\text{-}U \rightarrow -A\text{-}U_1 s \xrightarrow{e} C_o$

etiological
chain: $\quad\quad A \xleftarrow{a} -A: \quad S \xrightarrow{-i} -A\text{-}U \rightarrow -(-A\text{-}U_1\text{-}s) \left.\rule{0pt}{14pt}\right\} : \; : \; -e \; C_o$

$\quad\quad\quad\quad\quad\quad\quad\quad\quad\quad\quad\quad\quad \rightarrow A \quad U_1 \quad s \left.\rule{0pt}{12pt}\right\}$ (precipitating

cure: $\quad\quad\quad\quad\quad\quad\quad \approx S \xrightarrow{i} A\; U \rightarrow A \quad U \quad \text{-s} \quad$ factor)

The previous examples show that Guatemalan Indians understand and explain illnesses in different ways from those used by Western man. For them, the components of the causative chains, and the states of health are frequently related through semantic constants and inversions, thus forming paradigms. This is a rationalistic view of illness which contrasts with the empirical view prevalent in modern Western medicine. In the latter, a component of the curing chain, for instance, is thought to work not because of its semantic relation to other components in the etiological chain, but because of an empirical relationship.

The distinction between the two viewpoints could be made clearer by the following example. Fire, in view of previous experiences, may be thought to be extinguishable with water. But once fire and water are considered semantically opposed, people may begin to think that water extinguishes fire by a logical necessity. When experience is dealt with in "semantical" ways, we say that there is a rationalistic view of reality.

While the difference between a folk rationalistic and a Western empirical view is defendable in terms of the available data, and is likely to be useful in medicine, and yet more broadly, in technological research and action, one should be careful with its use. An analysis of Western medicine may surprise us all, as well as the physicians, with its abundance of rationalistic "arguments." On the other hand, a study of illness among Guatemalan Indians that is not focused on etiology may surprise us with the abundance of empirical views. Moreover, there is still the epistemological question as to whether all understanding requires the transformation of empirical knowledge into conceptual knowledge, thus implying the making of networks of semantic relations. Were this so, Guatemalan Indians would have a better understanding of their illnesses than most of us and our physicians have of our illnesses. Much of our empirical knowledge would have to be converted into rationalistic structures to arrive at the understanding the Indians have. This, of course, does not mean that such a conversion is necessarily desirable. One may think of an optimum point in which neither rationalism stifles new knowledge nor empiricism alienates the mind. Regardless of the way this philosophical problem is viewed, empiricism and rationalism are likely to be useful concepts in tackling issues like culture change, alienation, and social and regional differences.

To conclude, this article stresses the need for a new Guatemalan ethnology. We cannot "edit the past," as in the *akwas* of cracklings, and do now what we should have done at the beginning of the century. The theoretical interests and methodological procedures should be those of our times. It is hoped that in a very modest way this article contributes toward this end.

NOTES

1. Foster and Anderson (1978:4-8) cite ethnomedicine and international public health, among others, as the roots of medical anthropology. The dichotomous distinction here proposed is sharper and is based on theoretical and methodological premises, rather than on historical ones.

2. Wisdom (1952:131) also reports this illness for eastern Guatemala.

3. For a discussion on hot and cold elements see Adams (1952), Méndez-Domínguez (1971), and Cosminsky (1975).

4. Emotions may also act occasionally as agents, as in the case of distress because of the birth of a younger brother.

5. There are few mentions in the literature concerning this illness.

Haeserijn (1975) reports it for Chamelco, Avila (1977) for Coban, Terga and Vásquez (1977) for Tactic, and Rodríguez Rouanet (1971:18-19) for Chamelco, Cobán, and San Cristóbal Verapaz.

6. Rodríguez Rouanet (1971:18-19), however, reports an *akwas* of ants based on *vahos* in Cobán, a Kekchí city. Its being a regional urban center for northeastern Guatemala may account for a greater diversity of beliefs.

7. Lords of illness or sickness are also popular in the Quiché region, south of Chajul; see for instance Bunzel (1967:145) with regard to Chichicastenango.

8. Similar distinctions are made throughout the country, even in eastern Guatemala, for instance among the eastern Pokomam (Gillin 1958:308).

9. See, for instance, Saler (1969).

10. Encounters with minor deities like the *'ek* (the black one) usually do not produce illness.

11. This is a recurrent creature in eastern Guatemala (Wisdom 1952: 122; Gillin 1958:307).

12. From Latin and Spanish.

13. Rodríguez Rouanet (1971:237-39) reports it among Quichés, Mams, Ixils, and Chuj; Grollig (1959:176) among the Kanjobal; Maynard (1963:97-98) among the central Pokomam.

14. Why pigs and cows cannot give *ojo* has up until now not been adequately answered.

15. Cosminsky (1976:165-66) cites a relationship between hot and strong blood but denies an association with witchcraft in Santa Lucía Utatlán, a nearby town south of Momostenango and west of Patzún.

16. It should be noticed, however, that many forms of witchcraft should not be paired with cannibalism. Witchcraft could be carried out within the context of all the theories mentioned, and therefore should not be considered as an ethnomedical theory, but rather as part of a particular causative chain in a particular illness or medical case.

REFERENCES

Adams, Richard N.
1952   *Un analisis de las creencias y prácticas médicas de un pueblo indígena de Guatemala.* Instituto Indigenísta Nacional Publicación 17 (Guatemala).
1955   "On the Effective Use of Anthropology in Public Health Programs," *Human Organization* 13:5-15.

Adams, Richard N., and Arthur J. Rubel
1967   "Sickness and Social Relations," in *Social Anthropology*, ed. M. Nash. Vol. 6 of *Handbook of Middle American Indians*, ed. R. Wauchope (Austin: University of Texas Press).
Avila, César Augusto
1977   "Creencias populares sobre la etiología de las caries y el dolor dental en grupos de indígenas Kekchíes," *Guatemala Indígena* 12(1-2):5-51.
Bates, Marston
1953   "Human Ecology," in *Anthropology Today: An Encyclopedic Inventory* ed. A. L. Kroeber (Chicago: University of Chicago Press).
Bunzel, Ruth
1967   *Chichicastenango: A Guatemalan Village* (Seattle: University of Washington Press).
Cosminsky, Sheila
1975   "Changing Food and Medical Beliefs and Practices in a Guatemalan Community," *Ecology of Food and Nutrition* 4:183-91.
1976   "The Evil Eye in a Quiché Community," in *The Evil Eye*, ed. Clarence Maloney (New York: Columbia University Press).
1977   "Alimento and Fresco: Nutritional Concepts and Their Implications for Health Care," *Human Organization* 36(2):203-7.
Currier, R.
1966   "The Hot-Cold Syndrome and Symbolic Balance in Mexican and Spanish American Folk Medicine," *Ethnology* 5:251-63.
Douglas, B.
1969   *Illness and Curing in Santiago Atitlán, A Tzutujil Maya Community in the Southwestern Highlands of Guatemala* (Ann Arbor: University Microfilms).
Foster, George M.
1953   "Relationships Between Spanish and Spanish-American Folk Medicine," *Journal of American Folklore* 66:207-17.
Foster, George M., and Barbara G. Anderson
1978   *Medical Anthropology* (New York: John Wiley & Sons).
Frake, Charles O.
1961   "The Diagnosis of Disease Among the Subanum of Mindaneo," *American Anthropologist* 63:113-32.
Francis, Thomas Jr.
1959   "The Epidemiological Approach to Human Ecology," *American Journal of the Medical Sciences* 237:677-84.
Garcia, Bertha, Juan José Urrutia, and Moisés Béhar
1977   "Creencias y conocimientos sobre la biología de la reproducción en Santa María Cauque," *Guatemala Indígena* 12:53-81.

Gillin, John
1958   *San Luis Jilotepeque* (Guatemala: Seminario de Integración Social Guatemalteca).

Gordon, John E.
1958   "Medical Ecology and the Public Health," *American Journal of the Medical Sciences* 235:337-59.

Grollig, Francis X.
1959   *San Miguel Acatán, Huehuetenango, Guatemala: A Modern Mayan Village* (Ann Arbor: University Microfilms).

Haeserijn, Esteban
1975   "Filosofía popular de los Kekchí de hoy," *Guatemala Indígena* 10:44-54.

Hughes, Charles C.
1968   "Ethnomedicine," in *International Encyclopedia of the Social Sciences* 10 (New York: Macmillan, Free Press).

Hurtado, Juan José
1968   "El Ojo," in *Tradiciones de Guatemala,* vol. 1 (Guatemala: El Centro de Estudios Folklóricos, Universidad de San Carlos).

La Farge, Oliver
1947   *Santa Eulalia: The Religion of a Cuchumatan Town* (Chicago: University of Chicago Press).

Maynard, Eileen
1963   *The Women of Palín: A Comparative Study of Indian and Ladino Women in a Guatemalan Village* (Ann Arbor: University Microfilms).

Mendelson, Michael
1965   *Los Escándalos de Maximón* (Guatemala: Seminario de Integración Social Guatemalteca).

Méndez-Domínguez, Alfredo
1971   "Consideraciones socio-económicas en la introducción de nuevos alimentos," in *Recursos protéicos en América Latina,* ed. Moisés Béhar and Ricardo Bressani (Guatemala: Institute de Nutrición de Centroamérica y Panamá).

Norge, Ethel
1958   "Etiology of Illness in Guinhangdan," *American Anthropologist* 60:1158-72.

Oakes, Maud
1951   *The Two Crosses of Todos Santos* (New York: Pantheon Books, Bollingen Series XXVII).

Paul, Benjamin
1959   *La vida de un pueblo indígena de Guatemala.* Cuadernos del Seminario de Integración Social Guatemalteca (Guatemala).

1963   "Anthropological Perspectives on Medicine and Public Health," *Annals of the American Academy of Political and Social Sciences* 346: 34-43.

Paul, Benjamin, and Lois Paul
1952   "The Life Cycle," in *Heritage of Conquest: The Ethnology of Middle America,* ed. Sol Tax (Glencoe, Ill.: Free Press).

Reina, Ruben
1966   *The Law of the Saints* (New York: Bobbs-Merrill Co).

Rodríguez Rouanet, Francisco
1971   "Aspectos de la medicina popular en el area rural de Guatemala," *Guatemala Indígena* 6(1):3-330.

Rogoff, Barbara
1977   "Etnografía del desarrollo del niño en una comunidad maya en proceso de modernización," *Guatemala Indígena* 12:207-34.

Rubel, Arthur
1964   "The Epidemiology of a Folk Illness: Susto in Hispanic America," *Ethnology* 3:268-83.

Saler, Benson
1969   *Nagual, brujo, y hechicero en un pueblo quiché.* Cuadernos del Seminario de Integración Social Guatemalteca (Guatemala).

Schult-Jena, Leonhard
1945   *La vida y las creencias de los indígenas quichés de Guatemala,* trans. Antonio Goubaud Carrera and Herbert Sapper, Anales de la Sociedad de Geografía e Historia de Guatemala, vol. 20 (Guatemala).

Stoll, Otto
1938   *Etnografía de Guatemala* (Guatemala: Tipografía Sanchez y de Guise).

Suchman, Edward A.
1968   "Epidemiology," in *International Encyclopedia of the Social Sciences,* vol. 5 (New York: Macmillan, Free Press).

Terga, Ricardo, and Emilio Vásquez Robles
1977   "Tactic, El Corazón del Mundo," *Guatemala Indígena* 12: 67-206.

Termer, Franz
1957   *Etnología y Etnografía de Guatemala* (Guatemala: Editorial del Ministerio de Educación Pública).

Wisdom, Charles
1952   "The Supernatural World and Curing," in *Heritage of Conquest: The Ethnology of Middle America,* ed. Sol Tax (Glencoe, Ill.: Free Press).

Woods, Clyde
1968   *Medicine and Culture Change in San Lucas Tolimán: A Highland Guatemalan Community* (Ann Arbor: University Microfilms).

12

Robert Redfield's Culture Concept and Mesoamerican Anthropology

John Hawkins
Brigham Young University

Language is a form and not a substance.
—Ferdinand de Saussure (1959:122)

The culture concept is central to anthropology. Indeed, it has often been remarked that the ethnographic pursuit of culture is what distinguishes anthropology from other disciplines. Moreover, the impact of an anthropologist's definitions, assumptions, models, and theories upon fieldwork and writing has long been recognized. With culture indeed central to anthropology, then the way culture is conceived will have great consequence for the study of society.

This paper explores the impact of the culture concept in Mesoamerican anthropology. In this regard, Robert Redfield stands central. He was among the first professional investigators of the broadly defined Mesoamerican region and early published his important social and cultural monograph on Tepoztlán (1930b). Later he was instrumental in the training of many students who, along with Redfield, studied a more narrow region centering in Guatemala, Chiapas, and Yucatán. Although there are prior intellectual tributaries that flow into Redfield and into other Mesoamericanists that were not directly Redfield's students, Redfield is an intellectual main channel that feeds the delta of more recent and somewhat varied theoretical studies. Therefore, we can fruitfully explore Redfield's culture concept and its impact on Mesoamerican research.

I shall, however, critique Redfield's culture concept and the impact it has had on Mesoamerican studies. In brief, I will show that his behavioral view of culture has obscured the social and cultural interconnections within the region. In its place, I suggest that a rigorously ideational, meaning-oriented approach to culture offers some hope for a unifying appraisal of the region's social and cultural complexity.

Robert Redfield's Culture Concept

Robert Redfield developed and expanded his idea of culture during the thirty-year span of his publications. His first writings suggest an initial focus on material and behavioral traits; however, this view of culture progressively included more and more ideological content. Yet Redfield's culture never became exclusively ideational. It always retained a simultaneous material and behavioral reference.

In his first article, published in 1926, Redfield assesses the state of anthropology. He suggests that anthropology should move away from its primary interest in description toward studies of process. In the course of his comments on other anthropologists, it is apparent that, for Redfield, culture consists of an assemblage of items which distinguish a group. The terms *culture elements, defined cultures,* and *culture traits* are used with comfort, though they are drawn out of an analysis of the works of others (Redfield 1926:5,9). Separating identifiable cultures was an intellectual trend of the time.

Redfield's first article based on his own field experience is a description of the financial organization and collection methods of the Tepoztecan festival days. This article contains no explicit theory, no definitions, and only a slight hint of the problem of mixed Spanish and Indian origins of the Tepoztecan lifestyle (Redfield 1927). The word *culture* is not used.

In 1928, Redfield proposes that the Tepoztecans are a nonprimitive folk in contact with the cities. "The folklore of present-day Mexico," observes Redfield, "is a close compound of Indian and early Spanish elements. . .," though their folk medicine is "probably more Indian than European" (Redfield 1928c:217). Still, there is no mention of "culture." The article, however, describes medical belief, curing practice, plants, and plant knowledge. In it, Redfield foreshadows the major elements of his definition of culture: beliefs, behavior, and objects.

In another article in the same year, Redfield places the Tepozteclans more precisely with his emerging notion of a continuum. More important in this context, Redfield makes an oblique reference to culture.

Moreover the Mexicans constitute a whole series of ethnological and sociological problems to themselves, because of the cultural gulf between the small educated class and the great majority of ignorant peons. This uneducated majority is largely Indian in blood, and its representatives preserve many ancient customs. But they are not a primitive, tribal people, like those First Americans, now largely on reservations in this country. Neither are they as sophisticated as those later Americans of Chicago and elsewhere. They are a mixture, already centuries old, of colonial Spanish elements and of ancient Indian elements. They are an intermediate kind of people, illiterate, rather than pre-literate. They are Middle Americans culturally as well as geographically (Redfield 1928a: 243-44).

Thus for Redfield, culture is elemental and discrete, a "mixture" rather than a fusion. His focus is on skills (literacy/illiteracy) and on behavior ("customs") rather than on the "regnant" (Schneider 1976: 204) and fundamental conceptual system. In the absence of close travel routes, "contacts" with nearby Mexico City "introduce no more than a dilution of modern city ways into a peasant village" (Redfield 1928a:244). Thus by 1928 Redfield has set the major course of his life work: culture is elemental, focused on behavior, but including belief; culture process is acculturation, principally through contact diffusion; the result is an intermediate "folk."

Culture considered as artifact and as behavior has a particularistic tendency. This view subdivides systems. As a result, Redfield speaks of the "obviously different cultures" of the barrios or wards in the town center:

Thus, Santo Domingo is the most civilized barrio, and the most patriotic (i.e., most nearly conscious of national feelings—their chapel is decorated with Mexican flags; a modern orchestra was organized here, etc.) Santa Cruz is strongly primitive—Catholic, exclusive and independent—Santa Cruz governs itself like a little republic. San Pedro is a barrio of poor, illiterate people who reserve to a marked extent ancient mentality and resent the presence of outsiders;and so forth (Redfield 1928b:292).

Continued focus on traits (1929:615-16), on diagnostic material culture (1930a:146-47), and on diffusion as borrowing across a cultural boundary (1930a:148) are characteristic of Redfield. Yet, he observes that simple trait maps are inadequate because they leave out the complexities of culture entailed in "custom" and "everyday conduct" (1930a:148). Redfield's culture is a primarily behavioral process. Though there is certainly a mental or ideological aspect to the natives' "patriotic" attribute, their "consciousness" is immediately recast in the behavioral terms of decoration, and in the act of having organized an orchestra.

Nineteen-thirty marks his first explicit recognition of the crucial importance of meaning or significance in culture. Before this time, beliefs, attitudes, or consciousness were simply thrown in with material objects and behavior. Now, however, meaning is central.

Anthropologists may talk as if the culture fact were the shape of the tool they collect or the form of the ritual they record. The cultural fact, however, is not merely the form of the tool or of the overt behavior, but rather the significance that tool or behavior has to the people who use or perform it. So understood, the culture area is the geographic area within which dwell persons to whom objects and acts seem about the same (Redfield 1930a:149).

Even so, in this perspective the meanings are attached to the "objects and acts." As a result, a system of meaning per se cannot emerge, for each meaning is isolated from the other meanings by virtue of being attached to an act or object. The system then derives from the relations between acts and objects rather than from the relations among meanings. As a result of this view, Redfield quickly slips back to the behavioral definition of culture. A few paragraphs later he asserts that "the culture of Tepoztlán is a well-integrated combination of Indian and Spanish elements . . . [which] is now in a process of change." The cultural evidence of this change consists in the fact that "the more sophisticated, city-wise persons . . . often referred to as *los correctos* . . . often wear shoes, occasionally read newspapers, go on occasion to Mexico, and, in a word, have a role in life outside the valley" (Redfield 1930a:150).

Another result of this material and behavioral reference point is the isolation it introduces into the various communities of the region. Because the diacritical differences between communities are conceived to be defining features of a culture, there is a plurality of "folk cultures," each of which is individually a coherent, integrated whole. In Redfield's words, "the local world is, then, separate, complete, distinct" (Redfield 1935:178). Since the local world is folk by definition of its local orientation, the "folk cultures" are thus "separate" from the "city-wise" in their midst. Both the behavioral focus and the tendency to view the community as a self-sufficient unit are manifest as late as 1940, when Redfield observes,

> To the anthropologist "a culture" implies an integral. The phrase has reference to organized, traditional ways of life in which all members of a self-sufficient, continuing, and complete society participate and which are adequate for all recurrent needs of the individual from birth to death and of the community through successive generations (Redfield 1940:739).

Later in the same paragraph, Redfield implies that the Indian community he studied was such an isolate. But in order to do so, one must either ignore the *correctos* living in the municipio of Tepoztlán, or use the diacritical and characterizing aspect of a behavioral culture to isolate one group, which then becomes the "community."[1]

In spite of Redfield's later commitment to regional study, beginning in the early 1930s and flowering in 1941 with the publication of his classic, *The Folk Culture of Yucatán,* and in spite of his explicit linkage of the peasant to the city (1953:31), Redfield's separate, complete, and local view of the folk encouraged the study of but one distinctive status group, namely the Indians of each community. The Mesoamerican ethnography has many examples of this approach.

In *The Folk Culture of Yucatán,* Redfield presents his best, as well as his most extensive, definition of culture. Indeed, the first three of the following sentences nearly preempt and certainly foreshadow the recent semiotic emphasis on culture as ideology, symbol, and meaning:

> In speaking of "culture" we have reference to the conventional understandings, manifest in act and artifact, that characterize societies. The "understandings" are the meanings attached to acts and objects. The meanings are conventional, and therefore cultural, in so far as they have become typical for the members of that society by reason of intercommunication among the members. A culture is, then, an abstraction: it is the type toward which the meanings that the same act or object has for the different members of the society tend to conform. The meanings are expressed in action and in the results of action, from which we infer them; so we may as well identify "culture" with the extent to which the conventionalized behavior of members of the society is for all the same. Still more concretely we speak of culture, as did Tylor, as knowledge, belief, art, law, and custom.
>
> For we find it natural and convenient to deal with the culture of any particular society in terms of separably denotable entities: this form of calendar, that marriage custom, this belief as to life after death. At the same time, in attending to the whole of those conveniently separable elements which taken together characterize that society, we feel it to be not simply an aggregation but an organization. There is no society the conventional life of which may be described realistically in terms of a series of accounts of customs and beliefs taken one by one so that each is completely reported without reference to any one of the others. The items into which we separate the whole are not, we feel, really separate. In describing one we find it necessary to describe others.
>
> So the quality of organization among the conveniently separable elements of the whole of a culture is probably a universal feature of culture and may be added to the definition: culture is an organization of conventional understandings manifest in act and artifact (Redfield 1941:132-33).

In the end, Redfield never surpassed this definition and discussion. Indeed, in some writing, his contrast of culture with world view and ethos tends to deprive culture of its newfound ideological content (Redfield 1953:84). Despite this tendency arising from a contextual contrast, ideas do remain in his subsequent definitions of culture. But so does behavior. In spite of the fact that the last two quoted lines of his 1941 definition are, as Singer has pointed out, "structural" (Redfield's "organization") and "semiotic" (Redfield's "understandings") (Singer 1976:223), behavior is usually reintroduced in the form of acts or activities, while objects enter culture through close attention to artifacts.[2]

The promise inherent in the semiotic approach was subverted by a key phrase that subordinates ideas to acts and objects. To repeat, "The meanings are expressed in action and in the results of action . . . so we may as well identify 'culture' with the extent to which the conventionalized behavior of members of the society is for all the same" (Redfield 1941:132). The task becomes one of identifying the social-behavior boundaries rather than of explicating, elucidating, or discovering a system in the meanings or understandings. Meaning is subordinated and lost in the task of discovering the sameness of behavior.

Why did Redfield undermine his idea-oriented approach with this behavioral emphasis? Redfield does not seem to have considered in print the issue of meaning and its theoretical sources. This does not prevent him from having a theory of meaning. For Redfield, meaning is a significance attached to an act or object. In spite of his dictum that a mere listing of cultural attributes is insufficient and that organization is essential, the "convenience" of separating elements, the ease with which one can interrelate objects, as opposed to ideas, and the goal of diacritically "characterizing" separable groups subverts the developmentof a system of meanings. His central question is not how objects have meaning, but how a unique distribution of objects and their significances mark out and distinguish a group or level in a society. Moreover, it is not at all certain that the concept represented by the word "understanding" is the crucial aspect of a system of meanings. For Redfield, the natives' "understanding" of an object seems to entail their realization of its implications as an index of social relations or as a utilitarian implement. This is quite different from abstracting the system of beliefs or ideology in terms of which each object is made meaningful. Redfield's early interest in native beliefs might have served him better, had he sought the system in them. But his move to understandings attached to objects appears to have been counterproductive, for the objects, and the organization among them, are a manifestation of *parole*—single speech texts. The objects, or their distribution, are not the same as the *langue,* the system from whence and out of which contextually appropriate acts of communication are constructed.

Highlights of Subsequent Mesoamerican Research

It would be incorrect to suppose that Redfield is the sole source of these concepts which have limited Mesoamerican research. In the first place, not all of the first or second generation Mesoamericanists were students of Redfield. Second, cultural particularism, aboriginal origins, acculturation, diffusion, and the act-and-artifact approach to culture were generalized concepts. Thus, while Redfield is an important source for the ideas that channeled many Mesoamerican researchers, his work serves here as a type or model of ideas that other researchers may have acquired rather independently. Ideas "in the air" are inhaled and exhaled by many.

While Redfield's later work pays considerable attention to both modern and primitive, as well as folk, cultures, a number of subsequent anthropologists continued to separate the national, city-oriented, "westernized" culture from that of the Indians of any particular region. This may be seen to derive from Redfield's early notion that the "folk" were "local," "distinct," and "separate."

A classic statement of this separatist tradition is given by Redfield's student, Sol Tax, in *Penny Capitalism.* Although the term *culture* is not explicitly defined by Tax, his use of the word is trait-oriented in the Redfieldian tradition:

> Panajacheleños speak a dialect, wear a costume, and have certain beliefs and ways of life distinct from those of the Indians of other towns; they are a social and cultural unity (Tax 1953:7-8).

Elsewhere, Tax defines culture as "the characteristic way of life in general" (Tax 1952b:66). Here too, Tax shows special concern for the "recognizably Indian groups." Tax thus follows Redfield in characterizing the Indians by traits. Neither Redfield nor Tax sought for the meaning of the traits by considering them as a system with relations to each other that cross both community and ethnic boundaries.

Like Redfield, Tax uses the term *ethnic group* to refer to the Indians of the Guatemalan region. Because of the behavioral variations among the Indians from community to community, each municipio or community is considered a separate ethnic group.

> The people of Guatemala live in municipios which are territorial administrative divisions commonly recognized in all governmental matters, but which are also—as it happens—the basic ethnic divisions and cultural groups into which the country is divided (Tax 1937:425).

Ethnic group and culture are equated and linked to the municipal unit. This has the effect of fragmenting the study of Guatemalan society into a multiplicity of disconnected community studies, each considered a separate culture. Much of our literature fits this pattern.

The equation of culture and community is possible, however, only by ignoring the presence of the Ladinos residing in almost every municipio. Although Ladinos are mentioned by Tax at several points in *Penny Capitalism,* they are treated in asides, as though they are intruders from some other society.

> The distinguishing characters of Ladinos and Indians, the two classes of people officially recognized in Guatemala, differ to some extent in different parts of the Republic, but in general a Ladino is anybody who is not an Indian, and an Indian is defined on the basis of cultural and linguistic criteria rather than on physical features (Tax 1953:6-7).
>
> In Panajachel the Indians are distinguishable from Ladinos because their mother tongue is Indian and their command of Spanish relatively poor, because they wear a costume distinct from that of the Ladinos (which is pretty uniform over the whole country), and because their surnames are usually of Indian rather than of Spanish origin. . . . It must be borne in mind that since the distinction is cultural rather than physical, Indian and Ladino are not primarily thought of as race designations in the sense that Negro and White are in the United States. But there are important economic and social differences between the two classes and each constitutes in large degree a community apart from the other. This study is concerned primarily and almost entirely with the *Indians* of Panajachel (Tax 1953:7 [emphasis his]).

This separatist approach is adopted in spite of the fact that Indians are defined in opposition to Ladinos, that Ladinos comprise one-third of the population in the community (Tax 1953:6), that Ladinos own 63 percent of the lands most valued by the Indians, which the Indians rent, and 81 percent of the total lands in the community (Tax 1953:60). Road work, plantation labor, and wage-labor relations with Ladinos further complicate the picture. The basic problem is that culture, conceived as overt behavior, too easily leads to a separation of Ladino from Indian and community from community. This separation, however, vitiates analysis of the system as a system.

Sol Tax is by no means alone in this cultural separatism. Indeed, in *The Heritage of Conquest,* there is remarkably little mention of the conquerors and their ethnic affiliates, the Ladinos. While the book is about the "peoples of Mexico and Central America" (Tax 1952a:2), it treats mainly Indians. For example, Kirchhoff's lead article treats, by title, the ethnic composition and cultural characteristics "of Mesoamerica." Yet nowhere are Ladinos or nationals mentioned. His interest is in "native cultures"; "ethnic composition" is considered only "at the time of the conquest" (Kirchhoff 1952:17, 20).[3] Nor do Redfield and Tax consider present-day Mesoamerican society. Rather, they confine themselves to the "General Characteristics of Present-Day Mesoamerican Indian Society." With the exception of references to Catholicism and the penetration of Christian ritual, the context of the Indian society in the national system is noted in only three sentences:

> The controls which shape conduct characteristically include, however, regulations which are imposed upon people from outside the local community; these originate in natural (sic; Did he intend "national"?) law. Everywhere there is wider integration than the tribe; the truly isolated community is exceptional. There is a hierarchy of market, political and religious centers extending over large areas (Redfield and Tax 1952:31).

Yet, the "hierarchy" that "shapes" and "controls" is not explored at all. Consequently, one cannot determine to what degree the "general characteristics" of Indian society are a result of that shaping.

Guiteras Holmes begins her paper by observing,

> In discussing social organization in Mesoamerica, I am referring especially to Indian groups; only in that which concerns *barrios* and ritual kinship is there participation by non-Indian groups (Guiteras Holmes 1952:97).

Even granting a restricted definition of social organizations as kinship, marriage, and household, and the fictive extensions of these, it is doubtful that this separation of Ladino and Indian is warranted. While marriage and common law union remain somewhat within the ethnic boundary, concubinage, occasional congress, and forced intercourse bridge the ethnic boundaries in highly directional patterns.

Wisdom treats the supernatural and curing practices in a review article that appears to be limited to the Indians or the syncretic, non-standard peasant religion. In a discussion note from the conference, Tax queries Wisdom to see if he meant that one of the typologies is used by the Indians. Wisdom replies, "I suppose I do." Later in the note, Guiteras questions Tax's suggested revision of the typology by noting the revision would not work "if you want to include Ladino culture." Tax's unchallenged response is, "We have to draw the line somewhere" (Wisdom 1952:135 n2). The fact that Wisdom could write a general article on the subject of religion specifying only once (p. 119, line 12), and at that very obliquely, the people to whom the article applies, suggests how strongly the participants focused their interest on the Indians as a separable unit of study. Finally, Benjamin and Lois Paul portray a separate life cycle for the Indians, mentioning the non-Indians only once.[4]

Three papers in *The Heritage of Conquest* treat the Ladino and the Indian simultaneously, explicitly, and extensively. In addition, SolTax's paper on Indian economics discusses aspects of Indian relations to Ladinos. Nevertheless, in each of these papers the cultures of the two groups are considered distinct and separately analyzable. Tax notes that "all the Ladinos may be considered one culture and one kind of community" against a background discussion of the many differences among the Indian communities (Tax 1952b:49). De la Fuente discusses the class and ethnic hierarchy among Ladinos and Indians. Though he considers ethnic "passing," he focuses on the distinctiveness of the groups. Thus, the "two principle groups" are identified by "ethnic distinctions . . . made primarily on the basis of cultural differences" which are largely "differentiating traits" of a material or behavioral type (de la Fuente 1952:77-79). Even Gillin, whose paper is the volume's most balanced in detailing Ladinos along with Indians, sees "Indians and Ladinos each still preserving separate and distinguishable cultures" (Gillin 1951:195). Gillin's work is particularly interesting, for it is the only paper in the symposium that treats culture as ideological and mental. While beliefs are mentioned in some of the other chapters, they are treated at negligible length. With Gillin as exception, a Redfieldian material and behavioral approach to culture is the dominant emphasis of this symposium.[5]

The balanced treatment of Ladino and Indian in Gillin's paper represents a transition that was taking place in the late 1940s, when one begins to find community studies seriously attempt to encompass both Ladinos and Indians in a broader perspective. Of course, Redfield was a forerunner of these through his regional study of Yucatán as a folk-urban continuum.

In Guatemala, Ladinos and Indians are brought jointly into systematic analysis in the works of John Gillin (1951) and Melford Tumin (1952). These two authors have collaborated and communicated throughout their careers, and they suggest that their works should be considered as a single unit (Tumin 1952). But with the training of Gillin in anthropology and of Tumin in sociology, their differences in focus are instructive. Gillin accepts separate aboriginal and European origins as an explanation for the manifest differences between Indians and Ladinos. In the tradition of Redfield, Gillin observes:

> At one end of the road, so to speak, are Indian tribes still practically untouched by European civilization; at the other end stand communities in which Iberian colonial beliefs and customs have so completely amalgamated with contributions from the Indian cultures that neither the people themselves nor the outsider can readily recognize which is which: consolidation of the several traditions into the Modern Latin American culture has been practically completed.
>
> San Carlos [San Luis Jilotepeque] is a way station, one might say, along this road, but typical of many other communities of its kind. Here the absorption of one culture into the other or of both into a new blend has not been completed. In San Carlos the Indians and the Ladinos each have their own mode of life, although many elements overlap (Gillin 1951:1).

The behaviorist view of a "culture" as a "mode of life" which one practices intrudes here. For Gillin, a culture is an institutionalized system by which needs are satisfied. The sum of need satisfactions constitutes the degree of "security" of the individuals. Gillin describes the security needs of each ethnic group in chapters on land, habitation, food, clothing and ornament, and money. The differentiated ways of life of Ladino and Indian are shown to procure adequate, though quantitatively different, degrees of security. The institutions providing "social structure" (meaning "caste" relations), and "political and control structure," however, impinge upon each group differently. In the face of a subordinate relation to Ladinos, Indians adapt their culture so as to achieve security through insulation. Orientation toward a solitary household (Gillin 1951:51-53); communication of place in the structure by surname, deference behavior, and other devices (1951:53-54); ties of ritual kinship (1951: 60-61); and submissiveness to authority (1951:69-76) are each viewed as protective adaptations of the basic Indian heritage to the threatening social superiority of the Ladinos.

What surprises Gillin is that the local Ladinos are the most frustrated in spite of the fact that they acquire the bulk of the benefits of the local system. This points to the weakness of Gillin's approach. The community-oriented study does not place the local elite in a context where elite behavior may be adequately interpreted. That requires a regional and national focus. But the regional or national focus cannot be expressed in simple material needs or limited social relational terms. In material terms (to which a fair share of need theory reduces), the poor Ladino in San Luis should be the most frustrated because his material conditions are substandard relative to his status. It is quite clear in Gillin's monograph, however, and corroborated by Tumin (1952), that the wealthiest Ladinos in the community are the most frustrated.

The unhappy town elite can be interpreted better within a national framework, from a symbolic, structural viewpoint. The capital, Guatemala City, is symbolically central while San Luis is peripheral. Wealth is central in the sense that is it valued, especially in the form of land, while poverty is marginal. The poor Ladino in the town of San Luis is marginal both in residence and in wealth. Those aspects of his system are symbolically intact, if not the most desirable. But the rich Ladino in San Luis is central in wealth but marginal in residence. His interaction position is disjoint with respect to the overarching conceptual scheme, and he is frustrated. Only a move to the capital can reintegrate his symbolic system. This is precisely what Tumin says the richer San Luis Ladinos wish to do.

The analytical shortcoming arises from treating the community as separable from the national system. Thus in several regards, Gillin preserves the Redfieldian perspective: communities are local entities; culture is behavioral and descriptively accessible through topical chapters; acculturation is the crucial culture change process. As a result of this view, Gillin was not able to see that his extraordinary *Heritage of Conquest* analysis—in which Ladinos and Indians are shown to be opposites at nearly every point in their ideology—is, in fact, evidence of a particular kind of semantic unity.

If Gillin, as an anthropologist, holds the initial cultures as basic and sees the institutional constraints of stratification as modifying the cultures, Tumin, as a sociologist, holds the institutional constraints of caste as basic. For Tumin, the local culture is just another way of decorating the common framework of all caste systems.

> The community in question does represent, however, a kind of variation on the general theme of societal stratification which is likely to be found duplicated to some degree by many societies presently on, or about to move onto, the fringe of the influences of westernization and Europeanization (Tumin 1952:5).

Tumin's institutional articulation of Indians and Ladinos through "caste" relations does view the community as a single unit.[6] But, perhaps because of this prior focus on stratification, it is often difficult or impossible to tell whether certain statements about the lower reaches of the society refer just to Indians, or to Ladinos, or to a hypothetical poor class containing both Indians and Ladinos. The ethnic populations frequently tend to disappear as a result.

A number of later Mesoamerican scholars have attempted to overcome the limitations of the narrow community study by broadening their investigations to encompass a region, or even a nation, as the context for interpreting ethnic relations. The regional-national view has been expressed in the Guatemalan context by four principal authors—Nash, Colby, van den Berghe, and Richard N. Adams.

As a basis for studies in economic development, Manning Nash has elaborated the notion of a "multiple society with plural cultures"

(Nash 1957:826, 1964:228).[7] He advises that "the unit of study for economic development is a political one—the nation . . ." and that "the anthropologist who studies only one of the cultural traditions, and makes generalizations about the process of culture change and economic development for the whole country, errs conspicuously. . . ." (Nash 1957: 825). Nash is quite correct in adopting this wider perspective. It has enabled him to place Guatemalan Indians within a larger context. As a result, *Machine Age Maya* (1958b) emerges as one of the finest case studies of the changing relations between an indigenous people and the wider economic sphere in the Latin American literature.

Nash absorbed the notion of "two distinct cultural traditions," perhaps from his teacher, Sol Tax:

As a social type, the multiple society with plural cultures is marked by the presence of at least two distinct cultural traditions, each significantly different in breadth of integration. Although the entire population of the national territory is included in a single system of political and economic bonds, only a part of the population is fully aware of the national entity, participates significantly in its cultural and social life, or has control over resources and communications of nationwide scope or impact. That part of the population which carries the national variety of culture is in fact the national society (Nash 1957:826).

The other components of the society are separate social enclaves, mini-societies awash in the flux of the national system.

This national . . . segment of the multiple society . . . is superior to those small-scale societies with different cultural traditions within the same national territory. These subordinate societies are locally organized; economic resources are small compared to the national society; political power is not vested in them; and the cultural cleavage between the national segment and its plural cultures is marked by many symbolic pointers of dress, language, occupation, custom, and perhaps even the physical features of the members (Nash 1957:826).

There is indeed a sharp distinction between the national perspective of Ladinos and the local perspective of Indians. Nash further develops this observation in his "Political Relations in Guatemala"

(1958a). What presumably prevented Nash from viewing these opposite political interests as systems of inverse status ideologies is his assumption that the differences come from "two distinct cultural traditions." The too easy assumption of origins, the idea of a "cultural cleavage," and the apparent equation of "distinct" and "different" with "separate" precluded the observation of a single cultural system that systematically relates the different ethnic perspectives and behavior. In these respects, Nash fell heir to the limitations that had blocked Redfield from making the leap to a semiotic system analysis.

Colby and van den Berghe draw on Furnivall (1944) for the parallel idea of a "plural society." Such societies unite discrete subsocieties or sectors in a single political domain. The sectors are "corporate" and are composed of "distinguishable" though "noncomplementary" sets of functionally "parallel" institutions (Colby and van den Berghe 1969:7). The cultures of the two or more groups "frequently" (1969:8) are different and Guatemala is one case of "maximal cultural pluralism" (1969:9).

> We call a society pluralistic to the extent that it is divided into socially, and in most cases culturally, distinct groups, with a compartmentalized institutional structure of *duplicatory* (as distinguished from functionally differentiated) sectors. Thus a society is pluralistic if it consists of several interacting ethnic, "racial," or caste groups linked through a set of economic and political ties, each group having its own set of kinship institutions, religious and cosmological systems, voluntary associations, child-rearing practices, and so on (Colby and van den Berghe 1969:vii [emphasis his]).

The plural society approach is coupled with a relatively behavioral notion of culture. Colby speaks of van den Berghe, his sociologist coauthor, as placing stress "on 'social structure' as distinguished from the specific cultural forms of interaction" stressed by the anthropologist. On the other hand, "the wide cultural range of behavior" typifies Colby's anthropological approach (Colby and van den Berghe 1969:1).

Because some of the differences are parallel and noncomplementary, yet distinct, they are described in isolation, to a degree. To be sure, Colby and van den Berghe have given us perhaps the best description we have of ethnic interaction in Guatemala or Chiapas. Yet, because behavior is the cultural criterion, domestic and ritual differences mark several cultures, each of which by definition is integral. Thus, artificial boundaries are introduced and a plural culture is analytically created. Since interaction and some degree of integration is apparent, points of linkage are sought. The government, the market, and the Catholic church are the institutional structures through which the cultural groups are linked, though they each stand at different social levels. The analysis of ideological correspondences and oppositions, however, is impeded by the assumption of noncomplementarity. Being different, the world views and cultural values are to be analyzed separately. And because the ideologies differ, force and economic need are thought to hold the system together at a few points while the other institutions run separately.

A difficulty with this view is that many Guatemalan Indians are quite accepting of their situation. The implication is that they share a considerable body of concepts with the Ladinos about the social place of each. Another more severe difficulty is that the differences in the related ethnic ideologies penetrate and condition the domestic and ritual systems. Domestic and ritual life in turn shape ethnic behavior and hold each group more sharply in its place. Thus, even the domestic domains of the two groups are not parallel. Rather, they are functionally linked, contradicting the original plural society assumption.[8]

The plural society model, despite its different source, preserves many of the Redfieldian liabilities. The approach assumes plurality when institutions are distinguishable, without searching for system. Redfield also had manifold local folk societies for which he sought the characterizing traits, a case of nearly parallel concepts addressed in different words.

Richard N. Adams's early work separates the ethnic cultures on account of behavioral differences. This is manifest in his *Encuesta sobre la cultura de los ladinos en Guatemala* (1956) and in other sources. In his later work, *Crucifixion by Power* (1970), Adams analyzes the social structure of power and production relations. Like Tumin, Adams as a result loses the ability to distinguish Indian from Ladino peasants and fails to analyze adequately the Indian and his many manifestations of distinctiveness.

Perhaps for reasons of national social policy, several Mexican an-

thropologists have developed more thoroughly satisfying national perspectives that encompass the Indian. One of these approaches is
Aguirre Beltrán's notion of a refuge region. In certain respects Aguirre
Beltrán's work is a regional extension of Gillin's idea of adapted and
self-protective Indian culture. According to Aguirre Beltrán, in the
contest between the cultures of Europe and America, the native system lost politically and economically. The Indians were subjugated.
The only place the Indian system could remain even somewhat intact was in refuge regions. Aguirre Beltrán defines a refuge region as
an area made economically and politically marginal to the superordinate national system by its severe landscape and considerable distance from the politicoeconomic center of the colony or nation
(Aguirre Beltrán 1967). The refuge region provides the isolation
within which the Indians can maintain and elaborate their half of
the dual economy and ideology. They thereby escape some of the
onerous aspects of their political subjugation and status reduction.
Although Aguirre Beltrán focuses on the geographical aspect of
marginalized relations, he also works with the economic and political differences. It is not difficult to see here a parallel to Redfield's
isolated tribal Mayas of Quintana Roo.

Rodolfo Stavenhagen, by contrast, focuses on the political subjugation of the Indians and on the economic consequences of this subjugation through internal colonialism (Stavenhagen 1970, 1975).
For Stavenhagen, the conquest brought about the political basis for
economic class exploitation carried out in the guise of ethnic difference.

Adams, Aguirre Beltrán, and Stavenhagen complement each other.
None of them emphasize one aspect of geography, polity, or economy exclusively. The authors share the regional-to-national-level
focus, and they examine the objective circumstances of political
power, economic assets, and geographic marginality of the ethnic
groups. Yet in the work of each, the distinctive peculiarity of the
two sectors is derived from each group's original cultural sources,
their respective Spanish and Mayan heritages (Aguirre Beltrán 1967:
21; Stavenhagen 1975:172). Since these cultural differences are not
the substantive aspects of the real system, however, the differences
are accorded a greatly diminished analytical focus. As happened in
Tumin's stratification analysis of one town, the regional stratifica-

tion approaches tend to drain both Indian and Ladino of their distinctiveness. The ethnic terms become markers for social classes differentiated by politicoeconomic conditions. Differences in ideological culture nearly disappear, bleached by the focus on material circumstances.

Two recent studies carry this trend even further. According to both Judith Friedlander (1975) and Barbara Margolis (1975) the appellation of Indian is rejected by the people they studied. The natives prefer occupational or market class designations such as campesino (peasant), *obrero* (worker), or *pobre* (poor). This convergence of class and ethnic status in Mexico is not to be doubted.[9] But one must not suppose that the "objective" aspects of class relations bring about the maintenance of ethnic categories. The class relations are not "objectively" dichotomous. Actually, the set of oppositions in the preexisting categorical system is being used to conceptualize and define a continuous and multifaceted class relation into a dichotomous ethnic relation. The concepts make the class conditions objective via the use of symbols, not the reverse.

In dealing explicitly with conflict and with the untoward consequences of supremacy, Adams, Aguirre Beltrán, Stavenhagen, Friedlander, Margolis, and other authors of the genre depart from Redfield's perspective. As Oscar Lewis has ably shown, Redfield had a theoretical disposition to ignore the harsher aspects of peasant life. Yet, these authors parallel Redfield in their dependence on material circumstance. The focus shifts from social-group characterization to social-class structure. To be sure, these studies definitely benefit from using the structural, rather than the acculturational, approach to regional linkages. Nevertheless, the approach obscures the analysis of ethnic belief and ideology. This consequence is unacceptable, if, as Sahlins contends, the material organization of society is the symbolic expression of a cultural ideology (Sahlins 1976).

Yet the stratification approaches, taken together, do capture the gross outlines of the social conditions of Ladinos and Indians. They are thus valuable, although they do not deal well with the finer points of actual circumstance. There are, for example, apolitical Ladino peasant agriculturalists in refuge regions. There has been an Indian president of both Mexico and Guatemala. And there are Indian communities in the heartlands of Mexico and Guatemala. How are we to deal with such circumstances? A satisfying analysis does not seem to lie in causal theories based on objective conditions, for these studies virtually ignore ethnic differences in a given class's perceptions, as they pursue the objective circumstances thought fundamental. Nor does an adequate analysis derive from the behavioral and material definitions of culture, for these have led to unacceptably fragmented studies of peoples that are clearly linked. What is needed for a more penetrating anthropology of Mesoamerica is a different, non-Redfieldian concept of culture.

Culture: An Ideological System

Culture is at once the guiding concept of anthropology and the source of many of anthropology's weaknesses.[10] In order to avoid the liabilities of the behavioral view of culture that has constrained research in Mesoamerica, I shall use a more restricted definition of culture—one that focuses on ideas. Culture is here defined as a structured system of ideas. This definition of culture can be more clearly understood by comparing and contrasting it with those of David Schneider, Raymond Smith, and Clifford Geertz.

In Schneider's work culture is defined as a "system of symbols and meanings." Schneider elaborates this phrase. For "symbols and meanings" he offers "ultimate values, the collective representations" (Schneider 1976:208), the "basic premises," the "units" of life, their "order or classification," and the "parts" and "premises" with which the world is structured (Schneider 1972:38). Schneider's expansion of his notion of culture has been a major source of my definition of culture.

There is a difference, however, with regard to the word *symbols,* which is present in Schneider's definition but absent in mine. Throughout his writings on culture, Schneider persuasively asserts that behavior must be kept analytically separate from culture. Unfortunately, the word *symbol* frequently refers to behavior that is patterned and meaningful, what Milton Singer (1972) has termed *cultural performances.* The idea that symbols are a part of culture focuses our attention on the devices used to portray a system of ideas, however, rather than on the system of the ideas portrayed. If used in this way, the inclusion of symbols in the definition of culture contradicts Schneider's dictum of the separation of behavior and culture. This appears to be the central issue behind Raymond Smith's assertion that he is concerned with culture as a system of ideas and not with the particular forms by which the system is represented:

> Schneider has shown that it is both possible and fruitful to treat a kinship system as a system of inter-related cultural symbols which define and differentiate the domain of kinship (Schneider 1968 cited). Such a system is analytically separable from the lower level system of norms which define the rights, duties and obligations and proper modes of action of kinsmen toward each other. It consists of the most basic *ideas* about the nature of kinship; . . . The nuclear family as a cultural symbolic system is deeply rooted in Judeo-Christian "western" culture. The *idea* of a man and a woman, united in carnal love for the production of children who are the embodiment of the physical substance of both parents is a fundamental *assumption* about the nature of the reproductive process, and the *conception* of "the family" of parents and children is embodied in religious doctrine and symbolism. In this sense it is concretized into vivid images such as those of the Holy Family, even though this symbol represents the spiritual rather than the carnal aspect of kinship. When we speak of the nuclear family as a cultural symbol we do not refer to these more dramatic presentations, which of necessity objectify the system by adding to it; we refer to the very elementary *ideas* which define what kinship is (Smith 1970: 57-58 [emphasis mine].

Here Smith attempts to disentangle the idea or conceptual system from the symbolic or presentational system, but the attempt is partially obscured by the use of "cultural symbol" to refer to the ideas rather than the symbols.

By contrast, Clifford Geertz's definition of culture sometimes focuses directly on the performance aspect of symbols. Thus, culture is "meanings embodied in symbols," the symbols being "forms by means of which men communicate" (Geertz 1973a:89). Too much emphasis on the performance aspect of culture (as symbol) may lead to the dismembering of different statuses within a society. If the members of one particular status perform distinctively, in order to represent the idea of their differing positions, the two might be construed as separate cultures. As we have seen, precisely this tactic dismembered Guatemalan socie*y into the culture of the Ladinos and the many cultures of the Indians. Moreover, the focus on forms makes it very difficult to speak of a "Mediterranean culture" (Peristiani 1976:1), where parallel ideas are presented through distinct symbols from country to country. To be sure, Geertz elsewhere emphasizes the idea matrix by means of which performances are interpreted:

> The concept of culture I espouse . . . is essentially a semiotic one. Believing, with Max Weber, that man is an animal suspended in webs of significance he himself has spun, I take culture to be those webs, and the analysis of it to be therefore not an experimental science in search of law but an interpretive one in search of meaning. It is explication I am after, construing social expressions on their surface enigmatical (Geertz 1973b:5).

In this perspective Schneider, Smith, and Geertz are in essential agreement. I would add simply that the meanings arise out of the structuring of ideas. Symbols merely help us to perceive the structure. But the same structure of ideas may be acknowledged by one segment of a society through reverence for the Holy Family and by another segment through regular attention to the Walton family.[11] Culture is a form and not a substance.

It is precisely a structural and systematic concept of meaning that Redfield lacked, for meaning or, in his words, "significance" or "understanding" was attached to individual things, whether acts or objects. As we have seen, this approach deprives ideas of structural relations to each other. Saussure, however, provides the roots of a structural approach to meaning.[12]

According to Saussure, the meaning of a linguistic sign is not intrinsic to a single sign but arises out of a system of relations within the entire corpus of other signs. Furthermore, the sense or value of a term is a product of a kind of negation. Meanings often arise out of binary opposition. In more complex sets of signs the meaning of one term is a kind of leftover or remainder in relation to the other terms:

> Language is a system of interdependent terms in which the value of each term results solely from the simultaneous presence of the others. . . .

Within the same language, all words used to express related ideas limit each other reciprocally; synonyms like French *redouter* 'dread,' *craindre* 'fear,' and *avoir peur* 'be afraid' have value only through their opposition: if *redouter* did not exist, all its content would go to its competitors (Saussure 1959:114, 116).

If I may use my own metaphor, the value of a sign is achieved in a process that parallels the expansion of several small balloons within a larger container, each balloon inflating into the unoccupied space. The space becomes wholly occupied and the balloons shape each other in a single system.

Subsequent research has shown that even binary opposition is a highly complex phenomenon. In dealing with two-term paradigmatically opposite signs (high-low, white-black, man-woman, etc.), Linda Waugh (1979), following Jakobson, has noted that distinctive feature opposition in the Levi-Straussian sense of plus and minus features is not usually correct. Rather, one member of the polar opposition is either unmarked or negatively marked, while the other term is positively marked. Thus, in the set [man, woman], [man] in its unmarked superordinate status may refer to either a male or a female person. [Woman] is the marked or restricted term, referring only to a female. [Man] used in the environment of [woman] takes negative marking as the opposite of the positively restricted term, in short, a [nonwoman]. These are exemplified, for example, in "Man cannot live by bread alone" versus "First a woman ascended in the elevator and then a man." In the latter phrase there is marked opposition; in the former there is no marking. Further, we note that the unmarked form of the ambiguous term (either unmarked or opposite of marked) may often be replaced by an explicitly neutral term, in this case [person].

A second source of meaning consists in the syntagmatic relations generated by language. Syntactic rules bring lexical concepts into relationships with each other. Sometimes the relationships may be anomalous because of incompatible feature structures of the syntactically joined lexical items. Thus, "He is a good man," is permissible while "He is a good woman," is usually not permissible.[13] It is discordant. Yet it is sayable and it is ungrammatical in quite a different sense from "Man good a is he."

The above notes do not pretend to be a full explication of meaning. Yet it is certain that meanings are not individually attached to single sign vehicles. Rather, meanings or ideas arise out of oppositions among a set of ideas (paradigmatic relations for which particular terms are merely placeholders) and out of the relations among ideas induced by a set of speech production rules (syntagmatic relations). This is the essential Saussurian notion: though each term and each context is different and unique, no term and no context has meaning or significance in and of itself. The meaning of any term derives from the oppositions and context considered as a total system.

The Structure of Guatemalan Culture: Inverse Status Ideologies

The Saussurian approach to meaning can be applied to Guatemala.[14] First, the people are subdivided into the basic social categories of Ladino and *indígena*. The categories are opposites in several senses of race, social status, occupation, and education. Each group is frequently defined as the opposite or negation of some characteristic of the other. While the term *ladino* does not encompass *indígena* in its unmarked form, its relation of markedness with respect to *indígena* is interesting. Ladino is unmarked for status, in its general sense. Thus a Ladino can be either high or low status, a president or a peasant, in the neutral or unmarked form. Indian, however, is marked as low status. Nevertheless, in the environment of a discussion of Indians, Ladino is the opposite of the marked low status. Thus Ladino is also high status, especially in the western half of the country where Indians are more contrastively present.

A similar pattern emerges in the concept of urban affiliation. Ladinos are unmarked as to urban residence and may be either city-wise urbanites or country peasants. This is most obviously the case in eastern Guatemala, where Ladino peasants abound. Indians, however, are marked as peasants; as rural, uneducated, manual laborers.[15] In the environment of a discussion of Indians, Ladinos are urban, urbane, and professional, depending on whether the rural residence, the education, or the agricultural occupation of the peasant is the issue in focus.

There are several social implications of this conceptual structure.

First, the city itself is the symbolic manifestation of the urban ideology attached to high status. Thus the city, especially the capital city, will gut the hinterland of its human resources as individuals move to capture the symbols of central high status. This is manifest in absentee finca landlordism at one end of the social scale and in the vacant-town phenomenon among the Indians at the other. It is further manifest in the process of ladinoization that tends to affect the Indians who leave their marginal municipios and move to the larger town centers. In each case, people are integrating their categorical social status with their symbolic productions in actual circumstance.

Attached to these opposed social statuses is a system of inverse ideologies. The inversions of ideology correspond to the mutual negations of Ladino and Indian as marked categories. The Ladinos orient toward the city, to the center, to power, and despise manual labor. Indians orient to the field, the *campo,* the periphery. They flee power and see manual labor not only as their lot but as their preference. The ideological oppositions run deeper yet. Attached to Ladino status is an ideology of social interconnection. The Ladinos both tend to have, and intend to seek out, protections and favors through a system of friends. Indians, on the other hand, isolate themselves more. They are less able to maintain multiple friendships. They invite fewer friends or potential friends to their parties than Ladinos. Indeed, Indians evince an ideology of disconnection or of atomization, preferring to do things on their own, as separate family households and as politically unprotected and largely unassisted local communities. Ladinos, by contrast, involve the government and seek out help. Ruben Reina (1959) has earlier noted the inability of Indians to form multiple or enduring friendships, in contrast with the multiple linkages among Ladinos.

Just as the marked linguistic category is "restricted," so is the marked social category of Indian. To be sure, the restrictions on the Indians were worse in the Colonial period, and have only begun to be relaxed with the reforms beginning in 1944. Yet sharp restrictions remain. At least in western Guatemala, the Indians of the peripheral communities are arbitrarily recruited for military service. Such is not the fate of the Ladinos, except, perhaps, the near derelict. The restrictedness of Indians is further manifest in the political domain in the Indian orientation to a closed corporate community. In the domestic domain Indian restrictedness is manifest in community endogamy and in precise rules of postmarital residence. In the domain of religion, Indian men participate more than Ladino men. Whether as orthodox or unorthodox Catholics, the Indian men and women have manifest their submission to Catholic government through symbols of suffering. As individuals they have traditionally supported the fiesta system in a structural parallel of encomienda taxation and repartimiento labor service.

Ladinos, by contrast, conceive of themselves as fluid and adaptable. They are unrestricted and ideally (but only in contrast with Indians) above the law. Ladino friendships are open; Ladino political affiliations span the nation; Ladino marriages link communities; Ladino postmarital residence is conditional upon self-interest. Ladino religious participation—a symbol of subordination as well as of restrictedness—is considerably downplayed among the Ladino men, though appropriate for Ladino women.

The system of ideologies is symbolically manifest in the patterns of indexical behavior such as clothing use and language preference. In clothing, Indians are conceptually uniform from individual to individual and varied from community to community. Ladinos on the other hand are varied from individual to individual within a community and uniform from community to community. Similarly, Ladinos speak one language across many communities while Indians speak many languages across a few communities and yet more numerous dialects each in a particular community. While each language and clothing difference indexically marks the individual and his community, taken as a whole, the systems symbolize the underlying ideologies of Ladino interconnection versus Indian atomization. The inversions of Ladino and Indian are pervasive and systematic.

Certainly I am not the first to note such contrasts between Ladino and Indian. Gillin's *Heritage of Conquest* paper, "Ethos and Cultural Personality in Mesoamerica," is a masterful display of such ideological oppositions. For convenient presentation I have drawn out the high points of his analysis in tabular form (unbracketed phrases are quotes):

Page	Line	Indian	Page	Line	Ladino
196	7	effect a peaceful adjustment or adaptation of men to the universe	196	8-9	effect control of the universe by man
196	9-10	wishes to come to terms with the universe	196	10	wishes to dominate it [the universe]
196	13-17	man is in a world [of] laws [which are supernaturally controlled] ongoing and immutable	196	27-28	universe . . . can be manipulated by man
196	17-21	man must learn certain patterns of action and attitude to bring himself into conformity with the scheme of things . . . [to] receive the minimum amount of punishment and misfortune and the maximum rewards	196	29-38	control and power . . . over things . . . animals . . . other men; . . . man has a will of his own . . . destructive force . . . is the legitimate and ultimate technique for the removal of barriers to the individual's control
197	5-7	individual . . . counts less than the group. Individual exists as a member of the group	197	10	individual personality . . . has the higher value . . . group, . . . family, . . . exist to promote the individual
197	16-17	uninterrupted routine practice of traditional patterns	197	18-22	routine is intensely boring . . . periodic change of power . . . adds zest to life. Oscillation of power
197	23-27	universe . . . restricted [to] local community or region	198	12-40	universe . . . expanded both in space and time. . . . Have kinship, political, and economic connections with the capital and other towns. Cultivate a concept of nationality [as] part of the republic

Page	Line	Indian	Page	Line	Ladino
198	3-9	restricted time space . . . a timeless present	198	29	strong sense of history
199	12-20	interested in owning land so that they personally can work on it. . . . No Indian ever tries to acquire wealth or skill so that he can retire from the land but rather the reverse	199	21-26	personally works the land only when all other means of livelihood are unavailable . . . Control of land . . . enables the owner to master the lives of his tenants and workmen
199	36-39	[from] physical toil . . . one receives the approval of his fellows.	200	3-4	toil is not only unbearably wearisome, but also disgraceful
200	7-8	adjustive and permissive	200	8	ordering, dominating
200	8-9	ranking or stratification . . . not characteristic	200	10	[ranking or stratification] always present
200	11-13	leadership [positions] throught of as obligations [not] striven for	201	28-30	political advancement [in] own interest
200	17-18	envy and competitiveness . . . an anomaly or a crime	201	21	competition or conflict [appropriate]
200	30	group decisions . . . by consensus	201	12-14	domineering or ordering behavior [with unequals] factions [among equals]
201	38-39	husband is officially dominant [but] patterns require a reciprocal division of labor and of authority	202	29-30	husband's authority is definitely superior
201	1	wife shares the honors and the responsibilities [of public life]	202	32	does not expect his wife to share . . . public life
203	15-17	religion . . . tends to permeate all of life	203	18	much more secular

Page	Line	Indian	Page	Line	Ladino
204		[religious devotions with group orientation]	205	7-8	organized support for the Church is striking by its absence
204		[men and women religiously involved]	205	4-5	In contrast to Indian women, Ladino women show more devotion than men
206	16	relatively more secure [personality structure]	209	18	much less secure [personality structure]
206	19-22	compulsive following of the approved patterns without any strong motivation	209	18-20	no feeling of certainty that any of his available culture patterns will produce satisfactions
206	32-33	calmness and comparatively little affect, or show of emotion	209	13-15	much more emotionalism . . . likes and dislikes more demonstratively expressed . . . mood swings
207	1-9	little show of aggressiveness [except with alcohol or special offense]	209	25-26	much more aggressive . . . both toward themselves and toward members of the other caste
207	18-20	child rearing . . . quite permissive	210	13-14	the higher one goes in the Ladino class system, the greater is the rigidity of child training

Gillin found the oppositions, yet he maintained the cultures were distinct. Indeed, his language is laced with words connoting structural opposition: "in contrast," "on the other hand," "quite the opposite is true of." Other sentences balance on a comma, contrasting one group with the other. Yet, Gillin presumably failed to see the single-system implications of the pattern because, like Redfield, he treated the meanings of each ethnic segment in isolation as attributes attached to objects or behavior (1951:205). Furthermore, behavior is typed, discrete, elemental, and diacritically characterizing of a culture's participants. "San Luis," he says, "happens to be a community which contains both Indians and Ladinos, each still preserving separate and distinguishable cultures" (Gillin 1951:195).

But the Saussurian perspective of meaning analysis forces us to a quite different conclusion. First, culture is a system of meanings. Second, meaning arises from a system of oppositions. Thus, categories of opposite meaning are elements of the same culture. Since Indian and Ladino are opposed categories, and take meaning in reference to each other, they are elements of the same culture. Moreover, these categories are structured in a status hierarchy. Associated with these status-linked positions of Indian and Ladino are two sets of basic premises about how to live one's life. These I have called status ideologies. According to Schneider's definition of culture, they constitute a portion of the cultural system for they establish the basic premises of world view. Inasmuch as these status ideologies are also opposed to each other in a systematic pattern of inversions or negations, they, too, constitute elements in the same culture and take their meaning from their relationship to each other.[16] The apparent variability of the Guatemalan institutions arises from the differentiating impact of the inverse-status ideologies on the various institutions of each status group. Not in spite of their differences, but rather because their differences are opposed and structured as they are, Ladinos and Indians are members of a single culture.

Mesoamerica has produced its share of classic studies, and has had an impact on anthropology generally. I would cite Redfield on regional relationships and peasant subordination to the city, Lewis on conflict and family interaction, Foster on the image of limited good, Wolf on the nature of peasant society and on the theory of the closed corporate community, and there are others. Indeed, the community study approach was essentially pioneered and mastered in Meso-america.[17]

Yet the literature is subject to criticism. I have attempted to es-tablish why this is so for two important styles of Mesoamerican re-search. In the first genre, the widely accepted behavioral approach to culture has dismembered the region and cut asunder the social and cultural relationships existing between the ethnic groups. As a result we have a plethora of community studies largely about one or another ethnic group. But linkages seem to be one of the most im-portant aspects of each group's character. One reaction to this has been the second genre of regional studies. But because of the en-trenched behavioral definition of culture, attempts to define the re-gional social relationships rely on power and economic dependency models. Such studies tend to be flat textured, because the force-need approach tends to discount and eliminate the richness of cultural data.

Yet all of us have experienced firsthand the richness, the complexi-ty, and the vibrancy of some part of Mesoamerica. To capture this richness and resolve the dilemmas—as Kuhn (1962) has shown for any discipline experiencing contradictions of its established para-digms—we need new theoretical approaches. If Kuhn is right, we will cast about for new models. The direction I have chosen to take, for a while and until persuaded otherwise, is based on the assump-tion that the enigmas of Mesoamerica will tend to be resolved if we treat its culture as a single system of ideas—as a form and not as a substance.[18] There is evidence of others casting about, both in this conference and in the Mesoamerican literature. While I do not think that anthropology operates with the clean sweep of all rivals model that Kuhn posits for the physical sciences, it is probable that a more successful theoretical approach to the complexities of Mesoamerican life would serve well in other ethnographic areas. That is the poten-tial in the pleasure of Mesoamerican research.

NOTES

1. Also in this paragraph one finds reference to "the people who share those common understandings we call culture" (Redfield 1940:739). This, of course, is a clear reference to culture as something mental, though it does not employ the idea that the understandings are a system. They are potentially just a tally list of common ideas.

2. For example, in 1953. "The culture of a people is, then, its total equipment of ideas and institutions and conventionalized activities "(Redfield 1953:85). There is, however, one unusual definition which shows a close affinity to Bennidict: "As an alternative perspective it seemed that the activities of the people were obedient to a limited number of prevailing and influential general ideas about the nature of things" (Redfield 1955:23). Redfield, however, never followed this suggestion with a configurational rendition of the society or societies inquestion.

3. The material and behavioral trait orientation is also sharply manifest in Kirchhoff. Beliefs are treated in segments of two sentences comprising less than two lines of print (Kirchhoff 1952:25).

4. In addition, focus on the community as a social unit is manifest in the selection of ten community reports which, along with his own report, are the basis of their study.

5. Part III, the conclusion of the symposium, takes a less descriptive tack. But in assessing or summing up, the conclusions flow largely in the direction of acculturation analysis and historical derivation. For Redfield, diffusion was one of the principal forms of acculturation. The acculturation process, indeed, is the principal analytical mechanism throughout his writings after 1930. We recall that his first published paper called for a move toward process analysis in anthropology. For Redfield, process consisted of differential acculturation. The result was his famed folk-urban continuum. In this regard, the final section of *Heritage of Conquest* is an extension of a direction taken by Redfield, though it would not be correct to say that the participants took the idea of acculturation analysis just from Redfield. Chapter 14, the concluding chapter of the concluding section, returns to the topic of social interaction.

6. The "objective" correspondences between Asian caste and Guatemalan "caste" are numerous. There are restrictions on intermarriage, with privileged access of higher-status males to lower-status females. Residence tends to be caste grouped. Social distance and forms of deference are maintained. Occupations differ and are viewed as caste related though not caste exclusive.

There are differences, however. The most significant seem to lie primarily at the symbolic and conceptual levels rather than in the objective circumstances. In Guatemala, origin symbols map a set of secular status categories with a secular degree of honor onto secular fields of interaction. The Guatemelan symbols link secular to secular. In India, the origin symbols map a set of sacred status categories, with sacred degrees of honor, onto secular interactions. In short, the Indian symbols link sacred to secular. This divergence seems to make changes in objective interaction circumstance less significant for the reorientation of categories in India than in Guatemala. Furthermore, the community definition of group in Guatemala versus the kinship definition of group in India makes it easier for a Guatemalan to escape a low-status community and, by physical movement, rejoin society in a more central-status community. In India, by contrast, kinship closes off the return to society at a higher level. In India one escapes the restrictions of lower status by stepping out of society and orienting toward the symbolic center, as a religious ascetic. In Guatemala one escapes by stepping out of one community and reentering another one conceptually closer to the symbolic as well as politicoeconomic center in Guatemala City. Movement is thus greater in Guatemala because status concepts and interaction circumstances are mutually adjustable by virtue of their both being secular.

7. Nash also uses the phrase "non-national state composed of plural cultures" (1958).

8. For a detailed analysis of the functional complementarity of Ladino and Indian domestic systems, see Hawkins (in press).

9. Indeed, Guatemala appears to be headed in the same direction of change.

10. As James Boon put it, the concept of culture is a center "of and for debate, . . . difficult to talk about and impossible to agree upon . . ." (Boon 1973:1).

11. This reference to a current television program may be difficult to interpret outside American culture, or in a few years even in our own. "The Waltons" is a currently popular program about an honorable, easygoing, caring, problem-solving family, cast a nostalgic forty or fifty years ago.

12. I do not develop a complete theory of meaning. Rather, I shall draw on a few principles which seem essential to a theory of meaning.

13. It would be acceptable in reference, say, to a homosexual partner in a men's prison.

14. For a more thorough analysis of the following issues, see Hawkins (in press).

15. Of course there are exceptions. Many of the Indian inhabitants of San Pedro Sacatepéquez and several communities in the region of Quezaltenango-Totonicapán-San Francisco el Alto are more successfully commercial. Yet because their inhabitants do not fit the marked expectation, they are remarkable and remarked upon communities.

16. For the ethnographic documentation of this briefly stated position, see Hawkins (in press).

17. In the original conference presentation I compared the Mesoamerican

region unfavorably with other ethnographic areas for not having produced many classics and being a bit tedious. Robert Kemper, Norman Schwartz, and Barbara Tedlock thought the position rash, and they were right. With a year to mellow since the conference, I have realized that I try to skim the classics from the other ethnographic areas while I try to read anything on the Mayan region. The result is the other areas subjectively look better written. But the perception resulted from the selective bias of my research interests.

18. This paper attempts to offer a new perspective on Mesoamerica. To the degree that a new perspective is needed, it is a critique of the acknowledged masters. Yet, I am acutely aware that in gaining this enhanced view (if it be such) I have, as it were, stood on the shoulders of the very persons I critique in order to see a bit further. Though there is something rude in the process of standing on my mentors to see further and yet criticizing them for not having seen as far, the question of whether the perspective offered here is indeed an improvement for certain purposes seems to emerge best by contrasting the basic assumptions of this approach with Redfield and selected later Mesoamericanists. If this perspective is valuable, then it should serve as a platform on which others will stand to see even further. To be sure, I shall also receive criticism, hopefully for not having seen as far as possible rather than for having looked in the wrong direction. But in either case that is how our studies progress.

My thanks to Sol Tax and Manning Nash for having been solid enough to stand upon, to Raymond Smith for many helpful comments on my earlier work, to Rex Cooper and John Sorenson for several useful conversations and criticisms, to Norman Schwartz, Barbara Tedlock, and Carl Kendall for their encouragement and comment, to Arthur Rubel for a thorough critique, to Suzie Goodfellow and to Jan Lowman, each with an eye for editorial detail, to Brigham Young University for continuing research support, and to many Guatemalans for their tolerance, friendship, and insight.

REFERENCES

Adams, Richard N.

1956   *Encuesta sobre la cultura de los Ladinos en Guatemala.* Seminario de Integración Social Guatemalteca, no. 2 (Guatemala: Editorial del Ministerio de Educación Pública).

1970   *Crucifixion by Power: Essays on Guatemalan National Social Structure, 1944-1966* (Austin: University of Texas Press).

Aguirre Beltrán, Gonzalo
1967   *Regiones de refugio: El desarrollo de la comunidad y el proceso domini-
cal en mestizoamerica* (Mexico: Instituto Nacional Indigenista).

Boon, James A.
1973   "Further Operations of 'Culture' in Anthropology: A Synthesis
of and for Debate," in *The Idea of Culture in the Social Sciences*, ed.
Louis Schneider and Charles Bonjean (Cambridge: Cambridge
University Press).

Colby, Benjamin N., and Pierre L. van den Berghe
1969   *Ixil Country: A Plural Society in Highland Guatemala* (Berkeley
and Los Angeles: University of California Press).

de la Fuente, Julio
1952   "Ethnic and Communal Relations," in *Heritage of Conquest: The
Ethnology of Middle America*, ed. Sol Tax (Glencoe, Ill.: Free
Press).

Friedlander, Judith
1975   *Being Indian in Hueyapán: A Study of Forced Identity in Contemporary Mexico* (New York: St. Martin's Press).

Furnivall, J. S.
1944   *Netherlands India: A Study of Plural Economy* (Cambridge: Cambridge University Press).

Geertz, Clifford
1973a   "Religion as a Cultural System," in *The Interpretation of Cultures:
Selected Essays* (New York: Basic Books).
1973b   "Thick Description: Toward an Interpretive Theory of Culture,"
in *The Interpretation of Cultures: Selected Essays* (New York: Basic
Books).

Gillin, John
1951   *The Culture of Security in San Carlos: A Study of a Guatemalan
Community of Indians and Ladinos*. Middle American Research
Institute, Publication 16 (New Orleans: Tulane University).
1952   "Ethos and Cultural Aspects of Personality," in *Heritage of Conquest: The Ethnology of Middle America*, ed. Sol Tax (Glencoe,
Ill.: Free Press).

Guiteras Holmes, Calixta
1952   "Social Organization," in *Heritage of Conquest: The Ethnology of
Middle America*, ed. Sol Tax (Glencoe, Ill.: Free Press).

Hawkins, John P.
in press *Inverse Images: The Meaning of Culture, Ethnicity and Family in
Postcolonial Guatemalan Society* (Albuquerque: University of New
Mexico Press).

Kirchhoff, Paul

1952   "Mesoamerica: Its Geographical Limits, Ethnic Composition and Cultural Characteristics," in *Heritage of Conquest: The Ethnology of Middle America,* ed. Sol Tax (Glencoe, Ill.: Free Press).

Kuhn, Thomas

1970   *The Structure of Scientific Revolutions,* 2d ed. (Chicago: University of Chicago Press).

Margolis, Barbara

1975   *Princes of the Earth: Subcultural Diversity in a Mexican Municipality* (Washington, D.C.: American Anthropological Association).

Nash, Manning

1957   "The Multiple Society in Economic Development: Mexico and Guatemala," *American Anthropologist* 59: 823-36.

1958a   "Political Relations in Guatemala," *Social and Economic Studies* 7: 65-75.

1958b   *Machine Age Maya: The Industrialization of a Guatemalan Community* (Chicago: University of Chicago Press, 1967).

1964   "Social Prerequisites to Economic Growth in Latin America and Southeast Asia," *Economic Development and Cultural Change* 12: 225-42.

Peristiani, Jean G.

1976   *Mediterranean Family Structures.* Cambridge Studies in Social Anthropology, no. 13 (Cambridge: Cambridge University Press).

Redfield, Robert

1926   "Anthropology, A Natural Science?" in *Human Nature and the Study of Society: The Papers of Robert Redfield,* vol. 1, ed. Margaret Park Redfield (Chicago: University of Chicago Press, 1962).

1927   "The Cerahpa and the Castiyohpa in Tepoztlán," *Mexican Folkways* 3: 137-43.

1928a   "Among the Middle Americans," *University of Chicago Magazine* 20: 242-47.

1928b   "The Calpolli-Barrio in a Present-day Mexican Pueblo," *American Anthropologist* 30: 282-92.

1928c   "Remedial Plants of Tepoztlán: A Mexican Folk Herbal," *Journal of the Washington Academy of Sciences* 18: 216-26.

1929   "The Material Culture of Spanish-Indian Mexico," *American Anthropologist* 31:602-18.

1930a   "The Regional Aspect of Culture," in *Human Nature and the Study of Society: The Papers of Robert Redfield,* vol. 1, ed. Margaret Park Redfield (Chicago: University of Chicago Press, 1962).

1930b   *Tepoztlán* (Chicago: University of Chicago Press).

1935   "Folkways and City Ways," in *Human Nature and the Study of Society: The Papers of Robert Redfield,* vol. 1, ed. Margaret Park Redfield (Chicago: University of Chicago Press, 1962).

1940   "The Folk Society and Culture," *American Journal of Sociology* 45:731-42.

1941   *The Folk Culture of Yucatan* (Chicago: University of Chicago Press).

1953   *The Primitive World and Its Transformations* (Ithaca, N.Y.: Cornell University Press).

1955   *The Little Community* (Chicago: University of Chicago Press).

Redfield, Robert, and Sol Tax
1952   "General Characteristics of Present-day Mesoamerican Indian Society," in *Heritage of Conquest: The Ethnology of Middle America,* ed. Sol Tax (Glencoe, Ill.: Free Press).

Sahlins, Marshall
1976   *Culture and Practical Reason* (Chicago: University of Chicago Press).

Saussure, Ferdinand de
1959   *Course in General Linguistics,* ed. Charles Bally and Albert Schehaye in collaboration with Albert Riedlinger, trans. Wade Baskin (New York: McGraw-Hill, 1966).

Schneider, David M.
1972   "What is Kinship All About?" in *Kinship Studies in the Morgan Centennial Year,* ed. Priscilla Reining (Washington, D.C.: Anthropological Society of Washington).

1976   "Notes Toward a Theory of Culture," in *Meaning in Anthropology,* ed. Keith H. Basso and Henry A. Selby (Albuquerque: University of New Mexico Press).

Singer, Milton
1972   *When A Great Tradition Modernizes* (London: Pall Mall Press).

1976   "Robert Redfield's Development of a Social Anthropology of Civilizations," in *American Anthropology: The Early Years,* ed. John V. Murra (St. Paul: West Publishing Co.).

Smith, Raymond T.
1970   "The Nuclear Family in Afro-American Kinship," *Journal of Comparative Family Studies* 1:55-70.

Stavenhagen, Rodolfo
1970   "Classes, Colonialism, and Acculturation: A System of Inter-ethnic Relations in Mesoamerica," in *Masses in Latin America,* ed. Dwight B. Heath (New York: Oxford University Press).

1975   *Social Classes in Agrarian Societies,* trans. Judy Adler Hellman (New York: Doubleday, Anchor Press).

Tax, Sol
1937   "The Municipios of the Midwestern Highlands of Guatemala,"
        American Anthropologist 39:423-44.
1952a   "Preface," in *Heritage of Conquest: The Ethnology of Middle Amer-
        ica,* ed. Sol Tax (Glencoe, Ill.: Free Press).
1952b   "Economy and Technology," in *Heritage of Conquest: The Ethnol-
        ogy of Middle America,* ed. Sol Tax (Glencoe, Ill.: Free Press).
1953   *Penny Capitalism: A Guatemalan Indian Economy.* Smithsonian
        Institution, Institute of Social Anthropology,Publication 16
        (Washington, D.C.: Government Printing Office) (Photo-
        reproduction, New York: Octagon Books, 1972).
Waugh, Linda R.
1979   "Marked and Unmarked: A Choice Between Unequals in Semi-
        otic Structures," unpublished paper.
Wisdom, Charles
1952   "The Supernatural World and Curing," in *Heritage of Conquest:
        The Ethnology of Middle America,* ed. Sol Tax (Glencoe, Ill.: Free
        Press).

IV

An Afterword: Assessing the Field of Mesoamerican Anthropology

13

The Second Heritage of Conquest: Some Observations[1]

Norman B. Schwartz
University of Delaware

No doubt it is risky trying to comment on a diverse group of papers and then trying to relate it to an earlier, equally varied set. Aside from simply misunderstanding someone, there is the danger of imposing false unities on divergent themes, approaches, and conclusions. It is also possible to exaggerate differences, particularly between the first and second symposium. With all this and more in mind, I have tried to do several things here.

First, I have attempted to outline a background for the papers in this symposium by making some observations about past and contemporary anthropological research in Mesoamerica. Second, the various methods, ethnographic coverage and conclusions of the authors are noted. Throughout there are comparisons drawn to the first *Heritage of Conquest*. Finally, I think it is necessary to observe the absence of certain subjects in the present symposium, for example, ethnohistory.

Background

To oversimplify somewhat, the history of modern (roughly 1930-60) anthropological field studies in Mesoamerica begins with Redfield's study of Tepotzlán. "It is the first clear example of a detailed study focused on a single community" (Chambers and Young 1979: 47). Community studies predominated in the modern period, and most of them were holistic, functionalist, and synchronic investigations of Indian towns and villages. While holistic functionalism may be properly understood as a field method as well as or even more than as a species of equilibrium theory, its use in Mesoamerica often made the Indian community appear as an isolated, bounded entity insulated from macrosocial processes and structures (Carmack 1973: 219). Indians, it seemed, had a self-sealing set of customs, values, and objects, and their own distinctive identity, social organization, and economy. Tax's discovery that ethnic and municipio boundaries coincided reinforced the attractiveness of the community-study method. Consistent with all this, it was often assumed that (Indian) behavior was determined largely by psychocultural factors, and studies guided by this assumption appeared to confirm it.

Many data collection techniques were used, but participant-observation and interviewing were then, as now, the main ones (see Chambers and Young 1979:50). As the papers in this symposium show (e.g., Early, Bossen, Corbett, and Whiteford), other techniques, such as surveys, are used mainly when anthropologists go, as Boissevain (1975) puts it, "beyond the community."

In the early years of this period there was a shift from a previous emphasis on culture history to one on social anthropology, and "social anthropologists and cultural historians had little overlap in problem selection, in concepts, and in evaluation of results" (Nash 1967:4). The nature of the community-study approach probably made the divergence inevitable. But at the same time, limited personnel in both areas could hardly have failed to reinforce the situation. On the other hand, Nash noted that in the 1960s the two types of scholarship were converging (e.g., Vogt's Chiapas project), and the trend is growing (see Jones 1977; Carmack 1979; Chambers and Young 1979).

The first *Heritage of Conquest* was profoundly concerned with delineating culture area boundaries and traits and with problems of acculturative change among Indians, leaning heavily at all times on community studies—the most common form of investigation at the time (Paul 1952:293). Of course, the participants at the first symposium did not concentrate exclusively on these matters. Few of the issues which were to become important in the contemporary period were completely ignored in the symposium. Rather, when the participants began to discuss topics and concepts that were to loom large in the 1970s, they tended to be short-circuited and quickly brought back to problems of acculturation, trait distribution, and so forth. To take just one example, there is an interesting discussion in the *Heritage of Conquest* of whether the cultures of pre-Conquest Mesoamerica can be described without the inclusion of city and state structures (Tax 1952:254-55). If culture is defined in ideational and affective terms, then it may be described with minimal attention paid to structures of power and inequality. If, on the other hand, these factors determine, condition, or somehow enter into culture, then no analysis of pre-Conquest Mesoamerica is possible without detailed consideration of city, state, and stratification. This view also makes the need for ethnohistory, colonial history, and the like all the more urgent. But commonly, discussions along these lines are truncated, and there is a return to the major themes of the conference.

By 1967 Nash, writing in the *Handbook of Middle American Indians,* was able to note some significant developments in Mesoamerican studies, several of them foreshadowed in *Heritage of Conquest.* For example, Wolf's understanding of group relations in a complex society directed attention to ecology, conflict, and brokers who mediated tensions among groups. This was part of the recognition that certain types of community study could not deal adequately with part-whole relations or satisfactorily explain patterns of behavior observed within local units.

The work was becoming more problem oriented, too, taking up the issues of sociocultural change linked to urbanization, industrialization, acculturation, and "directed change" (see Nash 1967:8-9). With this, there were fewer holistic community studies. Simultaneously, "from the efforts to see patterns and structures in Middle America as a whole, along with regional differences or subcultural variations, investigators moved to making other sorts of typologies or categorizations of Middle American societies" (Nash 1967:7; see also the June 1955 issue of the *American Anthropologist*). Today, problem-oriented studies not only continue to proliferate (Chambers and Young 1979), they predominate, while the typological approach has more or less dropped from sight save in certain urban investigations. Incidentally, when anthropologists tracked their rural subjects into the city, they tended to examine their adaptations or "cultures of poverty" with insufficient attention paid to the city as a form of sociocultural organization with its own adaptation to the surrounding society, economy, and polity and with its own ideological style (see Basham and DeGroot 1977; Fox 1977; Kemper, this volume). Simply put, the traditional community-study method has survived more intact in urban than in rural research.

While it may be "virtually impossible to typify" contemporary (roughly 1969-79) work in Mesoamerica (Chambers and Young 1979:47), several developments are relevant to this conference.

The concern with macrosocial-microsocial links and all this implies for new approaches to the community is salient. This is often connected with an interest in "developmental" processes—"modernization" having fallen on hard times. In this context, there is a marked tendency to give primacy to political economy and to make culture secondary to the analysis of customs and patterns of behavior. The incorporation of local units into larger ones is now a major focus of research (see Corbett and Whiteford, and Moore below), although in some ways this trend goes back at least to the 1956 publication by Steward, et al. on Puerto Rico. It also is useful to recall that in fact Mesoamerican communities are less isolated than before.

> Most of the peasant communities . . . described by anthropologists
> from a decade to a generation ago have changed almost beyond
> belief, as a consequence of roads, emigration to cities, improved
> schooling, radios and television, and many other intrusions—and
> opportunities—of the modern world (Foster 1976:711).

New approaches to Mesoamerican society and culture involve a recognition of this fact as much as they result from dissatisfaction with older theories.

So-called dependency research is growing at a geometric rate and has some consequences similar to those noted above. While none of the authors in this volume directly addresses the topic, I believe it has become part of the background for a general perspective on Mesoamerica. This holistic and historical approach not only changes understanding of the relations among state, city, and countryside, but it also makes community and ethnic groups less distinctive than ordinarily is the case in anthropology. It reduces the causal efficacy of culture, for example, in dealing with ethnic and sexual identity. Dependency theory helps clarify the degree to which all subnational groups are influenced by the same set of national and international political and economic processes, although the specific consequences for subordinate groups may differ. Scholars from the U.S.A. have contributed far less to this literature than Latin Americans have, but the situation is changing (Jackson et al. 1979).

The concern with macrosocial processes and dependency reinforces an increasingly marked tendency to see traditions as adaptive, opportunistic responses to the environment rather than as rule-bound, inherently conservative expressions of values, ideas and world views. Just as historians (Chambers and Young 1979:53-55) are demonstrating that some Indian groups reacted in expedient ways to the Conquest, ethnographers (e.g., see Collier 1975) are showing how native traditions are dynamic, adaptive responses to conditions in "regions of refuge." These perspectives help sharpen definitions of culture even though they may lessen its power to account for behavior. Making culture part of the "superstructure" also disentangles it from behavior and objects thereby highlighting its ideational nature (see Hawkins, this volume). Of course ideational analyses have other roots (Keesing 1974), but the approaches mentioned here do help clarify the lines now drawn around culture.

This purification, if that is what it is, of the culture concept along with macrosocial, adaptive theories also tends to bifurcate work on topics such as sexual, ethnic, and status identity. Thus sexual identity may be examined in terms of political economy, with relatively little attention paid to ideology (see Bossen, this volume). On the other side, ethnic and (by implication) sexual identity may be derived from a superordinate set of ideas about humankind (see Hawkins). From one angle, Corbett and Whiteford (this volume) do outline a framework which may permit combining political economy and ideational analysis, but in general the lines are increasingly divergent, and this is a genuine departure from at least one anthropological tradition (see Cohen 1969).

Studies of change in particular are said to mark the contemporary period (Chambers and Young 1979:51). In fact, many of the topics Chambers and Young discuss under other headings also can be placed in this category, for example, national policy for the community, economic development, agrarian reform, urbanization, and so on. Most of this work is done with Indian populations—clearly a continuity with the past. If the first *Heritage of Conquest* stressed acculturative changes among Indians, contemporary reviews emphasize developmental change among pretty much the same groups (see Cline 1952; also Chambers and Young 1979). While the geographic distribution of groups studied by anthropologists is wider than in the past, the most favored regions and peoples have not changed all that much over the past thirty years.[2] Of course, there are discontinuities as well—new topics (e.g., women's roles), old issues seen in new ways (e.g., ethnicity), and so forth. Some topics are still relatively neglected, for example, kinship, intercommunity comparisons, urban-based unions, elite networks, and so on. Several of these neglected topics are examined in this symposium, often within a framework of change.

Finally, it is hard to avoid noticing that every time a review of Mesoamerican anthropology appears, it is remarked that research in the area has increased tremendously. What Tax noted twenty-seven years ago—"In the past fifteen or twenty years the amount of anthropological field work in Middle America has probably increased more rapidly than in any comparable area" (1952:8)—sounds as if it were written today. Along with the proliferation of scholars and studies, symposia have become increasingly specialized and restricted. This, as much as anything else, helps account for the absence of ethnohistorians, linguists, and other specialists on this panel which, by current standards, casts a fairly wide net.

In short, there are several background factors for a conference of this sort. There is the growing interest in relating macro- and micro-social processes, usually within a political economy framework. The latter is often but by no means inevitably informed by dependency theory. Coincident with this is a growing split between ideational and political economy research, and scholars working in both areas express dissatisfaction with traditional community study methods. While there are new topical interests, there also are direct links with the past, especially the continuing focus on the various dimensions of change among Indian populations.

Topics, Methods, Coverage, and Results

One theme of the conference, then, is an attempt to examine the ways in which national and international processes determine or set parameters for local events. Rather than describing how the urban center's world view diffuses out to the "little community" in a Redfieldian manner, the stress is on how the central state and capitalist sectors penetrate into and condition behavior at the local level. It is assumed that both superordinate and subordinate groups act in adaptive, rational ways, and any given group seeks to enhance or secure its political and material position in relation to other groups. Actors are acted upon, but they also act; the emphasis is more on "smart" adaptive behavior than on "proper" cultural conduct. Now, a from-the-top-down approach often washes out inter- and intra-community differences, but fortunately this does not occur in the papers presented here (e.g., Bossen, Corbett and Whiteford, Moore, and others).

Corbett and Whiteford observe that Mexican state penetration has accelerated in recent years (see Adams 1970 for a parallel study of Guatemala). The Bonapartist and developmental goals of the state require an increase in its ability to extend integrative control and a uniform ideology down to the lowest level of Mexican society. As elsewhere in Latin America, this is linked to plans for urban industrial capitalist growth (Roberts 1978). Corbett and Whiteford construct three global categories to describe these processes—cultural penetration, institutional transformation, and structural penetration. The utility of the scheme is illustrated by examining state penetration and economic development in Oaxaca and Puebla, demonstrating, among other things, how state activity weakens cargo systems in Oaxaca and differentially affects several communities in Puebla. Although microecological variations partly account for differences between settlements in Puebla (see Corbett and Whiteford on seasonal workers from marginal ejidos), the situation cannot be fully understood without considering the interventions of the state. Rather than compartmentalizing descriptions of communities (e.g., organized cane workers and poorer unorganized laborers living in different villages) the way traditional community study methods often do, the Corbett-Whiteford approach demonstrates that there are critical connections between them. The same single set of state actions helps account for intercommunity similarities and differences. The authors also show that what I would call a structure-function vocabulary can be used to examine dynamic processes. If nothing else, the scheme sorts out and organizes what would otherwise be an overwhelming amount of data in a rapidly changing situation.

Interestingly, in view of Moore's paper, the first example Corbett and Whiteford give of structural and cultural penetration is a school designed to teach Spanish in an Indian community. To achieve national integration the state tries to create a more homogeneous population, hence it attempts to inculcate the "dominant sectors' values and behavior" (Corbett and Whiteford) at all levels of society, using the school as one mechanism for this purpose. Moore (1973, and this volume) examines the limits of this method, although he concentrates on Guatemala rather than Mexico in his description of different forms of education and enculturation. He points out that formal, nationally directed education programs reach only a small number of people. Moreover, these programs may be misarticulated with local, traditional forms of enculturation such as career learning through cycles of rituals among Indians and patronage among Ladinos. Indeed Corbett and Whiteford make it clear that learning patron and client roles is an adaptive necessity in Puebla, as it is for Guatemalan Ladinos. Although formal education may be more effective in achieving national ideological integration in more economically developed towns (Sexton 1979), Moore's paper suggests a question which Corbett and Whiteford do not explore in any detail, namely, whether the various forms of incorporation may not contradict each other at several points. For example, some national state regimes devote so much energy consolidating their hold on their societies and homogenizing their people that they are forced to neglect socioeconomic problems and so cannot satisfy the demands that the homogenizing (or enculturating) processes generate. This cultural modernization leads to changes in demands, but economic and/or political development have/has not gone far enough to cope with them. Often described as a transitional phase in development, the situation may also become one of enduring instability in some countries.

Bossen treats another but related type of penetration—capitalist modes of production. One typical result is increased sexual inequality. Bossen argues that sexual stratification is more a matter of political economy than "cultural tradition and family roles," an observation also made by others. Thus Burawoy, discussing Warner and Low's 1947 Yankee City study, notes that "by allocating jobs on the basis of gender and ethnicity, management creates antagonistic divisions within the labor force and thereby undermines its collective strength" (1979:239; see Saffioti 1977 for a Marxist interpretation). Whether Bossen has too quickly put aside cultural contributions to sexual stratification is, in my opinion, still an open question. Apparently, Mexican regimes, for example, believe it is very important to get people, including the have-nots, to accept the cultural legitimacy of a particular system of stratification and inequality.

Bossen describes how peasant modes of production more closely relate the sexes to each other than do capitalist systems. "Where a man is tied to his land in order to be productive, and where he cannot effectively farm it without female partnership," sexual stratification is minimized, as in traditional Indian communities of Guatemala. Sexual inequality is greater among Ladinos, who "even if peasants, are typically less confined (than Indians) to subsistence production." Moore's work (1973) on Indian and Ladino "careers" might be seen as the enculturative complement to Bossen's descriptions. Of course the association between mode of production and sexual inequality and ethnicity, may only be taken for granted if it also is assumed that the cultural traditions of each ethnic group are not powerful, independent determinants of social relations and family roles. If so, precisely insofar as Bossen is correct, then there should be instances of Indian machismo and also of Ladino couples living in relative equality; it would depend on their mode of production rather than on ethnic culture. Unfortunately, we lack data on this and similar matters, for it appears that most kinship studies in Mesoamerica neglect the topic of sexual stratification and concentrate mostly on Indian systems (see Salovesh, this volume), although Gross and Kendall (this volume) in a different context offer some data on all this.

It would also be useful to know how social-class position and sexual inequality are related. Does social-class membership affect women's own definition of their situation? Do women in one class desire to maximize income while those in another prefer (Bossen might challenge the use of "prefer" in this situation) to increase power within the family, and so forth (see Saffioti 1977)? No doubt family and gender statuses and income are objectively related to each other, but it would be interesting to know more about the symbolic and subjective side of the relationship, something anthropology is well suited to examine.

Bossen is careful to place local units within the context of the nation. Her synthesis of ethnographic and survey data permit her to describe the impact of a macrosocial process on sexual stratification in the village, plantation (about which we know too little), city, and nation. This "healthy and growing emphasis" on larger contexts (Chambers and Young 1979:64) is also manifest in the papers by Early, Kemper and Royce, Moore, and Corbett and Whiteford.

Early's reassessment of Guatemalan census and ethnographic data is a case in point. He, along with others, demonstrates that ladino-ization can occur without loss of ethnic identity and, more importantly, that different aspects of acculturation are linked to each other; that is, he uses census data in analytic ways.[3] His paper, moreover, shows how national census data help locate over- and understudied regions, and that there are serious limits to the validity of small-group research in increasingly integrated national sociopolitical systems.

Granting the necessary qualifications about the differences among them, the preceding papers contend and demonstrate that cultural systems, community institutions, urban enclaves, patterns of sexual and ethnic status, and so on, are shaped by or are more flatly functions of macrosocial (economic, political, and demographic) processes. The perspective permits us to make intercommunity and intersector comparisons, something not often done in Mesoamerican anthropology despite the proliferation of empirical studies (but see DeWalt 1975). At the same time, the approach shifts attention away from cultural and onto societal processes.

A second group of papers in this volume take a different tack, concentrating more on culture (broadly conceived): the logic of native medical beliefs (Méndez); rituals, symbols, and domestic groups

(Crumrine); normative kinship structures (Salovesh); the intellectual dialectics of religious change (Tedlock); and the semiotic analyses of culture, community, and ethnicity (Hawkins). Since these papers tend to focus on Indians, we are in some sense back on familiar anthropological ground. Of course, the state penetration papers are also anthropological, deal with symbols, pay attention to Indians, and so on. But at the same time, they tend to make culture a superstructural phenomenon and/or concentrate on society, economy, and polity. There is no need to exaggerate the point; no paper falls completely or neatly into either camp. Thus, Moore or Gross and Kendall span both, but most of the papers move more toward one than the other side. Saying that a given group of papers falls on this or that side of a line does not mean they are all alike. Investigations of symbols, rules, and ideas are as diverse as the studies of societal processes.

With these cautions in mind, it may be noted that Hawkins argues that tying culture down to group-specific behavior isolates local groups from relevant macrosocial and macrocultural contexts and also from significant others in their own communities. Defining culture as an awkward combination of ideas, acts, and objects imposes a false separatism on Indians and Ladinos. If Hawkins is correct, our understanding of Indian and Ladino culture is fundamentally altered. Today, there is general agreement that Indians and Ladinos form a single integrated polity and economy, but even those who stress the point contend that each group has its own distinct world view (Pitt-Rivers 1967; Stavenhagen 1975), hence each set of ideas may or must be examined apart from the other. The problem, Hawkins says, is that this position cannot fully account for what now appear as anomalies in the data, for example, that mestizos and Indians share many cultural traits (see Beals 1952:66, 227) or that Indians may become presidents of Mexico, and so forth. The way to cope with this, Hawkins says, is to use a semiotic definition of culture. Culture is a system of ideas not to be confused with behavior or with devices (symbols) that express it. Meaning emerges from structural opposition between the ideas. Ideational oppositions between Ladino and Indian world views make sense only when seen as subsets of a single cultural system. Just as Indians and Ladinos participate in the same political and economic system, so they share a single (Guatemalan in this case) culture. What others have done to the economics of "penny capitalism," Hawkins does to the logic of cultural separatism.

In Guatemalan culture there are opposed and inverted ideas about Ladino and Indian. "The inversions . . . are pervasive and systematic" (Hawkins), and status ideologies may be derived from them. In a very real sense, to be a Ladino is to be what an Indian is not and vice versa (see Warren 1978). This approach permits Hawkins to resolve certain empirical problems, for example, the observed discontent of the more affluent Ladinos of San Luis Jilotopeque. What may be called Indian and Ladino reference groups (Rubel 1977) are like the opposite ends of one telescope. Since the Ladino reference group is the national urban elite rather than the local provincial unit, San Luis's upper-class Ladinos are unhappy with their lot even though it is "objectively" comfortable. In short, Hawkins argues that the proper way to interpret this and similar data is to disengage culture from community and then to treat the former in semiotic terms.

Tedlock's preliminary examination of the internal dialectics of Quiché Maya religion complements Hawkins's argument. Tedlock points out that Quiché religious ideas change according to an internal intellectual dynamic of their own and without necessary reference to culture contact. Without denying that situational and ideational factors intersect at various points and mutually influence each other, both Hawkins and Tedlock maintain that the latter have an autonomous status. Hence, certain types of changes (for example in religious conceptions) cannot be explained by reduction to environmental constraints and societal experiences.

Hawkins's approach, even more than Tedlock's, I think, must affect a reading of several other papers in this symposium, although each is strong enough to stand by itself. For example, after mapping the distribution of Indian medical beliefs in Guatemala, Méndez begins to work out the logic behind them, and the analysis has important implications not only for ideational or structuralist approaches to culture but also for applied anthropology (see also Cosminsky's paper). (It would, by the way, be intriguing to make overlay maps of Méndez's and Early's data.) Nevertheless, from Hawkins's perspective—close as it is to Méndez's—rather than contrast the etiological focus of Indian empiricalistic medicine with the agent-centered view of Western rationalistic medicine (the terms are from Méndez), it might be more appropriate to contrast the former with local Ladino folk medicine. The logical structure of the beliefs might turn out to be a variant of Western medicine, but it may also be an inversion of the Indian belief system. Somewhat the same comments apply to Moore's work; that is, perhaps ritual cycles and patronage networks are educational and enculturative inversions of each other and components of a single intellectual system. If they are, does this mean that the national educational system is the inversion of a superordinate concept which synthesizes the oppositions between ritual cycles and patronage concepts? To take a step in another direction, Hawkins's analysis suggests that even in monoethnic Ladino communities there may be found the ideational, symbolic, and social equivalents of Indians, and vice versa in all-Indian settlements (see Schwartz 1979).

Crumrine explores the properties of symbols, particularly ritual ones, in the context of domestic groups. It appears that the ways in which modern objects and new experiences are coded into traditional rituals are increasingly the subject of close analysis. It is another question whether similar investigations will be extended to non-Indian rituals, for example, Easter pageants in places like Antigua, Guatemala. A possible implication of this paper is that the ideas about self and society expressed in rituals may not be congruent with the strategies people use to cope with the political and economic environment. As part of the polarization of meaning in symbols of which Crumrine speaks, ritual symbols may voice compromises between cultural ideas (and ideals) and tactical action, much the way folk literature can (see Taggert 1979).

Cultural ideas and symbols have normative as well as expressive and existential aspects, and it is the normative side of kinship that Salovesh describes. As he points out, kinship is a relatively neglected topic in Mesoamerican anthropology. Salovesh, and Gross and Kendall fill in some of the gaps in our knowledge about the subject, and the papers by Crumrine, Moore, and Bossen help supplement what they discuss.

Salovesh surveys and summarizes a great deal of material on Indian kinship systems, and he pays more attention than most to the question of cultural boundaries. The latter was, of course, a major concern in the first *Heritage of Conquest*. Salovesh suggests that cultural boundaries should be drawn in terms of types of social relationships and cultural events rather than with historically dated artifacts or geopolitical lines. For example, if the life-styles and social relations of Chicanos living in Chicago are "Mexican," then the cultural boundary of Mesoamerica extends far north of the Rio Grande. This adds an interesting note to the idea of "heartland and frontiers" (see Helms 1975).

Salovesh then goes on to outline the reasons why kinship, something at the heart of Mexican culture, has been a neglected topic. Among other things, the stress on community, and the belief (or discovery) that community was more important in ordering social relationships than kinship is or was a major contributing factor. Even if it is true that Mesoamericanists have not produced as much "world-class" literature (Hawkins, note 17) as, for example, Africanists have, (I am not sure it is true but the comment makes sense in the context of Hawkins's paper) even a hasty review of introductory anthropology textbooks strongly suggests that Mesoamericanists have generated many, if not most, of the influential ideas about community current in anthropology and related fields. In any case, Salovesh helps balance things by his review of kinship terminologies, marriage forms, residence and descent rules, kinship relations, and compadrazgo (ritual kin ties). He concludes by noting that people interact with "groups and institutions through networks of interpersonal ties of kinship." Kinship, and according to Salovesh that includes compadrazgo in Mexico, is not only the "interface" between the individual and the larger society, but also the "prerequisite to understanding all other social interactions" in Mexican society. I am not sure if Salovesh means that kinship is the template for all social relations in Mexico (the papers by Bossen and Corbett and Whiteford surely qualify that idea), but there is clearly an overlap between kinship and patronage. In this sense, Moore's paper nicely takes up where Salovesh's leaves off.

Salovesh's review is very useful, but there is one point in particular that I do not understand: his comments about "optative structures." Salovesh writes, "The rules of kinship interaction in these (Mexican) cultures are much more complex than those of simple unilineal systems." I suppose that "simple" systems of any sort are, of course, simpler than complex systems whatever their rules, but most unilineal systems seem complex enough, for example, the

Trukese (Goodenough 1956). Furthermore, to say that this is related to the fact that "alternate rules" come into play in some situations and that there are metarules that define which of the subrules takes "priority in given circumstances" does not distinguish the Mexican from any other system. Salovesh does not have the space in this essay to detail the operation of some of these metarules, but the point is that all systems have optative as well as fixed aspects. For example, I imagine that even in unilineal systems where lineages control access to land and where land is scarce, people may be more precise about genealogical connections when someone lays a claim to a share in the estate than when that same individual expresses a willingness to pledge his loyalty to the same descent group in a political fight. In the latter instance, all sorts of optative structures may emerge. If, on the other hand, Salovesh means that the rules of the game and the tactics players use in playing the game cannot easily be derived from each other, that still would not distinguish Mexican from any other culture. It must be that patterns of behavior and choices between alternatives are everywhere the result of a complex interplay between ideas, rules, psychological and material resources, and situational circumstances. Furthermore, none of these factors may be congruent with each other. I believe that several of Salovesh's observations can be read this way.[4] Gross and Kendall show how different postmarital residence choices can be squared with the rules when sufficient contextual material is taken into account, but they do not do so by raising what I think is the spurious issue of "optative structures."

The paper by Gross and Kendall also nicely complements the many data Salovesh has pulled together, detailing several of the more general points he makes. In addition to some interesting specifics like the position of the *ch'ip,* Gross and Kendall link up the approaches taken by others in this conference. They illustrate what a synthesis of normative and statistical methods can accomplish and, by extension, what an integration of semiotic and political economy methods might look like. Significantly, in view of the many reproaches aimed at community studies, in order to achieve this goal Gross and Kendall do "intensive ethnography" in a local community.

In another way, Cosminsky also spans political economy and normative approaches in her review of studies on alternate medical systems in Mesoamerica, although this statement comes at least as much from personal communications as from her paper. Cosminsky sets out to determine the criteria people use to make selections from a wide array of medical practitioners. She finds that the standards of choice reflect or result from both situational and cultural factors. Although the practitioners and their clients make use of elements from different traditions, it might be interesting to think about the data in the way Tedlock does about Quiché religious events. Mesoamerican medical systems may change and even incorporate new elements according to an inner dialectic of their own, and perhaps Méndez suggests some of the relevant structures at work in this process.

Just as the topics and approaches of the contributors to this symposium vary greatly, so do their research techniques. Some of the research tools are relatively new in Mesoamerican anthropology (e.g., Early's use of national census data), others are applications of older procedures (e.g., Méndez's distributional study), but perhaps an important point is that the study of macrosocial units and contexts calls for training and methods that are not part of the traditional anthropological kitbag. Possibly we should have taken the time to discuss the matter at the symposium. In any case, most of the authors still rely on familiar ethnographic procedures, strengthened where appropriate by the addition of techniques borrowed from other disciplines.

Generally, there is a relationship between an author's overall approach and the sociocultural level of the units under investigation. Thus, those primarily concerned with ideational approaches and analyses—and despite the necessary qualifications let me include here studies of normative structures, symbols, and rituals—also tend to concentrate on microsocial units. Scholars using political economy methods focus more on macrosocial units. There are, of course, exceptions; for example, Hawkins deals with Guatemalan national culture, hence no iron dichotomy is intended here, and some contributors combine micro- and macrosocial analyses and data. Within this framework, a very wide range of specific "objects" are examined—gender categories, domestic groups, local communities, ejidos, plantations, cities, regions, and entire nations. As indicated above, the range of topics and processes is equally broad (see Table 1).

The relatively new approaches, treatment of new and neglected topics, and so forth affect, I believe, the ethnographic coverage of this symposium compared to that of the original conference in 1952. I have some sense that we know or seem to know less ethnography than our predecessors. We have not even gone too much beyond the traditionally favored regions and ethnic groups (see Helms 1975). Whatever else is going on, the situation may be related to dissimilar theoretical interests. Working through problems in acculturation, community culture, trait distribution, and ethnological comparison rests on a mastery of ethnographic detail. On the other side, the concerns of several of the participants at the present symposium require that more attention be paid to different levels of society rather than to distinct local groups. In all fairness, then, it may be more accurate to say that the present writers command different types of, rather than lesser amounts of, information compared to the older group. In short, there is more vertical and perhaps less horizontal coverage, but when it is all said, the contributors to the first symposium possessed an enviable control over the literature.

Concluding Remarks

Implicit and explicit conclusions of the two symposia differ in several ways. They have been noted at various places above, but some brief observations are in order.

One of the more obvious differences concerns the position of the community-study method in anthropology. Whatever the merits of the approach, by itself it is not adequate to satisfy contemporary interests and theories. As anthropologists place local units within broader contexts or directly study those contexts, at least some of them also emphasize the structure and distribution of economic and political power within society rather than distinctive cultural traditions within ethnic or local groups. This is related to a revised understanding of the locus and nature of sociocultural change. Identity, tradition, and culture become tactics in a game of power rather than primary irreducible determinants of change and continuity. Tradition is no longer a manifestation of a particular world view but rather an expression of sectarian interests, a labile adaptation to an environment, and a dependent variable. All the way down the line, change is generated by political and economic interests, alliances, and conflicts at superordinate national and international levels. Insofar as this view is accepted, there is less inclination to see the sources of change coming from within the community or from the shared psychocultural orientations of the people, and instead to root them in macrosocial structures and the clash of material interests. This viewpoint also necessarily lessens interest in acculturation and the other processes highlighted at the original conference. Of course, state penetration and like processes involve the "diffusion" of new standards from a center, but in the long run does it really make much difference if these standards are internalized (acculturated to) or more simply complied with for reasons of expediency? In short, there has been a shift in study away from acculturation over to power, from culture to strategic poses, and from community to the state and marketplace. It is as if the first symposium centered on heritage, and this one in part on conquest.

Table 1.   A comparison of topics discussed at the first and second
Heritage of Conquest symposia.[a]

First symposium	Second symposium
Culture area boundaries and traits	Culture area boundaries
Economy and technology	Political economy of the state and capitalist penetration
Ethnicity	Ethnicity
Kinship	Kinship
World view	World view; semiotic, phenomenological, and structuralist approaches
Religious systems and structures (including cargo systems)	Rituals, religion, cargo as rite of passage, medical systems
Dance and acculturation	Dance and identity[b]
Life cycle	Personality formation, "careers," and educational systems
	Women's roles
	Urbanization and demographic analyses

[a]The table does not stress, even if it implies, certain central concepts utilized or challenged at the respective conferences, for example, the emphasis on acculturation at the first meeting, the attention paid to political and economic power and macrosocial contexts at the second, and so on. As noted in several places, linguistic analysis, ethnohistory, and colonial history receive relatively little attention in both symposia. In the first session, the neglect seems related more to a lack of available studies and scholars than theory. In the second, it may be an artifact of the tremendous growth of Mesoamerican scholarship in recent decades.

[b]Discussed at the symposium, even though the planned paper did not materialize.

In part, for there is obviously more to the story. There also are relatively new, for Mesoamerica, ways of looking at culture—phenomenological, semiotic, structuralist. Although they diverge from the perspective outlined above, they too revise understanding of community, tradition, and change. Here the interest is not so much in patterns of behavior, but rather the ideological and conceptual structure of which they are a manifestation. Culture in this sense is not to be confused with community, and the criteria people use to decide what is and what is not "community" are not to be confounded with an administrative-territorial unit which may be called the town (see Warren 1978). In fact, the people living in a given town may not operate with a concept of community at all, something which surely has serious implications for traditional research strategies. In this perspective, the ideological or ideational system in terms of which people order their universe is not a direct response to the practical pressures and pulls of the environment (see Alter 1979), which is not identical with saying that an ideology or its derived rules and beliefs are untouched by feedback from the environment. As Kensinger (1979:2) puts it,

> . . . probably all aspects of ideological systems, may result in behavior which can be both adaptive and maladaptive . . . (and) belief systems which consistently produce maladaptive behavior significantly reduce the survival chances both of the societies and their belief systems.

Nevertheless, the viewpoint lessens interest in the sort of change that results from culture contact. Conceptual systems and probably symbolic or other devices for voicing them are in the main self-referential, hence they must change in large measure in terms of their own inner logic, for example, in some dialectic fashion or some equivalent to linguistic drift, and so on. Just why a given people should prefer one way of ordering the world over another is a different matter, but the choice is not a reflection of social and material circumstances. All in all, neither heritage nor conquest are as important in this context as is discovering the structure of meaning of which community, tradition, and belief are expressions.

When this conference was planned in Mérida, three questions or problems were put forth as organizing themes or goals. The first dealt with definitions of the Mesoamerican area and its subdivisions.

In different ways Salovesh and Kemper and Royce take this up, but the issue itself has less vitality than it had a generation ago. The second goal was a synthesis of recent studies in the region, a very difficult task given the proliferation of publications on Mesoamerica and increasing professional specialization. Just think of how much longer the list of periodicals and scientific series on the area (p. 303, *Heritage of Conquest*) is today. Nevertheless, most authors do respond to the challenge—Bossen, Cosminsky, Gross and Kendall, Hawkins, Kemper and Royce, Moore, and Salovesh. From a different angle, Early and Méndez also summarize a great deal of empirical material.

For the third goal, the authors were to deal with the implications of anthropology for Mesoamerica (the conference did not take up the implications of recent events in the region for anthropology). On the one hand, the work of Cosminsky, Méndez, and Moore has direct, immediate implications for applied anthropology. The papers by Bossen and Corbett and Whiteford offer some ideas about how to evaluate the applied work. On the other hand, all the papers raise methodological and theoretical issues which have been touched on above and which will affect future research in Mesoamerica. Salovesh suggests a way of defining a culture area that has implications for where Mesoamerican research is done. Thus, the location as well as the conceptions of future Mesoamerican research are treated at length in the symposium. In all of this there is a manifest sense of responsibility toward the people of the area, questions about the position of women in a changing world, about new forms of education, or about the new approaches and directions anthropologists must take to fulfill their mission.

Just as in the original *Heritage of Conquest,* here, too, there is a tacit agreement that anthropology is an holistic discipline with both scholarly and moral responsibilities. Whatever the new achievements, perspectives, and directions, there is a continuing and deep concern for knowledge and for people, none of which would be possible without the work of our predecessors.[5]

NOTES

1. This symposium, planned in Mexico in 1978, was held August 1979 at the Congress of Americanists, Vancouver. I mailed my paper to Dr. Kendall, symposium organizer, December 11, 1979. Since then several participants have rewritten their papers, some making minor changes

and others substantial revisions. In view of this, the problem was whether to rewrite my paper or let it stand as originally written. The editors and I chose the latter course in the hope that this would give readers some idea and sense of what all of us did in Vancouver. More is gained, we decided, by retaining one initial response to the symposium than by improving a paper with the benefit of additional information. Had this essay been rewritten, the major change would deal with applications of Mesoamerican anthropology to practical problems of politics and development. For some, current anthropology must be concerned with the status of the culture concept (in broad terms, challenged by cultural ecology and cultural materialism on one side and strengthened by ideationalism on the other). But I believe the central problem is whether anthropology will split into applied (or sectional) and academic divisions, perhaps after the fashion of social work and sociology, or retain its now battered unity. This may, however, be a topic for another symposium.

2. Despite all the interest in macrosocial processes and structures, development, urban life, and so on, there are relatively few anthropological descriptions of, for example, unions, specific state bureaucracies, urban elites, the impact of the CACM on various sectors of the population, or similar matters. There are partial exceptions (see Adams 1970; Helms 1975), but they do not come close to matching the amount of work done in familiar places with familiar peoples. Of course, building on past research permits one really to refine problems and hypotheses, but new theoretical orientations do require a look at the types of organization Corbett and Whiteford examine.

3. Although the point may not be pushed too far, the papers mentioned here indicate that until processes like state penetration, capitalist expansion, and urbanization began to accelerate, earlier concepts and descriptions of Mesoamerican communities were quite accurate.

4. Incidentally, the *y* between patronyms not only signals to "outsiders" that "the father's patronymic is a surname, rather than a middle name" (Salovesh), but also, as is well known, indicates to "insiders" that one claims aristocratic, or at least very distinguished, ancestry.

5. For a variety of reasons beyond anyone's control, I was not able to see complete drafts of some papers (by Cosminsky, Crumrine, and Kemper and Royce) before my own comments were sent to the editor.

REFERENCES

Adams, R. N.
1970   *Crucifixion by Power: Essays on Guatemalan National Social Structure, 1944-1966* (Austin: University of Texas Press).

Alter, R.
1979   "A New Theory of Kashrut," *Commentary* 68:46-52.
Basham, R., and D. DeGroot
1977   "Current Approaches to the Anthropology of Urban and Complex Societies," *American Anthropologist* 79:414-40.
Beals, R.
1952   "Notes on Acculturation," in *Heritage of Conquest: The Ethnology of Middle America,* ed. Sol Tax (Glencoe, Ill.: Free Press).
Boissevain, J.
1975   "Introduction: Towards a Social Anthropology of Europe," in *Beyond the Community: Social Process in Europe,* ed. J. Boissevain and J. Friedl (The Hague: European-Mediterranean Study Group, University of Amsterdam).
Burawoy, M.
1979   "The Anthropology of Industrial Work," in *Annual Review of Anthropology,* vol. 8, ed. B. J. Siegel, A. R. Beals, and S. A. Tyler (Palo Alto, Cal.: Annual Reviews).
Carmack, R. M.
1973   *Quichean Civilization: The Ethnohistoric, Ethnographic and Archaeological Sources* (Berkeley and Los Angeles: University of California Press).
1979   *Historia social de los Quichés.* Guatemala: Seminario de Integración Social Guatemalteca, Publicación 38 (Guatemala: Seminario de Integración Social Guatemalteca).
Chambers, E. J., and P. D. Young
1979   "Mesoamerican Community Studies: The Past Decade," in *Annual Review of Anthropology,* vol. 8, ed. B. J. Siegel, A. R. Beals, and S. A. Tyler (Palo Alto, Cal.: Annual Reviews).
Cline, H.
1952   "Mexican Community Studies," *Hispanic American Historical Review* 32:212-42.
Cohen, A.
1969   "Political Anthropology: The Analysis of the Symbolism of Power Relations," *Man* 4:215-35.
Collier, G. A.
1975   *Fields of the Tzotzil: The Ecological Basis of Tradition in Highland Chiapas* (Austin: University of Texas Press).
DeWalt, B.
1975   "Changes in the Cargo Systems of Mesoamerica," *Anthropological Quarterly* 48:87-105.
Foster, G. M.

1976   "Reply to Schryer," *Current Anthropology* 17:710-13.

Fox, R. G.

1977   *Urban Anthropology: Cities in Their Cultural Settings* (Englewood Cliffs, N.J.: Prentice-Hall).

Goodenough, W. H.

1956   "Residence Rules," *Southwestern Journal of Anthropology* 12:22-37.

Helms, M. W.

1975   *Middle America: A Culture History of Heartland and Frontiers* (Englewood Cliffs, N.J.: Prentice-Hall).

Jackson, S., B. Russett, D. Snidal, and D. Sylvan

1979   "An Assessment of Empirical Research on *dependencia,*" *Latin American Research Review* 14:7-28.

Jones, G. D., ed.

1977   *Anthropology and History in Yucatan* (Austin: University of Texas Press).

Keesing, R. M.

1974   "Theories of Culture," in *Annual Review of Anthropology,* vol. 3, ed. B. J. Siegel, A. R. Beals, and S. A. Tyler (Palo Alto, Cal.: Annual Reviews).

Kensinger, K. M.

1979   "Food Taboos as Markers of Age Categories in Cashinahua," paper presented at the Seventy-eighth Annual Meeting of the American Anthropological Association, Cincinnati.

Moore, G. A.

1973   *Life Cycles in Atchalán: The Diverse Careers of Certain Guatemalans* (New York: Teachers College Press).

Nash, M.

1967   "Introduction," in *Social Anthropology,* ed. M. Nash. Vol. 6 of *Handbook of Middle American Indians,* ed. R. Wauchope and G. R. Willey (Austin: University of Texas Press).

Paul, B. D. and L. Paul

1952   "The Life Cycle," in *Heritage of Conquest: The Ethnology of Middle America,* ed. Sol Tax (Glencoe, Ill.: Free Press).

Pitt-Rivers, J.

1967   "Words and Deeds: The Ladinos of Chiapas," *Man* 2:71-86.

Roberts, B. R.

1978   *Cities of Peasants, Explorations in Urban Analysis, I* (Beverly Hills, Cal.: Sage Publications).

Rubel, A. J.

1977   " 'Limited Good' and 'Social Comparison': Two theories, One Problem," *Ethos* 5:222-38.

Saffioti, H. I. B.
1977   "Women, Mode of Production, and Social Formations," *Latin American Perspectives* 4:27-37.
Schwartz, N. B.
1979   "Culture, Social Structure and Community in Petén, Guatemala," paper presented at the Annual Meeting of the Northeastern Anthropological Association, Henniker, N.H.
Sexton, J. D.
1979   "Education and Acculturation in Highland Guatemala," *Anthropology and Education Quarterly* 10:80-95.
Stavenhagen, R.
1969   *Social Classes in Agrarian Societies* (New York: Doubleday, Anchor Press, 1975). (Spanish ed., 1969).
Steward, J. H., ed.
1956   *The People of Puerto Rico: A Study in Social Anthropology* (Urbana: University of Illinois Press).
Taggert, J. M.
1979   "Men's Changing Image of Women in Nahuat Oral Tradition," *American Ethnologist* 6:723-41.
Tax, S.
1952   "Preface," in *Heritage of Conquest: The Ethnology of Middle America,* ed. Sol Tax (Glencoe, Ill.: Free Press).
Warren, K. B.
1978   *The Symbolism of Subordination: Indian Identity in a Guatemalan Town* (Austin: University of Texas Press).

Note: All other references are to papers presented at the second Heritage of Conquest symposium.

EDITOR'S NOTE: We regret that discussion and debate could not be included in this volume as they are in the original Heritage symposium volume. The symposium planners were not able to secure funding for a separate conference and the transportation costs that that would have entailed. Unfortunately, the time constraints on presentation and discussion at the International Congress of Americanists forced the participants to make short oral summaries and limited both the audience's questions or comments and the author's responses. As a result, upon transcribing the tapes of the conference interactions, we found that most exchanges were truncated to the point of being enigmatic; the editors therefore decided to include none of them. All the participants, we feel sure, will remember and therefore join us in thanking Ralph Beals, whose participation throughout the symposium enlivened our efforts and made more immediate our sense of heritage.

Index